Juana the Mad

The Johns Hopkins University Studies in
Historical and Political Science

123rd series (2005)

1. Stephen G. Alter, *William Dwight Whitney and the Science of Language*

2. Bethany Aram, *Juana the Mad: Sovereignty and Dynasty in Renaissance Europe*

3. Thomas Allison Kirk, *Genoa and the Sea: Policy and Power in an Early Modern Maritime Republic, 1559–1684*

Juana the Mad

Sovereignty and Dynasty
in Renaissance Europe

Bethany Aram

The Johns Hopkins University Press
Baltimore and London

This book was brought to publication with the generous assistance of the Program for Cultural Cooperation between Spain's Ministry of Education and Culture and United States' Universities.

Originally published as *La reina Juana: Gobierno, piedad y dinastía*
© 2001 Marcial Pons Ediciones de Historia, S.A.

The Johns Hopkins University Press
2715 North Charles Street
Baltimore, Maryland 21218-4363
www.press.jhu.edu

Library of Congress Cataloging-in-Publication Data

Aram, Bethany.
  [Reina Juana. English]
  Juana the Mad: sovereignty and dynasty in Renaissance Europe /
  Bethany Aram.
    p. cm.
  Includes bibliographical references and index.
  ISBN 0-8018-8072-6 (hardcover : alk. paper)
  1. Juana, la Loca, Queen of Castile, 1479–1555. 2. Queens—
  Spain—Castile—Biography. I. Title.
  DP143.6.A73 2005
  946'.042'092—dc22   2004013498

A catalog record for this book is available from the British Library.

Contents

Preface

International moviegoers have admired and pitied Queen Juana in the Spanish film *Juana la loca*, released in English as *Mad Love* (2002). Styled "a bodice-ripper for intellectuals,"[1] the movie combines fact and fiction to depict a passionate queen who inherited but never ruled the kingdoms of Castile and Aragon. Inspired by the libretto of a romantic opera, the film features Juana's tumultuous relationship with her husband, Philippe "the Handsome." A subsequent opera, *Rage d'amours* (Rob Zuidam, 2003), emphasizes Juana's supposed attachment to the corpse of her deceased husband after 1506.[2] Such productions, informed by conventional accounts, leave much still unsaid about Juana five hundred years after she became Queen of Castile.

The troubled legacies of Juana "the Mad" (1479–1555) and her mother, Isabel "the Catholic" (1451–1504), have intrigued artists since the nineteenth century. In *Doña Isabel the Catholic Dictating Her Testament* (1864), Eduardo Rosales depicts the elder queen upon her deathbed, with only her face and hands protruding from a kerchief and bedclothes. Surrounded by her husband, scribe, confessor, nobles, and friends while dictating her last will and testament, Queen Isabel provides for the eternal realms that will survive her mortal body.[3] A related composition, Francisco Pradilla's famous *Doña Juana la Loca* (1877), features Isabel's daughter Juana alongside the coffin of her husband, Philippe "the Handsome." Regarding the two paintings, critics have noted a resemblance between Rosales's *Doña Isabel* and Pradilla's *Doña Juana*.[4] In the second and more famous romantic composition, Philippe's dark coffin with the Habsburg coat of arms acquires dramatic agency alongside the widowed Queen, visibly pregnant, in the midst of a violent landscape. The coffin, signaling Philippe's premature death, also evokes the parallel fates of three previous heirs to the thrones of Castile and Aragon. In this sense, Queen Juana's personal loss incorporates the tragedy of her bereaved kingdoms.

For present-day observers, these powerful images may efface a sixteenth-century reality that merits consideration on its own terms. Aiming to recover the earlier historical period, the present study explores the nature of royal authority and the transition to Habsburg rule in early modern Spain. Considering Juana neither a heroine nor a victim, this portrait depicts her struggles amid individuals eager to govern her and her realms.

My efforts to uncover Juana's historical experience have received support from the Program for Cultural Cooperation between Spain's Ministry of Culture and United States' Universities (1994–95), the Singleton Travel Fund (1997), the Belgian-American Educational Foundation (1997), and the Fulbright Commission (1998). Among numerous individuals contributing to this project, I owe many thanks to the staffs of the Archives du Département du Nord at Lille and the Archivo General de Simancas. I am especially grateful to the personnel of the Biblioteca Nacional in Madrid, the Archives Générales du Royaume in Brussels, the Archivio Segreto Vaticano, and other archives and libraries that have helped me access a wealth of new information about Juana and her time. These findings, used to reinterpret familiar sources, entirely transform conventional views of the "Mad Queen."

This book has benefited from conversations with many scholars, including James S. Amelang, Isabel Beceiro Pita, Fernando Bouza Álvarez, Rafael Domínguez Casas, Georgina Dopico Black, Antonio Feros, Juan Gil Fernández, María del Mar Graña, Peggy Liss, Sabine MacCormack, Sara T. Nalle, José Manuel Nieto Soria, Joseph Perez, María del Pilar Rábade Obradó, Cristina Segura Griaño, Peer Schmidt, Eddy Stols, María Isabel del Val Valdivieso, and Lee Palmer Wandel. Ángel Casals i Martínez, Jean-Marie Cauchies, and David Lagomarsino have kindly allowed me to consult their unpublished work. With similar generosity, Juliet Glass and Rafael Pérez García have shared archival documents and early printed sources. I am also grateful to Ruth MacKay, who offered helpful advice for revising the Spanish text.

At the Johns Hopkins University, Orest Ranum patiently guided my study of early modern constitutional thought and kindly read my first chapters. I owe particular thanks to Richard L. Kagan for his tireless efforts to improve the Ph.D. thesis. David A. Bell, Rita Costa Gomes, Henry Maguire, and Stephen G. Nichols have contributed their thoughtful suggestions and remarkable expertise. Offering further insights, a reader for the Johns Hopkins University Press has made invaluable contributions, as have Brian R. MacDonald, Claire McCabe, and Henry Tom.

Since 1993 this project has benefited immensely from the advice and encouragement of Geoffrey Parker, who has commented on individual chapters as well as various versions of the full typescript. He has recommended innumerable sources, consistently urging me beyond my own limitations. My parents, Dorothy and John Aram, have provided equally indispensable support. To them I dedicate this book.

Juana the Mad

Introduction

Juana "the Mad," though the subject of numerous biographies, remains little understood. In 1868 Gustav A. Bergenroth awakened historical interest in Queen Juana and provoked a storm of controversy by depicting her as disloyal or extremely indifferent to the Catholic Church—a heretic rather than a lunatic. Arguing that Juana's father and son had prevented her from ruling, Bergenroth described the queen's madness as "the foundation stone of the political edifice of Ferdinand and of Charles, which would have immediately crumbled to pieces if she had been permitted to exercise her hereditary right."[1] Bergenroth made Juana's *locura* a confessional issue, and it remained one for his opponents. Among those who rushed to disprove Bergenroth, Belgian scholar Louis Prosper Gachard criticized the German author's interpretations of archival documents[2] and emphasized Juana's ultimate reconciliation with God.[3] Another leading historian of the day, Antonio Rodríguez Villa, found representations of Juana as a heretic and a lunatic equally erroneous. Arguing that Juana could not be considered crazy in the "general and proper sense of the word," Rodríguez Villa pronounced her simply devoted to Philippe "the Handsome."[4] In the same spirit, Constantin von Höfler opened his 1885 biography of Juana with a reference to Dido, the Phoenician queen, who, consumed with passion, ended her own life after losing Aeneas.[5]

In the midst of the romantic movement, artistic representations further popularized Juana's alleged *locura de amor*. Lorenzo Valles portrayed the queen at her husband's deathbed (1866) even before Francisco Pradilla depicted Juana alongside Philippe's coffin (1877).[6] Tournaisian artist Louis Gallait (1810–87) represented Juana entranced with the visage of her deceased spouse as a fallen scepter lay beside them.[7] An opera in four acts, *Doña Juana la loca* (1848), and a drama, *Locura de amor* (1890), both by Manuel Tamayo y Baus, further canonized the legend of Juana's eternal connubial passion.[8]

Whereas nineteenth-century artists and writers emphasized Juana's attachment to the deceased Philippe, twentieth-century authors applied the fashionable diagnoses of their own time. In 1930 and 1942, Ludwig Pfandl and Nicomedes Sanz y Ruiz de la Peña asserted that Juana and other members of her family suffered from schizophrenia.[9] Writing in the same tradition, in 1969 American scholar Amarie Dénnis attributed evidence of Juana's rationality to occasional "moments of lucidity"[10]—a diagnosis that art historian Miguel Ángel Zalama has recently affirmed, along with that of schizophrenia.[11] Succumbing to an opposite but equally presentist temptation, English historian Michael Prawdin sought modern rationale for all of Juana's actions.[12] Most recently, authors have portrayed Juana simply as a victim of political machinations: Juana *la Desventurada* (the Unfortunate), as Manuel Fernández Alvarez has labeled her.[13] Other accounts have mixed fact and fiction.[14] The pitfall of psychological anachronism, always inherent in the genre of biography,[15] seems particularly dangerous in the case of a "Mad Queen."

The historiography on Juana thus appears inconclusive, providing little insight into the queen's apparent failure or refusal to exercise royal authority. Although Bergenroth, Gachard, and Rodríguez Villa published many relevant documents, other important sources have remained unexplored. Beyond the need to incorporate such new material, this study draws upon recent scholarship in four areas: Spanish constitutional thought, female sovereignty, princely courts and households, and cultural understandings of madness. It considers advances in each of these areas as theories to test against the data while reconstructing different periods in Juana's life. The argument, although it often takes the form of narrative, continually attempts to engage these theoretical issues.

The first area of present academic inquiry deals with Spanish exceptionalism—specifically whether late medieval Castilian constitutional thought should be considered part of a European norm. To date, the fundamental concept of "the king's two bodies" has received scrutiny mainly in Renaissance England and France. In a 1957 groundbreaking study, Ernst H. Kantorowicz detailed the importance of this political theory for the English monarchy. While depicting "the progression from Christ-centered kingship to law-centered and man-centered rulership,"[16] Kantorowicz explored the nature of a medieval ruler's double persona. According to Kantorowicz, the king's two bodies, united during his reign and separated upon his demise, comprised individual as well as corporate identities. While the king's personal body could suffer infirmity or death, his mystical body never died. This immortal, political self corresponded to the royal *dignitas* as well as to the kingdom's corporation. Although Kantorowicz found the idea of the king's two bodies more pervasive in England than anywhere else, his student, Ralph Giesey, successfully revealed the theory at work in French royal funeral ceremony.[17]

As early as 1973, José Antonio Maravall emphasized the central belief in a unifying mystical body for political groups throughout the history of Western culture, and specifically in late medieval Spain. Maravall traced the idea's development in Iberian jurisprudence with reference to specific texts, particularly the *Siete partidas*.[18] Apparently unaware of Maravall's contribution, in 1984 Teófilo Ruiz raised the specter of Spanish exceptionalism by contending that the Castilian monarch embodied only personal, and neither corporate nor mystical, authority.[19] In subsequent studies, José Manuel Nieto Soria has contested that assertion by pointing to mystical, corporate components of sovereignty expressed in late medieval royal propaganda, including royal entries, oaths, and funerals.[20] In addition, Nieto Soria has examined a shift from the hidden king (emphasizing the corporate body) to the exhibited king (highlighting the personal body) in late medieval Castile.[21] From a different perspective, Adeline Rucquoi has argued that medieval Castilian monarchs, unlike their French and English counterparts, had little need for coronation or healing rituals to impress cosmopolitan, Catholic subjects deeply familiar with Roman law. Instead, the "reconquest" of Islamic-ruled territory, envisioned as a crusade, enabled the rulers of Castile to assume the role of defenders of the Catholic faith and wise guardians of their territories, even bypassing the need for clerical intervention.[22]

Building upon such divergent insights, the pages that follow highlight the role of Castilian practices (hand-kissing and pennant raising) and the royal identification with the land that Rucquoi mentions, without overlooking their sacral, even "magical," dimensions. The tension between royal display and concealment, drawing upon and alluding to church ritual, may have enhanced the Castilian sovereign's mystique. As Habsburgs succeeded Trastámaras, Juana's seclusion and Charles V's absences from Spain favored a return to the "hidden king" and a more corporate, less personal monarchy. Because the exercise of royal authority normally involved the conjunction of individuals and corporations, Juana's situation as a proprietary queen who never ruled provides an ideal opportunity to detect the two royal personae usually distinguishable only upon a ruler's death.

By sanctioning delegated authority, the idea of the king's two bodies may have also provided a foundation for what J. H. Elliott has identified as the "composite monarchy"—a single ruler's possession (or incorporation) of distinct multiple crowns.[23] Ideally, in medieval theory the corporate body of a realm contained its monarch's personal body. In the case of Queen Juana and eventually her son, Charles, a split between their individual and corporate persons may have enabled other individuals to rule in their names. The divergence of Juana's personal and institutional selves upon her accession in 1504 appears to have shaped depictions of her "madness" alongside related perceptions of her religiosity. Extending analysis of a monarch's two personae into the early Habsburg period, this study points to ambiguous, contested aspects of royal authority. It also challenges claims to Castilian exceptionalism in another sense by illuminating Juana's Pan-European contacts and experiences.

One of the books that Juana owned, also cited by Maravall and Nieto Soria, the *Glosa castellana al regimiento de príncipes* (ca. 1344) by Juan García de Castrojeriz,[24] revealed a profound understanding of mystical bodies' cohesive force in political life.[25] García de Castrojeriz explained that the prince served as the head of his kingdoms, with wise men as his eyes, judges as his ears, lawyers as his tongue and mouth, gentlemen as his hands, and farmers as his feet.[26] According to García de Castrojeriz, the prince should successively govern himself, his household, and his realms. Self-government required controlling one's passions and practicing moderation. Ruling the household, a community of persons rather than a physical structure, entailed directing one's wife, children, and servants. To describe the task of governing a city or a kingdom, García de Castrojeriz adopted a corporate conception from Aristotle's *Politics* (books 4 and 5) and *Rhetoric* (book 1), which described the ruler's human body as a microcosm for the macrocosm of his realms. According to García de Castrojeriz, "the health of the kingdom and the city" rested upon obedience to the king, "the life and health of the kingdom."[27]

Due, in part, to a common reliance on Aristotle, Iberian thinkers predating García de Castrojeriz also developed the theory of a ruler's two bodies. Incorporation of the faithful community in the person of a king has been seen as an innovative feature of the thought of Isidore of Seville.[28] The *Siete partidas* described the monarch's individual person as guarded and counseled, even governed, by his officers.[29] In corporate terms, the sovereign represented the heart and the head of his realms: "For as the senses of the head govern all members of the body, in this way all subjects of the Kingdom are ordered and guided by the sense of the King: and therefore he is called Head of the People [*Pueblo*]. Moreover, as the heart resides in the middle of the body to give life to all of its members, in this way God placed the king in the middle of his People, to administer equality and justice to all in common, so that they can live in peace."[30] In this way, the *Siete partidas* depicted the monarch's personal body within the corporate body of his kingdoms.

In fourteenth-century Aragon, King Pedro "the Ceremonious" extended the bicorporal concept by comparing his court to the human body and then to the mystical corporation of his realms. Upon issuing comprehensive ordinances for his household in 1344, Pedro declared: "The variety of offices nobly and beautifully distributed among diverse persons in the government represents a beautiful body, and the manner of the government is pleasant when the variety of offices are distributed among many persons, resembling the human body in which the variety of members are assigned diverse functions, resulting in the whole body's elegant beauty."[31] While comparing his court to the human body, King Pedro modeled his own behavior on that of Christ. He claimed that the king, like the Savior, would distribute "diverse graces" among many persons, while remaining "their only true head and lord."[32] Identifying the royal household with himself as well as his kingdoms, King Pedro also described the household as directing ceremonies that connected the mortal ruler to an immortal *dignitas*.[33]

The presence of a dual royal persona in key juridical and prescriptive texts nevertheless raises a number of questions. Were the sovereign's two bodies anything more than a figure of speech? Might a scholar read the corporal metaphor too literally? Or, rather, does the slippage between literal and metaphorical interpretations provide an appropriate hermeneutics for the late fifteenth and early sixteenth centuries? And, most crucially for the present study, how did a doctrine developed for native male sovereigns apply to a foreign consort or proprietary queen?

The rulers of Castile and Aragon, I argue, invoked "the king's two bodies" in declarations and ceremonies according to traditions and political exigencies. Their claims to exercise divinely sanctioned authority seem to have depended on a fluidity between material and metaphorical modes of understanding. Aspiring rulers, including Queen Juana and the Empress Isabel, wife of Charles V, appropriated regal symbols and sought to emphasize their continuity in the immortal *dignitas* that Isabel "the Catholic" had occupied. Juana faced particularly formidable challenges.

With certain notable exceptions, the concept of a king's two bodies reflected a late medieval and early modern preference for male authority. Building upon such a corporate conception of the political community, Catalan author Francesc Eiximenis described "how bad governors destroy the public good" (ca. 1383): "The effeminate and weak [body politic] is governed by women and by other people similar to them or worse, who have no shame or determination or virtue in their affairs or who care for useless things."[34] Rather than governing in their own right, queens ideally secured alliances and ensured corporate continuity by producing legitimate male heirs. Regulation of a queen's personal body, particularly her sexuality, appeared essential for a kingdom's well-being.

In France and, to a certain degree, Aragon, Salic law allegedly barred women from inheriting the throne or even transmitting the right of succession. Indeed, sixteenth-century writer Claude de Seyssel praised this custom for preventing France from falling beneath "the power of a foreigner."[35] Seyssel's contemporaries shared "the general understanding that a wife, by definition, was subordinate to her husband's authority, and her own authority was subsumed in his."[36] Hence the danger that a queen would marry a foreigner who, subverting the laws and customs of her lands, would favor those of his own.[37] The transition to Habsburg rule in Castile, effected through Juana's marriage to Philippe of Burgundy in 1496 and subsequent motherhood, illustrated precisely such a risk.

Relatively successful female sovereigns, including Isabel of Castile and Elizabeth Tudor, appear to have emphasized their male corporate selves more often than their female identities. Queen Isabel, often praised as a "manly woman,"[38] sought acclaim for her "heart of a man, dressed as a woman."[39] Elizabeth Tudor employed a similar strategy. As Carole Levin has shown, the "Virgin Queen" resolved a conflict between femininity and rule by claiming that her individual female body could contain a kingly body politic.[40] Female rulers, sometimes identifying themselves as male,[41] illustrated what Louise Olga Fradenburg has termed a "plasticity of gender in the field of sovereignty."[42] According to Ian Maclean, by virtue of her birth, a princess could be considered male.[43] If suc-

cessful rulers such as Isabel I and Elizabeth I managed to transcend their gender, others, including Juana, may have embodied female stereotypes. Their political debility might become associated with a "natural" personal condition.

While the basis for claims to royal authority, the idea of a sovereign's two bodies could also limit a female proprietary ruler. Marie Axton has argued that Elizabethan lawyers developed and popularized the theory of the king's two bodies
to restrict the powers of the Virgin Queen.[44] Other queens may have encountered personal circumstances that prevented them from exercising political power.
In a provocative article, Charles T. Wood has discussed Elizabeth of York's loss
of political authority in England after her marriage to Henry Tudor. According
to Wood, by allying with the lawful heiress to the English throne, Henry Tudor
usurped her sovereignty. Foreshadowing Queen Juana's historical experience,
Wood explains: "The queenship of Elizabeth of York teaches further lessons
about women and sovereignty, lessons which suggest that if a woman wanted to
have influence and to exercise genuine power, then it was far better not to have
any legitimate claim to them. Such claims were dangerous and a clear threat to
male hegemony. Few males could have ever accepted them comfortably, least of
all a man whose own rights were as dubious as those of Henry Tudor."[45]

Wood's suggestion that an early modern queen with unquestionable rights to
the throne might be prevented from exercising practical authority certainly
rings true for Juana's case. Neither Isabel of Castile nor Elizabeth Tudor had as
clear a hereditary right as Juana of Castile or Elizabeth of York. Accordingly,
Isabel of Castile forced her niece and competitor for the throne, Juana *la Beltraneja*, to enter a Clarisan convent,[46] and Elizabeth Tudor imprisoned her
cousin, Mary Stuart, for twenty years.[47]

A look at the process of governing Juana "the Mad" points to the political
importance of the royal household, in line with recent work on other courts. For
late medieval Portugal, Milan, and Burgundy, Rita Costa Gomes, Gregory Lubkin, and Monique Sommé have depicted an integration of personal service and
conciliar administration.[48] The role of sovereigns' households in early modern
times nevertheless remains contested. For Tudor England, Christopher Coleman and David Starkey have already challenged a "supposed eclipse" of household government long associated with the development of modern bureaucratic
administration.[49] From negotiating marriages to inciting rebellion, the members of Juana's household played crucial roles in the political events of her time.
Simultaneously, they may have used their positions within the queen's household to enhance their own authority, even at Juana's expense. By treating polit-

ical events alongside the daily workings of the household, I hope to illuminate the interdependence of these domains.

Juana's experience may also help clarify the fuzzy distinction between a household and a court. C. A. J. Armstrong has rightly asserted that households comprised appointed officers, whereas courts included welcome as well as unwelcome visitors and hangers-on.[50] In medieval Castile and Leon, the king's household comprised an executive organ with its members chosen by the sovereign, exclusively dependent upon him, and exercising no territorial functions—in contrast to the deliberative, more inclusive nature of the court.[51] In another formulation, Ronald G. Asch and Adolf M. Birke have suggested: "The household can exist and operate in the absence of the ruler, but a court only exists where a prince 'holds court.'"[52] Highlighting the difficulty of separating *casa* and *corte* in the Spain of Philip II, M. J. Rodríguez Salgado has identified the monarch's "residual authority" as the "prerequisite of a court."[53] In the Low Countries, Juana's Burgundian household comprised a part of Philippe's court. Many of the servants who cared for Juana's physical person owed their offices to Philippe and consequently sought to protect his interests rather than Juana's. Even when physically separate from Juana's household, Philippe and his councillors continued to direct it. After Philippe's death, Juana's father, Fernando, and her son, Charles, successively attempted to exercise authority over the queen's household. Thus, in Juana's case, the Burgundian and Castilian courts appear to have become centers of authority directing a household that circumscribed the queen's sphere of action. Juana had a household but never a court of her own.

Since Juana's earliest years in the court of the Catholic kings, her servants owed primary loyalty to other members of the royal family. Juana's marriage to Archduke Philippe "the Handsome" of Austria (1478–1506) literally separated her from the kingdoms of her parents. From Juana's marriage in 1496 to her husband's death in 1506, Philippe and his councillors directed Juana's household. Her inability to win the principal allegiance of her own servants constituted the essence of Juana's incapacity to rule—a problem that emerged within her household before her succession or "madness." Juana's tacit delegations of authority to other members of the royal family took concrete form in the Tordesillas household, which Fernando "the Catholic," Juana's father, established for his daughter in 1509. Forming a semipermeable barrier between Juana and the outside world, the members of her household controlled access to the queen.

An etymological link between the Spanish word *corte*, the court, and Cortes, the representative assembly of Castile and Leon, reveals the common nature of both corporate bodies, which, in theory at least, represented the realm.[54] This study seeks to demonstrate that Juana's household, serving the kingdom as well as the queen, regulated the relationship between them. According to the interests of their patrons—successively, Isabel, Philippe, Fernando, and Charles—members of Juana's household represented the queen to the world, and the world to the queen. Historians, like Juana's contemporaries, rely upon the household for information about her.

Because so many of the data available about Juana appear biased and mediated, the present study aims to avoid the pitfalls of either condemning Queen Juana as "mad" or defending her as "sane." To this end, it draws upon scholarship that considers madness a socially constructed discursive category rather than an objective transhistorical condition. Starting with Michel Foucault's *Histoire de la folie à l'âge classique* (1965), various studies have suggested that the definition and treatment of madness can reveal more about a given historical moment than about the "mad" individuals themselves.[55] A recent analysis of late medieval juridical texts found that persons considered insane (*demens*) had offended basic norms of their families and communities, thereby providing insights into those norms.[56] Other studies have suggested that the testimony of "mad" individuals who faced inquisitors reflected larger social and religious conflicts of their time.[57]

Troubled relations with God detected in "mad" behavior became all the more serious in the case of a proprietary ruler entitled to govern "by the grace of God." Given the ever-present analogy between individual and corporate persons—Juana and her kingdoms—the queen's contemporaries asserted that her personal sins threatened the health of her realms. By the same transitive principle, the queen could personally undertake penitence or suffer retribution for transgressions committed within her realms. Rather than judging Juana sane or insane, pious or heretical, the present study attempts to interpret representations of her infirmity. Such an effort involves particular attention to the way that Juana's contemporaries described her physical, moral, and spiritual condition.

With respect to troubled princes in Renaissance Germany, H. C. Erik Midelfort has proposed a periodization of treatment that coincides little with Juana's experience. According to Midelfort, demented German princes were not considered sick or subjected to humoral and religious therapies (from dietary restraints to exorcism) until the mid-sixteenth century, at which point "the prince in his physical body had become essential to the structure of authority."[58] Concerns about Juana's health suggest that princes may have been more central to the structure of authority in early sixteenth-century Castile. Although sources first mention Juana's "sickness" in 1503, its treatment by physicians and exorcists—discussed in chapters 3 through 6—fluctuated with political circumstances. Thus, resistance to Habsburg rule in Castile from 1516 to 1521 involved attempts to "cure" the queen. Subsequent attention to Juana's spiritual health reflected the larger efforts of her son, Charles V, and her grandson, Philip II, to promote Catholicism in their dominions. Indeed, the queen's relationship to God lay at the center of both dynastic and therapeutic considerations. Midelfort's formulation nevertheless remains useful in that it allows for changes in the perceptions of and responses to ailing princes. The fact that Juana's case does not fit Midelfort's periodization invites further questions about the impact of political centralization and confessional conflict, which Midelfort does not link explicitly to anxieties about princes' health.

Midelfort's most important contribution to the historical study of madness perhaps lies in moving beyond hereditary or genetic explanations. Historians have long blamed the unfit rulers of early modern Europe on their families' endogamy, which would accentuate any genetic defect. According to this interpretation, Juana inherited "madness" from her maternal grandmother, Queen Isabel of Portugal (ca. 1432–96), and then transmitted a double dose to her great-grandsons, don Carlos (1545–68) and Sebastian of Portugal (1557–78).[59] Yet the rash, ambitious behavior of don Carlos and Sebastian bore very little resemblance to the devout seclusion of Isabel and Juana.

After the respective deaths of their husbands in 1454 and 1506, Isabel and Juana, reportedly overwhelmed with sadness, took refuge in solitude.[60] Isabel's and Juana's retreat from the world, a common practice among royal widows, may have drawn upon precedents from Visigoth times.[61] In the sixteenth century such pious enclosure, termed *recogimiento*, became increasingly popular among women.[62] Indeed, many of Queen Juana's practices after the death of her mother in 1504—fasting, frugal dress, silence, solitude, and vigils—may be associated with this type of voluntary and/or enforced confinement.[63] Although the defense of Christian poverty might seem inappropriate for a queen, the Aragonese royal family had a long tradition of ties to beguines, holy women, and Franciscan tertiaries.[64] The fourteenth-century Pope John XXII even reprimanded one regent of Mallorca, Felipe, for "not ruling, but, rather, being ruled" and a "retired life that made him invisible to his subjects."[65] In spite of such censure, Felipe and his sister, Queen Sancha of Naples, continued to protect and to emulate poor Franciscans. Another royal model, Saint Isabel of Portugal (1271–

1336), resided alongside the Monastery of Saint Claire of Coimbra after the death of her husband, King Dionis.[66] Such precedents suggest the need to consider Queen Juana's *recogimiento* as part of a trend rather than an aberration. Spiritual withdrawal may have enabled Juana to negotiate the conflicts inherent in royal concealment and display, proprietary queenship, and the impositions of household personnel.

New perspectives on corporations, gender, courts, and madness inform the theme of governing a queen. At the intersection of these concerns lies a tension between individual and collective agency. While Juana's servants worked to marginalize her, I have attempted to maintain the queen at the center of this study. The effort has led me to consider royal authority as depending upon the governed as well as the governor or, rather, through a tantalizing inversion, subjects who could govern the monarch. A struggle emerges between individual and collective protagonists—Juana's household, its various members, and the queen herself. Indeed, during certain crucial moments, Juana's household may have governed the queen by regulating her sphere of action. Hence, the act of governing, rather than an exercise of arbitrary rule, entailed compliance with a set of traditions and expectations. Occasionally and notoriously protesting such norms, Juana usually gained more by negotiating the conditions of her compliance. The extremely limited options available to Queen Juana, however, do not prevent recognition of her choices at crucial historical junctures in 1504, 1506, 1509, and 1520.

Although Juana never fully governed her household or her realms, she exerted a measure of influence on the individuals who attempted to rule in her name and their officials. Political correspondence, chronicles, and household records depict a process of negotiation between the queen and her governors. These sources also reveal conflicts over the appropriate manner for governing the queen, which most individuals defined in accord with their own personal and political ambitions. Areas of particular tension included Juana's religiosity, movements, and possessions, precisely because of their importance for a proprietary ruler. Controversy over the queen's ability to worship and travel, while retaining her own belongings, suggests that these activities, among others, may have expressed the relationship between Juana as an individual and her corporate kingdoms.

Each chapter of this study explores a theme related to royal authority and the sovereign's double persona. The 1469 marriage between Juana's parents, Isabel of Castile and Fernando of Aragon, which subsequently joined their realms, provides a point of departure for interrogating the relationship between individuals and corporations in late medieval Castile and Aragon. Beginning with Queen Isabel, chapter 1 discusses Juana's models for appropriate female and regal conduct. As the third of five children born into her parents' itinerant court, Juana received training in music and Latin. She became acquainted with her parents' realms while being groomed for a foreign marriage that would separate her from them forever. In 1496 her parents sent Juana to marry Duke Philippe of Burgundy, as the lesser half of an alliance that also joined her brother, Juan, to Philippe's sister, Marguerite of Austria.

Chapter 2 suggests that competing Burgundian and Castilian agendas left Juana little room to develop, much less to pursue, her own priorities. After reaching the Low Countries, most of Juana's escort returned to Castile with Marguerite. The household that Archduke Philippe appointed for his bride governed her so successfully that Juana's parents soon began to question her piety and loyalty to their interests. Because Juana's dowry was never assigned in rents, she remained dependent upon her husband for revenues. As Juana made concessions to accommodate Philippe's councillors and subjects, she risked disappointing her parents. Her authority and, indeed, sustenance depended on her relationship to Philippe. The records of Juana's Burgundian household, alongside more general accounts, illustrate the dynamics of this dependence.

Conflicting demands upon Juana's physical person—her mortal, natural body—only escalated. The unexpected deaths of three heirs to her parents' realms left Juana their successor by the summer of 1500. Her elevation to the rank of Princess of Asturias and direct heiress to the throne, confirmed by the Cortes of Toledo and Zaragoza in 1502, further increased the constraints upon Juana. By asserting her own will and demanding a reunion with her husband in 1504, Juana contravened her parents' wishes and lost access to the divinely sanctioned authority that they claimed in Castile and Aragon. The Burgundian household still surrounded her. Representations of Juana from 1503 to 1506—recorded by Desiderius Erasmus, Antoine de Lalaing, Pietro Martire d'Angleria, Jean Molinet, Vicenzo Quirini, and others—ranged from chaste to lustful, dignified to degrading. Placing them alongside political developments, chapter 3 examines these images in terms of Renaissance views of the passions.

After Philippe's death on 25 September 1506, the image of Juana's extreme devotion to her husband favored her father and son. Chapter 4 explores how Juana's legendary attachment to Philippe's corpse secured the government of Castile for Fernando and the succession for Charles. Fernando and Juana disseminated masterful propaganda to discourage her suitors, including Henry VII of England and the Duke of Calabria. Juana's installation in Tordesillas, which Fernando supervised in 1509, entailed compromises with the queen and many of her former servants. Led by Fernando's adherent, Mosen Luis Ferrer, the restructured household aimed to preserve Juana's life and her father's authority.

Upheavals at Tordesillas following Fernando's death in 1516 continued intermittently until 1521. In documenting these struggles, chapter 5 highlights attempts to identify the queen's person with her kingdoms. The new governor of Juana's household, Bernardo de Sandoval y Rojas, Marquis of Denia and Count of Lerma, led the imposition and restoration of Habsburg authority. Denia used his position as governor in Tordesillas to enhance his influence on the council of state. His concerns about the plague culminated in Juana's journey to Tudela de Duero in 1534—a previously unknown episode of her life. Governing Juana's contacts with the outside world, the Denias linked their fortunes to those of the Habsburgs.

During the last fifteen years of her life, Juana's relationship with God received particular scrutiny. Chapter 6 examines these later struggles to interpret the divine and demonic forces at work within the Tordesillas household. Estrangement from God had long justified Juana's exclusion from power. The Protestant Reformation, however, made her presumed lack of spiritual health increasingly problematic. Although the queen insisted on her Catholic devotion, only in death could she fully regain divine favor and rejoin the corporate body of her kingdoms. Following Juana's demise on 12 April 1555, her household continued to mediate the relationship between the queen's body and the body politic. Transferred to other members of the royal family even before her death, Juana's servants and possessions conveyed her residual claim to legitimate authority.

The exercise of royal authority depended on the conjunction of individual and corporate selves. Preventing Juana's person from wielding such authority, Cortes, councillors, and members of her household sanctioned and enforced the queen's alienation from her realms. Having internalized the values of her society, Juana may have accepted and even welcomed this state of affairs, which her spiritual withdrawal facilitated. Serving family interests from her earliest years, as queen Juana apparently permitted kin to rule in her name. Rather than revealing only a single royal body, Juana's separation from the government suggests a Castilian concept of two bodies strong enough to justify governing a queen.

CHAPTER ONE

From Isabel "the Catholic" to Juana "the Mad"

An *Infanta*'s Education and Inheritance

Two landmark events in the political history of late medieval Castile illuminate an indigenous concept of the king's two bodies at the center of political life. The 1453 execution of the Constable of Castile, don Álvaro de Luna, and the 1465 deposition in effigy of King Enrique IV both turned upon the question of the king's dual persona. In the first case, King Juan condoned the death of his favorite, Álvaro de Luna, whose personal influence fell victim to a corporate monarchy that the constable himself had strengthened.[1] The intimate adviser, who had long bolstered royal authority, found consequently that he could no longer govern the king. Twelve years later, in the so-called farce of Ávila, a band of nobles and prelates deposed an effigy of Juan's successor, Enrique IV; conferred the royal insignia (crown, scepter, sword, and throne) upon Enrique's half brother, Alfonso; and proclaimed the eleven-year-old king. Angus MacKay's analysis of this ceremony highlights the constitutional transfer of the eternal royal *dignitas* from one mortal king to another.[2]

The crucial events of 1453 and 1465 paved the way for the accession of a female proprietary ruler—Queen Isabel—in 1474. Proving quite mortal, indeed, Enrique's half brother and Isabel's brother, the eleven-year-old Alfonso, died of pestilence within three years of his acclamation. Unlike her younger sibling, Isabel refused to allow the nobles to recognize her as proprietary ruler during Enrique IV's lifetime.[3] Reinforcing her even more tenuous claim to the throne, Isabel astutely positioned herself to inherit Castile and Leon after Enrique's death. Against Enrique's will, Isabel married Fernando of Aragon, the closest male heir to the throne that she coveted, in 1469. In spite of their brilliant alliance, Isabel and Fernando faced a long civil war after Enrique's death against his supposed daughter, Juana, and her partisans to secure their rights to the throne.

With the peace in her realms barely established, on 6 November 1479, Queen Isabel gave birth to Juana of Castile, her second daughter and third child. Although Isabel did not expect the newborn to succeed her as queen, she anticipated an important role for the child advancing her family's interests in a foreign court. A minstrel of the day celebrated Juana's birth in Toledo:

> There God sent us the second
> daughter of our illustrious kings,
> blessed with many of their gifts
> on which the present treatise bases itself.
>
> And they gave her the name of that glorious
> Juan, he whom God had chosen
> among men, and in her birth
> [she] was chosen for a copious gift;
> and this lady they named Juana,
> so that if only for this great calling
> Of His perfection God would give her
> the best share of the human race.[4]

Through identification with her family's male patron saint, the newborn approached perfection. The birth of another daughter probably disappointed Fernando and Isabel, who hoped for a second son to secure the succession.

In the winter following Juana's birth, the Cortes of Castile and Leon confirmed her brother, Juan, as their mother's heir. The children's matching names, claiming both John the Baptist and John the Evangelist as guardians, would ensure the appellation's continuance even if one of the children did not survive into adulthood, a likely prospect in that age of high infant mortality. Seeking another male offspring, Fernando and Isabel produced only more daughters—

María, born in 1482, and Catalina (Catherine of Aragon), in 1485. Juana's eldest sister, Isabel, had been considered the Princess of Asturias and direct heiress to her mother's kingdoms of Castile and Leon until Juan's birth in 1478 reduced her to the rank of *infanta*—a royal daughter without direct rights to the throne. Nevertheless, young Isabel remained important and regained the title of princess upon her engagement to the Prince of Portugal in 1490. In the case of Juan's premature death, the queen would have to depend on her eldest daughter, appropriately married to the Portuguese heir, to succeed her.

Such dynastic considerations and the status of a second daughter shaped Juana's youth, while her mother struggled to rule Castile and Leon. Since the queen governed her children with equal resolve, Juana's connections to her mother's servants, including the Dominican Andrés de Miranda and Beatriz Galindo, "the Latinist," appear particularly important for her early instruction. Contemporary financial accounts, complemented by more expressive but less reliable literary works, help illuminate these ties.

A copious literature on the governance of Renaissance elites informed Juana's education. These texts, from Isidore of Seville (d. 636)[5] to the *Regimiento de príncipes* by Juan García de Castrojeriz (1344), emphasized the divine source of royal authority invested in the governed as well as their governor.[6] They pointed to the ruler's Christian conduct, inculcated from an early age, as the basis of good government. Developing an analogy between the king's personal body and his corporate realms, the governance-of-princes genre raised implicit questions about the suitability of a female head of state. Hence we encounter the problem that Garret Mattingly posed with respect to Juana's sister, Catalina (Catherine of Aragon), and the education of her daughter, Mary: "But how if the prince be woman?"[7] Yet Juana, less than a princess, remained one of three *infantas* with no direct right to the throne during her most formative years. In fact, she would be the only one of her parents' daughters to leave their court without the title of "princess" and attendant plans to become queen consort of another kingdom. Juana, like Queen Isabel, would confront a gap between her childhood education and her eventual inheritance.

Isabel's Tenuous Claim to the Throne

Isabel refrained from assuming the title of queen upon her brother Alfonso's death in 1468. Isabel's gender, rather than her age of seventeen, made her a less suitable candidate to oppose Enrique IV. Aware of this limitation, Enrique IV's opponents supported Isabel as his heiress, in place of Princess Juana, Enrique's daughter, whom they claimed was illegitimate. The final six years of Enrique's life enabled Isabel and her partisans to formulate a justification of her rights as his successor. In addition to supposed homosexuality, the king's politically emasculating customs included an alleged preference for Moorish dress, Moorish and Jewish company, and unorthodox eating practices.[8]

Beyond attacks on Enrique IV, the defense of Isabel's rights included an early argument in favor of elite women's education. The Augustinian friar Martín de Córdoba dedicated his *Jardín de las nobles donzellas* to Isabel after her brother's death (July 1468) and before her marriage (October 1469), seeking to inspire her to study in order eventually to rule. As the friar declared, he composed his treatise to refute individuals "less learned, and perhaps not knowing the natural and moral causes, nor considering the chronicles of past times, who believe it evil when some kingdom or other polity falls to a woman's government. I, as I will declare below, hold the contrary opinion."[9] Following García de Castrojeriz, Martín de Córdoba enumerated the importance of sound instruction in order to govern oneself, one's household, and one's kingdoms. Citing learned queens, goddesses, and sibyls of antiquity, the friar marveled at the lack of contemporary *exempla*, "especially in letters, because now, in this, our century, women do not give themselves to the study of liberal arts and other sciences; rather it appears to be prohibited."[10]

But how to explain this sorry lack of female erudition? Turning to *El libro de las antiguedades* by the Roman author Marcus Terentius Varro, Martín de Córdoba drew upon a tale about the naming of Athens. According to this account, Apollo informed the supposed leader of that republic that he could name the city after either Minerva or Neptune. An assembly of all citizens—which allegedly included women—then voted to select their patron. Although the men unanimously favored Neptune, the women, supporting Athena, outnumbered them by one. The sea god, enraged, flooded their city with waters, which he only withdrew when the Athenians promised to exclude women from future council. Because women could not provide counsel, reasoned the friar, they had no need for moral philosophy, theology, or other sciences. He noted, however, that the exclusion from council pertained only to common women and not to the illustrious, "as is our lady, the princess." Isabel's royal descent, the Augustinian argued, made her exceptional among womankind.[11]

Among exceptional females, Córdoba compared Princess Isabel particularly to the Virgin Mary, whom he also considered a daughter of kings. For Córdoba,

Mary redeemed mankind from the sin of her eternal antithesis, Eve. If God created Eve in paradise, he made the Virgin paradise itself.[12] As Córdoba's analogy between Mary and Isabel gained force, he described three degrees of female chastity: virginal purity, marital fidelity, and honorable widowhood. Citing examples of female saints, the Augustinian encouraged Isabel to guard her virginity.[13] Yet Isabel's political ambitions dictated another choice.

Fernando of Aragon proved the husband that Isabel needed for the first of her conquests—that of the throne itself.[14] In 1469 Fernando and Isabel secretly married with a forged papal dispensation for their kinship as second cousins. In October 1470 their first offspring, a daughter, entered the world. Upon the death of Enrique IV in 1474 Isabel claimed the title of Queen of Castile and Leon. Taking advantage of Fernando's temporary absence from Castile, Isabel paraded through the streets of Segovia with the naked sword of justice raised before her. The gesture, which proclaimed her proprietary queen, offended certain subjects, who found it inappropriate for a woman to appropriate the masculine symbol of the sword.[15] Negotiations over Fernando's and Isabel's respective powers in Castile and Leon grew tense. Fernando's partisans considered him, as a male, the legitimate heir, whereas Isabel's supporters argued that a woman could, indeed, inherit those kingdoms. Moreover, Isabel contended that the sex of their only child at that time made it necessary to establish a clear precedent for female succession. In the end, according to contemporaries, Isabel insisted on her great "conformity" with Fernando.[16]

The theme of perfect harmony between Isabel and her husband became a favorite among their chroniclers, enabling Isabel to distance herself from previous proprietary queens of Castile, Urraca and Berenguela, whose marriages had produced discord and were ultimately annulled.[17] Isabel and Fernando presented a united image on letters, seals, and coins—"for if necessity separated their persons, love joined their wills."[18] Although Fernando continued to father illegitimate children, the idea of consummate unity with his queen contained particular implications for her sexual conduct: "In the absence of the king, until now she always slept in the common dormitory of certain young ladies and maidens of her household. Now she sleeps in the company of her daughters and other honorable women in order not to give root to gossip that could blemish her reputation for conjugal fidelity."[19] According to a later account, Fernando shared not only Isabel's realms but all of her virtues as well: "King and queen together, they were chosen by God, united by Him, who, joined together in this way, ruled and governed thirty years, and although two in body, in will and unity they were only one."[20] The monarchs further confirmed their providential election by exercising divinely sanctioned justice.

Of the three virtues—justice, liberality, and affability—that Isabel needed in order to rule, fray Martín de Córdoba stressed the role of justice in the organic or corporate conception of Isabel's realms. A kingdom, according to the friar, functioned like a body, with the monarch as its "head" and justice its "spirit." He explained:

> It was determined that the kingdom was like a body with its head as the king, and justice as the spirit of the kingdom. Thus, as life descends from the head and spreads through all of the body, in this way justice must descend from the prince and run through all of the realm. Wherefore, as the body without a head is dead, so is the realm without a prince; and, like a body with a head that has no sense, a kingdom with a king who does not exercise justice is dead and buried.[21]

As Isabel strove to wield the sword of justice, an interdependence emerged between her individual, mortal person and the corporation of her realms.

Like much that the chroniclers report, a potentially apocryphal tale about Isabel's exercise of justice illuminates the transitive relationship between Isabel's body and that of her kingdoms. According to Hernando de Pulgar, in 1480 a dispute arose in the queen's court between two young noblemen, the Admiral of Castile's eldest son, don Fadrique, and the Lord of Toral, Ramir Núñez de Guzmán. Despite Isabel's orders to refrain from violence, three masked men accosted and beat Núñez de Guzmán in the public square. Exercising one of her favorite maneuvers, the queen set off on horseback at once for the fortress of Simancas, which belonged to the Admiral of Castile at the time. When the admiral pleaded ignorance of his son's whereabouts, Isabel demanded that he surrender the fortresses of Simancas and Rioseco to the crown in place of the young man. The admiral could only obey. On the following day, the queen remained in bed. When asked about her ailment, Isabel allegedly proclaimed, "My body suffers from the blows that don Fadrique delivered yesterday against my guarantee." Thus the queen purportedly drew a direct analogy between the well-being of her physical person and that of her realms. Although don Fadrique was a cousin of Isabel's husband, Fernando, the queen refused to return the admiral's fortresses until his son accepted just punishment.[22]

Isabel and Fernando's allegedly perfect union masked neither differences between the spouses nor the respective interests of their realms.[23] Because the possibility of female succession remained doubtful in Aragon, that kingdom's union with Castile and Leon could only be attained in the person of a male heir, Prince Juan, born to Isabel and Fernando in 1478. The queen's much-emphasized love for Prince Juan highlighted his potential as a unifying force in her family as well as her kingdoms. Juan de Flandes's *Adoration of the Kings*, which depicts the Virgin with Child—or might Isabel "the Catholic" appear enthroned with her newborn son?—includes Fernando alongside the Moorish king, paying homage to a common savior.[24] Emphasizing ties to her husband, son, and corporate kingdoms, Isabel appeared determined to overcome her gender and otherwise dubious rights to the throne.

The Quest for Spiritual and Territorial Unity

The concept of Isabel and Fernando's realms as a single corporate body based on the model of a Christian community united in the body of Christ, as seen in the works of Martín de Córdoba and Hernando de Pulgar, deeply influenced the monarchs' religious policy. Once securely seated upon their thrones, Isabel and Fernando petitioned Pope Sixtus IV for the right to name inquisitors who would root out heresy, particularly Jewish practices among recent converts to Christianity, in their realms. Although various ecclesiastics have received credit for persuading Fernando and Isabel to request a stronger weapon against heresy,[25] the role of Dominican Andrés de Miranda, who eventually became the personal tutor of Isabel's daughter, Juana, requires attention.

Although virtually unknown today, a treatise by Andrés de Miranda, "Declaration Regarding Heresy and Other Things Pertaining to This Matter," offers insight into the mind of Juana's instructor and the preoccupations of his time. Written in Castilian and never published, Miranda's text provided Queen Isabel with a precise, canonically informed method for extirpating heresy from her realms.[26] Drawing upon a corporate conception of Isabel's kingdoms, Miranda argued that relapsed heretics, if tolerated among good Catholics, could infect the faithful with pernicious beliefs. Citing Saint Jerome's instructions for separating rotten from good meat, the case of a rabid lamb who infected an entire flock, and a single bolt of lightning that destroyed all of Alexandria, Miranda argued that the community's spiritual health demanded the elimination of non-Catholics.[27] He conceded that human government, derived from and begun within divine government, should allow heretics to embrace the faith bit by bit. Nevertheless, according to the Dominican, individuals who converted to Catholicism, then returned to Jewish practices, committed a greater sin than

Jews who had never accepted the Catholic faith. Thus, a contradiction emerged in Miranda's thought between the demand for a unified corporate body and the recognition that the Inquisition could not prosecute Jews who had never joined the church.[28]

A dramatic attempt to resolve this disjunction between secular and ecclesiastical corporations—the expulsion of 1492—failed to guarantee spiritual unity in Fernando and Isabel's realms. The monarchs' "reconquest" of the kingdom of Granada, from 1482 to 1492, achieved a type of territorial integrity, while bringing thousands of Moorish subjects under their rule. How might such dramatic events have impacted Isabel and Fernando's second daughter? As a member of their itinerant court during the entire war, she would have inherited her parents' obligation to continue the "reconquest," even to the Holy Land.[29]

The "reconquest" of Granada inspired Pedro Marcuello, mayor of Calatorau, to compose a militant and prophetic *cancionero* or book of songs for Queen Isabel and her second daughter. After commending the work to Isabel, Marcuello addressed Juana:

> And I beg you to be served
> by the present treatise,
> very perfect *infanta*,
> furnished with virtues
> and prudent at a very tender age;
> in much you follow the shining
> great Queen of Castile
> who is the fountain of virtues
> and the bridge of this conquest
> in goodness the chief.
>
> And because you are devoted
> to the Mother of Jesus,
> I glossed the *Salve* sung
> with the rest, so that imprinted
> in the mind you carry the cross,
> and you securely find the steps
> of the high Queen Isabel,
> you, with the other daring [maidens],
> and let you be well indoctrinated
> to serve Emanuel.[30]

In this way, Marcuello emphasized the importance of Juana's doctrinal training. If properly developed, religious principles inherited from Isabel would enable Juana to continue her mother's work.

Marcuello nevertheless admitted that Juana, unlike Isabel, was destined for marriage abroad. However perfect, the union between Juana's parents had also proved somewhat disappointing. In Marcuello's elegy, King Fernando received honorable mention for his role in the "reconquest" as Isabel's divinely chosen spouse:

> I say: God has joined you
> to lift up his cross
> the two of you in one flesh:
> don Fernando, very great king,
> with the great queen, strong
> column of faith, and by one accord
> in order to augment His law.[31]

But why had such mystically inspired leaders been blessed with only one son? In Marcuello's device of a dialogue between Saint James and Mary, the Virgin declared that her Son had sent them many daughters in order to pacify their realms by winning the adherence of foreign sons and lands.[32] The task of securing such alliances would prove as difficult for Juana as for any of her sisters.

Marcuello composed his collection of songs and prayers in an attempt to convince Queen Isabel and Juana to accept his daughter, also named Isabel, into the *infanta*'s service. The queen, the *infanta*, Marcuello, and his daughter, Isabel, appear throughout the manuscript. Interestingly enough, Marcuello addressed his plea to Queen Isabel, the supreme governess of Juana's household, as well as to Juana herself.

Education within the Itinerant Court

To say that Juana had a household of her own, while a questionable assertion at any moment during her lifetime, would be particularly misleading and inaccurate before 1496. Rather, Queen Isabel selected members of her own itinerant court to care for Juana and the other royal children. In the shadow of her parents and older siblings, the *infanta* cultivated a few, although surprisingly few, loyal servants. Her training involved not only music and Latin, in which she excelled, but also instruction in religious conduct and decorous self-presentation. Above all, Juana learned that she should serve the corporate interests of her parents' realms. Carefully governed from her earliest years, Juana received an education that would both help and hinder her as Archduchess of Burgundy.

A manual for female instruction contained in Juana's library, *Carro de las donas* by the Catalan Franciscan Francesc Eiximenis, emphasized the need to govern young girls with particular care. Because Eiximenis believed that good morals and customs were imbibed through mother's milk, the fourteenth-century humanist urged noblewomen to nurse their own infants, or at least to choose their daughters' nurses with caution.[33] Eiximenis further directed parents to instruct their female offspring in the precepts of Christianity as soon as the girls showed "some sign of sense." The young girl should learn to cross herself, to recite the *Pater Noster* and *Ave María*, the *Credo*, and the *Salve Regina*, kneeling before the image of Christ or his mother. Eiximenis also advised parents to keep their daughters away from Moors and Jews, refusing any food that non-Christians might offer them. According to the Franciscan, a daughter should accompany her mother to church with her head covered, as Saint Paul ordered. Eiximenis added that the female child should always carry a rosary and dedicate a portion of each day to prayer.[34]

At the age of ten or twelve, Eiximenis considered the daughter a young lady. Able to exercise some discretion, she also grew increasingly subject to discipline.[35] The young lady ought to fast with her parents on the eves of principal holidays, choosing prayers according to her devout inclinations. Also by ten or twelve, she could begin to understand the mystery of the Holy Trinity and to select a patron saint who would intercede for her with God. To inspire fear and respect in their daughters, Eiximenis advised parents not to spare the rod:

> Punish them and wound them on the back with some switch rather than on the head. For as Solomon says: The switch is medicine for the madness [*locura*] of girls . . . so that they always maintain silence and do not speak but little and when questioned . . . nor should they play with boys or take anything that the boys give them. Order them not to speak loudly or to laugh dissolutely. Admonish them to carry their eyes low, never staring anyone in the face, but responding modestly if addressed, then lowering their eyes to the ground.[36]

While respecting her parents and even her brothers, Eiximenis explained, the well-governed daughter should learn to supervise servants in preparation for ruling her own household one day. Above all, the Franciscan directed, young women should avoid idleness. Eiximenis considered weaving, sewing, and prayer their proper occupations.[37]

To what extent did Queen Isabel follow Eiximenis's precepts in educating her own daughters? The accounts of her treasurer, Gonzalo de Baeza, reveal that the queen carefully selected and consistently remunerated her children's instructors. Status taboos in conjunction with the demand for male heirs made it unlikely that Isabel herself would nurse any of her offspring. Juana's wet nurse, doña María de Santistevan, served her until the age of six, when she went to Juana's younger sister, María.[38] The nurse and her servant, Catalina, received a variety of cloth from London scarlet to Flanders linen, coral, ribbons, pins, thread, footwear, and, of course, coins (maravedíes, hereafter mrs), for themselves and the young *infantas*.[39] Although Juana lost her nurse at age six, she simultaneously obtained a governess, doña Teresa Manrique. Besides modeling proper behavior and overseeing Juana's conduct, doña Teresa provided rose sugar for the young charge on special occasions.[40] Also at six, Juana began sleeping in a wooden bed, receiving formal table service, and traveling in style on a raised platform carried by peons.[41] A bout of sickness in the same year led Queen Isabel to donate a total of 34,000 mrs to the friars of Saint Francis of Carmona and the bishop of Leon for prayers on Juana's behalf.[42]

In accord with Eiximenis's recommendations, Isabel taught her daughters piety and charity. When the court passed through Córdoba in early 1485, the queen donated two bundles of wax, each the weight of one of her youngest daughters, to the local patron, Saint María de la Fuente. In the Church of Saint María de la Fuente, under their mother's guidance, six-year-old Juana and her three-year-old sister, María, each offered a castellano (485 mrs) to the saint.[43] A few years later, Juana would receive a certain sum to offer at the traditional monument commemorating the burial and resurrection of Christ during Holy Week—a custom that she would continue throughout her life.[44]

At age seven, Juana began studies with her long-term *maestro* or tutor, Doctor Andrés de Miranda, from the Monastery of Santo Domingo outside the walls of Burgos. In addition to special gifts and cost-of-living supplements, Juana's professor received 50,000 mrs per year.[45] In 1490 and 1491, before Catalina turned six and could begin her studies, María joined Juana in classes with Miranda. The Dominican's salary, however, only increased in 1495, when Juana became engaged to Philippe, Archduke of Austria, and thereby assumed the title of archduchess.[46] Under Miranda, Juana received Latin training in addition to the Christian instruction that Eiximenis had recommended. Household accounts provide some indication of the curriculum that Miranda followed with Juana. In her first year of lessons, the *infanta* received a box for carrying letters and a large book of hours, embellished with a silver lock and gold-lined pages.[47] By age ten, Juana owned not only printed prayer books, but her own edition of Boethius's *De Consolatione*, a philosophical guide for combining faith and reason.[48] The *infanta* could probably read Latin by age fourteen, when she received Latin editions of the *Lives of Church Fathers* and the *Lives of the Saints*. Visiting Queen Isabel's court in the fall of 1494, German voyager Hieronymous Münster heard Andrés de Miranda praise Juana's skill in reciting and even composing Latin verses.[49]

In addition to Miranda's instruction, Juana may have received guidance from Queen Isabel's tutor and friend, Beatriz Galindo.[50] The *infanta*'s expenses in 1487 included blouses, a skirt, and a bed for the distinguished Latinist.[51] As the author of commentaries on Aristotle as well as a book of Latin verses,[52] Galindo may even have inspired Juana to try her own hand at poetry. Among 116 tomes that Juana accumulated during her lifetime, however, only a volume of Cicero suggests the slightest humanist inclination.[53]

Was the education of Juana's brother, Juan, much different? Alonso Ortiz, a canon in the Cathedral of Toledo closely associated with the royal court, composed a treatise on the prince's training that espoused much of Eiximenis's educational philosophy.[54] While recognizing the advantages of birth under the right stars and a good humoral composition, Ortiz proved as ready as Eiximenis to prescribe strict discipline, "which makes a man's soul turn good, that is, impedes the soul from falling into dementia."[55] Also following Eiximenis, Ortiz pointed to religious practices and doctrine as the foundation of early education.[56] In another similarity, both siblings studied music—the prince singing tenor and the *infanta* playing clavichord.[57] Yet books and music comprised only one dimension of their education.

A crucial component of Juana's training involved instruction in appropriate self-presentation. Gonzalo de Baeza's accounts reveal that the *infanta*'s largest expense by far comprised the purchase and adornment of cloth and numerous articles of clothing. Along with her royal siblings, Juana received the services of tailor Fernando de Torrijos and shoemaker Juan de Sahagún.[58] The *infanta* owned *verdugos* to provide the appearance of wide hips as early as age five and began wearing locks in her hair by age nine.[59] From fitted vests to fashionable hats, Juana particularly favored the color crimson, which more than doubled an item's price.[60] By 1488 Juana's accumulation of clothing and other possessions required a convoy of mules, appropriately garnished, to carry her luggage.[61] The fact that a kindly farmer presented Juana with pet rabbits that same year did not prevent the *infanta* from wearing a cloak lined with the pelts of ninety-one rabbits or another trimmed with the fur of cats as she matured.[62] Juana's self-presentation involved the display of her person within an entourage of well-attired servants. In Queen Isabel's itinerant court, dress highlighted not only a royal body but also the retinue around it. Juana, her siblings, and their servants formed part of a court pertaining to the queen who governed them all.

In comparison with her older brother and sister, Juana received a rather modest education in public ritual. Queen Isabel and King Fernando devoted more attention to the ceremonial training of their first offspring, Isabel, and Juan. During the ten-year war preceding the conquest of Granada in 1492, the queen often selected her eldest daughter and other distinguished ladies to accompany her public appearances, while Juana and her younger sisters remained behind.[63] The young Isabel's ceremonial instruction culminated in fifteen-day festivities celebrating her betrothal to the Portuguese prince, Alfonso, in 1490. During these celebrations, the princess and the queen attended jousts accompanied by up to seventy exquisitely attired noble ladies.[64] Juana appeared only briefly, staging skits in a small theater built from serge and poles in honor of her sister's engagement.[65] Princess Isabel's departure for Portugal in 1490 enabled Juana to take her sister's place alongside the queen until the death of the Portuguese heir precipitated young Isabel's return to Spain three months later.[66] Juana's brother, Prince Juan, while always preeminent, appeared increasingly with his father. In late 1490 King Fernando knighted the prince and permitted him, in turn, to knight other lords. Like his older sister, Juan learned to honor the distinguished nobles of his own sex.[67] In contrast, Juana's limited public appearances confirmed her status as an unlikely heiress in Castile.

Although Juana's military training fell far short of her brother's,[68] she became a skilled equestrian. At age ten, royal accounts indicate that Juana received a mule, complete with reins, stirrups, and saddle covered in silk and brocade.[69] Her mule's trimmings cost nearly as much as the *infanta*'s own dress.[70] Both undoubtedly required renewal after a mishap outside Aranjuez in 1494. According to Gonzalo Fernández de Oviedo, as the itinerant court waded through the Tagus River, Juana's mule lost its footing and dragged the *infanta* away with the current. "As red as a rose" and "with great spirit," Juana clung to her saddle until Queen Isabel sent a stableboy to rescue both her daughter and the mule. King

Fernando accordingly promoted the stableboy to keeper of the silver and also provided him with other rewards.[71]

Through the course of Juana's education, equestrian and otherwise, Fernando and Isabel maintained authority over the retainers surrounding their daughters. By selecting, rewarding, and governing Juana's servants, the monarchs limited her ability to exercise patronage and win personal adherents. Which servants, if any, could develop lasting attachments to Juana? As early as 1485 Juana's accounts mention three "Canarias de la infanta," or female slaves from the Canary Islands, possibly Guanche natives, attendant upon her person.[72] Baeza's accounts occasionally list Queen Isabel's gifts of cloth, dresses, skirts, blouses, shoes, and capes for these slaves.[73] One of them, named Catalina, received linen for a bed and wool for mattresses in 1488.[74] Seven years later, Baeza's records indicate that Juana's entourage included four female servants or *criadas*, at least three of them former slaves.[75] Whatever the reasons for their apparent manumission, these women, Juana, Inés, Anastasia, and Catalina, remained with Juana and displayed greater loyalty toward her than other members of Isabel's court. Indeed, their initial lack of status may have made these *criadas* more dependent on Juana for the type of favors—usually unrecorded—that she could provide. Unlike former slaves, most of Juana's attendants owed their positions to Queen Isabel.

In 1496 the queen appointed official households for Juana and her brother Juan. After religious personnel (confessor, sacristan, almoner, chaplains), each child received administrative officials led by a *mayordomo mayor* (governor), *camarero mayor* (principal chamberman), *cavallerizo mayor* (first horseman), accountant, and secretary. In selecting officers to serve her children, Queen Isabel may have relied on the guidelines recorded in *Las siete partidas* (ca. 1369). Citing Aristotle's instructions for Alexander, the *Siete partidas* explained the role of royal servants using an analogy between the king and his kingdom:

> And from the lesser world [microcosm] that resembled man, he [Aristotle] made another comparison, in which he likened the king to the kingdom. In this way he explained how each should be ordered and showed that just as God placed understanding in the head of man, which is over the body, in the most noble place, he made it like the king, and wanted all of the senses and the members . . . to obey and to serve him as lord, and to govern the body and protect it like the kingdom. In addition, he showed that the officials and the shepherds should serve the king as lord, and protect and maintain the kingdom like his body.[76]

According to this text, household officials served the ruler "to guard and maintain and govern his body." In *Las siete partidas*, and probably for Isabel as well, governing royal individuals included such important tasks as providing them with clothing, food, and drink.[77]

The household that Queen Isabel gave Prince Juan 1496 remains better known than that which she assigned to Juana, thanks to an account by one of the prince's chamber boys. Nearly fifty years after Juan's death in 1497, his former servant, Gonzalo Fernández de Oviedo, idealized Juan's household as a group of officials sharing and implementing the royal will. According to Fernández de Oviedo, the office of *camarero mayor*, which he may have coveted in the household of Philip II, entailed particular intimacy with the prince. Fernández de Oviedo claimed that the prince secretly entrusted a bag of money to the *camarero*, so that only the two of them knew how that money was spent. After the prince undressed each evening, the *camarero* had the right to keep the belt that had encircled the royal person that day, or to grant it to someone else if he wished.[78] Whenever the prince desired new cloth or clothing, the *camarero* would summon the tailor to purchase the requisite items, then present them to the prince for approval. When selecting other goods such as canopies, seats, and liveries, the *camarero* had no need to disturb the prince, "because he already knows the will of His Highness, who has already consulted him and given orders on what should be done."[79] Such a model alliance between ruler and servant would prove far from Juana's antagonistic relationship with her own *camarero mayor* (discussed in chapters 3 and 6).

Nor would Juana comply with the norms that Queen Isabel established for her brother's household. According to Fernández de Oviedo, the *camarero*'s access to the prince also entitled him to the royal person's extra footwear and clothing. Because the prince usually ordered two new pairs of shoes each month in addition to at least two new pairs of slippers, moccasins, and Moorish boots each week, the *camarero* acquired whatever the prince did not use. Caps, hats, and other clothing, after Prince Juan had worn them three times, also supposedly belonged to the *camarero*, although Fernández de Oviedo claimed that the prince could bestow them on other servants and compensate the *camarero* in coin or favors. When Queen Isabel learned that her son had not been distributing his clothing among the servants, she allegedly ordered him to disburse all of the articles that he had accumulated in the last year. In this way, Fernández de Oviedo explained, the queen taught her son the virtue of liberality. Exhibiting the prince's clothing, members of his household visibly became extensions of the royal person.[80] Years later, Juana would hoard and even destroy her clothes rather than share them with servants she found unworthy.

Not only clothing, but food, required careful distribution among members of the prince's household. The principle of calculated abundance that governed Juan's wardrobe also applied to his menu. Any birds that His Highness did not consume went back to the *cocinero mayor* or principal cook. Two *vallesteros de maça* (standard-bearers) received the back of a roasted lamb or a hen in addition to their wages for entering the dining room with the royal arms before the master of the hall and the meal. Led by the *vallesteros de maça*, the public presentation of meals placed the prince and his household on display.

As extensions and protectors of the royal body, servants performed the *salva*, or ceremonial tasting, whenever the prince's food or drink changed hands. The distribution of bread and wine, invoking the sacrament of communion, also figured prominently in these ceremonies. The baker would emerge from the kitchen with a large plate of buns and rolls, publicly consuming one of them. Each of Juan's doctors, standing behind the prince and advising him throughout the meal, would also receive a roll.[81] After approaching the prince with a covered cup of wine, his principal cupbearer would execute a reverent bow, remove the lid, and then pass the cup to a gentleman who would sample the beverage.[82] Not surprisingly, the *Siete partidas* referred to princely meals as "governamiento assi como comer e bever"—government as [in] eating and drinking.[83] Castilian dining etiquette highlighted both of the king's persons: one, individual and mortal, another, encompassing the household and, by implication, the entire kingdom. The rituals of eating and dressing, like the domestic ceremonies that Juana would encounter in the Low Countries, appeared designed to illustrate ideal relations between subjects and their rulers.

Fernández de Oviedo's account also listed certain personnel that Juana apparently shared with Juan, most notably the chaplain and composer, Juan de Anchieta.[84] After Juan's death, Juana inherited a number of her brother's former servants, including master of the hall, Hernán Duque de Estrada; the physician, Doctor Nicolás de Soto; and *camarero mayor*, Pedro Núñez de Guzmán, later *ayo* (master or governor) of Juana's second son, Fernando.[85] Family continuity appeared crucial. As governor or *mayordomo mayor* of the prince's household, don Gutierre de Cárdenas, *Comendador Mayor* of Leon, ordered its members paid and settled any quarrels that arose among them. The *comendador's* eldest son, don Diego de Cárdenas, one of Juan's former pages, would later inherit his father's post in Juana's Tordesillas household. The transmission of such offices from brother to sister and from generation to generation illustrated the household's capacity to serve both the mortal prince and the royal dignity. The death of heirs did not prevent personnel from ensuring continuity in the royal household.[86]

Although far less detailed than Fernández de Oviedo's account, a memorial describing the selection of officials who would accompany Juana, now titled the Archduchess of Austria, to the Low Countries in 1496, suggests that court connections and experience counted more toward gaining posts than specialized skills or favor with Juana. After appointing don Rodrigo Manrique, second son of the Count of Paredes, *mayordomo mayor* of Juana's household, Queen Isabel granted Manrique's son the household office of his choice. She then distributed remaining posts among other nobles' relatives and clients.[87] The important appointment of *camarero mayor* went to Diego de Ribera, who had previously served young Isabel, the Portuguese *infantes* at court, and even the queen herself.[88] Juana's quartermaster of the chamber since 1485, Martín de Moxica, obtained the office of treasurer.[89] Of six stableboys who had served Juana during her early education, only Antón de Molina and Alonso Pacheco remained with her in 1496.[90] According to chronicler Lorenzo de Padilla, Queen Isabel further "ordered" her daughter's household by "giving" the archduchess eleven noble ladies to accompany her.[91] The extant documentation provides no sign of any role for Juana herself in the selection of her household staff.[92]

Unlike Juana, her brother began to take charge of his household in preparation for governing his future realms. Before granting Juan his own servants, Queen Isabel gave the prince possession of the city of Oviedo and other territories in Asturias, along with the tax revenues from those areas and civil and criminal jurisdiction over them.[93] The queen also named Juan president of his own council, so that he would "learn to exercise justice, which is the reason that God places kings and princes on earth."[94] Juana's household, on the other hand, lacked a council or any equivalent structure. It taught her to obey rather than to rule.

Marriage Strategies

Juana and Juan both received their own households as a prelude to marriage. Prince Juan began to govern his servants with the expectation of governing his bride. In contrast, the extent of Juana's domestic influence would depend largely on her husband. One of the books in Juana's library, *Visión delectable de la filosofía y artes liberales . . .*, an extended allegory in which the Liberal Arts and the Virtues progressively enlighten Human Understanding, instructed the husband to rule his wife differently from his servant and his son. If his wife proved prudent, the husband should commend the household government to her, accepting her counsel on many occasions.[95] Thus Juana might look to her husband for authority independent of her mother's.

Fernando and Isabel, like most rulers of their time, negotiated their children's marriages to advance diplomatic and strategic aims. They educated their daughters to represent their interests abroad, aware that Juana's skill in Latin and appreciation of music would serve her in any European court. In 1490 the monarchs sent Juana's older sister Isabel to marry the Portuguese prince and, upon the death of her husband, accepted Isabel back into their court. Determined to maintain the Portuguese alliance, within a few years the Catholic sovereigns persuaded their eldest daughter to marry King Manuel of Portugal.[96]

Fernando and Isabel used Juana to attain related ends. In 1488 the Holy Roman Emperor, Maximilian of Austria, sought a political alliance with Fernando and Isabel and offered to marry their eldest daughter. By this date, however, the monarchs had already promised Isabel to Portugal. Nevertheless eager to strengthen their ties with Maximilian, Fernando and Isabel offered Juana to his son, Philippe of Burgundy, in exchange for Maximilian's daughter, Marguerite of Austria, as a spouse for Prince Juan.[97] This double alliance, essentially designed to curtail French expansion, rested upon Austrian and Spanish animosity toward the Valois monarchs.[98] According to the terms of the ensuing treatises, the two brides would forgo the usual dowries from their parents. Instead, Juana and Marguerite were each to receive an annual income of 20,000 escudos, to be paid out of revenues collected in their husbands' respective territories.[99] Bowing to the wishes of her parents' realms, Juana could only accept their refusal to assume financial responsibility for her person.

Whatever Juana's thoughts about her betrothal to Philippe, one fact stands out: she was the only daughter of Fernando and Isabel to wed a duke rather than a ruling king or a prince awaiting the throne. The idea that Juana might marry beneath her station surfaced in a series of verses written to celebrate the alliance. In an attempt to elevate Philippe's status, the anonymous poet granted him the elective title of "King of the Romans" that pertained to Philippe's father, Maximilian, implying that Philippe could likewise become emperor and make Juana empress.[100] When Burgundian ambassadors visited the Castilian court,[101] the poet claimed that doña Juana appeared at her window:

Whereof the courtiers
took joy in the beauty

Of her animated face
with the clarity
of a virtuous stone
clear and brilliant
her beauty shining
her great ability
well worthy
of the high aspiration
to be more than empress.

Her Highness adorned
I will tell you how I saw her
with a dress colored
in very rich scarlet
trimmed with crimson
she wore a great ruby
and other brilliant stones
which gave such light
that they would brighten
the darkest nights.[102]

Impressed by Juana's resplendent beauty, one of the ambassadors allegedly requested a portrait of the *infanta* to share with the people of his homeland.[103] Although unidentified, the portrait in question may have resembled that attributed to Michael Sittow, presently in the collection of the Marquis of Santillana. In the preceding verse as in that painting, Juana wore her trademark ruby pendant suspended from a simple black ribbon.[104]

The anonymous verses also attempted to enhance Juana's status by emphasizing her monarchical virtues of clemency and magnanimity. Given a high level of tensions with France, the poet explained, Queen Isabel prepared an impressive armada to escort her daughter from the port of Laredo to Flanders.[105] According to the poet, Juana's fleet supposedly encountered enemy vessels off the coast of La Rochelle:

And after setting sail
on the ocean with her men

they saw many ships and caravels
depart from La Rochelle
with a great fleet of Bretons
whose false beliefs
brought them a bad turn
for in the end
the Spanish armada
took their fleet.[106]

Although, according to the poet, the Frenchmen deserved death, Juana allegedly persuaded her gentlemen to exercise clemency and to send the prisoners to Castile. This apparently fictional episode, which appears in no other source,[107] suggests a dramatic shift in Castilian ideology since the war on Granada against the Moors. Unbelievers now appeared in the guise of Frenchmen, and Juana would lead the crusade against them.

Had Juana's education prepared her to secure an anti-French alliance? Could she, guided by only a few loyal Spaniards, successfully represent her parents' policy in the Burgundian court? As Juana sailed toward Flanders in August 1496 with her escort of up to 133 vessels and 15,000 men,[108] the corporate interests of Castile and Aragon must have weighed heavily upon her small frame. Juana's ability to fulfill her role, like that of Queen Isabel, would depend largely on her husband.

CHAPTER TWO

Competing Court Cultures and the French Menace, 1496–1502

Juana suffered a number of setbacks as she traveled to meet a fiancé who shared neither her language nor her culture. Troubles began when contrary winds forced the ships that were escorting Juana to the Low Countries to take shelter at Portland, England, on 31 August. The Spaniards reembarked 2 September, but only to endure five days stranded in still waters.[1] When the fleet finally could approach the port of Middelburg in Zeeland, one of its ships, a Genoese carrack carrying seven hundred individuals, Juana's wardrobe, and many of her personal effects, hit a sandbank and sank.[2] The loss of part of the *infanta*'s crew and most of her possessions represented a serious reversal but was only the first of many misfortunes awaiting Juana. Her future husband's failure to welcome Juana when she stepped ashore at Middelburg also presaged enduring problems.[3]

Philippe's absence at Middelburg stemmed from the deep-rooted antipathy of some of his closest advisers, notably François de Busleyden, the archbishop of Besançon, and Guillaume de Croy, seigneur de Chièvres, toward a union between the houses of Burgundy and Castile. Although Juana's parents had envisioned her marriage to Philippe as an alliance against France, she quickly discovered that many of Philippe's advisers supported close relations with the

French court. Castilian and Aragonese interests required one set of policies, whereas Juana's potential Burgundian subjects demanded another. Caught between opponents and allies of France, Juana risked disappointing both. Whereas Juana's education in the court of the Catholic monarchs underlies her difficulties in the Low Countries, her experiences as Archduchess of Austria, Duchess of Burgundy and Brabant, and Countess of Flanders offer insights into her subsequent failure to rule Castile and Aragon. The sources rarely, if ever, provide direct access to Juana's thoughts but nevertheless make it possible to examine the conflicting demands upon her.

The Spanish-Burgundian alliance designed to isolate the Valois monarchs of France was largely the brainchild of Philippe's father, the Emperor Maximilian. In 1495 Maximilian contracted the marriage of his children, Philippe and Marguerite, to Fernando and Isabel's offspring, Juana and Juan. Opposing these marriages, Philippe's advisers convinced him to travel to Germany, in the first of many efforts to separate him from Juana. As late as 1496, Philippe's Francophile advisers may have hoped to persuade the emperor of the virtues of an alliance with France rather than Spain. Thus, as Juana disembarked at Middelburg, she began a one-way journey into a web of competing interests that constituted the Burgundian court.

At the center of this web stood Juana's future husband, Philippe, Archduke of Austria, Duke of Burgundy, Brabant, Limburg, and Luxemburg, Count of Flanders, Habsburg, Hainaut, Holland, Zeeland, Tirol, and Artois, and Lord of Antwerp and Mechelen, among other provinces. From his birth in 1478, Philippe had enjoyed privileged status as the Burgundian heir. The death of his mother, Mary of Burgundy, in 1482, left Philippe, at age four, in the hands of councillors who steered their young charge toward an alliance with France. While governing Philippe's diverse provinces, these attendants and advisers entertained the boy with sports, banquets, and, eventually, women.[4] The ostentatious, pleasure-seeking atmosphere that surrounded the young Philippe radically differed from the devout, austere court that Juana had known in Castile.

Franco-Burgundian norms collided with Castilian attitudes toward eating, drinking, dress, worship, and sexuality. For Spanish observers, French influence in the Burgundian court indicated various levels of error, from personal betrayal to moral corruption. Previous Burgundian duchesses, Isabel of Portugal, who had married Duke Philip "the Good," and Margaret of York, the widow of Duke Charles "the Bold," who remained in Flanders until her own death in 1503, had periodically left the Burgundian court to pursue spiritual goals. On the other hand, Queen Isabel of Castile had made her court a nucleus of moral and spiritual reform. Accustomed to highly organized, elaborate splendor, the Burgundians failed to perceive dignity in Spaniards' sober simplicity. In short, the Franco-Burgundian and Castilian courts embraced different aspects of Renaissance humanism, which scholars have recently labeled "rigorist" or "moralist" (for Castile) and "hedonist" (for France and Burgundy).[5]

Philippe's attitudes toward his nobles and cities also contrasted with those that Juana had observed in her parents. Since 1480, political events in Burgundy had taken a different course from those of Castile. The great Burgundian nobles had prevented King Maximilian from influencing young Philippe's household, which they dominated. In contrast, as we have seen, Queen Isabel personally had selected servants to govern Juana. Whereas Fernando and Isabel had defended the cities and towns of Castile against the claims of landed magnates, Philippe had relied on his own nobles to punish rebellious municipalities. Amid various uprisings, the burghers of Ghent had held Philippe captive from 1482 to 1485, and the merchants of Bruges had imprisoned Maximilian in 1488. Yet noble support eventually forced even the most prosperous, independent-minded towns to recognize Philippe's sovereignty. The archduke's elite councillors correspondingly enhanced their authority over Philippe. Although known today as Philippe "the Handsome," in his own day the archduke received the epithet *croit conseil*, "believer of council," in allusion to his eminent governability.[6] Thus, in 1496, great nobles directed the government policy of the Low Countries more than that of Castile. Philippe's upbringing made him far more inclined than Juana to favor the high nobility.[7]

In the absence of Philippe and his entourage, only doña María Manuel, a Castilian noblewoman connected to the Burgundian court, welcomed Juana to Middelburg. During negotiations leading up to the Castilian-Burgundian alliance, doña María had married Maximilian's representative, Balduin of Burgundy, an illegitimate son of Charles "the Bold."[8] Together, doña María and Balduin formed the core of a potential pro-Spanish party in the Netherlands, albeit one that lacked influence with Philippe. Encouraged by doña María and Balduin, Juana retained a clear view of her mission: to secure the double alliance that her parents had arranged. Toward this end, Juana refused to lose time traveling to Bruges, where Philippe had organized a reception for her.[9] Instead, Juana went to Bergen-op-Zoom in order cultivate a family with pro-Spanish leanings led by Jean, seignior de Berghes, Philippe's first chamberlain and a member of the distinguished Order of the Golden Fleece. While enjoying de

Berghes's hospitality, Juana held his newborn daughter, christened Jeanne in her honor, over the baptismal font. Through such attentions, she confirmed the influential de Berghes family's support for the Spanish cause. Determined to reach Philippe as swiftly as possible, Juana departed, leaving most of her luggage on de Berghes's estates.[10]

Juana's visit to Bergen-op-Zoom entailed only a brief pause as she hastened to reach her groom and also to dispatch her brother's bride, Marguerite, to Spain in the fleet moored at Middelburg. After concluding her marriage to Philippe on 20 October 1496, Juana would pertain to and represent her husband's territories in addition to her parents' realms. A number of constitutional ceremonies, particularly joyous entries and solemn oaths, entailed competing attempts to govern Juana during her introduction to the Low Countries from 1496 through 1501 and her subsequent journey to Spain as heiress to the kingdoms of Castile and Aragon. Visiting the territories incorporated in her various titles, Juana established and reinforced fundamental ties between her realms and her person.[11] Franco-Burgundian and Spanish court cultures competed through public rituals and an ongoing struggle to control the household that would govern Juana.

Miraculous Entries, Ignominious Exits

Like any royal bride in a foreign land, Juana attempted to balance the demands of her parents against those of her groom. More responsible to Burgundian than Castilian subjects, Juana sought to please all parties during her first years in the Low Countries. In spite of her efforts, the members of Juana's Spanish escort suffered illness and even hunger. Most of those Spaniards who survived the winter of 1496–97 chose to return to Castile with Marguerite of Austria rather than remain with Juana. In turn, Juana became acquainted with the people of the Low Countries. She honored her subjects and received their homage through a series of inaugural entries into Philippe's principal cities and towns.

While continuing east from Bergen-op-Zoom in pursuit of Philippe, the aspiring archduchess reached the city of Antwerp on 19 September 1496. A chronicler associated with the Burgundian court described Juana's Antwerp entry in idyllic terms:

This very illustrious and virtuous lady . . . of handsome bearing and gracious manner, the most richly adorned ever seen before in the lands of monsignor the archduke, rode a mule in the Spanish fashion with her head uncovered, accompanied by sixteen young noble ladies and one matron who followed her, dressed in golden cloth and mounted in the same manner, having pages with rich adornments and 27 or 30 trumpeters who did everything possible to wake good courage in this entry.[12]

As she entered Antwerp, Juana represented her parents' desire to establish an alliance with Philippe. Her rich appearance and estimable entourage indicated that Juana was the daughter of important monarchs and alluded to the commercial promise of closer ties with Castile.[13]

Juana's quest for support in Flanders compromised her health as well as her reputation at home. Upon reaching Antwerp, Juana suffered from fever and took to bed for several days. The future archduchess nevertheless fared better than many of her travel-weary companions, including the party's leading ecclesiastic, the bishop of Jaén, don Luis Osorio, who died in Antwerp.[14] By far the worst casualties, however, occurred on the icy coast of Zeeland, where most of the fifteen thousand men who had accompanied Juana to Middelburg remained, awaiting Marguerite of Austria in order to return to Castile. Different sources roughly agree that up to nine thousand members of the Spanish crew perished from cold and hunger that winter.[15] When news of the company's high mortality trickled back to Spain, Juana received the blame for a tragedy that she could not have averted.[16]

In fact, Juana did her best to expedite Marguerite of Austria's departure for Castile. After receiving the future princess of Asturias in Antwerp in early October, Juana accompanied her to the small town of Lier.[17] On 12 October Philippe himself reached Lier. Six days later, Juana's first chaplain, don Diego Ramírez de Villaescusa, blessed the couple's union, which they consummated at once. On 20 October 1496 the bishop of Cambray and subsequent leader of the pro-Spanish faction, Henry de Berghes, brother of Jean (whose loyalty Juana had confirmed at Bergen-op-Zoom), performed the official marriage ceremony.[18] In addition to Marguerite of Austria and Margaret of York, the dowager Duchess of Burgundy, witnesses to the monumental if rather unglamorous event included Philippe's greatest vassals: Balduin, Marquis of Baden; Philippe of Ravenstein; Englebert, Count of Nassau; Balduin, "bastard of Burgundy"; Philibert of Burgundy; Jean de Berghes; Guillaume de Croy; Hughes de Melun; Balduin de Lannoy; Henry de Berselle; and Pierre de Fresnoy—all members of the elite chivalric Order of the Golden Fleece. The bride's party featured the Admiral of

Castile, don Fadrique Enríquez; his brother, Bernardino Enríquez, Count of Melgar; Rodrigo Manrique; Enrique Enríquez; Francisco Enríquez; Fernando de Cordoba; Sancho de Tovar; and Martín de Tavara.[19] Considering the Spanish fleet rotting in Zeeland, Juana and her attendants made every effort to hasten the requisite formalities. Following the marriage, they accompanied Philippe, Marguerite of Austria, and the court back to Antwerp.[20] Slightly north of that city, the new archduchess parted ways with her husband, who would escort Marguerite as far as Middelburg, and most of the Spanish nobles, who would return to Castile. Upon reaching Bergen-op-Zoom, Philippe feted the Admiral of Castile, granted the admiral's mother, doña María de Velasco, a large image of the Virgin with Child surrounded by twenty-seven pearls, and gave the Count of Melgar a cross of diamonds.[21] Although Juana may have wished to retain these Spanish nobles in her entourage, the interests of her parents' kingdoms took precedence over any such desire. Other important servants, including Juana's tutor fray Andrés de Miranda and the Countess of Caminas, doña Beatriz de Tavara, also may have left Juana at this time.

Lacking an alternative, Juana turned to her new subjects. Entering Mechelen and Brussels in December 1496, she continued courting the citizens of Philippe's most important cities and towns.[22] Juana's first visit to each community, termed a "joyous entry" (*blijde inkomst* or *joyeuse entrée*), involved her public presentation and recognition as countess or duchess. These inaugural events entailed Juana's reception outside each city or town, followed by her procession through streets hung with tapestries and past theatrical displays arranged in her honor.[23] Depending on the community's size and importance, its secular and ecclesiastical leaders then presented Juana with twenty-four to two hundred lots of wine, among other gifts.[24] Through this series of events, the townspeople acknowledged Juana's authority as Philippe's wife.

Vivid images of such inaugural ceremonies appear in a manuscript commemorating Juana's entry into Brussels, 9 December 1496.[25] The sixty-three-folio, exquisitely illuminated volume, recorded a citywide procession that included the archduchess. A series of corporate groups, including friars, scholars, royal councillors, mathematicians, and musicians, paraded before Juana and the people of Brussels. Other participants, including clowns and "wild men," enhanced the festive atmosphere. At the climax of the procession, Juana herself appeared. Lifted high by members of the halberdiers' guild, the archduchess shone in gold and red fabric that matched their torches. According to the manuscript record-

ing this event, Juana's presence "miraculously" (*ad miraculo*)[26] tamed the tumultuous multitude, "so that it could remain for posterity as a miracle" (*huisque ac
posteris miraculo fuisse potuerit*).[27]

Once Juana reached the Great Square of Brussels, she encountered a series
of theatrical scenes arranged to amuse and to instruct her. These representations,
featuring biblical, mythological, and historical heroines, were accompanied by
Latin inscriptions relating them to Juana. One of the first presentations, labeled
"Judith—Holofernes," depicted the Jewish heroine with a raised knife in one
hand and Holofernes's head in the other.[28] The accompanying inscription noted,
rather alarmingly: "Judith redeemed the people of Israel by killing Holofernes.
In this way our illustrious lady Juana will free her people from their adversaries."[29] This reference to "adversaries" presumably alluded to the French, who
had occupied Brussels in 1489. Subsequent scenes and comparisons encouraged
the archduchess to emulate other female champions, including Sara, the wife of
Tobias, Penthesilea, Semiramis, and Queen Isabel of Castile.[30] The city of Brussels, in short, provided its new archduchess with examples of heroines who had
exercised authority in ways that ranged from fervent prayer (Sara) to murderous
action (Judith).[31]

Following this spectacular entry, Philippe, having dispatched his sister to
Spain, met Juana in Brussels and traveled with her to Ghent. Their joint entry
into that city on 10 March 1497 differed from Philippe's last visit in 1482, when
local citizens held him hostage in a dispute over the regency.[32] In contrast, the
events of 1497 emphasized harmony and reconciliation. As in Antwerp, the
archduchess entered Ghent dressed in golden cloth and followed by her female
attendants, all mounted on rich saddles, "in the Spanish manner." By this time,
Juana's entourage also began to display signs of Franco-Burgundian influence.
Great hats typical of French fashion adorned the ladies' heads, while Juana's
new gentleman of honor, Jean, seignior de Berghes, and other members of the
chivalric Order of the Golden Fleece preceded the women.[33] On the surface,
Juana appeared to adapt well to northern fashions and customs. Once welcomed
into the city, Juana demonstrated the sovereign virtue of clemency by pardoning a prisoner found guilty of "dishonest conduct [*gouvernement*] with women
other than his own"—an offense she would later find more difficult to excuse in
her own husband.[34] Even with Philippe present, Juana appeared to cultivate
Burgundian ties without relinquishing her Spanish identity.

Beyond joyous entries into Ghent, Bruges,[35] and additional cities, the archdukes participated in other rituals designed to demonstrate the divine and pop-

ular mandate for their rule. By convoking regular meetings of the Order of the Golden Fleece, Philippe confirmed ties with his top vassals as a religiously sanctioned governing elite. For her part, the archduchess demonstrated her piety by visiting Franciscan convents in Brussels and Bruges.[36] Juana's participation in the Easter procession of Bruges also emphasized her identification with a wider spiritual and political community.[37]

Juana's involvement in joyous entries and religious processions, like that of any sixteenth-century consort, entailed quite limited contact with her subjects. Within the household, however, Burgundian nobles assigned to the archduchess gained direct access to her. Juana's daily interactions with attendants from Philippe's different territories enabled them to pressure her to favor their interests. In theory, these nobles offered the archduchess more personal ties to the people of the Low Countries. In practice, they attempted to reorganize Juana's household—a principal instrument for the acculturation of the archduchess and her attendants—in order to isolate and to govern her.

The Burgundian Model in Theory and Practice

Juana's household proved the focal point for competition between the Castilian and Burgundian customs represented, in principle, by servants native to each land. When, in September 1496, Juana entered the Low Countries, her household included ninety-eight Spanish men and at least eleven Spanish women.[38] The staff, initially led by eleven religious officials and nine nobles, soon underwent extensive changes. By March 1497 only sixteen of the original ninety-eight Spanish men remained with the archduchess. Seventy new Burgundian attendants had assumed positions in Juana's household, which they began to reorganize along Burgundian lines.[39] How could Queen Isabel's elite assembly undergo such a drastic transformation?

Although native Burgundians had traditionally served their own duchess,[40] Queen Isabel appeared surprised by the rejection of Castilian attendants she had selected for Juana. Informed of Burgundian attempts to replace Castilian servants, in October 1496 Isabel sent the bishop of Catania, Pedro Ruiz de la Mota, to Flanders "to ensure that the persons that the archduchess took with her for her service are not ousted from her household."[41] The queen also insisted that subsequent marriage agreements she signed with Henry VIII explicitly guarantee her youngest daughter, Catalina (Catherine of Aragon), the right to maintain up to 150 Castilian servants in England.[42] In a possible attempt to appease

Queen Isabel, Philippe's father, Maximilian, allegedly urged the new archduchess "not to let herself be defeated" and promised to help her combat the
Burgundian takeover.[43] Yet neither Juana nor Maximilian took any clear steps to
prevent Burgundians from pushing Castilians out of Juana's household.

Besides Juana's apparent inaction, cultural and economic factors may have
contributed to her loss of over eighty Spanish servants in six months. Castilians
voiced particular objections to what they perceived as low morals and high
prices in the Burgundian court. Juana's tutor, fray Andrés de Miranda, cited the
court's perilous moral atmosphere as his primary reason for leaving Flanders.[44]
Fray Tomás de Matienzo, one of Fernando and Isabel's ambassadors to Philippe
and Juana, agreed, claiming that the Burgundians "honor drinking well more
than living well." Matienzo emphasized the expense of his mission in Flanders
by declaring that he could live in Castile for the price of solely his lodgings at
the Burgundian court.[45] Conversely, Burgundians scorned the Spaniards' modest dress, frugal spending, and somber dining practices.[46] Unable or unwilling
to compete with the Burgundians, many of Juana's Spanish attendants simply
left Philippe's court.

The Spanish exodus, whatever its precise causes, enabled Philippe's intimates
to dominate Juana's household. Within two months of the Lier marriage, servants who had long attended Philippe began entering and restructuring Juana's
household.[47] Philippe's former governess, Jeanne de Commines, Madame de
Hallewin, became Juana's principal lady-in-waiting.[48] Similarly, two of Philippe's
squires, Charles de Lattre and Bonnet Desne, alternately took charge of Juana's
stables. Philippe's former household secretary, Jehan de la Chappelle, performed
that same office for Juana for several years before his promotion to her master
accountant and Philippe's counseler.[49] The archduchess also received one of
Philippe's tailors, Gilles le Monnier, and several of his lower-level officers.[50] Similarly, Christophe de Barronze, a Portuguese gentleman who had served Mary
of Burgundy and Philippe as master of the house, accepted the same charge
alongside Juana as early as 2 December 1496.[51] Along with another master of the
house, Claude de Cilly, Christophe de Barronze could attend councils of justice
and war, punish malefactors, control Juana's expenses, and direct ceremonies in
her household.[52]

These and other officers instituted structural changes in Juana's household,
which either eliminated or assimilated her Spanish attendants. Thirty-three
hommes espagnoles or *compagnons espagnards*, who accompanied Juana for five
months with fifty-six mules, disappeared from her household records by Febru-

ary 1497, presumably to return to Castile with Marguerite of Austria.[53] Other Spaniards remained with Juana and managed to secure positions in her new household. By 18 March 1497 individuals whom the wage lists previously identified simply as *espaignards* received Frenchified names—indicating some degree of recognition and even acceptance for the few surviving Spaniards. By assigning Frenchified names for convenience, Burgundian administrators may have indicated that they began to consider the remaining Spaniards less dispensable. Hence, Alonse de Burghes (Alonso de Burgos), Jehan de Orteghe (Juan de Ortega), and Pastromenis filled the offices of "chapelany espagnarts"; Francisque Gravi and Martin de Assasa became "varlets de chambre espaignarts"; and Anthoine de Moligne (Antonio de Molina) replaced "une saulsier espagnart." García de Camp became identified as "une huissier d'armes espagnart," and Alonse Pachicque (Alonso Pacheco) became "une garde linge espaignart." Other Spanish servants, including baker Fernando de Molina (Fernande de Moligne) and footservant Rodrigo de la Sal (Rodrique de la Salle), were named from the first available list of wages.[54] These potentially assimilating Castilians, along with new, Burgundian personnel, secured positions in Juana's Burgundian household.

In addition to new positions and personnel, Philippe and his councillors imposed Burgundian practices on Juana's household that differed from the relatively flexible etiquette that she had known in Castile. Such procedures included rotating terms of service as well as comprehensive accountability and control through ordinances and daily wages. Perhaps the most distinguishing feature of Burgundian protocol—disciplined rituals sacralizing the ruler's person[55]—involved strict procedures for dining and public appearances that honored the duchess yet clearly subordinated her to the duke. Together, such requirements made Juana's household dependent on her husband and his councillors. Perhaps most importantly, the new Burgundian etiquette enabled Philippe and his advisers to begin controlling access to Juana's person—an essential step in their efforts to govern her.

New household ordinances issued in March 1497 formalized the Burgundianization of Juana's entourage and its subordination to Philippe's. In these regulations, Philippe declared his intention: "To institute good order, rule, and conduct wherever necessary for our own good and that of our countries and subjects . . . we wish, as reason requires, to begin with our estate and household, along with that of our very dear and beloved companion the archduchess, so that we and she henceforth will be honorably accompanied." Updating the famous

"Burgundian model" codified by Olivier de la Marche in 1493 (more than fifty years before Gonzalo Fernández de Oviedo attempted to raise the household of Prince Juan to the same level), the 1497 ordinances presented order and good government in the archducal household as the foundation for the peace and unity of Philippe's realms. They reserved the most prestigious positions in Philippe's household for his most powerful vassals, led by "Cousin Albrecht, duc de Saxe."[56] They also required each of forty-one magnates to reside at court with three to six armed knights at all times in order to accompany the archduke, particularly during the celebration of Mass and "joyous" entries. In this way, Philippe ensured that he would always appear with a powerful entourage. At the same time, the quintessential Burgundian practice of rotating terms of service enabled other nobles to spend two-thirds of each year outside of the court, attending to their own affairs and reinforcing ties between different provinces and the archduke. Although the surviving documentation contains no specific provisions for Juana's household in 1497, the extant ordinances noted the political relevance of domestic regulations for rulers as well as for their consorts.[57]

As an extension of Philippe's entourage, Juana's household also connected her to his realms. Changes in Juana's records after the 1497 ordinances were issued indicate that the original regulations probably contained specific provisions for her household as well. For example, in 1496 Juana's dining service simply included cooks, a carver, and a cupbearer. On 16 March 1497, for the first time, her expenses listed Burgundian chiefs for departments or *états* mirroring Philippe's: "Panneterie [bakery] par Sidrac de Lannoy . . . Eschansonnerie [winery] par Ector de Meliades . . . Cuisine [kitchen] par Phelippe de Pontrewart . . . Escurierie [stables] par Charles de Lattre . . . Fourrierie [quartermaster] par Pasquier de Masieres."[58] Two days after this expense account, the first of many lists of wages for Juana's Burgundian household appeared—naming, in this case, eighty-six persons.[59] Certain key individuals, including Juana's first gentleman of honor, Monsieur de Berghes, and most of her female attendants, did not receive wages. These high-status servants, whose names do not appear on the regular payroll, obtained pensions and other gifts at Philippe's discretion. In accord with Burgundian tradition, Philippe and his advisers maintained direct control over the rewards that Juana's top-level officials received.

Philippe and his councillors gained and exercised control over Juana's household by appointing and rewarding her personnel. In addition to surrounding the archduchess with Burgundians, the archduke and his advisers attempted to co-opt Juana's remaining Spanish officials through a policy of gifts and offices. The

1497 ordinances listed, for example, an annual pension of 272 livres for Juana's confessor and first chaplain, Diego Ramírez de Villaescusa. Similarly, Juana's Spanish treasurer, Martín de Moxica, became one of Philippe's favorite ambassadors to the Catholic monarchs, attaining the rank of master of Juana's household by 1498 and the title *chevalier* by 1504.[60] Another of Philippe's ambassadors to Fernando and Isabel, Miguel Franco (known as "Granada"), Juana's herald and servant of the chamber, eventually received a post in the archduke's own household.[61] Franco and his wife also received silver cups after baptizing each of their two sons "Philippe."[62]

Ordinances issued in 1501—preserved for Juana as well as for Philippe—confirm that the Burgundian initiative also accommodated a number of less prestigious Spaniards in Juana's household. The Archives Générales du Royaume in Brussels contain two different plans for the structure of Juana's household in 1501.[63] The initial plan enumerated requisite offices without respect to the individuals who might fill them and calculated that wages, food, and pensions for Juana's household amounted to over 32,000 livres per year. The other plan attempted to accommodate those Spaniards who remained with Juana within the confines of this budget. In many cases, these servants, who would not easily fit into the Burgundian hierarchy or system of rotating service per term, required special treatment. In order to accommodate them, the scheme called for a reduction by approximately one-third in the projected wages of most Burgundian and Flemish officials. Such decreases in Burgundian pay made some degree of resentment toward Castilian servants nearly inevitable.

These salary adjustments enabled a minority of Spaniards to receive offices in Juana's Burgundian household. Of 144 individuals named in the 1501 ordinance, only 29 appear to have Spanish origins. The rest can be classified as either Flemish or Burgundian.[64] Somewhat mitigating this apparent imbalance, most of the Burgundians assigned to Juana served alternate six-month terms.[65] The Burgundian household, while excluding many Spanish customs, was forced to accommodate full-term service. Conversely, the inability of Spanish attendants to return to their homes every year or to exercise local offices may have helped them lose touch with Castilian interests. Overall, Juana's household involved roughly one-third the size and expense of Philippe's retinue, representing a customary distribution of human and economic resources in the Burgundian court.[66] Juana and her servants survived only by adapting to the new administrative procedures and cultural norms that they enshrined.

Philippe and his councillors also attempted to influence Juana's female attendants, including those appointed by Isabel of Castile. The 1501 ordinance promised to feed "slaves and other women" alongside Juana in compensation for their services.[67] In addition, Philippe made a point of granting gifts and pensions to doña Ana de Beaumont and fourteen other noble ladies serving the archduchess.[68] Nurses and cradle maids incorporated into Juana's household without wages following the birth of her children likewise depended on "extraordinary" pay that only Philippe could provide. As a result, it appears that Philippe's authority over Juana's female servants grew while Juana's dwindled.

Comparison with an earlier Duchess of Burgundy, Isabel of Portugal, points to Juana's failure to marry any of her Spanish maids to Burgundian nobles as an important departure from tradition, probably due to her lack of any funds to dower them.[69] Troubled by the situation, in August 1500, the family of one Castilian attendant, Beatriz de Bobadilla, arranged a Spanish marriage for Beatriz and summoned her back to Castile. Although Philippe claimed that Beatriz would marry a Burgundian gentleman, archival records show no evidence that he actually supported such a union.[70] In spite of the lack of marriage prospects, Beatriz and nine other Spanish ladies remained with Juana until 1504, when they would refuse to return to the Low Countries.[71] Despite the minimal incentives that Juana could provide these female attendants, they resisted the Burgundian takeover longer than her male officials.

Burgundian influence over Juana's household rested upon more than the home-court advantage that Philippe and his councillors enjoyed. Pushing out Juana's Spanish attendants, servants loyal to Philippe and his advisers gradually surrounded the archduchess and restructured her household along Burgundian lines. While Queen Isabel decried these changes, Juana herself showed little sign of resistance. For the most part, Juana lacked the funds and the personnel to sustain values, customs, policies, and institutions associated with the Castilian court in Flanders. Without economic resources, the archduchess could not govern her own household. Paradoxically, the situation, which horrified Juana's parents, represented a continuation of her experience in Castile.

Financial Straits: "In the Hands of Madame the Archduchess"

On the most basic level, Juana's absence of authority over her household rested upon a lack of financial autonomy. Although attempts to surround foreign brides with local personnel were nothing new, Juana's inability to access her dowry represented a startling innovation.[72] The marriage accord of 1495 had stipulated that Philippe and Juan would provide Juana and Marguerite with annual allowances of 20,000 escudos to maintain their persons and households.[73] Although Marguerite personally received the stipulated annual sum,[74] Juana found her promised income controlled by the Chambre des Comptes (House of Accounts) at Lille. The situation left her financially dependent on the whims of Philippe and his advisers.

When Juana received no funds, Fernando and Isabel unsuccessfully attempted to remedy her financial situation. In October 1496 they instructed an ambassador to Flanders, Pedro Ruiz de la Mota, to insist that Philippe pay Juana her allowance.[75] In addition, the Catholic monarchs set aside funds to help finance a pro-Spanish party at the Burgundian court. Assigning annual pensions to five key members of Philippe's household (Englebert, Count of Nassau; Philippe of Burgundy; Jean, seignior de Crumughen; Jean, seignior de Berghes; and François de Busleyden, archbishop of Besançon), the Catholic monarchs attempted to encourage these men to favor Juana's "things and interests."[76] Nevertheless, these pensions, ranging from 300 to 1,000 ducats, fell below those these same officials received from Philippe (from 600 to 3,000 livres).[77] The Spanish pensions were, moreover, rarely paid.[78] Consequently, the Catholic monarchs' attempt to help their daughter and to buy influence at the Burgundian court came to naught.

In response to Spanish complaints, Philippe's councillors eventually proposed to assign Juana's annual 20,000 escudos (an estimated 33,000 livres per year) to revenues and taxes from towns in different provinces.[79] During the 1497 negotiations over these payments, Fernando's secretary inquired whether Juana would obtain jurisdiction over the stipulated towns or simply revenue from them.[80] In the end, Juana received neither. Philippe's councillors retained authority over taxes and justice in the towns supposedly assigned to Juana. For example, the towns of Valenciennes and Ath, which were supposed to provide Juana with an annual 3,432 livres, remained in the hands of Guillaume de Croy, seigneur de Chièvres and grand bailiff of Hainaut.[81] Philippe and his advisers proved determined to deny Juana the independent economic and territorial power that previous duchesses had enjoyed.[82]

Although the subject of Juana's finances requires further study, money raised in Juana's name in fact appears to have gone to the general treasury. Celebrating the arrival of their new archduchess, in 1496 the États Générales voted an aid of 60,000 livres "on the occasion of the joyous entry of the Archduchess

Jeanne and for her [personal effects]" to be paid over three years. First collected in 1499, much of this money actually went toward compensations—kickbacks, to employ a more modern term—to monasteries and officials in regions that supported the tax. Of the 60,000 livres voted for Juana, only 1,356 were "paid and delivered in the hands of madame the archduchess to convert in her pleasures and affairs, for which she does not wish any other, more ample declaration."[83] Even accounts discharged at court flowed into the larger Recette Général des Finances, which Philippe and his councillors controlled.[84] Indeed, Juana's success in winning her husband's subjects proved a rather double-edged sword. As late as August 1504, Philippe refused to assign his wife any sum for incidental expenses. A document developed to estimate extraordinary costs, after assigning 2,600 livres to Juana's children, specified "regarding that of madame and her extraordinary estate—nothing, for it appears that monseigneur wants her to request assistance from the people [*demande ayde aux pays*]."[85]

In spite of rents assigned and taxes voted on her behalf, Juana herself seems to have obtained funds only at Philippe's discretion. During one sojourn in Bruges, the archduke ordered Simon Longin, *receveur général*, to deliver 200 livres "into Juana's hands for one time at this place to employ in certain customs and affairs at her good pleasure."[86] On 2 May and 13 November 1497, respectively, Simon Longin delivered 900, then 2,100 livres "into Juana's hands to do her pleasure."[87] On 31 January 1498, Juana signed for the receipt of 3,100 livres under the same conditions.[88] Later, when Juana resided in Ghent and Philippe in Bruges, the archduke sent his wife a special messenger with 800 livres "to employ in some of her affairs at her very noble pleasure," which the messenger delivered "in the hands of Madame."[89] Thus Juana's "good pleasure" depended on that of Philippe and his advisers. In turn, Juana acknowledged that she received such funds "by the commandment and ordinance of my said lord and by virtue of his letters patents."[90] Through this formula Juana recognized her economic dependence upon the archduke.

The Catholic monarchs' representative at the Burgundian court, fray Tomás de Matienzo, appeared less resigned than Juana in early 1499. In one letter to Fernando and Isabel, Matienzo noted that the Spaniards who remained with Juana complained that they were "paid badly" and that the archduchess did not "intervene in the governance of her household."[91] According to Matienzo, Juana "lived in such penury" that she could not even obtain "a single maravedí to give alms"[92]—perhaps exaggerating Juana's plight to reach the royal ear. When Philippe's councillors' remunerated and even selected her servants, the archduchess reportedly told Matienzo: "Let it pass this year, but next year I do not want them to make grants without me."[93] With little hope of Juana being able to assert such authority, the ambassador declared: "I believe that she will always remain needy, and her [servants] dying of hunger, and thus it will continue until Your Highnesses take action."[94] Matienzo's pleas on Juana's behalf ceased once his name appeared on the list of wages disbursed to members of Juana's household.[95] With Matienzo compromised, Juana retained few, if any, advisers encouraging her to resist Philippe's control.

As Philippe asserted his authority over Juana's household, he apparently appeased both Juana and her servants with occasional gifts. For example, on New Year's Day, 1497, he gave the archduchess a cross bearing five diamond tablets and a large pendant pearl that had once belonged to his mother, Mary, Duchess of Burgundy.[96] From Mary of Burgundy's former possessions, Philippe subsequently gave Juana a cross of Saint Adrian, an image of Saint Margaret, two lockets, two pearl necklaces, three paintings, and four coffers. According to the inventory, one of these coffers "contained no gold upon the demise of the deceased Madame Isabel of Portugal," suggesting that it had belonged to Isabel of Portugal before Mary of Burgundy.[97] Thus Philippe honored Juana by presenting her with objects that emphasized her rightful succession as duchess, even if she lacked an income in order to exercise the authority normally associated with that position.

Philippe's munificence extended to all branches of Juana's household. By investing in his wife's stables, the archduke attempted to please Juana's Spanish and Burgundian ladies while impressing local subjects. In August 1498 Philippe spent 24 livres for six ladies' saddles along with an additional 48 livres for twelve golden saddle covers, all of which went to Juana's stables.[98] One year later, the archduke paid a Brussels painter 190 livres to decorate two carriages with Philippe and Juana's arms and devices "to serve Madame at her very noble pleasure."[99] Then, on New Year's Day, 1501, Philippe gave 6 livres to each of Juana's guards of the chamber.[100] Philippe's calculated largesse magnified his authority.

In contrast with evidence of Philippe's bounty, very few records of Juana's generosity remain. Given her limited purse, the archduchess could rarely afford the expenditures necessary to guarantee the loyalty of her servants. One unusual source, a twenty-four-folio list of expenses that Juana's tailor, Gilles de Vers, incurred "at the command of my said lady" indicates that Juana did make an effort to reward faithful servants through gifts of clothing, so important in the Castilian court. In 1497 Juana gave two of her Spanish ladies, doña Blanca Manrique and doña Beatriz de Bobadilla, sober black dresses and provided clothing for Anne d'Assus, probably a young slave.[101] In 1499 and 1500 the tailor's accounts list the first articles of clothing for Juana's children, Leonor and Charles, along with corsets for their nurses, a collar for Madame de la Marche, and dresses with coats for [Anne de] Blaesfelt.[102] From April 1497 to January 1506 Gilles de Vers claimed to have prepared and delivered merchandise worth a relatively modest 885 livres at Juana's orders.[103] Philippe's refusal to pay the bills that Gilles de Vers submitted indicates that they may have reflected Juana's attempt to exercise independent patronage.[104] If so, the archduchess requested much of this clothing for her children and for herself. Perhaps teaching Gilles de Vers a lesson, Juana proved as demanding in 1497 as she would in later days, ordering the tailor to wash and to reweave a gray wool dress that she found unsatisfactory.[105] Although these records may reflect Juana's agenda, as distinct from Philippe's, it remains impossible to prove that Gilles really obeyed Juana rather than either of her first ladies, Jeanne de Commines (Madame de Hallewin) or Alienor de Poitiers (the Viscountess of Furnes). Once again, these accounts highlight the problem of Juana's agency in light of her economic debility. They also foreground the role of household servants who chose either to respect or to circumvent Juana's wishes. In short, the limited funds and articles that reached Juana's hands raise serious questions about the extent to which the archduchess developed her own image or, conversely, found it fashioned and tailored by others.

Juana's penury prevented her from exercising the sovereign virtue of liberality. By monopolizing that virtue, Philippe and his councillors controlled Juana's expenditures alongside the role of Spanish personnel and, thereby, the impact of Spanish culture in the Burgundian court. Rather than reflecting Juana's identity and authority, her household represented Philippe's. The expansion of Philippe's corporate persona thus prevented Juana from developing her own.

The Birth and Death of Heirs

The death of heirs in Castile and Aragon and their birth in the Low Countries entailed a series of unexpected events that transformed Juana's life and, indeed, European history. Although these events might have enhanced Juana's prestige, Philippe and his advisers ensured that Juana's economic dependency limited her authority. The archduke particularly denied Juana protagonism in matters related to her parents and her children.

Juana's lack of influence over her husband became increasingly evident after the death of her brother, Juan, 4 October 1497. On receiving the news of Juan's death, the archduchess went into mourning. Surviving records indicate that she ordered a great black cloak and dress for herself and distributed black cloth to the female members of her household.[106] Philippe, in contrast, received the news of Juan's death by presumptuously titling himself Prince of Asturias and seeking French support for his claim to inherit the Spanish throne.[107] In response to this affront, the Catholic monarchs hastened to have Isabel, their eldest daughter, and her husband, King Manuel of Portugal, confirmed as heirs to Castile and Aragon. On 23 August 1498, before the Aragonese Cortes agreed to accept a female heiress, Isabel died in the process of giving birth to a son, Miguel, whom the Cortes promptly confirmed as Fernando's successor. Meanwhile, Juana hoped to provide Philippe and his subjects with an heir of their own.

Aware of the preference for a male heir common to Spanish and Burgundian court cultures, Juana prepared for the birth of the first of her six children. Early reports of Juana's pregnancy elicited diplomats' wishes for a male child.[108] In August 1498 Fernando and Isabel's ambassador visiting Juana informed the Catholic monarchs: "She is so gentle and so beautiful and fat and so pregnant that the sight of her would console Your Highnesses."[109] On the other hand, Juana's childhood tutor, fray Andrés de Miranda, recognized the risks, as well as the promise, of pregnancy and childbirth. In a letter of 1 September, Miranda urged the archduchess to prepare herself for an experience that could threaten her life. He accordingly advised Juana to confess frequently with observant friars, so that she would not fear death:

> For I trust God to deliver you and guard you well and that you will give birth to a son, because God was asked to give you an offspring, and that it be a son. Write me, then, so that I may offer him to God and to our lady and to Saint Dominic and to Saint Peter Martir, and once, God willing, you have delivered the son, you must send me one of his dresses or shirts because this is promised to Saint Peter Martir.[110]

Thus Juana's tutor expressed sincere concern for her health alongside an equally open-hearted preference for a male child. Philippe and his father, Maximilian, also hoped for a boy. The emperor approached Brussels in order to attend the baptism in case Juana gave birth to a son but left the Low Countries following the birth of a daughter, Leonor, at Coudenberg Palace, 15 November 1498.[111]

Notwithstanding Maximilian's disappointment at the birth of a girl, Leonor's appearance proved that Juana could probably produce a male heir in the future. In accord with Burgundian tradition, the archduchess recuperated in a luxurious "chamber of honor" designed to emphasize her rank. Beneath a pavilion of green damask, Juana received noble visitors from a delivery bed (*lit de partement*) bearing a vast blanket of gold lined in ermine.[112] After Juana's "rising" from bed, a joust in honor of Leonor enabled the archduke to display his virility and Juana's fertility in a more public setting. Attending the event with Margaret of York and other important ladies, Juana watched Philippe himself enter the lists in rich brocade covered with green silk representing hope. The archduke's attendants appeared in green silk trimmed with yellow, or *jaune*, in a reference to Juana. After Philippe had impressed the company by breaking several lances and throwing an opponent to the ground, Juana sent him a message begging him to cease the violent contest. According to a Spanish informant, the archduke acceded to her wishes.[113] The costly display had enabled Philippe to exhibit princely liberality—providing members of his household with new liveries and taking repose upon his wife's request—as well as knightly prowess. The archduke had also honored Juana as the mother of his daughter. Nevertheless, in compliance with chivalric conventions, Juana acted mainly as a spectator.[114]

Chivalric rituals could barely mask Juana's inability or unwillingness to advance her parents' wishes at the Burgundian court. The archduchess initially encouraged the efforts of Fernando and Isabel's envoy, fray Tomás de Matienzo, to appoint doña María Manuel as Leonor's first maid of honor. Yet, ultimately, Burgundian reluctance to bankroll Spanish interests made concern for the infant's household largely irrelevant. Three months after Leonor's birth, Juana's daily records noted that her household had supported Leonor, her nurse, cradle maid, chamber ladies, and other servants for months, "hoping from day-to-day that monsignor the archduke would pay this expense, as he has still not done."[115] Finally, Matienzo heard reports that the archduke had declared: "Because this child is a girl, let the archduchess provide the estate, and then, when God grants us a son, I will provide it."[116] However degrading this policy may have been to Juana, the archduke and his councillors showed a shrewd determination to finance only their own political interests.

In spite of Philippe's selective parsimony, Juana maintained the outward appearance of marital accord. The archduchess, moreover, probably shared her husband's desire for a son. In a portrait from this period, Juana appeared with eleven female companions, including three reformed Franciscans, praying behind the Virgin Mary, who exposed her left breast. Originally part of a triptych picturing Philippe and his entourage behind Christ on the opposite wing, critics have explained that the painting, attributed to Colin de Coter and now in the Musée du Louvre, contained a prayer expressing the pious wish for a male child.[117]

The Franciscan sisters of Brussels pictured behind Juana may have asked God to grant the archduchess a son in exchange for her intercession with Pope Alexander VI on behalf of their convent of Bethlehem. On 4 September 1501 the pope authorized a Clarisan monastery "under regular observance and perpetual cloister . . . as we have been humbly beseeched by our beloved daughter in Christ, the illustrious Juana, Princess of Asturias, great Archduchess of Austria and Duchess of Burgundy, as well as the heretofore mentioned [nuns]."[118] While helping the Franciscan sisters of Brussels obtain papal permission to adopt the reformed order of Saint Claire, the archduchess visited their convent with her seven-month-old daughter Leonor, when Juana began expecting a second child.[119] Born in Brussels, Leonor may have represented her parents' bond with that city. For similar reasons, perhaps, the archduke determined that his next child—and potential successor—would see the light of day in Ghent. He seized the initiative in hopeful preparations for the birth of a son.

Philippe fully exploited the political benefits of his wife's parturition. Juana's transfer to Ghent for the birth of her second offspring entailed more than the usual pomp. For the occasion Philippe ordered two new carriages upholstered in black silk with velour covers.[120] Dedicating his usual attention to material display, in December 1499 Philippe recovered certain jewels in surety and a case of gold to display them after Juana's upcoming delivery.[121] At Philippe's request two friars from the abbey of Anchin brought the archduchess their most famous relic—a ring that the Virgin Mary allegedly had worn while giving birth to Christ,[122] thereby suggesting a parallel between Juana and the Virgin.[123] Philippe eagerly undertook expenditures to satisfy his longing for a male heir.

On 24 February, the vesper of Saint Matthew, Juana gave birth to a boy. Fireworks shot from the bell tower of Saint Nicholas in Ghent signaled the birth of a son and inspired popular celebrations in the streets.[124] At once Philippe sent triumphant announcements throughout his realms and summoned dignitaries for the baptism.[125] Responding to Philippe's eager summons, his sister Marguerite of Austria, the widowed Princess of Castile, reached Ghent in time for the baptism on 7 March 1500. In a gesture of courtesy, Philippe permitted his sister to hold the newborn over the baptismal font. Appearing in Spanish dress,

Marguerite recommended naming the newborn "Juan" in memory of her deceased spouse. Yet Philippe had the boy christened "Charles" after his own
grandfather, Charles "the Bold."[126] Philippe granted Marguerite, like Juana, status without authority. Once again, in other words, Burgundian political ambitions trumped Spanish interests.

The birth of a male child temporarily increased Juana's status at the Burgundian court, although it did little to augment her authority. Philippe treated his
wife with unusual solicitude throughout the year 1500. Thus, when Juana rose
from bed after the birth of Charles, Philippe presented her with a rich emerald
encrusted in a white rose worth 400 livres.[127] When Juana subsequently fell ill
in Brussels, the archduke ordered his best physicians to remain at her side for
over forty days.[128] Once the archduchess had regained her health, she, Philippe,
and Marguerite of Austria enjoyed the acrobatics of an Italian *joueur de souplesse*,
which included "Moorish dance"—the first hint of a Moorish fashion associated
with the Spanish succession in the Burgundian court.[129] Philippe temporarily
doted on Juana as the mother of his successor.

The Catholic monarchs and their representatives in Flanders hoped to see
Juana use her new status for political gains. On 4 August 1500 Spanish ambassador Gutierre Gómez de Fuensalida reported exhorting Juana "to take a greater
role in the governance of her estate and household than she had up to that point.
It was time for her to show herself mistress since she already had children who
were to be lords of this estate, and it seemed to me that she should no longer
countenance these people [the Burgundians], since they had no manners at
all."[130] Gómez de Fuensalida expressed disgust with Burgundian customs and
encouraged Juana to exploit her motherhood in order to intervene in political
matters, beginning with her own household. The archduchess nevertheless informed Gómez de Fuensalida that she could not influence political decisions
without her husband's favor. Juana reported winning Philippe's will when alone
with him, "because she knows that he loves her," yet found that Philippe later
shared anything that she told him with his former tutor, François de Busleyden,
archbishop of Besançon, a prelate known for his anti-Spanish views.[131] According to Juana, Busleyden's influence prevented her from informing Philippe "of
certain things that she believed should be said to him and that should be done."[132]
Even Gómez de Fuensalida recognized that the archduchess could not compete
with the archbishop of Besançon. In one letter, the ambassador noted, "everyone knows, or at least says, that he [Besançon] commands and governs ab-
solutely."[133] In a subsequent letter, Gómez de Fuensalida declared: "This lord

[Philippe] does not eat unless the archbishop of Besançon tells him to, obeying him more than I have ever seen a monk obey his superior."[134] To the detriment of Spanish interests, Besançon appeared capable of governing Juana's husband.

Besançon's authority caused even more pressing concern in Fernando and Isabel's court when the death of Prince Miguel, 20 July 1500, made Juana and Philippe the apparent heirs to Castile and Aragon. Fernando and Isabel immediately summoned Juana and Philippe to Spain, where the Castilian and Aragonese Cortes would confirm them as heirs. Nevertheless, Philippe procrastinated. According to Gómez de Fuensalida, "those who govern," notably Besançon and his ally, Philibert de Veyre, feared losing control of the archduke in Castile and sought all possible motives for postponing the voyage.[135] Philippe's councillors, moreover, hoped to safeguard their hard-won alliance with France before risking any approximation to Spain. For this reason, they demanded that the Catholic sovereigns approve a marriage alliance between young Charles and Claude, the sole offspring of Louis XII, the new King of France, before Philippe and Juana would leave the Low Countries.[136] Fernando and Isabel, in turn, refused to condone such an agreement.

Although Juana may have hoped to satisfy her parents' demand for a prompt journey to Spain, another pregnancy eventually delayed the voyage. On 5 November 1500, Gómez de Fuensalida read Philippe and Juana letters from Fernando and Isabel urging their swift departure for Castile. Apparently pleased with Juana's response, the ambassador informed Fernando and Isabel: "Since my capacities could not praise such a princess justly, I will silence myself upon saying that she is evidently the daughter of Your Highnesses in all things, and for her age has no equal in the world."[137] Nevertheless, in February 1501 it became clear that Juana expected another child and could not travel until she had given birth.[138] Juana even endured signs that Philippe's councillors considered leaving her in the Low Countries while Philippe traveled through France in order to ensure the archduke's prompt return. Praising Juana's fortitude, Gómez de Fuensalida claimed: "If Her Highness were not so equipped with virtues, she would not be able to suffer what she sees. Indeed, I do not think that so much sense [*tanta cordura*] has been seen in anyone of so few years."[139] Gómez de Fuensalida depicted Philippe's advisers, in contrast to Juana, as devoted "to the vices of the throat and its dependents"—gluttony, drunkenness, braggery, and slander, among other sins. He explained: "The archduke's governors dread the departure for Spain because they fear that he will be removed from their hands, and that they will not be absolute lords of him or his [goods] as they are now.

The gentlemen abhor this journey because their customs in all things are so different from Castilian customs as is good from evil."[140] The ambassador sensed that cultural differences informed and exacerbated the competition between Burgundian and Castilian policies reflected in Philippe's councillors' attempts to marginalize Juana. He praised Juana, moreover, for sharing her parents' values and customs.

The archduchess received further support from the bishop of Córdoba, Juan Rodríguez de Fonseca, whom Fernando and Isabel sent to expedite matters in Flanders during the summer of 1501. Describing Juana as "reputedly very sensible [*cuerda*] and very practical [*asentada*]," Fonseca reported diverse opinions about her influence over Philippe. While some observers believed that Juana could do more to favor Spanish interests, Fonseca wrote, others asserted that, "by attempting more, she would endanger herself and actually achieve less."[141] Burgundian control over Juana's household initially limited Fonseca's contact with her. Perhaps most significantly, the bishop found the archduchess entirely isolated, "so that she has no living soul to help her with a single word."[142] Attempting to remedy Juana's lack of pro-Spanish advisers, Fonseca himself played a crucial role in helping Juana adopt policies acceptable to her parents, especially during the subsequent journey through France. Shortly after Fonseca had reached the Burgundian court, on 16 July 1501, the archduchess gave birth to a second daughter, christened Isabel after Juana's mother, in a potential sign of Fonseca's influence. But had Queen Isabel sent her daughter too little help too late?

Rather than gaining authority through motherhood, Juana lost influence over her own children in the Burgundian court. As early as 8 February 1501, Juana had asked her mother to select "an agreeable and prudent woman, free of all fantasy [pretensions]" to care for the children in Flanders during her absence.[143] Juana may have objected to doña Ana of Beaumont, sister of the Constable of Navarre, who eventually received the post. Yet no alternative governess arrived from Spain. Philippe and his councillors imposed their authority over the children's household as easily as they had seized control of Juana's. Within four days of Isabel's birth, Charles de Lattre, previously Juana's first stableman, became master of the house for both Charles and Leonor.[144] In October 1501 Philippe sent all three children to join their grandmother and aunt in Mechelen under the direct supervision of Charles de Croy, Prince of Chimay.[145] Although assigned to Charles's household, Gómez de Fuensalida claimed that Burgundians prevented him from occupying the post of *maestresala*.[146] The officials who had marginalized Juana now asserted their authority over her children. Juana lacked the resources, and possibly the will, to resist such Burgundian advances.

Wayward Journeys and the Cortes of 1502

From 1496 through 1501 Juana had become acquainted with the provinces of the Low Countries and her northern subjects. After 1501, when Juana and Philippe became the heirs to the kingdoms of Castile and Aragon, the Catholic monarchs expected them to develop similar relationships with the lands and peoples of Spain. Philippe and Juana's status as heirs required confirmation through constitutional ceremonies including entries into principal cities and, especially, oaths before the Cortes in Toledo, the ancient seat of the Visigoth monarchy, and Zaragoza, residence of the *justiciar* (chief justice) of Aragon. The 1501 voyage to Spain marked the first occasion when Juana (advised by the bishop of Córdoba) successfully upheld her rights as proprietary heiress to the Spanish kingdoms. Philippe, on the other hand, adamantly refused to side with Fernando and Isabel against Louis XII.

Fernando and Isabel may have wished to forget the pro-French sympathies that Philippe unmistakably revealed in signing the Treaty of Paris with Louis XII, 23 July 1498. In that agreement, Philippe agreed to perform liege homage for Flanders and Artois and renounced his claim to the Duchy of Burgundy in exchange for the towns of Aire, Bethune, and Hesdin.[147] On that occasion, one of Fernando and Isabel's ambassadors informed them: "It is clear that those who govern intend to separate the archduke from the King of the Romans and from Your Highnesses and to make him lose Burgundy so that they will always be lords."[148] On the other hand, Juana's confessor noted popular support for the treaty in Flanders,[149] and Philippe's principal towns and cities provided surety for the accord.[150] Against such evidence, Fernando and Isabel may have hoped that Juana, as heiress, could finally persuade her husband to adopt policies favorable to Spain. If so, they would face yet another disappointment.

In 1501 Burgundian and Spanish policies clashed over the route that Philippe and Juana would follow to Castile.[151] Eager to deepen the archduke's alliance with Louis XII, Philippe's councillors urged him to travel overland through France. In contrast, Fernando and Isabel, on the verge of war with France, insisted on a sea voyage and even sent an armed fleet to Zeeland to transport the archdukes directly to Spain. When the bishop of Córdoba joined Philippe's admiral, Philippe de Bourgogne, to survey and provision the ships on 9 August

1501, a sea voyage seemed assured.[152] Ten days later, however, Philippe announced the engagement of his son, Charles, to Louis XII's sole offspring.[153] An
overland journey through France would cement the agreement. Even if the
announcement surprised Fernando and Isabel, Philippe may have decided on a
land journey months before. The Queen of France, Anne of Brittany, had sent
a delegation to reside with the archduke in April and May of 1501, presumably
promoting the marriage of their children and the journey through France.[154]

Having rejected the sea voyage, Philippe took calculated steps to stifle Spanish outcries against his decision. He sent the bishop of Córdoba gifts of silver[155]
and granted Juana's *camarero*, Diego de Ribera, a timely 35 livres.[156] Philippe
placated other Spaniards at the Burgundian court by paying them wages that
were long overdue. In a directive sent to the Chambre des Comptes at Lille, the
archduke ordered: "By this [memo] we wish to pay and to satisfy certain persons
of the Spanish nation in the household of our very loved and powerful companion, the archduchess, whose services she desires on her upcoming voyage with
us to Spain, with all that is due to them."[157] In accord with Philippe's instructions, more than 6,786 livres were tardily paid to Juana's twenty-eight "Spanish"
servants on the eve of their departure for Spain.[158]

Beyond paying overdue wages, Philippe expanded his and Juana's households
in preparation for their journey. The archduke appointed his councillor and
chamberlain, Hughes de Melun, Viscount of Ghent, as Juana's gentleman of
honor during the voyage.[159] On the eve of Juana's departure, increases in individual pay[160] as well as the number of servants nearly doubled the total daily
wages paid to members of her household.[161] In addition to seven Spanish ladies,
Juana's enhanced retinue included thirty-four Burgundian gentlewomen.[162]

The overland journey enabled Juana to visit the southern province of Hainaut for the first time. Two leagues outside of Mons, the archduchess and her
entourage paused at the Benedictine Abbey of Saint Gislen, which contained
the relics of Saint Leocadia, an early martyr from Juana's birthplace, Toledo.
According to an account published in 1591, Juana devoutly requested some part
of the saint's remains to restore to their common native city. The abbot, with
approval from Henry de Berghes, the bishop of Cambray, accordingly gave
Juana the right shin bone to convey to the city where she would be confirmed as
her mother's heiress.[163] While revealing a pious attachment to Toledo, Juana did
not neglect her northern subjects. On 9 November she staged an inaugural
entry into Valenciennes, whose inhabitants presented their countess two silver
pots and a bowl covered with flowers of gold.[164]

Burgundian chroniclers somewhat predictably emphasized Philippe and Juana's enthusiastic reception in France, which they entered 16 November 1501. The chronicle attributed to Antoine de Lalaing, one of Philippe's gentlemen, stated that local officials throughout France accorded the archduke the honors normally reserved for their king. Staging great receptions and expressions of joy, municipal representatives invited the archduke, as first peer of the realm, to intervene in matters of justice usually reserved for their sovereign—settling disputes and conceding pardons.[165] According to another chronicler, the people of Paris, in particular, loved Philippe "as if he were the king, for his beauty, bounty, and handsome train."[166] The provost of Paris delighted the archduke with a great banquet featuring flirtatious maidens, sweets, spices, dancing, and drink. Apparently less pleased, Juana left Paris the following morning.[167] Lingering in Paris four more days, Philippe basked in Franco-Burgundian pleasures before catching up with his wife just outside Blois, where the French king and queen awaited them.[168]

The visit to Blois offered Juana an important opportunity to uphold Spanish interests. Although her husband had pledged vassalage to Louis XII, Juana recognized no such subordination and managed to assert her independence as the rightful heiress to Castile and Aragon through a series of public gestures. What one historian has termed "petty conflicts aroused by feminine vanity" at Blois[169] actually involved contests over prestige and territory pertaining to neighboring kingdoms. The encounter, then, became a test of wills in which Juana, guided by the bishop of Córdoba, continually sought to defend her status without offending her hosts. Thus when asked whether she would kiss the King of France, the archduchess executed that Franco-Burgundian sign of friendship only after receiving prior approval from the bishop of Córdoba.[170] Perhaps in exchange, Louis XII, who had required Philippe to execute two bows before him, rushed to prevent Juana from making more than one curtsy in his presence.[171] Through this gesture, reported in a Burgundian source, the king affirmed Juana's dignity as the proprietary heiress to independent kingdoms.

Juana's greatest ceremonial challenge occurred at Mass with Queen Anne the following day. Toward the end of the service, the queen sent Juana a certain sum of money to donate to the church on Anne's behalf. Refusing to perform such an act of vassalage, Juana allegedly declared that she offered alms only for herself.[172] Although the queen waited for Juana to follow her after the Mass, the archduchess remained in the chapel long enough to demonstrate that she left it on her own accord.[173] Anne was furious. Not surprisingly, Juana found herself "ung[e] petit mal disposée" that evening. Demonstrating support for the arch-duchess and recognizing her social superiority,[174] the Duchess Valentinois, Ma-dame de Nevers, Germaine de Foix (Juana's future mother-in-law), and other ladies carried Juana "les espices dedens les dragoires"—spices with medicinal as well as intoxicating properties.[175] As if to excuse Juana's posture, Philippe dis-pleased the Spaniards in his company by dutifully offering coins on behalf of Louis XII at a separate Mass.[176]

Several days later, the archduchess attended a formal supper. She emerged from her rooms triumphantly laden with jewels and wearing a Spanish-style dress of gold cloth. After dining, Juana gratified the court by dancing "in the Spanish manner."[177] According to a Burgundian observer, Juana conducted her-self as "a virtuous and magnanimous princess" at Blois.[178] Her confident display of Spanish dress and dance challenged Franco-Burgundian assumptions of cul-tural superiority. Their hosts' ensuing discomfort required the archdukes to hasten their departure, as Juana probably desired.[179]

Traveling south from Blois, Philippe and Juana took different routes to Bay-onne, where King Juan of Navarre joined them. After hearing Mass, the King of Navarre left the church arm-in-arm with the archduchess.[180] During that brief encounter, Juana arranged to marry her youngest daughter, Isabel, to Enrique, Prince of Viana and heir to Navarre,[181] a match that her parents subsequently confirmed.[182] Far from engaging in meaningless ceremony, Juana attempted to use important encounters to shape her family's destiny.

The Burgundians found the Basque country, which they entered in January 1502, less familiar and less hospitable than France. In order to help the arch-dukes cross the Cantabrian Mountains, Fernando and Isabel had sent don Gu-tierre de Cárdenas, *Comendador Mayor* of Leon, to receive them with sturdy Vis-cayan mules and to escort Philippe and Juana to Toledo, where the Cortes of Castile would confirm them as heirs to that kingdom.[183] After abandoning their carriages at Fuenterrabia, the Burgundians faced an icy five-hour journey through the narrow passes of Mount Saint Adrian. Before reaching the town of Segura (south of Tolosa), many of them suffered great hunger and found themselves on the point of fainting. At the town gates, the party further endured a lengthy reception, in which several hundred Viscayans greeted Philippe and Juana "in the Spanish manner," kissing their delicate hands so many times that they became quite red.[184]

Having rested in Segura, the travel-weary retinue proceeded into Castile. As Philippe's company neared Burgos, which titled itself "the head of Castile," municipal guards mistook the Burgundian company for an invading army and closed the city gates. Only don Gutierre de Cárdenas could persuade municipal officials to admit the Burgundians.[185] The officials nevertheless demanded that Philippe swear to respect their city's privileges before entering Burgos. Once Philippe fulfilled this requirement, eighteen gentlemen dressed in red cloth raised a canopy of gold over the archdukes. Then, as another sign of sovereignty, Philippe's principal squire (*premier escuier*) raised the official sword pertaining to the heir to Castile, which Fernando and Isabel allegedly had sent Philippe.[186] By combining the princely sword with the sacred gold canopy, this royal entry— subsequently repeated in Valladolid, Medina del Campo, Segovia, and Madrid—publicly displayed the heirs' martial (personal) and transcendental (corporate) personae.

As Castilian cities and towns received their future rulers, the kingdom's principal nobles competed to ingratiate themselves. In Burgos, for example, the Constable of Castile, don Íñigo de Velasco, entertained the princely couple with bullfights and luxurious displays.[187] In Valladolid, the Admiral of Castile, don Fadrique Enríquez, offered them further diversions. The constable, the admiral, and other nobles found Philippe easy to please. Delighting in sports of all kinds, the archduke amused himself at bullfights by tossing leftover confections to crowds of people who scrambled after the morsels.[188] He also enjoyed appearing incognito among the crowds[189] and dressing as a Turk to reenact Moorish battles.[190] Meanwhile, keeping one eye on their nobles and another on their heirs, Fernando and Isabel discreetly remained in Andalusia, allowing Philippe and Juana direct contact with their future subjects.

From 18 March through 28 April 1502, Juana and Philippe resided in Madrid. During the Easter holiday they identified themselves with an expanding Christian community by sponsoring baptisms of Moors and Jews.[191] After the archdukes heard Mass on 21 April, Juana's confessor, the bishop of Malaga, baptized an old Moor with Philippe as godfather.[192] On 26 April the bishop baptized another "Saracen," his son, and his daughter. The son, whom Philippe held over the font, received his name. The daughter, sponsored by Juana, was renamed accordingly.[193] Accounts preserved in Brussels also list a gift of 18 livres 15 sous to a Jewish resident of Madrid, who accepted baptism, along with his two children.[194] By promoting the conversion of non-Christians, the archdukes joined Christ in redeeming lost souls.

After the Easter holiday, Juana and Philippe planned to meet the Catholic monarchs in Toledo, where Queen Isabel had summoned the Cortes to receive

Juana as her successor and heiress.[195] For his part, Fernando made every effort to win Philippe away from the French cause. When a bout of smallpox delayed Philippe in the village of Olias for several days, Fernando rushed to visit the archduke on his sickbed. Isabel, who was also ailing, did not travel to Olias. Nor did she meet the archdukes outside the gates of Toledo—*her* city—on 7 May 1502, after Philippe had recovered. Seizing the initiative once again, the Aragonese ruler positioned himself alongside Philippe beneath the golden canopy and pointedly left his daughter, Juana, to enter the city behind them.[196] As king consort himself in Castile, Fernando ceremonially honored Philippe, rather than Juana, the proprietary heiress to Isabel's realms. Philippe and Fernando thus collaborated to marginalize Juana and to undermine the principle of female inheritance that both sanctioned and threatened their authority in Castile.

Queen Isabel attempted to rectify this slight after the archdukes reached the house of the Marquis of Villena, where they would reside in Toledo. On 8 May the queen staged an elaborate Mass in the great hall of the Villena mansion with a golden canopy above the altar. After Fernando, Isabel, Philippe, and Juana took Communion, a table replaced the altar. Seated upon golden chairs beneath the very canopy that had covered the body of Christ, Fernando, Isabel, Philippe, and Juana "were served a lot of meat many times in the Spanish fashion."[197] By placing herself and her daughter beneath the golden canopy, Isabel reasserted her own position as a ruler divinely chosen and inspired and affirmed Juana's status as her lawful successor.

Isabel, supported by Castilian tradition, won the first round in the battle to establish Juana and Philippe's respective status. On 22 May the Cortes affirmed Juana as Princess of Asturias and heiress to the kingdoms of Castile and Leon and accepted Philippe as prince consort.[198] Two months later, apparently disappointed with his designation as consort and prolonged residence in Toledo, Philippe expelled Henry de Berghes, bishop of Cambray and leader of the pro-Spanish faction, from his entourage. Although both Juana and Isabel pleaded the bishop's case, Philippe restructured his own household and insisted that de Berghes and his followers return to the Low Countries.[199] Perhaps even more troubling to the queen, Philippe and his remaining homesick servants hastened to conclude their Spanish sojourn.

Tensions between Flemings and Spaniards continued to mount. On 16 August twenty or more armed Castilians assailed three of Philippe's gentlemen for reasons that went unrecorded.[200] Rather than placate Philippe, Queen Isabel attempted to pacify the local population by pardoning the Castilian aggressors.[201] The most devastating blow for Philippe, however, entailed the sudden death of François de Busleyden, archbishop of Besançon, on 24 August 1502.[202] Although many Flemings, including Madame de Hallewin, blamed their illnesses during the journey on the climate and the wine,[203] Philippe suspected that Besançon's opponents had poisoned him deliberately. Anxious to escape Toledo, Juana and Philippe traveled into Aragon, where their pages sacked a mosque, breaking lamps and everything in sight, to celebrate the day of Saint Luke.[204] Frustrated with their stay in Spain, the Burgundians had begun to behave more like an invading army than a disciplined court. Their violent discontent pressured Juana and Philippe to return to the Low Countries.

Meanwhile, Fernando prepared the Cortes of Aragon as the culmination of his strategy to force Philippe to side with him against Louis XII. On 26 October Philippe and Juana entered Zaragoza beneath a gold canopy and behind a naked sword, respectfully lowered when they passed King Fernando. The following day the Cortes of Aragon confirmed Juana as proprietary ruler and Philippe as king consort after Fernando's death, unless the Aragonese king fathered a legitimate male child.[205] Fernando then departed for Castile, claiming that Queen Isabel had fallen ill, and leaving Philippe to preside over the Cortes that were scheduled to vote subsidies for the war against France. Yet Philippe, having just received a safe-conduct from Louis XII, wanted to return to Flanders through France. The archduke galloped after Fernando, leaving Juana with the Cortes.[206]

Juana, well advanced in her fourth pregnancy, became the central pawn in the ensuing attempt to make Philippe side with Spain over France. Using Juana's condition as a pretext, Isabel and Fernando insisted that the archdukes remain in Spain until she had given birth. As Queen Isabel overcame her alleged fever, Philippe summoned Juana to Madrid. Instructing the Marquis of Villena to escort Juana as quickly as possible, the archduke accepted only those delays necessary to protect Juana's health.[207] At last, Philippe impatiently left Madrid to meet the archduchess. The Catholic monarchs, aware that Philippe insisted upon leaving Castile at once, urged the marquis to help Juana oppose his wishes: "Strengthen her so that she very vigorously impedes his departure and contradicts it as the most damaging thing possible for them and for us. Also, so that she does not receive pain or sorrow, assure her that we will help her, as we should, so that the prince does not leave her."[208]

As usual, Fernando and Isabel overestimated their daughter's and their own ability to influence Philippe. Regardless of Philippe's feelings for Juana, the

Catholic monarchs had failed to seduce him away from the court of Louis XII. More intimidated than dazzled by Philippe's court, Juana had accepted Franco-Burgundian customs and personnel in the Low Countries. Philippe, on the other hand, became increasingly irritated by Spanish efforts to refashion his Francophile tastes and orientation. Philippe fled Castile before understanding, much less adopting, the political culture that pertained to its heir.

Juana, for her part, may have found relief from such pressures at the Clarisan monastery of Reja outside Madrid, which she visited at least four times in 1502–3. The princess previously had accompanied her mother to the Franciscan monastery of Toledo while Philippe engaged in sport,[209] but appears to have approached the Claires of Rejas on her own. Juana ate and resided with the abbess and sisters of Rejas from 30 September to 1 October and again from 6 to 7 October 1502.[210] She dined with the same Claires on 9 December 1502 and visited them again from 15 to 16 January 1503, after Philippe had left Castile.[211] In exchange for spiritual guidance, Juana may have bequeathed the Claires of Rejas certain relics from the eleven thousand virgin martyrs that Pope Alexander VI granted her in 1500.[212] As late as 1587, the Clarisan monastery treasured the heads of some of the virgins who reputedly had gained martyrdom with Saint Ursula at Cologne.[213] Juana, like the daughter of King Enrique II of Castile and the wife of a previous Duke of Burgundy, Philip "the Good," turned to the Claires for guidance. These religious women probably appreciated and even shared the sober dress and customs that Burgundians had found dull and disdainful in the Castilian court.

The competing court cultures of Burgundy and Castile informed rival political agendas and attitudes toward France. At war with Louis XII, Isabel and Fernando displayed the martial, as well as the sacral, basis for their authority in 1502. Golden canopies for royal entries and meals, attendance at public Mass, visits to monasteries and convents, and the solemn confirmation of heirs in Cortes emphasized the monarchs' divine mandate to rule the territories they claimed. While extending the sacred ornaments of royal authority to their heirs, Fernando and Isabel expected Philippe and Juana to develop corresponding loyalty to the interests of Castile and Aragon. Nevertheless Philippe and Juana were already sovereigns of the Low Countries. The interests of those northern realms demanded peace with France and their rulers' personal presence. Marginalized with respect to each of two competing courts, Juana found herself trapped as she attempted to steer a course between them.

CHAPTER THREE

Renaissance Passions and Juana's Madness

"By Love . . . or by Fear"

Although Philippe had announced his desire to return to the Low Countries through France, Queen Isabel wanted Philippe and Juana to remain in Spain, among the subjects they would one day govern. Disturbed that Juana's husband would consider traveling through a kingdom at war with her own, the queen appealed to Philippe's feelings for his wife. She would not permit Juana, pregnant once again, to travel through enemy territory during the winter. Given Juana's "ardent love for her husband," Isabel allegedly suggested that her daughter would suffer a miscarriage, and might even die from sorrow, if Philippe abandoned her.[1] Queen Isabel attempted to arouse the prince's love and fear for his wife and, tacitly, her inheritance. Yet beneath Isabel's dramatic anxiety about Juana's health lay well-founded concern for the welfare of Castile and Aragon. Like many of her contemporaries, Queen Isabel linked the fate of rulers to that of their realms.

Love and fear, while ostensibly personal passions, could also express political interests. Employing a rhetoric of love and fear with respect to Juana and Philippe, early sixteenth-century authors may have used the language of amorous devotion to describe political loyalty. Analogies between rulers, their households, and their realms in contemporary political discourse made it natural to depict relations among rulers and between rulers, servants, and subjects in terms of love and fear.

In the treatise, *The Princes' Timepiece*, sixteenth-century theorist Antonio de Guevara recommended that the king love and fear his realms, just as the king's subjects should love and fear their ruler. Considering the prince "head of the republic" and his subjects the republic's body, Guevara declared that "the throat that joins the head to the body is the love between the king and the kingdom that constitute the republic." In this way, Guevara used a well-worn corporal metaphor to describe political ties of "love" as joining kingdoms to their ruler.[2] Elsewhere Guevara critiqued philistine manipulations of love and fear, stating: "Princes and great lords are feared for their power and loved for their generosity, so that, in the end, no one follows the king because he is apt, but rather, thinking him beneficent."[3] Generations of service in the Castilian and Burgundian courts gave the Guevara family privileged insights into the nature of love and fear as political passions.

Guevara's contemporary, Niccolò Machiavelli, also addressed the political uses of love and fear. In a famous passage of *The Prince*, Machiavelli wrote: "A controversy has arisen about this: whether it is better to be loved than feared, or vice versa. My view is that it is desirable to be both loved and feared; but it is difficult to achieve both and, if one of them has to be lacking, it is much safer to be feared than loved."[4] While attempting to inspire both fear and love, the ruler, according to Machiavelli, exercised greater control over fear as a political tool. Given the fickle nature of human affection, Machiavelli argued that the prince should strive only to avoid inspiring hatred. Fear, on the other hand, "sustained by a dread of punishment," would prove more reliable and efficacious.[5] Yet Machiavelli's predecessors, including the fourteenth-century theorist, Juan García de Castrojeríz, had favored love, a more noble emotion, over fear.[6]

Even before Guevara, Machiavelli, and García de Castrojeríz, rulers had employed affection and wrath to attain political ends. In Castile and Leon, the concept of *ira regis*, royal anger, allowed medieval kings to deprive vassals who lost their amity of honors, titles, lands, salaries, and goods, even ousting the unloved from their realms.[7] According to the *Siete partidas*, kings could banish vassals for treason, misdeeds, revenge, or dislike, lending particular force to royal anger, which inspired great fear.[8] Moreover, the exercise of love and fear—godly attributes that also comprised human passions—enabled monarchs to demonstrate their simultaneous divine and mortal natures.[9]

Love between subjects and their sovereigns formed part of a long-standing ideal of rulership. According to one study, in the Carolingian court "love and passion constituted a mode of expression for royal favor."[10] It follows that descriptions of amorous intercourse in official correspondence depicted not carnal but political affairs. The same concept may apply to accounts of Juana's and Fernando's relations with Philippe. If so, what has often been interpreted as evidence of Juana's excessive connubial passion alternatively might be understood as a public posture that she adopted in order to favor her husband and children. Juana's emotions may have become matters of public concern precisely because of their political implications.

In Juana's case, moreover, a Renaissance emphasis on human passions collided with long-standing uses of regal love and fear. According to two modern scholars, "Subsumed in Renaissance culture, perhaps more than generally appreciated, is a complex pattern of notions concerning the humours, love, the diseased imagination, and the pathological vulnerabilities of the body due to love."[11] Galenic medicine and Aristotelian philosophy popularized during the Renaissance linked female love and fear to infirmity rather than authority.[12] Many humanists shared the view of Desiderius Erasmus, who considered the woman "a stupid animal," albeit necessary to complement male reason.[13] Informed by such ideas, sources used in this chapter were the first to depict Juana as "sick" and "indisposed." Given the variable meanings of love and fear, Juana lost control of her image, if not her emotions.

From 1503 through 1506, Juana allegedly relinquished her capacity for self-government. Nevertheless, previous chapters raise the question of how much Juana really gave up. After all, the archduchess never had governed her own household or movements. Perhaps, however, her transgression lay in the attempt. The queen's "incapacity" emerges as her failure to comply with the wishes and conform to the expectations of the actors surrounding her. Long perceived as an obedient daughter and a submissive wife, beginning in late 1503 Juana increasingly refused to accept the rule of officials serving her mother and her husband.

Unruly Princes?

Renaissance texts depicted love as an expression of loyalty won through liberality, a political strategy, and even a debilitating condition. Love, like melancholy, became understood as a source of inspiration for men and, inverting medieval chivalric roles, a pathology for women. Isabel, Philippe, and Fernando all used love as a political tool, competing for adherents through patronage while making and breaking alliances allegedly based on "love." While human-ists tended to underestimate women in politics, Isabel and Juana themselves may not have relinquished tactical uses of love and fear. Juana, nevertheless, found Renaissance notions of the human passions employed against her.

An Italian humanist attached to the Castilian court, Pietro Martire d'Angle-ria, has provided some of the best-known details about Juana's excessive (and allegedly apolitical) love for her husband.[14] In missives dated 9 and 30 June 1501, Martire emphasized Juana's love for Philippe to alleviate Philippe's parti-sans' fears that she might oppose his (and their) political ambitions. After Prince Miguel's death in 1501, Philippe's ambassadors to Fernando and Isabel sug-gested that the Cortes of Castile and Aragon might be persuaded to accept Philippe as heir to the throne, even without Juana. Fernando and Isabel, not to mention the Cortes, would have balked at such a suggestion. Yet rather than emphasizing Juana's rights as the lawful heiress, Martire claimed that Juana would insist upon traveling with Philippe: "For the monarchs are convinced that their daughter will only agree to follow her husband."[15] Such a tactful interpre-tation stressed Juana's devotion to Philippe rather than her superior rights as heiress. In the later letter, Martire further emphasized Juana's exclusive devotion to her husband: "For she is lost in love for her spouse. Neither ambition for such kingdoms nor the love of her parents and other childhood companions would move her. Only attachment to the man, whom they say that she loves with such ardor, would draw her here [to Castile]."[16] Had Philippe's ambassadors, the archbishop of Besançon and Philibert de Veyre, begun to spread the legend of Juana's devotion for Philippe as early as 1501? Martire, taking his cue from these men, perhaps aspired to gain ducal favor by assuring Philippe of his primacy. More likely, Martire or his editor may have revised these letters at a later date, emphasizing Juana's amorous devotion to please either her father, Fernando, or her son, Charles.[17] The lack of any extant manuscript copy of these letters—first published in an error-ridden Latin edition of 1530[18]—makes them an excep-tionally problematic source.

During thirty years in the Castilian court, Martire sought and gained patron-age from nearly everyone but Juana. The Archives du Département du Nord at Lille preserves evidence of Martire's early contact with Philippe and his ambas-sadors. In 1502 Philippe's favor helped Martire obtain certain revenues from an abbey near Milan. The humanist subsequently reported that he erected an image of the archduke alongside the abbey's patron saints. On the death of Queen Isabel, Martire begged Philippe for further favors. Juana's presumed attitude aside, Martire himself appeared devoted to Philippe.[19]

According to Martire, neither Isabel's great sorrow nor Juana's great love could convince Philippe to remain in Spain in December 1502. The humanist claimed that Philippe's councillors, "whom, it is supposed, the French have bribed with their gifts, exercise such influence over him, that he does not appear to be his own master."[20] The more that Fernando and Isabel stressed the archduke's new obligations, the more, it seemed, Philippe strengthened his commitment to old duties in Flanders. Resentful of Fernando and Isabel's attempts to undermine his friendship with Louis XII, the archduke announced immediate plans to leave Spain for France. News of Spanish victories against the French in Naples only furthered Philippe's resolve to depart. When one of Louis XII's allies, the Duke of Calabria, reached the Spanish court as a prisoner,[21] Philippe had endured more than enough and fled Madrid.[22] Pregnant with their fourth child, Juana remained behind.

Philippe's departure allegedly devastated Juana. In a letter dated 4 January 1503, Pietro Martire claimed that the archduchess cared for neither riches nor power but exclusively for her spouse, "her only preoccupation, delight, and devotion." According to the humanist, Juana felt great sadness and "ardors for her husband."[23] Although Isabel assured Juana that she could depart for Flanders after the birth of her child, the archduchess soon suspected that her mother offered empty promises. Noting that Juana would soon give birth, the humanist pronounced: "If she does it well, perhaps the new child will relieve this woman's pain and her mind will not become disturbed [*nec turbine mentis obibit*]." Alluding to the dangers of menstrual retention during pregnancy,[24] Martire articulated a basis for the legend that subsequently emerged around Juana.[25]

Months after Martire supposedly noted Juana's extreme sadness, an individual close to the archduchess praised her happy virtues. Juana's confessor, Diego Ramírez de Villaescusa,[26] delivered a notable panegyric to celebrate the baptism of Juana's second son, Fernando, in March 1503. Taking the young princess as the theme of his joyful oration, the bishop praised her great Christianity, and the graces that God consequently conceded her. Recounting Juana's twenty-three years, the bishop discussed her childhood, her departure for Flanders in "the greatest armada ever seen," and the many children that God had granted her without pain or tribulation. Thanks to her great piety, Ramírez de Villaescusa claimed, Juana gave birth while laughing and playing, like the Virgin.[27] Finally, the bishop concluded with the admission that fifty days and nights would prove insufficient for him to enumerate Juana's excellent qualities.[28]

Ramírez de Villaescusa was only one member of the household that Philippe intended to govern Juana as long as she remained in Castile. Before leaving Spain, the archduke had provided Juana's personnel with a rigorous new ordinance. These regulations, limiting Juana's contacts, also sought to prevent new servants from infiltrating her staff. According to Philippe's instructions, gentleman of honor Hughes de Melun, along with masters of the house Claude de Cilly and Martin de Moxica, would govern Juana's household while she remained in Castile. Juana would receive and send letters only through her first *chevalier.* In a new form of rotating service, Cilly and Moxica would alternate months as master of the house.[29] The gentleman and masters could select individuals, including certain foreigners (*estrangiers*), to dine at their tables, symbolically close to the princess.[30] Because Philippe did not expect Juana to travel while she remained in Castile, the 1502 regulations also reduced her footservants to four or six. Juana's sojourn, like Philippe's, should remain as short as possible. Finally, the ordinance stressed that Juana's household would admit no servant without express, written orders from Philippe.[31]

The battle between Philippe and Isabel for Juana's "love" ultimately took the form of a struggle to influence her household. Isabel endeavored to inspire gratitude, if not affection, toward herself among Juana's attendants. In spite of Burgundian precautions, the queen took steps to win the allegiance of Philippe's personnel and to place servants of her own choice around Juana. Thus, when Juana gave birth to young Fernando, Isabel could order her daughter's servants to convey the news to Spanish nobles.[32] Isabel's success, much like Philippe's, depended on patronage. Burgundian lists of wages indicate that Juana's household shrank, rather than grew, over the course of 1503.[33] Nevertheless, Isabel's gifts of silk and cloth to Juana's servants suggested that the queen had her own idea about the members of that staff. Although Philippe left Juana with an entourage of some 128 individuals (not including most of her female servants),[34] on 1 November 1503 Isabel rewarded 171 members of her daughters' household (including 23 women, 5 of them slaves).[35] Perhaps most notably, Isabel's payments named 69 officers not previously mentioned in connection with Juana's household.[36] Distributing gifts from crimson velvet to London wool, depending on each attendant's rank, the queen spent a total of 1,688,349 mrs in one day to gratify her daughter's servants.[37] Competition for Juana's love and loyalty became a struggle to control her household.

The sixty-nine new attendants who appear to have entered Juana's service in spite of Philippe's instructions comprised mainly Castilians. Upper-level additions included a physician, Maestro Duarde, a surgeon, Maestro Jos, a pharmacist, Dirique, and a secretary long in the royal service, Sebastián de Olano. A new quartermaster of the chamber, Herrera, joined the valets who had staffed Juana's chamber since her days in Brussels. Not surprisingly, given their need for local contacts, both of the quartermasters charged with securing and preparing lodgings appear to have been new additions. Seven pages appointed to serve the princess included a "Loyola" who may have been "Jacques de Loyolle," listed on earlier payrolls, or Ochoa Pérez Loyola, brother of Ignatius de Loyola, future founder of the Society of Jesus.[38] Providing tangible signs of affection toward its members, Isabel, if not Juana, used the household to bolster her authority.

Juana seems to have tolerated Queen Isabel's efforts to reshape her household in contravention of Philippe's orders. In the same spirit, she had bowed to her parents' wishes and remained in Castile when Philippe left Spain against their will in December 1502. Although promised a reunion with her husband after giving birth, the princess stayed in Castile for more than one year after her delivery. These signs of Juana's respect for Spanish interests contrast with what humanist Pietro Martire depicted as Juana's exclusive devotion to her spouse.

Struggles between Mother and Daughter

Juana had made important efforts to uphold Spanish interests. Remaining in Castile for more than fifteen months after Philippe's departure, the princess had even given her parents another grandson—this time with a Spanish birthplace and name. In turn, she expected Fernando and Isabel to uphold their pledge that she could return to Flanders. Insisting on this short-term goal, Juana ultimately obtained it at the cost of her own credibility. Able to inspire neither love nor fear, the princess lost whatever autonomy she may have retained within the household.

Juana's demands for the promised reunion with her husband clashed with Isabel's efforts to prolong her daughter's residence in Spain. Since giving birth to her second son, Fernando, Juana had regularly sought her parents' permission to return to Flanders. Letters from Philippe likewise insisted upon Juana's immediate departure.[39] Yet Isabel stalled, alternately resisting such demands because of the war with France and providing signs of her daughter's upcoming leave. By June 1503 the princess became more insistent and confronted her mother directly. Juana made a clear choice to return to Flanders and mobilized all of her limited resources to attain that end.

According to Isabel's doctors, the ensuing struggles between mother and daughter endangered the health of both. Quarrels with Juana left the queen vulnerable to severe fevers and chest pains, they wrote:

> For the disposition of the lady princess is such that it should greatly pain not only those so affected and who love her so, but even foreigners, because she sleeps poorly, eats little, and sometimes nothing. She is very sad and quite thin. At times she does not wish to talk, in such a manner that, in this, as well as in certain acts, that reveal [her] to be moved, her sickness advances substantially. The cure is usually undertaken by love and entreaty or by fear. Yet she does not accept pleas or persuasion or anything else, and receives such alteration and at times such sorrow from any slight force applied, that to attempt it is a great shame, and no one wants or dares to.[40]

Without distinguishing between physical and psychological maladies, Isabel's doctors considered both love and fear as possible remedies for Juana's troubling and troubled behavior.[41] Neither approach, however, appeared particularly successful. The three doctors attending Isabel attempted to persuade Fernando to help the queen, in a fragile state herself, to manage their unruly daughter and heiress.[42]

The longer that war with France kept Fernando away from court, the more difficult it became for Isabel to prevent Juana from leaving Spain. In the summer of 1503, the women traveled to Segovia—presumably the first step in Juana's voyage north. According to one chronicler, however, Queen Isabel hid her intentions, "for in truth she did not want her daughter to go to Flanders just then, feeling badly disposed with the illness from which she died."[43] Juana apparently failed to recognize her mother's moribund condition—a crucial miscalculation easily condemned in retrospect.[44] Determined to expedite her departure for Flanders, the princess continued north to Medina del Campo, even when Isabel remained in Segovia.[45] Juana then ordered a naval captain to wait for her in Bilbao. The captain, rather than obeying Juana, informed Fernando of her intentions.[46]

Yet the princess would not give up. She ordered the members of her household to prepare for immediate departure. Informed of these orders, the queen sent Juan Rodríguez de Fonseca, the bishop of Córdoba, who had accompanied Juana in 1501–2, to detain her. The prelate accordingly instructed Isabel's servants to seal the fortress of La Mota where Juana was residing. Seeing her designs frustrated, Juana "gave him [Fonseca] very bad words" in a detrimental expression of *ira regis*. The bishop, even more offended, departed for the queen. Recognizing her error, Juana sent her valet, Herrera, to beg Fonseca to return. The prelate refused. Juana's attempt to inspire fear had only demonstrated her lack of authority.[47]

Queen Isabel still hoped to avoid a personal confrontation with her daughter. Upon receiving Fonseca's report, the queen wrote Juana, begging her to remain in Castile. Acknowledging important motives for Juana's departure, Isabel nevertheless argued that it would bring more harm than good until peace with France was secure. "With the love that I bear for you as my own daughter," Isabel demanded that Juana terminate preparations for her voyage until further notice.[48] Unmoved by the queen's pleas and commands, the princess continued her rebellion. As if awaiting an opportunity to escape from La Mota, Juana stationed herself on the ramparts of the fortress in the open air, "like an African lioness in a fit of rage."[49] At two o'clock in the morning Juana finally agreed to take shelter but violated the norms of her social condition by entering a kitchen on the edge of the fortress.[50] Juana had left the queen no alternative but to travel to La Mota and to confront her in person.[51]

Juana won the standoff with Isabel at the cost of her own credibility. According to the queen, Juana confronted her with "disrespectful words, which I never would have tolerated if not for the condition that she was in."[52] In response to Juana's outburst, Isabel insisted that she had no intention to separate Juana from Philippe ("de la descasar de su marido"), a reasonable fear, since two medieval proprietary queens, Urraca and Berenguela, not to mention a number of kings, used separations, then annulments, to free themselves from marriages that became political burdens. Queen Isabel further promised Juana that she could travel to Flanders as soon as her father returned from Aragon. Placated, the princess reentered her chambers.[53] In a subsequent letter to her ambassador at the Burgundian court, Isabel pledged that Juana could depart on 1 March by sea or, in the case of peace with France, by land.[54] Isabel's version of events, designed for Philippe, justified her actions in light of Juana's inappropriate conduct. Considering her daughter's "disposition," "health," and "passion," the queen requested that Philippe write the leading Burgundians with Juana, Hughes de Melun and Madame de Hallewin, "granting them full authority to hold her and restrain her in the things that her passion can make her do," adding that the Burgundians should prevent Juana from doing "anything that could endanger or dishonor her person" during the voyage.[55] Clearly, Juana had crossed the line of acceptable conduct by challenging her mother. The response from Burgundy, deeply regretting Juana's disrespectful words toward Queen Isabel, attributed Juana's misbehavior to her "great love" for Philippe.[56] Philippe, moreover, instructed Hallewin and Moxica to follow Isabel's orders "in matters regarding the governance of the person of the princess . . . governing her in the manner and according to the commands of the queen and ruler, and as befitting the honor of the princess, my wife, and my own."[57] Isabel and Philippe agreed that Juana could not govern herself and should return to Flanders.

In March the Catholic monarchs finally permitted their daughter to travel north.[58] Philippe's councillor and Juana's former master of the house, Jehan de Courteville, had left Brussels in December, and obtained safe conducts for the princess and himself from Louis XII in Lyon. After reaching Medina de Campo, Courteville accompanied Juana as far north as Burgos. From Burgos, she continued to the port of Laredo, while he returned through France.[59] Juana's decision to take the sea route when Philippe had made provisions for her to travel overland suggests that she sought an intermediate course between the wishes of her husband and those of her parents, whose relations remained tense with France.[60] Rather than blind devotion toward Philippe, Juana's tardy departure by sea reveals the extent to which she actually respected her parents' will.

Tensions erupted in Juana's entourage when the weather at Laredo delayed its departure for more than an additional month.[61] During this period, Juana dismissed eleven of her noble ladies, along with the more humble Marina Ruiz, sending them back to Castile.[62] Although the reason for their discharge seems unclear, these ladies, influenced by Queen Isabel, may have sought to dissuade the princess from continuing north. When the weather finally permitted Juana's household to set sail, another disagreement occurred. Juana's longtime chamberman, Diego de Ribera, refused to board her belongings until the princess had signed declarations for items that she had sold or given away in Spain. Juana apparently refused to offer such guarantees, insisting that the *camarero* was ultimately accountable to her and her alone. Once again, the princess attained her short-term goal. Servants boarded Juana's property, the fleet embarked, and Ribera remained behind.[63]

In Laredo, as at La Mota, Juana's tenacity severely strained the ideally affective relations between mother and daughter, mistress and servants. Although Isabel attributed her daughter's behavior to passion for Philippe, conflicts with Isabel and Isabel's servants raised questions about Juana's capacity to succeed her mother in Castile. With disastrous results, the princess had employed medieval *ira regis* to obtain a short-term goal. Queen Isabel, perhaps to her own regret, had trained her daughters to defend and safeguard their marriages. Juana refused to accept a potential separation from Philippe in 1503, just as her younger sister, Catalina (Catherine) of Aragon, would subsequently reject any effort to annul her own marriage to Henry VIII of England.

Discord between Husband and Wife

Events following Juana's return to the Low Countries in May 1504 cast further doubt on her ability to govern her mother's kingdoms. Hostility between Juana and Philippe boded especially ill for the future of their realms. Sixteenth-century thinkers envisioned not only the ruler, but also the royal household, as a microcosm of the kingdom. Ideally, the household provided a model for the realm, just as rulers served as a model for their subjects. Comparisons between ruler, court, and kingdom emphasized their interdependence to the point that sickness in the royal person or conflict in the royal household threatened the associated territories. In Burgundy as well as Castile, love and fear unified corporations and reflected political interests.

Expressions of popular affection marked Philippe's return to the Low Countries in the winter of 1504 (after a long illness in France) and Juana's arrival the following spring. Desiderius Erasmus, who subsequently received ducal patronage,[64] composed a jubilant discourse presented to Philippe on the day of the Epiphany. Erasmus employed an extended analogy between a wife's jealous desire for her husband and the Flemings' anxiety for Philippe's return. According to the humanist friar, Philippe's northern subjects had feared that he might love his new realms more than the old. Given Fernando and Isabel's "voracious and greedy love," Erasmus reminded the archduke that his generous presence in their realms "irritated rather than satisfied their passion to have you." And, yet, the Flemings loved Philippe even more. According to Erasmus, the ill jumped out of their beds and maidens rushed into the streets to witness Philippe's return.[65] To compete with such imagery, ambassador Gómez de Fuensalida reminded Philippe of the "great love" that Fernando and Isabel had shown him. Philippe's arrival in Castile had delighted that entire kingdom, the ambassador claimed, so that "the animals, the tress, and the rocks even seemed to show their joy."[66]

Erasmus, after favorably comparing the archduke to Hercules, Ulysses, Solomon, Alexander, and Julius Caesar, espoused similar praise for the archduchess. According to the humanist friar, Juana surpassed the heroines of antiquity in chastity, modesty, prudence, and love for her husband, not to mention reproductive success:

> Penelope was no more chaste, nor Claudia more religious, nor Cornelia, the mother of the Greeks, more noble, nor Lampido of Lacedemonia more happy, nor Aliestos a greater lover of her husband, nor more discreet and obedient Turia Emilia, nor Porci or Sulpicia more loyal, nor Zenobia more generous, Niobe more fecund. Already four times happily delivered, still such a girl, yourself such a boy, she made you father of a most beautiful progeny; so many times, with the tender offspring that she gave us, renewed the joy of Spain, Germany, and our own, giving us cause to celebrate the birth of a new prince. What could be more healthy for the empire, more sure to solder the concord of kingdoms, to bind world peace with the most solid ties, than the fecundity of good princes?[67]

The Augustinian's praise for Philippe and Juana also contained recommendations for their future conduct. By extolling Philippe's conjugal chastity as well as Juana's, Erasmus emphasized the importance of Christian customs among those who provided models for their subjects.[68] The humanist warned Philippe against the sins of ambition, arrogance, vanity, cunning, adulation, lust, violence, and luxury in his palace by commending Juana's efforts to extirpate such vices.[69]

The situation that Juana encountered upon her return to Flanders fell short of the humanist friar's ideal. Within one month of her arrival in Blankenburg, the princess came to suspect Philippe of a romantic attachment to a noblewoman at court. Pietro Martire, as usual, reported the scandalous gossip. According to Martire, Juana ordered the blonde locks of her husband's supposed lover severed. In retaliation, Philippe allegedly raised his hand against Juana.[70] Philippe's open infidelity made a mockery of the archdukes' twin chivalric device: Philippe's motto, "Qui voludrá?" (Who will dare?), which Juana answered "Je le veux" (I will), or "Moi tout seule" (I alone).[71] Juana had apparently lost her exclusive claim to Philippe's heart. The ensuing events would prove her quite alone, indeed.

News of connubial discord in Burgundy soon reached Castile. Philippe attempted to defend his actions by sending Martin de Moxica, whom the princess subsequently attempted to dismiss,[72] to Castile with a report on Juana's conduct since her return to Flanders.[73] In early November, Philippe sent the Catholic monarchs Claude de Cilly, his councillor and Juana's master of the household, to describe Juana's behavior while negotiating rights to Naples in exchange for custody of Juana's son, Charles.[74] With respect to the princess, Cilly received orders to "speak as Monsieur has instructed him."[75] From Castile, Isabel lamented "the discontent and lack of love that has begun between the prince and the princess" and urged her ambassadors to foster "love and agreement" between the spouses.[76]

The ambassadors nevertheless continued reporting Philippe's version of events. According to their accounts, Juana relied upon Moorish female slaves who bathed her and washed her head with such regularity that the practice supposedly endangered her health. Rejecting these slaves, Philippe sought to replace them with servants loyal to him, whom Juana refused to accept. While delighting in Moorish fashions and sports, Philippe and his court generally rejected persons of Islamic descent. This contradictory posture, which emerged in the 1502 Spanish sojourn, resurfaced in Philippe's vehemence against Juana's maintaining an aspect of her cultural inheritance, not to mention potentially loyal servants. Once again, the archduke's attempts to govern his wife centered on control of her household personnel. Now allied with Philippe,[77] ambassador don Juan Manuel ordered Juana's quartermaster of the chamber, Pedro de Rada, to inform her that Philippe would not visit the princess until she had dismissed her slaves. Exercising *ira regis*, Juana banished the quartermaster rather than her female captives. "With great anger," she ordered Rada to abandon the Low Countries within three days upon pain of death.[78] Philippe retaliated by ordering the doors to Juana's chambers sealed and refusing to see her. The princess, in turn, allegedly spent an entire night pounding on the floor of her bedroom and the ceiling of Philippe's, demanding her husband's attention. She refused, moreover, to eat a bite of food until the prince agreed to speak with her.[79] In pursuit of a concrete goal, Juana adopted drastic tactics similar to those that she had employed to summon Queen Isabel to La Mota.

Further evidence for the breakdown in marital relations comes from ambassador Gómez de Fuensalida's letter of 1 November 1504 to Fernando's secretary. The ambassador drew the commonplace analogy between princely households and realms. Seeing Philippe and Juana's domestic situation "in such discord," Gómez de Fuensalida wondered how they could ever agree to rule the many and great kingdoms that they were to inherit.[80] A few days later, the ambassador reported that Philippe had dismissed twelve of Juana's servants, including four slaves, the almoner Juan Íñiguez de Galarreta, a Valencian lady called *el ama* (the governess), her husband, Silvestre Perez, and Juan de Sepúlveda, quartermaster of the chamber of Juana's son, Charles.[81] According to Gómez de Fuen-

salida, Philippe allegedly sent these servants back to Spain to promote more har-
monious relations with his wife.[82]

Yet the conflict over Juana's household continued. Claiming to act with Juana's
consent, Philippe provided Friar Thomas Salazar, her Dominican confessor,
with 40 livres to return to Spain.[83] Apparently doubting the loyalty of Madame
de Hallewin, whom Queen Isabel had honored, the archduke then selected the
pro-French Viscountess of Furnes, Alienor de Poitiers, whom Juana refused to
accept as her first lady.[84] Seven other women, titled Juana's "girls of honor"
resided with her children when the princess refused to admit them into her own
household.[85] Another of Philippe's servants, don Alfonso, *infante* of Fez, began
to fulfill a mysterious function as Juana's "domestic servant" for four months at
a time.[86] Moreover, Philippe would no longer provide his wife with discretionary
funds. Complaining that he had not received the revenues due to him as Prince
of Asturias,[87] he also refused to pay Juana's extraordinary expenses.[88] Once again,
economic constraints prevented Juana from acquiring or maintaining the loyal
servants necessary to exercise authority. Without funds, she found it difficult to
inspire love or fear within the Burgundian household.

Juana lacked authority not only within her own household but even before
the Spanish ambassadors in Burgundy, who appeared to side with Philippe as his
marital conflicts intensified. Even Gómez de Fuensalida, who claimed no "passion" other than "love for the service and relief of their Highnesses [Fernando
and Isabel], along with love for the country and the public good,"[89] failed to
accord Juana the respect due to her as proprietary heiress. On 26 September
Fernando had written his ambassadors in Flanders that Queen Isabel's condition
appeared increasingly fatal. He instructed the Spanish diplomats to inform
Philippe and Juana that they should secretly prepare to travel to Spain by sea in
the case of Isabel's demise. Yet Gómez de Fuensalida failed to convey Fernando's
letter to Juana or to inform the princess of her mother's illness. In a letter of 11
November 1504, the king sternly reminded the ambassador "that she [Juana],
as heiress, is everything, and should receive your principal consideration." Although reports from Flanders portrayed the princess as "presently less healthy
than we desire" Fernando declared that he and Isabel maintained the hope "that
our lord will grant her health." If Isabel were to die, Fernando emphasized,
Juana would have to take possession of her kingdoms and govern them in person. The ambassadors should inform Philippe that he could not travel to Spain
without the princess and lawful heiress, for he would not be received. Fernando

further instructed the ambassadors to urge Philippe to treat Juana kindly, promoting "peace, love, and conformity" between the spouses.[90]

Queen Isabel confronted Juana's conflicts with Philippe in Flanders during the final month of her life. The queen's last will and testament, dictated on 12 October 1504, reaffirmed Juana's rights as her successor and proprietary heiress. By mid-November, however, such provisions appeared insufficient to prevent Philippe from leaving Juana in Flanders and seizing the Castilian crown himself. Reports from the Low Countries suggested that the princess, confined to her room and denied contact with Spanish servants,[91] retained little capacity for self-government. Thus, on 23 November, the queen added a clause to her testament stating that if Juana was absent from Castile at the moment of her mother's death or otherwise unable or unwilling to rule, King Fernando should govern on her behalf.[92] In other words, the queen moved to prevent Philippe from stealing power from Juana. In the case of Juana's incapacity, Isabel declared that Fernando—rather than Philippe and his cronies—should govern Castile. The queen died three days later.

Despite Isabel's precautions, Philippe assumed himself the queen's successor upon receiving news of her death.[93] On 12 December 1504 the bishop of Córdoba, Juan Rodríguez de Fonseca, reached Brussels with letters from Fernando confirming the queen's demise.[94] Although Philippe initially refused to inform Juana of Isabel's death on the pretext that she was pregnant again, within twelve days Philippe and allegedly Juana reportedly received the bishop and his news.[95] The would-be king's advisers designed a dramatic coup for 14 and 15 January, choreographing a ceremony that placed Philippe on center stage and relegated Juana to a secondary role if any.[96] With "the queen [Juana] present or absent," Philippe's councillors planned to raise the sword of justice and the arms of Castile, Leon, and Granada over the main altar in Brussels Church of Saint Gudule. The *roy d'armes* would then announce Philippe's and Juana's new titles as king and queen, removing Philippe's mourning hood and handing him the royal sword. As soon as Philippe took the sword of justice, the officers of arms and trumpeters were to shed his old insignia in favor of the new, distributing copies of the arms representing Castile, Leon, and Granada among all estates, "so that no one could remain ignorant" of the new possessions that Philippe claimed.[97]

The actual obsequies for Isabel in Brussels involved more than their initial plan. Juana chose to join the processions to and from Saint Gudule, probably to honor her mother rather than to support Philippe's designs. Next to two of her father's ambassadors, the princess preceded the Viscountess of Furnes, who carried her train.[98] The royal chapel, adorned with 250 large copies of Isabel's arms, also contained six angels, painted and hung. Six hundred smaller models of Philippe's new arms embellished the torches that paupers and town officials carried, while household personnel required 1,000 copies of the same images.[99] A more singular product, the richly illuminated missal containing portraits of Juana and Philippe, and a composition by Joaquin des Pres, "Philippeus rex Castillie," following Pierre de la Rue's more conventional "Kyrie Eleison," also may have been compiled for the occasion.[100] After reaching Saint Gudule, Juana joined Philippe at the altar. The herald, nevertheless, addressed only Philippe and handed him, not Juana, the proverbial sword. Once again, loyal personnel and generous spending magnified Philippe's authority.[101]

Having proclaimed himself King of Castile, Leon, and Granada, Philippe prepared a journey to take possession of those realms. In spite of a protracted rebellion in Guelders, Burgundian councillors announced that "the king is determined to go see his [new] subjects and kingdoms for a brief period, as short as his affairs will permit."[102] Fearful of death at sea, the self-proclaimed king dictated his last will and testament toward the end of December.[103] Notwithstanding such preparations, events in Castile led Philippe to delay his voyage for more than one year.

Rather than departing for Spain, Philippe became entangled in a propagandistic struggle with King Fernando, who had his own designs upon the crown of Castile. In early 1505, Fernando summoned the Cortes to hear Isabel's testament and to sanction his regency. In a statement directed to the Cortes on 23 January, Fernando claimed that Isabel's modesty and sorrow had prevented her from specifying the reasons that her daughter might not be able to rule. The representatives then heard Martín de Moxica's lengthy account of the "accidents, passions, and impediments that overcame the queen and had her outside her free will." By publicizing Moxica's report, Fernando used the record of conflicts between Philippe and Juana to obtain his own ends. Informed of "the illness that is such that the said Queen doña Juana our lady cannot govern," the Cortes unanimously declared her father, Fernando, guardian, administrator, and governor of Juana's kingdoms.[104]

Having declared Juana's incompetence, Fernando paradoxically also sought her mandate to rule. Secretly, Juan Rodríguez de Fonseca, Gómez de Fuensalida, and Fernando's secretary, Lope de Conchillos, secured Juana's written authorization for her father to govern Castile. Yet Aragonese valet Miguel de Herrera, charged with conveying the dispatch to Fernando, betrayed Juana and her father by delivering it to Philippe. Returning to Brussels, Philippe ordered Conchillos imprisoned and tortured, allegedly to the point that the secretary lost both his hair and (temporarily) his reason.[105]

While punishing Conchillos, Philippe tightened his control over Juana's household to ensure that she could not communicate with her father. Philippe's advisers charged Juana's vocal instructor, Juan de Anchieta, "to win the queen's conformity with the king, her husband," and to inform them of anything else that she might attempt to write Fernando.[106] Philippe also demanded that Juana's servants obey him rather than the queen. He even ordered the arrest of one attendant, Sebastián de Olano, who respected Juana's wishes by remaining with her in spite of Philippe's summons. When Gómez de Fuensalida meekly protested Olano's imprisonment, the archduke declared the intent to demonstrate that he was lord, "so that no one would say 'I must tell the queen' or 'the queen does not wish it done.'"[107] Thus Fernando's ambassador witnessed the results of Philippe's efforts to gain control of Juana's household: "All of the Spanish servants who came with Her Highness and have been with her since her arrival are all relatives of Judas; not one has remained loyal; each attempts to please the king, and none pays more attention to the queen than to me."[108] Philippe had used Juana's servants, whether Spanish or Burgundian, to attain full authority over her household. Governing Juana herself proved a more difficult task.

Confined to her chambers and prohibited any contact with the outside world, Juana could not use *ira regis* to her advantage. By April her gentleman of honor, the Prince of Chimay, had barred all Castilians from entering the queen's quarters, even when she summoned them. Ten to twelve archers stationed in Juana's first chamber enforced the regulation. In response to these restrictions, the queen summoned the Prince of Chimay. Fearing trouble, the prince asked his substitute, Monsieur de Fresnoy, to accompany him. According to one version of events, Juana greeted the gentlemen holding an iron bar. Chimay supposedly ran at once, leaving the elder Fresnoy to catch a blow from the angry queen. Juana then commanded one of her chapel boys to kill "the old traitor." As her elderly target escaped, Juana turned upon the responsible doorman, hitting his head, messing his hair, and "swearing that she would have them all killed." According to one report, the queen had inspired such fear that none of the Burgundians dared to visit her, and Juana remained entirely alone.[109] Her actions had provoked fright but not obedience.

Philippe, like Fernando, needed Juana's mandate to rule Castile in her stead. Thus dependent upon the authority that he undermined, the archduke sought a written declaration of Juana's love and loyalty toward him. Philippe's advisers claimed to have prepared six times a missive to this effect that Juana refused to sign but repeatedly edited. The document, they maintained, stated that even if Juana were mad, no one would govern her kingdoms but the king, her husband, whom she very much loved. Objecting to the word "love," Juana "undid it [the letter] five times, but in the end, she signed it that way," Philippe claimed.[110] Juana, in fact, never signed the letter.[111] Her husband's subsequent rights in Castile rested upon a forgery.

Suspecting that Juana had been forced to sign the letter supporting Philippe against her will, Fernando attempted to enter the marital fray on his daughter's side. Drawing upon reports from Gómez de Fuensalida, the Aragonese king presented a list of grievances against Philippe, which he threatened to publicize if Juana's treatment did not improve. He alleged that Juana had been held under armed guard, deprived of her freedom and of her Castilian servants, and forced to sign documents that she rejected.[112] Equally vehement, Philippe defended himself by claiming that Juana preferred not to receive visitors.[113]

Juana emerged from isolation only after 24 August 1505, when Philippe's father, Maximilian, arrived in Brussels determined to improve relations between his son and daughter-in-law. During Maximilian's visit, Juana attended jousts and met the Venetian ambassador Vicentio Quirini, who had solicited an audience with her for over five months. Quirini noted that he found the queen "molto bella," with the manner of "a wise and prudent lady."[114] During Maximilian's visit, Juana also joined in banquets that Philippe sponsored for his father.[115] Following the birth of Juana's third daughter, Mary, on 15 September,[116] Maximilian even held the newborn over the baptismal font.[117] Juana then helped Maximilian ensure the royal couple's voyage to Spain.[118] To expedite their departure, the queen transferred her household to Middelburg, close to the port of Vlissingen, where Philippe joined her by the end of December.[119]

Another source of marital tension surfaced at Middelburg, when Philippe selected and rewarded a new female escort for the queen.[120] Suspicious of the Flemish and Burgundian women loyal to Philippe, the queen sought more sober company and refused to accept them in her entourage. Juana insisted that the ladies disembark before she would set foot on the *Julienne*, the finest of forty or fifty vessels intended to convey the new monarchs to Spain. In light of Juana's objection, Philippe surreptitiously sent the women to another ship.[121] Juana apparently discovered their presence, however, when a storm forced the boats to take refuge on the coast of England.[122] From Windsor Castle, where Philippe rushed to meet Henry VII, the archduke informed his subjects that "a small incident" had prevented Juana from accompanying him "for the moment," although he hoped that she would join him soon.[123]

Juana's tardy and brief appearance at Windsor emphasized her differences with Philippe. While the queen shunned court festivities, Philippe delighted in them. In the midst of such celebrations the archduke pledged his son, Charles (now free of his engagement to Claude, who had married the future François I), to the English king's daughter, Mary, and his unwilling sister, Marguerite, to Henry VII himself.[124] Juana, in contrast, went to Windsor to approve an agreement for commercial cooperation between Spain and England and to see her sister Catalina (Catherine of Aragon), who resided with the English court.[125] According to Catalina, both she and Henry VII delighted in Juana's presence and lamented her hasty departure. Although Henry had wished to detain the queen, his councillors allegedly "told him that he should not intervene between husband and wife."[126] Two years later, Henry VII recalled his meeting with Juana: "When I saw her, she seemed very well to me, and spoke with a good manner and countenance, without losing a point of her authority. And although her husband and those who came with him depicted her as crazy, I did not see her as other than sane."[127] While relating a favorable impression of Juana, the English king recalled that Philippe and his entourage had portrayed her as mad.

Juana displayed similar disdain for Philippe and his councillors. Following her brief appearance at Windsor, the queen returned to Falmouth, where she welcomed seven ships that her father, Fernando, had sent to replace those damaged in the storm.[128] After two years of discord, Juana's political differences with her husband appeared irreconcilable. Far from senseless devotion to Philippe, Juana recognized an alliance with her father as her only means of frustrating Philippe's designs.

"Great Love between Father and Son"

Philippe, for his part, took measures to prevent Juana and her father from joining forces against him. Encouraging Fernando's love as well as his fear, the Burgundian maneuvered to exclude Juana by allying with Juana's father himself. Having established an accord of "strong love and friendship" with the Aragonese king,[129] the archduke nevertheless assembled two thousand German pikemen to accompany him to Castile.[130] The captain of this army described Juana as Philippe's worst enemy, after Fernando.[131] Yet Juana, following several unsuccessful attempts to secure a meeting with Fernando, ultimately found herself forced to compromise with Philippe.

In conjunction with the armed force at Philippe's disposal, the archduke's largesse discouraged servants from becoming intermediaries between Juana and Fernando. As a reward for past service and an incentive for future loyalty, Philippe named don Juan Manuel and Monsieur de Veyre, among others, members of the chivalric Order of the Golden Fleece.[132] Two of Juana's longtime servants, Diego de Ribera and Bertran de Fromont, likewise received gifts from Philippe before leaving Middelburg.[133] By reminding servants of his affection toward them, Philippe sought to deprive Juana of potential allies.

Under such circumstances, Juana's attempt to unite with her father failed miserably. When Juana and Philippe reached la Coruña on 25 April 1506,[134] Juana angered the local population by refusing to confirm local privileges, receive ambassadors, or undertake any act of government before meeting with her father.[135] According to Philip's ambassador at the papal court, the same story had reached Rome: "The Galicians approached the king [Philippe] and the queen to confirm their privileges and the queen wished to confirm them, yet responded that she would await the king, don Fernando, whom she considers king like herself."[136] Yet Fernando, rather than heeding Juana's summons, found himself deserted by the nobility and forced to side with Philippe at her expense. The elder king sent de Veyre to greet Philippe, with instructions to prevent Juana from disrupting "the peace and harmony" between the kings.[137] Juana's newly appointed master of the house, don Diego de Guevara, also represented Philippe's interests. Initially, Fernando questioned Guevara about his daughter and refused to abandon Castile before meeting with her.[138] Yet, as Philippe delayed his own encounter with Fernando, more and more grandees offered to support the Burgundian.[139] Just as decisively, the "Grand Captain," Gonzalo Fernández de Córdoba, a heroic commander in Italy, refused to back the elder king with troops from Naples.[140] By 9 June 1506 Fernando relinquished his demand for a meeting with Juana and emphasized solely his "great affection and desire" to see Philippe.[141]

Philippe and Fernando met on 27 June without informing Juana, who remained confined in the nearby town of Benavente. In Juana's absence, the kings conspired against her. Fernando promised to leave Castile in exchange for control of its military orders and one-half of the profits from the Indies.[142] In a second, secret, treaty Philippe and Fernando incapacitated Juana by asserting that she "in no way wants to occupy herself with or undertake any business of ruling or government or any other thing." Even if the queen wished to exercise authority, they stated, "it would be the total destruction and loss of these kingdoms due to her illnesses and passions, which are not expressed here for modesty." Should Juana attempt to rule on her own or be induced to do so by another party, the kings agreed to prevent her from governing.[143]

A desperate attempt to demand her father's attention only further marginalized Juana. Upon learning of the meeting between Philippe and Fernando, Juana escaped the castle of Benavente on horseback. Pursued by Philippe's guards, she took refuge in a humble home, where the German pikemen surrounded her. Juana's act of fleeing a noble castle and entering a residence beneath her station scandalized the court. Reportedly, the queen refused to leave the peasant's home until Fernando rescued her. Yet, rather than securing a meeting with her father, Juana's actions may have convinced Philippe of the need to confine her.[144] Juana protested her circumstances, as at La Mota and in Brussels, with increasingly unsuccessful results.

Having excluded Juana from the government, Philippe and Fernando emphasized their mutual affection. Philippe informed the city of Burgos that their accord entailed "ties and love" offering hope "that we will always remain in the union and conformity that interest and reason and peace require."[145] As Fernando departed for Aragon, he and Philippe met again in Tudela del Duero. According to the elder king, the second encounter entailed "acts demonstrating the great love that we share," in which he advised Philippe "as a true father to his true son," and the two remained "in great conformity and such love and such strong union that more would be impossible." After a private meeting that lasted one and one-half hours, the archbishop of Toledo, Francisco Jiménez de Cisneros, joined the two kings to witness "things of the greatest love between true father and son."[146] Such calculated displays of intimacy and affection served concrete political ends. Fernando wished to maintain the fiction that he left Castile of his own volition. Philippe, for his part, appreciated Fernando's unwillingness to champion Juana's rights. Juana had sent her first chaplain, Ramírez de Villaescusa, to Fernando with a letter begging him not to leave Castile before meeting with her. Yet Philippe, intercepting the letter, also imprisoned Villaescusa.[147]

Fernando's departure for Aragon and Naples without seeing Juana left Castilians opposed to Burgundian rule as Juana's most natural allies. As long as Juana remained confined, the bond of "love" between the foreign king-consort and his wife's lawful subjects appeared tenuous at best. According to one account:

> The people of these kingdoms hated the foreigners that Philippe had brought with him; and, since the foreigners were inclined to eat too much and to drink a lot, they committed disorders and misdeeds, so that justice began to weaken and expire.[148]

Another chronicler explained:

> Since the Flemish had a presumptuous manner of eating and drinking with respect to the Castilians, they killed each other for trivial causes and made great offense, there being less justice for the Flemish than for the Castilians.[149]

The Cortes of 1506, which initially met in the town of Murcientes, created a forum for opposition to the king. Although Philippe requested a legal mandate for Juana's imprisonment, the Cortes refused to provide it. In Murcientes, Pedro López de Padilla of Toledo and the Admiral of Castile, don Fadrique Enríquez, both interviewed the queen and subsequently refused to sanction her seclusion.[150] Even the Count of Benavente, don Alonso Pimentel, who had signed a petition to confine Juana, later protested that he had done so only under pressure from Philippe and swore to serve the queen with "entire faith, loyalty, and fidelity."[151]

Most dramatically, Juana herself appeared before the urban representatives in Murcientes in early July 1506. In response to their questions, she stated her support for Fernando's rule, agreed to dress in the Castilian manner, and refused to accept female attendants, "knowing the nature of her husband." Thus Juana implied that the company of ladies would dishonor her rather than enhance her regal status.[152] Then Juana revived her claim to royal authority by asking the procurators whether they recognized her as doña Juana, her mother's daughter and successor. Receiving an affirmative response, the queen attempted to move the Cortes to Toledo, where the same body had recognized her and her medieval predecessor, Queen Urraca, as proprietary heiresses.[153]

Philippe regained control of the situation by insisting that the Cortes continue in Valladolid rather than Toledo. On 10 July he and Juana entered Valladolid beneath a brocade canopy. Two days later the Cortes affirmed Juana as "true queen, legitimate successor and natural proprietary ruler of these said kingdoms and lands" and Philippe as "true king and legitimate ruler by legitimate marriage to the said queen, doña Juana." The procurators then swore loyalty to Juana and Philippe and performed the traditional acts of homage.[154] Another version of the same meeting recorded that the Cortes declared Juana's firstborn son and heir, Charles, her legitimate successor, and named Philippe "king and proprietary ruler of the said kingdoms."[155] Recognition as "proprietary ruler" gave Philippe the legal right to dispose of Castile and Leon as he wished. Indeed, an ambassador present noted that the ceremony's outcome delighted Philippe.[156] In the end, Juana may have decided to compromise with Philippe and relinquish the title of proprietary ruler in order to secure their son's subsequent rights to the throne. The precedent of Queen Berenguela, who assured the succession of her own son, Fernando, to the Castilian throne by ceding her sovereignty, once acknowledged, in 1217 may have influenced the outcome of the 1506 Cortes in the same city. By affirming first Juana, then Philippe, as proprietary ruler, the Cortes of Valladolid ultimately provided Philippe with legal authority to govern Castile.

After concluding the Cortes of Valladolid, Juana and Philippe proceeded to Burgos. In the midst of political pressures, Juana had not forgotten her early professor and confessor, the Dominican Andrés de Miranda, who resided in the monastery of San Pablo outside of that city. The queen donated eleven heads from the relics of the eleven thousand virgin martyrs, which the pope granted her in 1500, to Miranda's monastery, where they were hung 20 July 1506. By papal indulgence, individuals visiting San Pablo on this occasion, including Juana and Philippe, obtained complete remission of all their sins.[157] The indulgence that Philippe had achieved may have comforted Juana in the succeeding months.

Philippe, for his part, catered to the interests of his favorite, don Juan Manuel, in Burgos. After obtaining custody of that city's fortress, the favorite "who governed King Philippe at his will" sponsored a party for his benefactor.[158] During the course of the festivities, Philippe apparently overexerted himself, drank a large quantity of cool water, and soon fell ill.[159] Noting the king's fondness for women and games, one chronicler wrote, "through bad government he passed from this lifetime to the next."[160] As Philippe's condition worsened, the queen remained with him. Like the Duchess of Burgundy, Isabel of Portugal, and the future saint of the same name, Juana selflessly nursed her ailing spouse. Everyone but Juana, it seemed, expected Philippe to die.[161] On 24 September, one day before Philippe's death, the archbishop of Toledo, fray Francisco Jiménez de Cisneros, convened a council to form a provisional government. He also wrote Fernando, begging the king to return to Castile.[162] By summoning Fernando, the archbishop, like Philippe, denied Juana's rights.

Waiting for Fernando?

Historians have long assumed that Juana's behavior after her husband's death confirmed her inability to rule. Evidence for this interpretation derives principally from the queen's refusal to appoint an interim regent.[163] The archbishop of Toledo had asked for the post. Others pressured Juana to name either King Fernando or the Emperor Maximilian. Still others argued that the queen should convoke the Cortes of Castile and Leon.[164] Yet Juana granted none of these requests. Rather than a refusal to govern, Juana's actions after her husband's death indicated an unwillingness to let others rule on her behalf. After Philippe's death, Juana initially shunned royal councillors, ambassadors, and municipal delegates who demanded meetings with her.[165] Then, within three months of Philippe's death, Juana emerged from seclusion in order to govern in her own right.

In Juana's first attempt to rule, she issued a bold decree designed to restore the royal patrimony that Philippe had alienated through gifts to his friends and supporters. On 18 December 1506 Juana signed a provision revoking all of Philippe's grants in state bonds, revenues, and jurisdictions. The decree, countersigned by secretary Juan López de Lecárraga and four members of the royal council, stated that Philippe had distributed grants and privileges without Juana's knowledge or permission. The queen declared Philippe's favors "highly prejudicial and damaging to my royal patrimony and the public good of my kingdoms." She added:

> Since the said favors were not given by me as proprietary queen and natural lady of these, my kingdoms and lands, it would be a great burden on my conscience and a great harm and detriment to my said income and state and royal patrimony and to all of my said kingdoms and subjects and wards if this were not remedied. It pertains to me as queen and ruler to provide and restore them all by this, my letter, which I want to have the force and rigor of law, as if it were prepared and proclaimed in Cortes.[166]

The queen demanded that all lands and income alienated during Philippe's reign "be incorporated in my said crown and royal patrimony for now and forevermore."[167] In order to enforce this measure, Juana also attempted to restore her mother's council.[168] The widowed queen appeared determined to exercise royal authority.

Balancing these efforts to reverse Philippe's policies, Juana's most visible political initiative involved an attempt to escort Philippe's corpse to Granada. By placing Philippe's corpse alongside her mother's, as his testament stipulated, Juana probably hoped to secure her rights, and those of her eldest son, Charles, to that southern kingdom. Although King Fernando had instructed the cities of Castile "to serve and obey the most serene queen, our very dear and very loved daughter,"[169] he opposed Juana's desire to bury Philippe in Granada.[170] Juana nevertheless clung to practical reasons for attempting to reach lands that Philippe had never visited during his lifetime. The queen not only enjoyed a base of support among the nobles of Andalusia[171] but also needed to escape Philippe's former servants, who clamored for remuneration. Hence Juana sponsored a slow southward journey featuring elaborate obsequies for her husband to claim the inheritance that belonged to her and her son.

Historians have long depicted the queen's macabre procession as proof of her mad devotion for Philippe. The primary source for this legend—a more entertaining than accurate account—claimed that Juana regularly opened Philippe's coffin to kiss his feet.[172] Pietro Martire, who followed the queen, reported no such melodrama.[173] He nevertheless noted the strict exclusion of women from churches where the royal remains were deposited and speculated that Juana suffered from "the same jealousy that tormented her during her husband's life."[174] No chronicler recorded that Juana, in fact, complied with the rule of Carthusian monks who prayed for Philip's soul by barring nonroyal women from their presence.[175] Another courtier scornfully referred to Philippe's "holy body" and recorded Juana's rumored intention "to reveal in death how much she loved it in life."[176] However degrading to Juana, such accounts publicized her immortal bond to Philippe and, implicitly, Charles. While revoking Philippe's policies, Juana affirmed the rights of their common heir.

Descriptions of Juana's "excessive love" for Philippe enabled contemporaries to maintain the fiction of her two bodies—one corruptible, subject to passions, the other immortal and constant. The separation of the queen's human and transcendental persons became especially crucial for Philippe, Cisneros, Fernando, and others who sought to rule in her name. In the process of appropriating Juana's corporate identity, her contemporaries created a personality later termed "Juana the Mad." During Juana's lifetime, separation from her realms made the queen's love and fear personal liabilities rather than political tools. Indeed, controlling her image became a crucial aspect of governing the queen.

Nevertheless, the evidence suggests that the well-known passionate queen once coexisted with another Juana: virtuous, determined, and "molto bella." Alongside the representations that Juana's rivals used to bolster their authority, the historian glimpses a queen who attempted to pursue her own interests within the confines of those images. From such a vantage point, Juana's love and fear appear more misinterpreted than misdirected.

CHAPTER FOUR

Forging a Legend

The Triumph of Fernando's Paternal Authority

After the deaths of Queen Isabel and King Philippe, the idea of a well-ordered realm rested upon Juana's obedience to her father and Fernando's defense of his daughter. Assuming the obligation to defend Juana's subjects in exchange for their obedience, Fernando asserted the right to govern Castile, Leon, and Granada as his paternal duty. Drawing the analogy between Juana's person and her realms, the Aragonese king publicized his daughter's alleged submissiveness as a model for her subjects' conduct. From 1507 through 1518, Fernando craftily asserted paternal authority over Juana, her household, and her realms. Within the limits of filial submission, Juana confronted her father's rhetorical, diplomatic, and strategic initiatives—inspiring some, resisting others, and ultimately negotiating the conditions of her own retirement.

Juana accepted the prescribed role of an obedient daughter with notable reluctance. One of her books of hours, now preserved in the British Library, explicitly connected filial and Christian piety to elucidate the fourth commandment, "Venare parentes." According to this gloss, the household should educate children in order to restrain their irreverent hands.[1] Had Juana disobeyed her mother by returning to the Low Countries in April 1504? If the daughter retained any doubts about this action, then she may have interpreted subsequent events as retribution for offending Isabel and therefore God.

Six weeks before Isabel's death on 26 November 1504, the ailing queen dictated a last will and testament commanding Juana to obey Fernando. In order "to attain God's blessing, her father's, and mine," Isabel implored her heirs "always to maintain great obedience and subjection to the king, my lord, and not to stray from his obedience and commandment, serving and treating and respecting him with all reverence and obedience, giving him and having him given all honor that good and obedient children should grant their good father."[2] In addition to God's commandment, which required Juana and Philippe to venerate Fernando, Isabel emphasized that her heirs should respect the elder monarch for their own good as well as that of their realms, considering his great experience and services in those kingdoms.[3] Yet Philippe's subsequent actions, as detailed in chapter 3, revealed a blatant lack of respect for Fernando.

Juana, in contrast, presented herself as an obedient daughter, struggling for a measure of royal authority within the boundaries of this prescribed role. As we have seen, after her husband's death Juana took concrete measures to restore the royal patrimony as well as her mother's council. At the same time, the queen reformed her household to include Flemish chaplain and cantors while excluding other Burgundians.[4] Portraying herself as a competent mother as well as an obedient daughter, on 6 June 1507 the queen called her four-year-old son, Fernando, to her side.[5] Conversely, despite repeated supplications, Juana never summoned her father to help her govern Castile.[6] When nobles and prelates begged her to write Fernando, the queen took refuge in the guise of daughterly obedience, claiming that she could not trouble her father to abandon his own realms in order to govern hers.[7] Even when Fernando returned to the Iberian Peninsula in July 1507, Juana refused to write her father and sent members of the royal council to welcome him on her behalf.[8]

Sensitive to these slights, Fernando attempted to avoid offending the queen and her subjects. Disembarking at Valencia, the Aragonese king left his new wife, Germaine de Foix, in that city before entering Castile—a measure designed to appease Juana and other Castilians loyal to the memory of Queen Isabel.[9] As a further concession to Castilian sensibilities, Fernando ordered his Aragonese officials to remain in that kingdom and surrounded himself with Castilians.[10] Although the king wanted his daughter to approach the Aragonese frontier, Juana refused to leave the village of Hornillos de Cerrato (near Palencia) until her father had entered Castile. At that point, she traveled southeast to Tórtoles de Esgueva.[11]

Fernando and his partisans fabricated the support that Juana refused to provide for their government. Without presenting any evidence, they circulated rumors that Juana had written her father, welcoming him to Castile.[12] Fernando cast Juana in the role of a dependent daughter and portrayed himself as her defender. The seasoned monarch's triumphant return to Castile reflected, above all, the success of his own propaganda. Drawing on an idealized relationship between father and daughter, Fernando reasserted his authority in Castile. He presented the duty of governing Juana and her kingdoms as a paternal obligation.

The Health of Her Highness and Her Kingdoms

Fernando's partisans initially expounded on the analogy between Juana and her realms in letters urging the Aragonese king to succor both. As Philippe breathed his last breath, the archbishop of Toledo, fray Francisco Jiménez de Cisneros, addressed Fernando as "the true lord and father of these kingdoms," begging him "to come to govern and help them, as their true lord and father, and to console the very powerful Queen doña Juana, our lady, for the great loss and blow that the Lord has given her for our sins, because no one other than Your Highness, after God, can remedy such a great loss and misfortune."[13] Without consulting Juana, Cisneros turned to Fernando as the only ruler he believed capable of providing stability. Weeks later, royal secretary Lope Conchillos also implored the king to save his daughter and her realms: "Out of pity, please come in order to redeem and to rescue this daughter and these kingdoms, which risk being lost, placing all possible diligence in your arrival, since all good in this matter depends on it."[14] Juana's equanimity in late 1506 may have simply indicated a less apocalyptical view of events. Within one month after Philippe's death, the commander of Juana's guard noted, "it seems that the court and the kingdoms are in peace, although amid very different wills," while Juana refused to negotiate with prelates and officials she did not trust.[15] When the queen left Burgos for Torquemada with Philippe's coffin on 20 December 1506, Conchillos even feared for her life—a recurring concern he easily transferred to her kingdoms: "Now nothing remains to say but to ask God and the king our lord for mercy so that these realms do not perish."[16] Fernando's supporters filled the queen's obedient silence with desperate calls for paternal authority.

Such demands for Fernando's return to Castile from Naples, where he had gone upon ceding power to Philippe eleven months before, revealed deeply rooted distrust of independent female rule. One anonymous chronicle reported that, as soon as Fernando began to govern, Juana's realms "returned to their previous happy prosperity, because, as the sacred scripture reads, 'choose a man to govern the republic, and the people will live in peace.'"[17] According to this interpretation, the plague that assailed Spain in 1506–7 but abated with Fernando's return appeared to confirm God's choice of ruler. Meanwhile, another chronicler wrote that Fernando returned to Castile "in order to assume the government, as much of his daughter, Queen of Castile, as of all her kingdoms and affairs."[18] Once again, a parallel between the queen and her realms justified her father's authority over both.

Whether or not Juana wanted her father to return to Castile, she performed appropriate daughterly gestures when Fernando caught up with her in Tórtoles de Esgueva, southwest of Palencia, on 28 August 1507. The most credible account of the meeting remains one written by Jerónimo Zurita, a historian partial to the Aragonese king, in 1562. According to Zurita, on spotting Fernando, Juana rushed out of her apartments, accompanied by doña Juana of Aragon, Fernando's illegitimate daughter, and the Marquise of Denia. Catching a view of the queen, Fernando raised his hat just before Juana removed her mourning hood to reveal a modest white headdress. Then, in a kind of ritual designed to emphasize the diffidence of both partners, Juana moved toward her father's feet, as if she wished to kiss them, while Fernando humbled himself with one knee on the floor, embracing his daughter. Later, after the queen retired to her rooms, Zurita claimed that she showed even "greater obedience to her father" by requesting his permission to attend Mass in the local church. That same afternoon, Juana and Fernando met privately for two hours. The king emerged "very happy and-content" so that "it was understood that [Juana] desired her father's honor and good, possessing better sense and understanding than generally believed."[19] Whatever had transpired behind closed doors, Fernando seized interpretive control of events: "According to what the king himself ordered published, the queen had left everything regarding the government of those kingdoms to him."[20] A subsequent Aragonese historian expanded upon Zurita's interpretation of the Tórtoles encounter: "Everything assured the rule of the king and the well-being of the kingdom, because the eyes of Castilian loyalty saw great and solid sense in their queen's respect and obedience toward her father." After speaking with Juana for two hours, Fernando "began to rule as lord, either because the queen commended everything to him, as is thought, or because she should have commended it to him."[21] Once Fernando claimed royal authority, Juana could only assert her prerogatives at the price of disobedience.

Another, more contemporary, account of the same August meeting reveals how Fernando's supporters depicted the encounter as one in which Juana ceded royal authority to her father. The king's chief secretary, Miguel Pérez de Almazán, sent Fernando's ambassador in France the following version:

> The queen showed great reverence for her father and knelt on the ground, not wishing to rise until he gave her his hand [in order to kiss it], the king continually kissing her face and begging her to rise, while she continually insisted that he give her his hand. Finally, seeing that [Juana] did not wish to rise, [Fernando] gave her the palm of his hand. She granted him greater obedience than ever a daughter her father, and her father showed her as much love as a father could show a daughter. She begged him publicly to care for her and for the government of those kingdoms, leaving everything in his hands.[22]

Whether or not Juana actually kissed her father's hand, Almazán interpreted this humble gesture as an explicit declaration of obedience and vassalage. Yet the secretary's account of the meeting contained factual errors. First, the letter, supposedly written in Hornillos, claimed that the meeting occurred there rather than in Tórtoles, where it actually took place. One wonders if Almazán, an Aragonese official, even visited Hornillos, where he allegedly penned the letter, that year. It seems more likely that Almazán would have remained in the crown of Aragon, disseminating propaganda to secure Fernando's authority over Castile.[23]

Yet another account of the Tórtoles meeting and its aftermath came from Pietro Martire d'Angleria. While emphasizing Juana's obedience to her father, the humanist also indicated Fernando's deference and willingness to negotiate with his daughter. According to Martire d'Angleria, Fernando asked his daughter, as queen, to elect their next destination. Juana allegedly responded, "Children should continually obey their parents," so that, as Martire d'Angleria claimed, "Paternal respect triumphed."[24] In fact, invoking the ultimate paternal authority, Fernando had obtained a papal brief releasing Juana from the obligation to convey Philippe's corpse to Granada.[25] Fernando and Juana therefore moved north toward Burgos in order to recover its castle from a common enemy, don Juan Manuel. Although Fernando hoped to punish various nobles, Juana's long-standing opponent became the king's first target. While Fernando resided in Burgos, Juana chose to remain three leagues away in Arcos, where her father visited her two or three times each week.[26] Fernando's attentiveness to the queen encouraged her obedient posture.

Emphasizing the parallel between Juana and her realms, Fernando depicted Juana's subjects as equally respectful. In a November 1507 letter to Catherine of Aragon also intended for the English king, Fernando emphasized "the well-being and health and remedy of the most serene queen, my very dear and very beloved daughter, your sister, and of these kingdoms." In a passage reminiscent of tracts against Queen Isabel's predecessor, Enrique IV, Fernando described his celebratory reception throughout Castile: "Revealing that, after God, my return provided the good and health and remedy of the most serene queen, my very dear and very loved daughter, your sister, and of these realms, which were without any justice, in great upheaval and scandal before my return." Had he failed to return so swiftly, Fernando asserted, "without doubt the royal crown would have lost its patrimony, and these kingdoms would have been destroyed forever." He listed the recovery of Ponserrada in Galicia (an effort begun before his return)[27] and the appointment of new officials in many cities and towns, in consultation with Juana, as his most significant accomplishments. Overall, Fernando claimed to have restored "justice, peace, and tranquillity."[28]

Even municipal officials had to suspect that Fernando liked his own rhetoric. In the fall of 1507 Fernando began to assemble soldiers and an armada in Seville, claiming that he, himself, would lead the conquest of North Africa. Although the army may have been intended to enforce Fernando's authority in Castile,[29] the city councillors of Seville feared unrest if the king crossed the Mediterranean. The municipal officials asked Fernando to consider "his royal health, prosperity, and glory, as well as that of these realms," and placed their "consolation, peace, tranquillity, and life, and that of all of Spain in Your Highness." Since the relationship between Fernando's person and Juana's realms relied on a "natural" bond between father and daughter, the local councillors asked that Fernando "place before your eyes the natural love that you have always had and still have for the illustrious queen our lady, your very dear and very obedient daughter. Regard the state in which you would leave her and what she would do, say, or think. Consider that you are her father, and that she lacks a husband, so that your royal presence is her only consolation and remedy."[30] Drawing upon the analogy between Juana and her realms, the councillors suggested that Fernando's departure would upset both. Furthermore, the municipal officials reminded the experienced king of his obligation to protect his daughter as well as her kingdoms.

"The Queen Will Not Go without the Body"

Fernando's well-publicized efforts to defend his daughter's inheritance coincided with Juana's equally determined attempts to protect that of her own son. Both Fernando and Juana saw Philippe's uninterred corpse as an obstacle to the queen's remarriage and used it to ward off eager suitors, including Henry VII, Gastón de Foix, and the Duke of Calabria. Yet Fernando and Juana had very different motives for upholding Juana's widowhood and accordingly different plans for Philippe's corpse. Juana hoped to place her husband's body alongside that of Queen Isabel, as a reminder of her eldest son's right to the same throne. Fernando, in contrast, had his own designs on the throne of Castile and wanted to bury the memory of Philippe as king by interring his corpse as far north as possible. Thus, in spite of their common aversion to Juana's admirers, the queen and her father envisioned different destinations for Philippe's remains.

Juana's commitment to a widowhood spent defending her children's rights may have drawn strength from one of the *Letters* of Saint Jerome, a fundamental hermetic text contained in her library.[31] Praising the moral and political virtues of widowhood, Jerome counseled a young widow, Furia, to guard her chastity against "the rascality" of servants and the "mistaken kindness" of a father who encouraged her to remarry. Jerome recommended that the widow "quench the fire of the devil's shafts with the cold streams of fast and vigil" rather than accepting another husband to satisfy her lust.[32] Otherwise, Jerome predicted that the offspring of the widow's first marriage would suffer the consequences of her second union: "A mother sets over her children not a stepfather but an enemy, not a parent but a tyrant. . . . If it should happen that you have sons by your second husband, domestic warfare and internecine feuds will be the result. You will not be allowed to love your own children, or to look kindly on those to whom you gave birth."[33] Jerome's advice summarized the threat that Juana's remarriage would pose for her children, and particularly her firstborn son. Rather than remarry, she commemorated Philippe as the former King of Castile, Leon, and Granada in an attempt to assure her son's succession to those realms.

At Juana's insistence, Philippe would travel through "more of Castile dead than alive."[34] Although Philippe had never seen most of his subjects, Juana appeared determined that they would witness evidence of his presence. The queen's four nighttime pilgrimages with her husband's coffin from December 1506 through August 1507, surrounded by torches, presented her people with the image of Philippe as king and father of their future sovereign. Avoiding population centers and traveling at night, Juana allegedly claimed that a widow "should not be seen in cities or in principal parts," measures that also kept her company away from the plague.[35] The queen also oversaw prayers for the dead, a pious obligation often associated with *recogidas* and tertiary Franciscans.[36] Juana provided Philippe's former chaplains, whom she now called "my cantors," with robes of black camel hair and velvet appropriate for their office.[37] Intoning additional Masses, the Carthusian monks and prior of Burgos's Monastery of Miraflores, also accompanied Philippe's coffin. Granting the Carthusians alms, Juana also purchased "the wax that must burn alongside the body of the king, our lord, so that he may attain holy glory."[38]

While accepting the services of chosen friars, Juana demanded full authority over her husband's remains. The queen's attitude toward Philippe's corpse emerged in a letter of 28 October 1507 to Fernando from Mosen Luis Ferrer, who resided with the queen in Arcos, outside of Burgos. In a visit to the local church, Juana ordered her seat moved close to Philippe's coffin. She then instructed her chaplain, Alonso de Alba, to place fifty torches around the casket on 1 November, the Day of All Souls. The chaplain insisted that only thirty were necessary. Offended, the queen abruptly exited the church. She demanded respect for her orders and Philippe's memory.[39] If Juana had reached Granada with Philippe's corpse, she would have established her son's symbolic claim to a kingdom that Fernando had helped conquer and Philippe had never visited.

As Juana edged her way south, Fernando, loath to have Philippe's mortal remains interred in Granada before his own, advanced his own designs on Charles's inheritance. Fernando, unlike Juana, quickly remarried after the death of his first spouse. Fernando's 1505 union with Germaine de Foix—the youthful niece of his archenemy, Louis XII—appeared designed to produce a direct, legitimate male heir to the crown of Aragon. Any son born to Fernando and Germaine would supplant the rights of Juana and, eventually, Charles, to the Aragonese inheritance. On 3 May 1509 proponents of peninsular unity breathed a sigh of relief when a son born to Fernando and Germaine survived less than a few hours. Following this setback, the royal couple's desperation for a male offspring seemed to increase. In 1513 Fernando even resorted to a "virility potion" credited with ruining his health.[40] Fernando's attempts to produce a son suggest that he, unlike Juana, had little desire to bequeath the kingdoms he had ruled and conquered to Charles.[41]

While eager for a male heir of his own, Fernando apparently endorsed Juana's attempts to avoid a second marriage. The Aragonese king even publicized his daughter's attachment to the cadaver of her former husband. In late 1507 Fernando informed his ambassador in England, "you must know that the said queen, my daughter, carries the body of her husband, King Philippe, with her continually," and that she refused to consider remarriage until her former spouse was buried.[42] In a letter of 18 April 1508, Fernando repeated, "Until now it has not been possible to get her [Juana] to consent to bury the body of the king don Philippe, her husband."[43] Although Henry VII suspected Fernando of deceiving him, the Aragonese king, in fact, made several attempts to curtail Juana's journey with Philippe's remains.

Throughout 1508 Juana and Fernando vied for control over Philippe's corpse. While Juana insisted on keeping the cadaver in her possession, Fernando hoped to return it to the Carthusian Monastery of Miraflores outside Burgos. The Aragonese king simultaneously aspired to move Juana from the Arcos palace to a more secure residence in the town of Tordesillas, five leagues (twenty-eight kilometers) from Valladolid.[44] In January 1508 the king paid 74,560 mrs to transport his daughter's chamber and personal effects from Arcos to Renedo, then Tordesillas.[45] Yet the queen herself refused to budge without Philippe's corpse. Six months later Fernando tried again,[46] but Juana would not leave her husband's remains in Arcos. Exasperated, the king collected his young namesake, the *infante* Fernando, and departed for Andalusia, where he planned to castigate rebellious nobles who had supported Juana in 1506. Had the queen wished to send for her firstborn son, Charles, the king knew that she would have to provide young Fernando in exchange and effectively prevented her from making such a move.[47] When Juana protested the abduction of her son, the Aragonese king cited the *infante's* "health" as the motive for his removal.[48]

The Aragonese king took other measures to ensure his daughter's obedience. He left her in Arcos with a household of one confessor, ten chaplains, nineteen personal attendants, twenty-seven officers, and forty-seven armed guards.[49] To further enforce his authority, Fernando transferred troops loyal to him from the Navarrese frontier to the outskirts of Arcos.[50] The king also provided his former ambassador Mosen Luis Ferrer, now officially the queen's *cerrero mayor* or master of the wax,[51] with permission to authorize extraordinary expenses on Juana's behalf.[52] Taking charge of the queen's finances, Ferrer provided her Flemish chaplains and cantors with funds to return to the Low Countries.[53] Through this measure and with Fernando's consent, Ferrer began to dismiss servants the queen had maintained around Philippe's body since his death.[54]

A letter of 9 October 1508 from Juana's former confessor, Diego Ramírez de

Villaescusa, to Fernando indicates that the queen opposed the assertion of paternal authority over her household. Juana protested the seizure of her son and the imposition of new household personnel by refusing to eat, dress, wash, and worship appropriately. Since her father's departure for Andalusia, Ramírez de Villaescusa reported rumors that Juana had not changed her shirt or headdress, washed her face, or slept in a bed. Moreover, he warned:

> They have told me that she urinates very often—more often than ever seen in any other person. Of these things, some are signs of a short life and others causes. May Your Highness remedy them all. In my opinion, her health is in great danger and the government of her person should not be left to her disposition, for we see the results. Her face and everything else, they say, lacks cleanliness. She eats on the floor, without a tablecloth or glassware. Many days she misses Mass, occupying herself with eating so that noon arrives and she lacks time to celebrate [the Mass].[55]

The bishop provided this portrait of a disorderly queen—flagrantly disrupting household routines—in order to encourage Fernando to return to Castile. Juana's defiant conduct, reminiscent of Queen Isabel of Castile's supposed refusal to change her shirt until the fall of Granada, may also have been calculated to demand Fernando's attention. Begging the king to intervene, Ramírez de Villaescusa argued that Juana could not govern her body, much less her subjects. Considering the ever-present analogy between the ruler and her kingdoms, Juana may have adopted ascetic practices to benefit her realms. At the same time, her reported behavior violated royal, and even civilized, norms.

By suggesting that Juana's life might be in danger, Ramírez de Villaescusa offered Fernando an important motive to attend to his daughter. As the king knew all too well, Juana's death would terminate his right to rule Castile as her father. From Seville, Fernando ordered 12,000 mrs distributed among selected monasteries "so that they will beg God for the life and health of the queen and princess, my daughter." Although the king ordered this money deducted from that allotted to Juana's household, a comparison to Fernando's expenditures on prayers for his deceased wife (Queen Isabel) and children (Prince Juan and Princess Isabel) during the same year, 5,100 mrs in total, indicates the importance he attached to Juana's survival.[56]

Fear for Juana's health may have also motivated Fernando to reach a compromise with his daughter after returning to Arcos on 6 February 1509. Apparently, Juana agreed to move to Tordesillas if she could take Philippe's remains with her. On the evening of 15 February, Juana followed her husband's corpse out of

Arcos. In the words of a Venetian ambassador, "Her Majesty the queen will not go without the body."[57] Allegedly showing "great obedience and respect" toward Fernando, the queen proceeded to Tordesillas. On reaching that town, Juana deposited Philippe's corpse in the Royal Monastery of Saint Claire, alongside the palace where she would reside,[58] guarding her widowhood as well as her son's inheritance.

Paternal Diplomacy

The queen's seclusion in a small town of central Castile marked a crucial step in her father's efforts to limit Juana's contact with the outside world. From Fernando's standpoint, Juana's retirement to Tordesillas minimized his opponents' opportunities to communicate with her. Led by Henry VII of England and Maximilian of Austria, Fernando's adversaries contested his right to govern Juana and her realms. While Henry VII demanded Juana's hand in marriage, Maximilian aspired to rule Castile on behalf of Juana's son, Charles. In pursuit of such objectives, Henry and Maximilian even threatened to combine forces and to invade Castile.[59] Fernando kept them both at bay through astute diplomacy. Even more impressively, the Aragonese king secured international consent for governing his daughter and her realms.

Fernando's diplomatic and rhetorical offensive included depicting himself as a father to Charles, whom Marguerite of Austria, the erstwhile spouse of Prince Juan, raised in Mechelen. Although Fernando previously had encouraged the Duke of Guelders, who had likewise engaged Philippe, to rebel against Charles, he now withdrew support for the war in Flanders, declaring: "After the queen, my daughter, the Prince don Carlos [Charles] is my heir. For this reason, and because I consider him a son, I desire his good fortune and will procure it as if it were my own."[60] In another letter sent to England, Fernando affirmed "the Prince of Castile is my son and heir." Denying any intent to disinherit either Juana or Charles, Fernando insisted that he should be consulted regarding a proposed marriage between Charles and the daughter of Henry VII.[61] Notwithstanding his efforts to sire a son with Germaine de Foix, the Aragonese king appeared eager to exercise paternal authority over both of his successors.

In turn, Henry VII of England, while negotiating a marriage between his daughter and Juana's son, insistently solicited Juana's hand for himself. Although Fernando assured the English king that Juana would marry him before any one else, Henry became increasingly convinced that the Aragonese king impeded their union.[62] Outlasting the adamant suitor, Fernando emphasized the need for patience with Juana:

> I have done everything possible to persuade the queen, my daughter, to have the body of the king, her husband, buried. And I have not been able to conclude it [the matter], for each time she tells me, "Not so soon." Acting against her will in this [Philippe's burial] would be for her to take the sky with her hands, and to destroy her health entirely, because in this matter it is necessary not to contradict what she greatly desires, but rather to persuade her little by little through circumventions.[63]

Fernando shrewdly insisted that he would handle Juana with the requisite delicacy. Resentful of the ensuing delays, Henry VII blamed Fernando for Juana's alleged reluctance to marry him.[64] The aggressive suitor even considered invading Spain in order to wed Juana, "healthy or ill," and to rule Castile as her husband.[65] In spite of such ambitious plans, Henry VII died 21 April 1509, just two months after Juana had reached Tordesillas. Henry VIII's accession and the conclusion of his marriage to Catherine of Aragon removed any potential English opposition to Fernando's regency.[66]

Henry VII's demise left Maximilian as Fernando's principal opponent. Since 1507 Maximilian had threatened to convey Juana's son, Charles, to Castile, and then to rule the kingdom on his behalf. Maximilian recognized that any male offspring born to Fernando and Germaine would endanger the interests of the house of Habsburg. The emperor, moreover, found supporters in Castile, including the Duke of Nájera and the Marquis of Villena.[67] In the spring of 1507 Maximilian informed Castilian nobles and towns that he and Charles would arrive in Spain within one year.[68] Yet the emperor could secure neither custody of Charles nor the funds necessary for such a voyage.[69] Given his chronic shortage of cash, at one stage, Maximilian even offered Fernando the regency of Castile for his lifetime in exchange for an annual 40,000 ducats, and more in the case of Juana's death. He also requested that the Aragonese king send Juana's second son, Fernando, to the Low Countries in 1516 with a fleet that could then convey Charles to Castile.[70]

In the end, Maximilian could only reinforce Juana's efforts to protect the rights of Charles. The treaty that Fernando, Maximilian, and, nominally, Charles and Juana finally adopted in December 1509 specified that Fernando would govern Castile, Leon, and Granada during his lifetime unless Juana died, or Fernando and Germaine de Foix had a son. In either case, Charles would rule after attaining his majority.[71] A male child born to Fernando and Germaine would pose a clear threat to Charles by supplanting his rights in Aragon and Navarre. Yet Fernando and Maximilian also accepted the assumption that Juana's death would prejudice Charles. Their attention to that possibility reflected the fact that Juana's continued presence in Castile safeguarded her son's inheritance. In Fernando's favor, the agreement termed him "legitimate caretaker and administrator" of Juana's "person and goods."[72] It gave Fernando a clear mandate to govern Juana and her kingdoms. While excluded from these negotiations and treated as a permanent minor, the queen had already expressed her posture in favor of their outcome—fortifying the regency of Fernando and the succession of Charles. In order to facilitate such an accord, Juana had favored Fernando as he left Castile in 1506 and supported Charles after Philippe's death, consistently sustaining the weaker party. Juana's retirement in Tordesillas did not prevent her from influencing the fate of her kingdoms.

In compliance with the terms of the 1509 accord, the 1510 Cortes of Castile and Leon confirmed the Aragonese king as "legitimate administrator and governor for the very high and very powerful lady, the queen, doña Juana, our lady, his daughter," and affirmed Charles as his mother's successor.[73] Upon concluding the Cortes of Castile, Fernando led the ambassadors and nobles who had attended them to Tordesillas. Queen Juana, who had not been prepared to receive such visitors, shocked them by her humble clothes and surroundings. Although Juana attempted to change her appearance, the damage had been done.[74] The queen had adopted ascetic practices, as if following the model of Saint Claire, "who never had a bed or a mattress or anything soft [and] always went almost naked and barefoot," and Queen Isabel of Portugal, who subjected herself to three-day fasts and nightly vigils.[75] Such customs appeared highly inappropriate for a ruler, leaving nobles suspicious of Fernando no alternative but to approve the 1509 accord, as confirmed in the Cortes of 1510.[76]

Whether or not Juana knew about the political events of 1509–10, their outcome paralleled her sacrifice of the right to rule in order to confirm Charles's succession during the Cortes of 1506. Like Philippe four years earlier, Fernando legalized his personal right to act on behalf of the corporate body identified with Juana and, ultimately, with Charles. The 1509 agreement, while recognizing Juana as queen, officially deprived her of the ability to exercise royal authority. Female inheritance, while confirmed as a formal right, invited the assertion of potential male rulers. Fernando and Maximilian, each with his own paternal claims to govern Castile, agreed that a female heiress with clear titular rights should not wield political power. In the case of Juana's inability or unwillingness to rule, no one considered her younger sister, María, Queen of Portugal and herself a mother, as a possible regent of Castile, for the option interested neither Juana, Fernando, nor Maximilian. Although Maximilian eventually permitted Marguerite of Austria to govern the Low Countries, Charles would demote her upon his emancipation in 1515.[77] In the interest of their dynasty, Marguerite and Juana would endure such slights.

Royal Authority in Tordesillas

Fernando required local as well as international support to sustain the disjunction between Juana's titular rights and true authority. While ruling Castile in Juana's name, Fernando increasingly trusted his servant, Mosen Luis Ferrer, to govern Juana and her Tordesillas household in the paternal interest. Strengthening his control over Juana's household, Ferrer increasingly used its personnel to limit the queen's contact with the outside world. At times, however, Ferrer's mission of isolating Juana clashed with his need to guarantee her survival. Fernando's right to rule Castile rested on Juana almost as fully as Ferrer's ability to govern Juana depended on her father. Paternal efforts to defend the queen ultimately entailed the use of violence to procure her obedience.

Fernando had selected Tordesillas, a favorite residence among medieval queens of Castile, as a secure and secluded yet central permanent home for his daughter. Surrounded by walls and filled with low, solid churches, the town occupied a hill overlooking the Duero River, which provided local inhabitants with drinking water but did not admit navigation. Juana's palace, situated alongside the river, afforded a view of low, flat plains, extending as far as Medina del Campo (some twenty-three kilometers south) on a clear day.[78] Next to the royal palace lay the convent of Saint Claire, founded in 1365 by the daughter of King Pedro I, Beatriz, who entered it after renouncing her rights to the throne. In the fifteenth century, the royal convent became a locus of religious reform.[79] By the sixteenth century, it had acquired the right to tolls paid on the bridge crossing the Duero,[80] privileged access to scarce wood,[81] and custody of the staff of justice issued to royal officials.[82]

Juana appears to have taken a particular interest in the Royal Monastery of Saint Claire alongside her palace. Having visited the female Franciscans of Brussels as early as 1499, the Claires outside Bruges in 1501, and those of Rejas in 1502 and 1503, the queen developed a similar relationship with the Claires of Tordesillas. A desire to emulate Isabel of Portugal (1271–1336) may have even encouraged Juana to reside alongside the Tordesillas convent. As a widow, the Portuguese queen and subsequent saint had built her home next to the Monastery of Saint Claire of Coimbra, "which she frequently visited, and where she attended the divine office, disciplinary training, and other holy exercises with the other nuns and religious women."[83] Isabel of Portugal became particularly renowned for charitable practices,[84] which Juana may have made modest efforts to imitate.

Queen Juana exercised the degree of charity that her circumstances (not to mention her father) would permit. Before Fernando dismissed the Carthusians of Miraflores, Juana had given them important and personal gifts. According to the monastery's records, Juana donated clothing, curtains, and cloth, which the monks used to make ornaments, in addition to two rich carpets.[85] She also provided the vicar, García del Corral, with a plate of gilded silver and funds to convert the plate into a lamp. The queen herself even reportedly sketched the device that she wished engraved on the lamp.[86] Once settled in Tordesillas, Juana donated 100,000 mrs to two friars who visited her from the Royal Monastery of Guadalupe, a foundation renowned for its "great observance and *recogimiento*" where Queen Isabel's last will and testament had been deposited.[87] The Claires of Tordesillas, nevertheless, became the most regular recipients of the queen's charity. According to her household accounts, Juana personally donated 30 ducats to the Claires on Holy Friday in 1511, then 40 ducats in 1512 and again in 1513.[88] During Holy Week, the queen customarily ordered tapestries transferred from her own residence to the monastery and sponsored an annual monument there featuring the Host enclosed in a chest draped with cloth to represent Christ's body resting in the tomb three days before His resurrection.[89] Juana also made donations to the Claires on the day of Saint Sebastian[90] and to certain preachers who gave sermons at their convent.[91]

During her visits to Saint Claire, the queen apparently grew fond of certain aspects of the convent. In 1512, when the abbess and nuns moved an altar and image of Saint Francis, Juana paid 1,506 mrs to restore it.[92] Two years later, the abbess and nuns attempted to replace the same altar with a statue of Santiago, the patron saint of Spain. Again, the queen paid 408 mrs to return the statue to its original location.[93] Juana also objected in 1513, when the Claires planned to construct a new chorus in the middle of the main apse, "because it seemed to Her Highness that the said church was shortened." The queen accordingly sent the abbess of Saint Claire 60,000 mrs in order to help finance a new tribunal above the previous chorus.[94] Such expenses, recorded in royal accounts, suggest that Juana may have followed the spiritual model of Queen Isabel of Portugal, who had directed construction in the monastery of Coimbra,[95] with respect to the Tordesillas convent, where she exercised a measure of influence.

In contrast, Juana preserved very little authority within her own household. After installing Juana in Tordesillas, Fernando provided her with a household staff loyal to him. Payrolls that Fernando issued in Valladolid list a confessor and twelve chaplains, seventeen personal attendants, thirty-six officers, as many as twelve ladies-in-waiting, and forty-nine armed guards.[96] In fact these payrolls illustrate the fiction of Juana as queen, since Fernando and Ferrer selected and governed "her" servants. Certain officials listed as serving Juana, moreover, resided with her father.[97] Juana's official confessor, for example, fray Tomás de Matienzo, apparently earned 60,000 mrs per year without ever setting foot in Tordesillas. In addition, Juana was surrounded by a number of servants who never appeared on her payroll. Among these numbered six Franciscan friars charged with praying for Philippe's soul, who received clothing in lieu of pay.[98] The Franciscans' supervisor, fray Juan de Ávila, served as Juana's unofficial confessor in Matienzo's absence[99] and became the tutor of her youngest daughter, Catalina, in 1514.[100]

Prominent among the absentee members of Juana's household ranked the court humanist and gossip, Pietro Martire d'Angleria. Describing Juana as "entirely destroyed by Saturn," Martire d'Angleria claimed that she resisted movement and declared Tordesillas her permanent home.[101] Allegedly under the lethargic influence of a planet promoting either genius or madness,[102] Martire d'Angleria reported that the queen even refused to exchange her chamber overlooking the Duero River for one more protected from winter winds.[103] According to Martire d'Angleria, the stationary monarch rejected the comforts that Fernando and his adherents sought to provide:

> It was impossible for her father to uproot her from ramshackle and unhealthy rooms in order to install her in chambers prepared with royal sumptuousness. No one can persuade her to rest in a comfortable bed with mattresses, or to wear furs for the cold, or dresses appropriate for the season. She uses common furnishings. Through extraordinary evasions, she delays the hour for eating. At times she fasts for over three days, ignoring her servants' pleas to consume some food or drink.[104]

Martire d'Angleria portrayed Juana's ascetic self-mortification as the antithesis of proper regal behavior. Juana may have attempted to emulate the fasts and vigils that Saint Claire had modeled and Queen Isabel of Portugal had practiced.[105]

Whatever her pious intentions, Juana's refusal to sleep, eat, and dress according to royal norms nevertheless entailed a rejection of her new household and the routines that its members hoped to govern.

Martire d'Angleria expressed particular sympathy for Fernando's proxy in Tordesillas, Mosen Luis Ferrer. As *cerrero mayor,* Ferrer officially controlled the supply of wax in the church as well as the palace.[106] In practice, Ferrer approved all of the queen's "extraordinary costs," including the purchase of medicines,[107] linens,[108] and shoes,[109] as well as pious donations Juana chose to make.[110] Not surprisingly, townspeople became curious and concerned about the nature of Ferrer's authority.[111] Likewise resenting the burden of providing accommodations and clothing for "permanent guests" in the town, some residents even left Tordesillas.[112] Although Fernando issued orders to halt the expropriation of clothing, Ferrer postponed their enforcement until he could change the king's mind. Finally, the royal council granted Tordesillas an annual grant of 100 ducats "to assist in the expense of clothing."[113] Yet local residents remained troubled by the *cerrero mayor's* authority over their queen.

Notwithstanding these growing doubts about his behavior, Ferrer, with support from King Fernando, tightened his control over the Tordesillas household. Among Ferrer's antagonists, royal accountants refused to approve all of the extraordinary expenses that the *cerrero mayor* approved. King Fernando consequently informed the accountants that he had granted Ferrer full authority over Juana, "for everything necessary to our service, the governance of her royal person and household, and the administration of all of her offices and officials and costs, with which I fully entrust him."[114] Such unequivocal backing from the king enabled the Valencian *cerrero mayor* to select and to remunerate servants loyal to him. Not surprisingly, the names doña Francesca, doña Isabel, doña Margarita, and doña Violante Ferrer soon appeared on the list of Juana's female attendants receiving household salaries and cost-of-living supplements.[115]

Despite his growing clientele, Ferrer's authority rested almost exclusively on Fernando's. After the Aragonese king died on 23 January 1516, residents of Tordesillas and members of Juana's household unleashed their pent-up anger upon Ferrer. As soon as news of Fernando's death reached Tordesillas, local guards stormed the royal palace and expelled the *cerrero mayor.*[116] The bishop of Mallorca, sent to Tordesillas to investigate the turmoil, heard the villagers' complaints against Ferrer and forbade him further contact with the queen.

For his part, Ferrer insisted that he had governed Juana's household "like a monastery and religion of the most upright friars." The most serious accusation facing Ferrer was that he had employed force against the queen. The *cerrero mayor* did not deny this charge. Rather, he claimed that the queen's illness could not be cured, and that King Fernando had "ordered her given the rope [i.e., whipped] to maintain her life, so that she would not die from refusing to eat in order to enforce her will."[117] Such testimony suggests that Juana occasionally abstained from food in order to pressure her servants, and even her father, to respect certain demands. She succeeded, at least, in attracting attention.[118] Although no one recorded the queen's specific wishes in 1515, she may have sought greater freedom of movement, including more frequent visits to the neighboring convent of Saint Claire, as well as increased opportunities for contact with her subjects.[119] In spite of Juana's efforts, Ferrer had treated her like anything but a proprietary queen.[120]

Upon Fernando's death and Ferrer's expulsion from Tordesillas, Juana's servants sought spiritual remedies for her health. Welcoming a "very honorable cleric" into the royal palace, first chamberman Diego de Ribera joyfully declared: "Friday, the first of February, the cure of the queen, our lady, began." In particular, the priest exorcised Juana, blessing the queen and saying prayers as she ate.[121] Ribera claimed that the cleric had recognized Juana's illness and promised to cure her "so that she confesses this Lent." The queen, for her part, spent hours consulting her Franciscan confessor, fray Juan de Ávila.[122] In contrast to Ribera's enthusiasm, Juana's first lady, doña María de Ulloa, declared herself skeptical about the methods of the cleric, whom she described as a "witch." According to Ulloa, the exorcist left Tordesillas before producing any change in Juana.[123] In this way, Fernando's authority over Juana's health gave way to a short-lived attempt to cure the queen amid varied assessments of her condition.

Ferrer's obedience to Fernando's paternal authority had established a crucial precedent for governing the queen in Tordesillas. This situation would endure irrespective of any fluctuations in Juana's health. When informed of "diverse opinions" regarding the queen, her son and heir Charles ordered Juana placed under rigorous guard: "Because the queen's honor, contentment, and consolation pertain to me more than any one else, and persons wishing to intervene [in this matter] will not have good intentions."[124] Citing filial duty instead of paternal authority, Charles would inherit the household and beliefs that had enabled Fernando to deprive Juana of sovereignty. Having pushed Marguerite of Austria aside, Charles remained at the mercy of his own governors in Brussels, his first chamberlain Guillaume de Croy, seignior de Chièvres, and Chancellor Jean

Sauvage. They allegedly decided to withhold from Charles reports that Queen Juana was recovering her health. According to one source, Chièvres and Sauvage discussed the queen's well-being, "and not because they desire it."[125] Guided by such advisers, Charles would follow Fernando in claiming the right to govern Juana so fundamental to ruling her kingdoms.

Two Regents?

In a testament dictated the day before he died, Fernando sanctioned a continuing rift between his daughter's titular status and actual authority. While affirming Juana's rights as Queen of Castile, Leon, and Granada, as well as his heiress in Aragon, Naples, Sicily, Navarre, and other territories, Fernando confirmed his belief in Juana's inability to rule: "According to what we have been able to know about her during our lifetime, [she] is very far from governing or ruling kingdoms, nor does she have the disposition that would be suitable for it, which Our Lord knows how much we regret."[126] Juana's incapacity and Charles's absence had justified Fernando's rule of Castile as regent for nine years. Now, these same factors enabled the Aragonese king to select different regents for Charles in the kingdoms of Aragon and Castile. Until Charles could rule in person, Fernando appointed his own illegitimate son by a Catalan noblewoman, don Alfonso, archbishop of Zaragoza and Valencia, as regent in the crown of Aragon. After many doubts and an attempt to leave Castile to Juana's second son,[127] the moribund king finally named Cardinal Cisneros regent of Castile.[128] In fact, Cisneros governed alongside Charles's representative, Adrian of Utrecht, until Juana's eldest son reached Spain in late 1517. By appointing different governors—however provisionally—for Castile and Aragon, Fernando took a step toward separating the crowns that his marriage to Queen Isabel had united.[129]

In spite of Fernando's provisions, the *justicia mayor* (chief justice) of Aragon, Juan Lanuza III, prevented Alfonso of Aragon from assuming the Aragonese regency and insisted upon preserving those kingdoms for Charles.[130] Before an apostolic notary, Lanuza declared Charles his mother's legal guardian, for the duration of the "illness, mental alienation, and dementia" that Juana "notoriously and manifestly" had suffered since 1508.[131] Although Fernando had bequeathed don Alfonso the regency of Aragon, Lanuza blocked the appointment.[132] Ironically, an Aragonese official's resistance to the last will of an Aragonese king led to Habsburg rule of those kingdoms. Thus paternal authority, which appeared to establish the law in the Castile, carried less weight than the law in the crown of Aragon. In this case, Spanish unity persisted in spite of Fernando's efforts.

Once united, Fernando and Isabel's realms had become an entity of their own—the corporate body corresponding to Juana and, eventually, Charles. Fernando's continual use of the analogy between Juana and her realms emphasized his unique capacity to defend and to care for both of them. With remarkable dexterity, Juana's father manipulated the concept of a dual royal person for his own ends. He claimed paternal authority over Juana as well as her kingdoms. Yet Juana's conditional obedience ensured that paternal authority overshadowed legitimate dynastic right for only one lifetime. Ultimately, Fernando could not prevent the Habsburg succession.

CHAPTER FIVE

Promoting Family Interests

The Denias and the Habsburgs

Juana's sixteen-year-old son Charles assumed the title of King of Castile, Leon, and Aragon in Brussels on 14 March 1516. Against the advice of Spanish councillors, Charles and his governors, led by first chamberlain Guillaume de Croy, seigneur de Chièvres, claimed monarchical authority without the consent of the affected realms. During the next four years, Charles further upset his new subjects by granting foreigners royal offices and benefices, exporting silver and gold, and demanding increased taxes to finance his election as Holy Roman Emperor.[1] Castilians protesting such measures identified their kingdoms with Juana rather than Charles and championed the queen's rights alongside their own. Charles, meanwhile, attempted to adopt Fernando's claim to a unique, personal right to protect Juana and her realms.

Without trusting Juana, Charles and his councillors would use the queen to sanction their exercise of royal authority in Spain. Hence, after disembarking on the northern coast in the fall of 1517, Charles proceeded to Tordesillas to obtain his mother's blessing. Visiting Juana again the following March, Charles appointed the Marquis of Denia, don Bernardo de Sandoval y Rojas, and his wife, doña Francisca Enríquez de Cabrera, to govern the queen's Tordesillas household. To the dismay of many Spaniards, in May 1520 Charles hastily left Spain to claim the imperial crown. Three months later, Comunero rebels against Habsburg rule overtook Juana's household. Hoping that the queen would endorse their decrees to "remedy" her realms, they even expelled the Denias from Tordesillas.

Since the nineteenth century, liberal historians have depicted Denia as a brutal villain[2] and the Comuneros as Juana's—and Spain's—last chance for salvation.[3] While the Comuneros demanded an accessible ruler tied to their lands, the Denias supported the Habsburg imperial project. With contrasting visions of the monarchy, whether dynastic or territorial, both the Denias and the Comuneros pursued their own interests. On behalf of these interests, the Comuneros, like the Denias, attempted to deceive and to govern the queen. Although Juana could have supported the Comuneros in opposition to Charles, after punishing the Denias she chose to remain loyal to her own dynasty. In the end, Juana trusted neither the Denias nor the Comuneros. Resisting their attempts to control her, the queen defended her family as resolutely as the Denias promoted their own.

Sixteenth-century elites, from the former dukes of Burgundy to the future dukes of Lerma, sought to protect and to increase familial wealth across generations. Ideally, a noble family's possessions attained the same perpetuity as the royal crown and would be transmitted, undiminished if not augmented, to lawful heirs. The Comunero rebels, in contrast, envisioned their kingdom as a united territory resisting foreign usurpation. After the Comuneros' defeat in 1521, corporate family interests took precedence over those of the corporate kingdom in Juana's household as well as her realms.

Maternal Honor versus Paternal Authority

Even before Charles reached Castile in September 1517, Spaniards opposed to Habsburg rule defended Queen Juana's rights and attempted to uphold their own. Royal councillors, nobles, and ecclesiastics reluctant to accept a young Burgundian ruler promptly reminded Charles of the obligation to honor his mother. Yet Charles defiantly adopted the royal title, only to find local officials in some parts of Castile delay proclaiming him king. Aragonese representatives, for their part, also questioned the Burgundian's right to rule their kingdoms. Facing such opposition, Charles and his governors asserted the new king's privileged ties to his mother and therefore to her realms.

Following King Fernando's death on 23 January 1516, Spanish opposition to

Burgundian pretensions focused on the defense of Juana's honor as proprietary queen. On 4 March 1516 the royal council of Castile wrote Charles, urging him not to assume the title of king during his mother's lifetime. Such an act, the councillors warned, "would diminish the honor and reverence due to the queen our lady, your mother, by divine and human law, and would contravene God's commandment to no effect or benefit." The councillors begged their prince, "for the fear of God and the honor that a son owes his mother," to administer Juana's realms without infringing on her title. According to these councillors, Charles could govern freely on his mother's behalf without claiming personal possession of the realms that he would inherit after her death.[4] Disregarding the councillors' advice, Charles adopted the title of King of Castile and Aragon on 14 March 1516, following elaborate obsequies for Fernando in Brussels's Church of Saint Gudule.[5] The Burgundian ceremony, emphasizing continuity from Fernando to Charles in a single immortal office, entirely overlooked Juana's rights as proprietary queen. Castilian grandees felt equally excluded. Indignant, the Admiral of Castile, don Fadrique Enríquez, considered granting Charles the royal title tantamount to "calling the living queen dead."[6]

In defense of his right to regal status, Charles, or, more accurately, his Burgundian governors, invoked papal and imperial authority. In letters sent to Castilian grandees on 20 March, the newly proclaimed king described a compromise between paternal ambition and maternal honor. According to these letters, the pope and emperor, along with "other excellent, prudent, and wise men," had urged Charles to assume the title of king of Castile and Aragon. Nevertheless, Charles added: "Because some object to our consequent aggrandizement [*acrescentamiento*], it suits me to adopt the name and title of king together with the Catholic queen, my mother." Employing a combination of the Burgundian "we" and the Castilian "I," these letters sought to assure Castilian magnates that Charles's succession would not prejudice them or the queen.[7]

Given Charles's determination to rule as king, cardinals Francisco Jiménez de Cisneros and Adrian of Utrecht convoked a meeting to discuss the situation. At this gathering, the Admiral of Castile and other grandees expressed sorrow that the prince, poorly advised, had assumed the royal title. In particular, they asserted that Charles could only receive the title he claimed in consultation with the nobles and kingdoms concerned, presumably in Cortes.[8] Confronted with these arguments, Lorenzo Galíndez de Carvajal, a leading member of the royal council, detailed historical precedents for joint rule that would allow Charles to adopt the sovereign title in conjunction with Juana. According to Carvajal, sons had ruled during their parents' lifetimes by various means: usurpation (don Gar-cía from Alonso "el Magno"), parental consent (Alonso VI for doña Sancha in Leon), public consent in Cortes (Fernando "the Saint" for doña Berenguela), and/or parental incapacity, possibly requiring Cortes (Alonso VII for doña Urraca).[9] Implicitly, these *exempla* encouraged Charles to avoid illicit usurpa-tion by fulfilling the other conditions that could authorize shared rule.[10] Al-though Carvajal saw no alternative to accepting Charles as king, when the meet-ing concluded, the Admiral of Castile, the Duke of Alba, and other grandees still opposed the Habsburg's accession to the throne.

Despite this opposition, as regents of Castile, Jiménez de Cisneros and Adrian of Utrecht presented the Habsburg succession as favorably as possible in letters sent to nobles, cities, and towns on 3 April 1516. These letters emphasized the prince's concern for the public good, rather than his desire to enhance his status and estate. The regents echoed Charles's claim that the pope, the emperor, and other Christian potentates had insisted that Charles alone assume the regal title:

> Yet, His Highness, first considering God and the honor and reverence that he owes the very high and very powerful Queen doña Juana, our lady, his mother, more than his own, did not and does not wish to accept it [the title] other than jointly with her, placing her first in the title and in all other things and royal insignia, pay-ing the debt that he owes his mother as an obedient son, deserving her blessing and that of his other progenitors, taking this measure only for the service of God and the public good, and for the authority and reputation necessary for these realms and all the others of his succession.

The regents argued that Charles could have excluded Juana entirely, but accepted the royal title only to serve his mother, God, and their realms. With respect to Juana, the regents emphasized the king's "intention and firm objective to obey and respect and honor her in everything as mother, queen, and natural lady of these realms." Finally, Jiménez de Cisneros and Adrian concluded with the promise and warning that Charles soon would travel to Spain.[11]

Once Charles had assumed the regal title, Castilian custom entailed raising the royal pennant in his honor. This practice, which originated in the Christian conquest of Al-Andalus,[12] retained sacral dimensions and identified a commu-nity with its new ruler. Certain cities performed the pennant ceremony and accepted Charles more promptly than others.[13] In Murcia, for example, muni-cipal officials led by the Marquis of los Vélez, raised the royal pennant and pro-claimed Charles king on 10 April 1516, only a few days after receiving instructions from the regents. The town crier promulgated the official orders from a stage in the plaza of Santa Catalina, raised the regal pennant, and repeatedly declared: "Long live the very high and very powerful lady, the queen doña Juana, our lady, and the very high and very powerful lord, the king don Carlos, her son, our lord, Queen and King of Castile, Aragon, the two Sicilies, Jerusalem, and all of their other kingdoms and lordships." The list of royal possessions had grown too long for even the most dedicated crier to recite. To the sound of trumpets and drums, local officials then marched to the Church of Santa María, whose clergy assembled to receive the pennant and to sing "Te Deum laudamus." Clerics also offered to recite daily prayers for Charles's safe arrival, which the local authorities deemed unnecessary. Marching back to the plaza, municipal officials read the royal instructions again and reraised the pennant, repeating "long live the very high and very powerful lady the queen, doña Juana, our lady, and the very high and powerful lord the king, don Carlos, her son, our lord" three more times. Following these acclamations, the instruments sounded, church bells tolled, and canons fired, as the city officials marched back to Santa María. Finally, the assembly proceeded to the Alcázar, where the royal pennant was raised in a tower, and shouts proclaiming both Juana and Charles echoed once again. From the plaza to the church to the fortress, the people of Murcia had supposedly declared their loyalty to both Juana and Charles.[14]

Yet, in contrast to the people of Murcia, other subjects delayed the act of proclaiming Charles king. Doña María de Ulloa, Juana's first lady, waited one month before ordering her vassals to acclaim Charles. Upon receiving Ulloa's instructions, the governor of the fortress of Miranda on the Ebro River had one of his servants raise a pennant and proclaim, "Castile, Castile, Castile, for the queen doña Juana and for the king don Carlos, our lords," before firing a cannonade.[15] Even slower to accept Charles as king, municipal officials in the city of Zamora postponed its pennant ceremony until 18 May, and those of Plasencia waited until 25 July.[16] The belatedness of these ceremonies, intended to demonstrate immediate and unified support for the new king, suggested a reluctance to accept his accession to the throne.

Nor did the Aragonese rush to acclaim Charles king. The fact that the Aragonese Cortes had confirmed Juana as princess and heiress in 1502 presented their four "arms or estates"—ecclesiastics, high nobles, lower nobles, and urban patriciates—with a constitutional dilemma. Some observers argued that accepting Charles as king during his mother's lifetime would violate local laws and privileges (*fueros*), which accorded the oath (*juramento*) to Juana in 1502 a nearly sacramental value. Yet other members of the Cortes argued that Juana had been affirmed as heiress only on the condition that her father produced no legitimate male offspring. They suggested that Juan, the short-lived son of Germaine and Fernando born in 1509, invalidated Juana's claim to the throne. By alternately questioning and affirming Juana's rights, the Aragonese undermined those of her son.[17]

Determined to overcome Castilian and Aragonese opposition to the Habsburg succession, the young king's governors prepared to escort him to Spain. Since Juana had made the same journey, both as princess and queen, Charles sought to learn from her experience. On 11 July 1517 Charles instructed the Chambre de Comptes at Lille to provide copies of his mother's expenses in both 1502–3 and 1505–6.[18] Drawing on the records of Juana's former master of the dispense, Charles acquired a rough idea of the cost of maintaining his own household abroad on "days of fish" as well as "days of flesh." He also obtained the names and salaries of the individuals who had accompanied his mother and might still prove useful in his own entourage. Having acquired this information, on 8 September 1517, Charles finally departed from Zeeland.[19]

After reaching the coast of Asturias on 19 September, the young king and his sister Leonor journeyed to Tordesillas, where they arrived on 4 November. This visit enabled Charles to discharge his filial obligations to his mother, while avoiding a meeting with Cardinal Jiménez de Cisneros, who died 8 November. According to Laurent Vital, the chronicler who accompanied Charles, Guillaume de Croy, seigneur de Chièvres, organized an eight-day visit including an audience with Juana and her daughter, Catalina, as well as a funeral service for Philippe in the Royal Monastery of Saint Claire.[20] Dutifully, Charles had honored his mother, and, in return, appeared to have gained her approval for his rule. Demonstrating Charles's respect for the queen, Chièvres had set the stage for the Cortes of 1518–19, which would formally declare Charles king in all his Spanish kingdoms.

Cortes of 1518–1519

Concern about Juana's rights as proprietary queen in 1518–19 reflected apprehension about Burgundian attitudes toward Castilian and Aragonese laws, customs, and privileges. The Cortes, representing individual cities and towns as well as each corporate kingdom,[21] provided crucial forums for attempts to impress such concerns upon the would-be king. In Valladolid and Barcelona,

Charles found it necessary to make conciliatory gestures toward his mother, leading nobles, and even local traditions. In spite of such efforts to win Spanish loyalty, the new king's hasty departure in 1520 left the impression that Charles valued his paternal inheritance more than his mother's kingdoms.

After visiting Juana at Tordesillas, Charles traveled to nearby Valladolid, where he convoked the Cortes of Castile and Leon. In January 1518 delegates to these Cortes from eighteen cities and towns presented Charles with eighty-eight petitions. The representatives' first three demands reflected their identification with the queen and her progeny. First, the delegates requested that Juana receive "the household and estate that pertains to Her Majesty as queen and ruler of these realms"—presumably a well-funded, well-governed establishment that would make Juana accessible to her subjects. In response, Charles promised to provide for Juana's household, claiming that he had "no greater or more principal concern than matters touching the queen, his lady."[22] The representatives' second petition urged Charles to marry and to produce an offspring as soon as possible. Finally, the delegates requested that the king's brother, Fernando, remain in Spain until Charles provided them with another heir to secure the succession.[23] Through such demands, the urban representatives demanded continuity in the government of their kingdoms.

The delegates also voiced specific complaints against the Burgundians. Along with the export of gold, silver, and other coins, they condemned the alienation of offices, benefices, dignities, fortresses, and estates to foreigners as a ruinous policy.[24] The new king's selection of Chièvres's seventeen-year-old nephew, Guillaume de Croy, for archbishop of Toledo after the death of Jiménez de Cisneros had exacerbated resentment on this point. While demanding that Croy reside in their kingdoms, the procurators requested that only native Castilians receive subsequent appointments. They also emphasized the need for Charles to establish personal ties to his new subjects, learning Spanish and welcoming Castilians into his household.[25] In short, the delegates wanted a monarch who understood and favored the interests of their realms.

In response to the delegates' demands at Valladolid, Charles attended to Juana's household by inviting some of the late King Fernando's most important supporters into his own service. On 15 March 1518 Charles officially named don Bernardo de Rojas y Sandoval, Marquis of Denia and Count of Lerma, governor of Juana's household as well as the town of Tordesillas.[26] The leader of an influential Valencian family, don Bernardo had inherited the noble title his father received for service in the war on Granada. A close confident of Juana's father, don Bernardo became Fernando's principal governor (*mayordomo mayor*) in 1504 and obtained a seat on the royal council in 1512. King Fernando further rewarded don Bernardo by naming his son, don Luis, a retainer (*contino*) of Juana's household in 1514.[27] In 1516 the marquis witnessed Fernando's last will and testament before personally escorting the king's coffin to Granada.[28] After depositing Fernando's corpse alongside Queen Isabel's, Denia offered his services to Charles.[29] Charles's decision to appoint Denia head of Juana's household thus signaled a continuity in service from Fernando to Charles. Denia would help Charles legitimize his rule, and Charles, in turn, would enable the marquis to maintain his privileged status.

Although don Bernardo de Rojas received the official title of governor and administrator (*gobernador y administrador*) of Juana's household, he actually shared the office with his wife, doña Francisca Enríquez. A member of the powerful, well-connected Enríquez clan led by the Admiral of Castile, the marquise had entered Queen Isabel's household in 1504, shortly before the sovereign's demise.[30] Although the marquise had served barely four months, in 1515 King Fernando restored and continued her annual salary of 40,000 mrs.[31] Under Charles, the Denias jointly earned an impressive 3,000 ducats, or 1,125,000 mrs per year.[32] Charles sent their predecessor, Hernán Duque, who had reportedly pleased Juana, into retirement with an annual pension of 200,000 mrs. The new king also dismissed Catalina's governess, doña Beatriz de Mendoza, and her husband, don Diego de Castilla, principal keeper of the stables (*caballerizo mayor*), who had attracted suspicion in local uprisings after Fernando's death.[33] In this way Charles ensured that the leading members of Juana's household would favor his interests.

Beyond these top-level appointments and dismissals, Charles avoided immediate changes in Juana's household personnel. He may have adopted this policy after a disastrous attempt to remove Catalina from her mother's care in January 1518. Upon noting her daughter's disappearance, Juana began a fast that forced her son to return Catalina to Tordesillas within three days.[34] Charles promoted Juana's Flemish quartermaster, Bertrand de Fromont, who had helped him abduct Catalina, to lieutenant governor of the household, but refrained from further appointments.[35] Rather than offend Juana by changing her personnel, Charles trusted Denia to govern approximately two hundred servants whom Fernando had appointed for his daughter since 1507.

Having satisfied two important noble families and otherwise assured continuity in Juana's household, Charles left Valladolid for Zaragoza, where he sought confirmation as the King of Aragon. Once again, Charles found himself forced to accommodate local demands. If sworn in as co-ruler with his mother, Charles promised to convene the Cortes and to remain in Aragon as long as necessary. In exchange for acceptance as proprietary king, rather than Juana's caretaker or administrator, Charles pledged to satisfy Aragonese complaints and swore to honor the *fueros* of the Aragonese kingdoms.[36] Before receiving news of the Emperor Maximilian's death on 22 January 1519, Charles concluded the Cortes in Zaragoza and departed for Barcelona.[37]

In Barcelona, as in Zaragoza, Charles promised to honor the *fueros* in exchange for recognition as king. However, until April 1519, the municipal Consell de Cent refused to accept Charles as co-ruler. Invoking Fernando's testament, these councillors argued that Juana's "impediment and indisposition" only entitled Charles to become her caretaker (*curador*).[38] The councillors also objected to the fact that Charles had convoked their Corts before swearing to guard Catalonia's laws and privileges. Finally, the Burgundian agreed to revoke and reconvene the Corts in order to attain acceptance as co-ruler.[39] Adhering to procedure, Charles obtained the royal status that he desired.

During the Corts of Barcelona, Charles made additional bids for local support. As Ángel Casals has demonstrated, the royal address to the Catalan Corts, delivered on 15 February and repeated, in summary, on 13 May, highlighted aims that Charles, his Aragonese predecessors, and his Burgundian ancestors shared. This address proposed a full-fledged struggle against the Turk for control of the Mediterranean.[40] In support of the same aim, Charles convoked a meeting of the chivalric Order of the Golden Fleece in the Barcelona Cathedral that March and inducted ten Spanish grandees, including the Duke of Cardona, a leading Catalan nobleman.[41] Many Spaniards nevertheless found such concessions inadequate evidence of the new king's commitment to their lands and interests, which they continued to identify with Juana.

The news that Charles had been elected Holy Roman Emperor on 28 June reached Barcelona by 7 July.[42] Eager to receive the imperial crown, Charles inspired rage by sending Adrian of Utrecht to Valencia to hold Cortes in his stead. In an equally unpopular decision, the emperor-elect also announced that henceforth official correspondence would grant his imperial title precedence over his mother's royal dignity. Once again, Charles had to insist that the measure would not prejudice Juana or her kingdoms. The emperor-elect explained that the demands of reason, rather than personal desire, led him to favor the imperial title. Regarding Queen Juana, Charles repeated: "With all reverence and respect we honor her and desire to respect and honor her." Then, Charles stated that the Spanish kingdoms would retain their political independence. With authority exceeding his mother's, Charles would rule Spain as king and Germany as emperor.[43]

Fictions of the Denia Regime

Thanks to the Marquis of Denia, Juana remained ignorant of her son's experiences in Valladolid, Zaragoza, and Barcelona. The correspondence between Denia and Charles reveals that the king and the marquis developed a complex strategy to govern Juana and her kingdoms by minimizing communication between them. Denia's efforts to isolate the queen entailed restricting her movements, controlling the people around her, and shaping the information that she received about the outside world. Although Charles encouraged the marquis to deceive his mother, the king approved the use of physical force against Juana only as a last resort.

Governing Juana's household, Denia served as an intermediary between Juana and Charles. With the king's approval, Denia invented a fictional world for Juana. He claimed, for example, that King Fernando and the Emperor Maximilian survived, urging Juana to write them.[44] Denia then relied on Juana's ladies and elite guards (*monteros*) to confirm his stories about Juana's relatives and kingdoms. Rather than a straightforward account of don Bernardo's interactions with the queen, his letters entailed part of a larger strategy to promote his family alongside that of the Habsburgs.

The officers that the Denias supervised most closely formed two rings of security around the queen, separating her from the outside world. Although the royal court ideally connected the sovereign to her subjects, the marquis and Charles appeared determined that Juana's household would serve the opposite function. To fulfill this mission, Denia considered Juana's ladies and elite guards indispensable, repeatedly informing the king that reforms considered for Juana's household should leave the women and the *monteros* under his direct, personal control.[45]

Twelve ladies attending to Juana's personal needs constituted the initial barrier between the queen and the outside world. The marquis relied on these women, led by his wife, doña Francisca, to limit the queen's movements and to keep her isolated. Apparently resenting the women's role, Juana reportedly attacked two of them with a broom in April 1518, shortly after Charles had left

Valladolid. According to the marquis, Juana claimed "that she could not endure these ladies."[46] Denia, for his part, sought increased control over them.

After residing at Tordesillas for several months, Denia developed his own objections to Juana's female attendants. Reporting that certain ladies left the palace too often, the marquis complained: "There is not a wedding or baptism or funeral that touches them in the fourth generation that they do not attend."[47] Denia explained that the women who tended the queen could share palace secrets with their husbands, relatives, and friends. In particular, the marquis asserted that royal councillors had written him regarding information that they could only have received from Leonor Gómez, one of Juana's attendants.[48] To make matters worse, Denia claimed, the ladies returned with news from the outside world that "unsettled" the queen. In order to remedy this situation, Denia requested powers to dismiss and appoint Juana's female servants.[49] Rather than granting the marquis such authority, Charles sent Juana's ladies orders to obey Denia and his wife.[50] Charles also allowed Denia to place his sister, doña Elvira de Rojas, alongside Juana. Starting with his wife and his sister, the marquis—like Ferrer before him—began to surround the queen with female members of his own family.[51] Denia apparently found promoting his own relatives and clients an effective strategy for governing the queen.[52]

After Juana's ladies, twenty-four royal guards or *monteros de Espinosa*[53] circumscribed the queen. Denia expected these elite guards, twelve serving at once, to prevent anyone from reaching Juana without his express approval.[54] In turn, the marquis guaranteed the salaries, rations, wardrobes, and mattresses traditionally granted them.[55] To assure their loyalty, Denia protected the *monteros'* positions and promised to employ their sons, reminding Charles that, "since Your Majesty relies so much upon them, it does not seem reasonable to me to upset them at all." With respect to the elite guard as well as other household positions, Denia ceaselessly reminded Charles that children should inherit their parents' offices.[56]

While Denia tightened the rings of security around Juana, the queen, for her part, attempted to circumvent them. According to Denia, Juana requested a meeting with the grandees in order to remedy her isolation. Listening to the queen's "fine words," Denia claimed, "it frightens me that someone who is like Her Highness says them."[57] The marquis also reported that Juana repeatedly begged him for permission to attend religious services at the Royal Monastery of Saint Claire, which he refused to grant.[58] Informed of Juana's desire to visit the neighboring convent, Charles agreed that she should remain in the royal palace.[59] The king, however, insisted that Juana's forced confinement must not impede her religious obligations. Because Juana refused to hear Mass within her chambers,[60] after a three-month test of wills, the marquis reluctantly permitted the queen to enter an exterior corridor for that purpose.[61] Juana had won a small victory within the confines of her palace.

The onset of plague in Tordesillas in August 1518 and again in May 1519 required Charles and Denia to formulate plans for Juana to evacuate the town. Fearing that the queen might refuse to leave Tordesillas, Charles and Denia developed elaborate means to avoid recourse to physical coercion. First of all, the king recommended that Denia rigorously guard the town and the palace to prevent the spread of disease. If Juana had to move and wished to take the corpse of her husband, Charles instructed Denia to build an imitation coffin, since he soon hoped to send Philippe's body to Granada.[62] As another strategy to overcome Juana's potential resistance, Charles asked the marquis to emphasize the danger of plague for Catalina's health. On the other hand, if the queen wished to travel to Valladolid, Medina del Campo, or another principal town, Charles ordered Denia to inform her that the pestilence had left those places depopulated. The king further advised the marquis to prepare Juana for the move by claiming that individuals infected with plague died within two days. To make the story more convincing, Denia should order clerics with crosses to pass alongside the royal palace several times each day, as if carrying dead to burial.[63] Although Denia feared that removing Juana from Tordesillas would require violence,[64] the king authorized such measures only as a last resort.[65] Conversely, Charles not only permitted but instructed the marquis to confine Juana in a fictional world.

Denia quickly complied with most of the king's orders. In case the plague actually required Juana to abandon Tordesillas, the marquis gathered information about nearby towns with houses appropriate for her *recogimiento* or seclusion.[66] When Charles recommended that Juana travel to Arévalo, Denia noted that the queen would not accept the destination due to its fortress and her grandmother's former confinement there. He nevertheless offered to deceive the queen by taking her to Arévalo and claiming that it were some other town.[67] When Juana expressed a desire to go to Valladolid, Denia explained that she could not because that city was infested with plague.[68] Several months later the queen reiterated her wish to visit Valladolid. Denia informed her that mortality in the neighboring city remained high, assuring Charles, "Even if it were healthy I would tell her that many died."[69]

While gathering information about other towns, the marquis assiduously worked to prevent the spread of plague in Tordesillas. He closed all but two of the town's gates, where he placed *monteros* to bar merchants and travelers coming from infected areas from entering the town.[70] When local individuals died of plague, the marquis, in a desperate effort to prevent further contagion, ordered their houses sealed and their families expelled from Tordesillas.[71] Lamenting the policy—which entailed force—the marquis stated that he personally had compensated some of the poor cast out of their homes.[72] The expulsion of these subjects, combined with Denia's other efforts, enabled Juana to remain in Tordesillas and helped assure her isolation.

Representations of the plague composed only one aspect of the fictional world that Charles and Denia created for Juana. Initially, when Juana asked about "the prince," or Charles, Denia explained that he had gone to Aragon "to remedy certain scandals with his presence," rather than to receive confirmation as king.[73] Following a suggestion from Charles,[74] in the fall of 1519, Denia informed Juana that the Emperor Maximilian had abdicated the imperial title in favor of her son and retired to a monastery, as if to encourage Juana's parallel *recogimiento*. The marquis even urged Juana to write the deceased Maximilian and Fernando—acts that would have testified to her "madness."[75] Rather than accepting such a trap, in both cases Juana requested that Denia write on her behalf.[76] When Juana asked about her younger son, Fernando, Denia asserted that he had gone to Flanders and would probably marry a daughter of the King of France.[77] Whether or not the marquis regretted deceiving Juana, on two occasions he asked Charles to destroy holograph letters recounting such exchanges with the queen, eliminating evidence of his efforts to mislead her.[78] To prevent Juana from receiving conflicting information or seeking allies, the marquis and Charles agreed that no servant other than Denia should speak with her.[79]

Although Denia exercised close control over Juana's ladies and guards, he found it impossible to prevent other household officials from communicating with the queen. When Juana's daughter, Catalina, suffered from "the itch," the marquis found himself obliged to admit Juana's doctor, Nicolas de Soto, to treat the *infanta*. Under such circumstances, Denia could not prevent Soto from speaking with the queen.[80] Juana further breached Denia's rings of security by summoning her chief steward, Fernando de Arzeo (an official later implicated in the Comunero revolt)[81] so often that the marquis admitted that he could not always prevent contact between Juana and Arzeo.[82] Finally, in October 1519, the queen refused to eat until Denia allowed her to speak with her treasurer, Ochoa de

Landa. Juana's drastic tactics left the marquis little choice but to update Ochoa on Juana's fictional world and admit him into her chamber. Testing her governor's assertions, the queen quizzed Ochoa on her father's whereabouts. The treasurer confirmed Denia's version of events and declared that King Fernando had gone to Málaga.[83] In spite of Ochoa's collaboration, Juana appeared to question aspects of the fictional enclosure that Denia and Charles created for her. Claiming that Juana "said words that would move stones," the marquis also requested and received a royal cipher to minimize the risk of anyone intercepting their correspondence.[84]

Denia may have emphasized the hazards of his contact with Juana, at least partially, to encourage Charles to reward his dedicated service.[85] As governor of the queen's household, the marquis benefited from privileged access to the king. In addition to his salary as governor, Denia obtained an annual discretionary allowance of 300,000 mrs for household expenses in Tordesillas,[86] 225,230 mrs due in taxes on his lands in 1519, and 5,375,000 mrs in general taxes voted at la Coruña the following year.[87] The marquis also continued receiving 100,000 mrs per year as a royal councillor.[88] In spite of these earnings, Denia informed Charles that his duties as governor required expenditures that still exceeded his income.[89] Letters ostensibly about Juana gave Denia frequent opportunities to encourage Charles to recompense his loyalty.

Disturbed by popular uprisings throughout Castile in 1520, Denia recommended that Charles act to stifle the nascent Comunero rebellion. First, the Marquis suggested that Charles encourage the grandees to distance themselves from rebellious cities and towns by using the leading nobles as intermediaries. The rebels would then recognize their isolation and the magnates' ability to punish them on the emperor's behalf. Second, the marquis asked Charles to publicize any accord with the King of England—an alliance that Denia had always encouraged—in order to gain support among Castilians.[90] An agreement to marry Mary Tudor, another of Queen Isabel's grandchildren, would promise the future heirs requested in the Cortes of 1518 and divert attention from Juana.[91] Finally, Denia warned Charles of the rebels' desire to take Juana from Tordesillas to another town, where they could consult with her.[92] The marquis realized that political turmoil threatened to explode Juana's fictional world.

Weeks later, Denia informed Charles that the rebellious cities had voted to move Juana from Tordesillas to Toledo. According to Denia, the situation threatened Charles as well as his crown, since the rebels might induce the queen to commit "some error worse than any other." Referring to the king's dual identity,

Denia lamented "the disrespect to your imperial person and the damage to your kingdom if this continues." The marquis encouraged Charles to return to Castile to pacify the situation there immediately after receiving the imperial title. Moreover, Denia assured Charles that God had chosen him to govern "so many kingdoms and lordships at such a tender age" and that "great things cannot be held or maintained without great effort." The marquis served the Denias and the Habsburgs, if not Juana.[93]

Comunero Deceptions

Denia had correctly predicted rebellion throughout Castile. Charles's departure from la Coruña on 20 May 1520, after demanding a large extraordinary tax, proved the catalyst. The emperor-elect's appointment of a foreigner, Adrian of Utrecht, to govern Castile in his absence violated his pledge to reserve offices for natives and inspired further ire. Presenting themselves as the Santa Junta, or "Holy Assembly," representatives of distinct cities and towns banded together to defend the interests of their corporate kingdom.[94] Given the king's absence and the queen's captivity, the rebels declared themselves the repository of sovereignty and attempted to convoke the Cortes of Castile and Leon. Considering Queen Juana, like her realms, a victim of Flemish rapacity, the Comuneros needed her to sanction their seizure of power. Juana, while using the Comuneros to expel her governor and female attendants from the royal palace, found it increasingly difficult to identify the rebels' interests with her own. Ultimately, the queen disappointed the Comuneros by upholding the rights of her family. The rebels, for their part, proved no more truthful than Denia had.

Troubled that the Comuneros claimed to act on Juana's behalf, in August 1520, the president and several members of the royal council went to Tordesillas themselves. They presented Juana with a decree condemning the popular rebels and asked her to sign it. Yet Juana, finally receiving confirmation of her father's death, used the occasion to criticize the Marquis of Denia for deceiving her. Once accurately informed about the state of her realms, Juana asked the councillors to return another day. Following a second, private six-hour session, the queen ordered the councillors to travel to Valladolid, consult their colleagues, and prepare different provisions for her to sign. Nevertheless, before the royal councillors could return to Tordesillas, the town rose up against them and summoned the Comunero captains.[95]

On 29 August 1520 the Comunero captains reached Tordesillas with the pro-

fessed goal of swearing loyalty to the queen. Certain members of Juana's household welcomed the rebels, and the queen's *monteros* failed to combat the intrud-
ers.[96] From a corridor of the palace overlooking the plaza where their armies
assembled, Juana waved at the captains and "manifestly appeared to order them
to ascend."[97] Juan de Padilla, Toledan leader and son of Queen Isabel's general
captain of Castile, addressed Juana on his knees. He explained that the Comunero forces had come to kiss Her Majesty's hands and to inform her of the "great
evils and scandals and injuries" in her kingdoms "due to their bad government"
since Fernando's death. Thanking the captains for their attention, the queen
agreed that they should serve her and punish the evils in her kingdoms, expressing a degree of interest, which the rebels publicized as miraculous approba-
tion.[98] In a similar meeting three days later, Padilla professed respect for Juana's
"powerful, illustrious" son,[99] while asking the queen to grant them "favor and
authority." Again, Juana affirmed her desire for the Comuneros to join her in
Tordesillas.[100] Circulating notarized copies of their exchanges with the queen,
the enthusiastic Comunero captains summoned official representatives of the
cities and towns. Under Juana's authority, they hoped to assemble a Cortes capable of redressing the kingdoms' ills.

Early reports from Tordesillas euphorically proclaimed Juana's capacity to
govern. According to Padilla and his associates, Juana's servants and ladies informed them that no one (except Juana's governors) had seen the queen in the
last seven years.[101] Juana's attendants further alleged that she was as fully capable of ruling, "as was the queen doña Isabel, her mother."[102] Beyond such claims,
royal officials favoring the Comuneros defamed Philippe, Fernando, and Charles
by stating "that Her Highness had been aggrieved and detained by force in that
castle for fourteen years as if she were insane, having always been as sensible and
prudent as she was at the beginning of her marriage."[103] Attempting to assess
such rumors about Juana's health, the Portuguese ambassador reported that the
queen exhibited important signs of sanity: eating and dressing properly, wearing
new clothes, and inhabiting clean, well-furnished quarters.[104] The Comuneros,
however, wanted more from Juana.

The self-titled "Holy Assembly and Cortes," comprising representatives from
thirteen Castilian cities, reached Tordesillas 19 September 1520. Within five
days, the Holy Assembly expelled the Denias from Juana's palace[105] and attained
a public audience with the queen. Among other Comuneros, Doctor Alonso de
Zúñiga from Salamanca fell to his knees, asked Juana for her hand, and begged
her to claim her hereditary right to govern. Addressing the queen at length,

Zúñiga accused foreigners, "whom Your Highness knows better than anyone," of despoiling her kingdoms. The doctor implored Juana "to take strength to rule and govern, and to command your kingdoms, since there is no one in the world to forbid or prevent it."[106] In response, Juana emphasized her family obligations. While encouraging the Comuneros to punish any misdeeds committed in her realms, Juana explained that she might refrain from action only to mourn her father and to protect her children. Promising to undertake whatever measures she could, Juana instructed the Comuneros to name four representatives who could meet with her whenever necessary.[107]

Juana's reluctance to provide substantial support for the Comunero program encouraged the rebels to become increasingly skeptical about her sanity. By 26 September the Comuneros alluded to Juana's "lack of health," listed her cure among their principal goals, and ordered processions for her well-being in all of the cities under their control.[108] Claiming that bad spirits tormented the queen, the rebels recruited priests to exorcise her. At Juana's request, they subsequently removed the female servants constituting Denia's first ring of security from her household.[109] Yet, even when the Comuneros met Juana's demands, she persistently refused to sign documents denouncing her son's policies and collaborators.

Differences between Juana and the Comuneros had become unmistakable. Among their principal aims, the rebels hoped to oust the governor, Adrian of Utrecht, and to punish the royal councillors abetting Charles. In defense of Adrian of Utrecht, Juana noted that the cardinal, "although a foreigner, was a good man, with good intentions and habits."[110] With respect to the royal council, Juana insisted on consulting all of its members before signing any act of government.[111] In one attempt to dissuade Juana from summoning the royal council, the Comuneros claimed that its president, Antonio de Fonseca, wanted to move the queen to a stronger fortress and to separate her from her daughter, Catalina.[112] When Juana remained skeptical, the Comuneros blamed the councillors, among others, for advising her son poorly and destroying her kingdoms. Determined to meet with the royal council, Juana retorted: "Since those of the council were from the time of the Catholic king [Fernando], they could not all be bad, and at least some of them would be good. For this reason she wanted to speak and communicate with them because they were experienced persons who knew the form of good government from the time of the Catholic monarchs."[113] By summoning the royal council, Juana rejected the would-be Cortes's exclusive claim to represent her realms. Indeed, the queen's attitudes toward Cardinal

Adrian and the royal council demonstrate that she disagreed with two of the Comuneros' basic aims.

Unable to lure the royal councillors to Tordesillas, the Comuneros employed increasingly desperate tactics to induce the queen to provide them with written support. Adrian of Utrecht repeatedly warned Charles that a single signature from Juana would cause him to lose Castile.[114] In early December, two nights before royal troops recaptured Tordesillas, the rebels allegedly threatened not to feed Juana or Catalina until the queen signed orders for the constable and other grandees to disband their troops.[115] Moreover, the Comuneros invented fictions that rivaled those of Charles and Denia. Once surrounded by troops loyal to Charles, the junta gave Juana quill and ink, claiming that only her signature would prevent the emperor from burning the town and sending her to the fortress of Benavente.[116] Unconvinced, Juana ordered the town gates opened to welcome the grandees to Tordesillas.[117] Grasping her daughter, Catalina, by the hand, the queen took refuge in an interior patio of her residence as 160 imperialists and even more Comuneros perished in the ensuing battle. Once the victorious nobles reached Juana's palace, she reportedly spoke to them "with great sense."[118]

Juana's apparent support for the imperialist cause accompanied her progressive disillusionment with the Comuneros, particularly after Juan de Padilla left Tordesillas on 11 October. The queen had used the Comuneros to free herself of unwanted servants—namely, Denia, and her female attendants—and to gain greater contact with her subjects. While temporarily attaining these goals, Juana never strayed from her declared intention of supporting her children, including Charles V. When the Comuneros informed Juana that her son called himself king and endangered her kingdoms, Juana defended his right to the royal title and proclaimed: "No one turns me against my son, for everything that I have is his."[119] Noting that Juana defended the emperor and prevented the Comuneros from speaking against him, Adrian of Utrecht reminded Charles of "the singular love" that the queen "has always shown toward your person and succession."[120] Her relationship with the Comuneros ended in mutual disappointment.

Denia versus Enríquez

Although initially sympathetic to Comunero grievances, Queen Juana, together with most of Castile's landed magnates, ultimately clung to patrimonial interests.[121] Juana's restraint before the Holy Assembly, combined with Charles's timely concessions to leading nobles, turned the tide of the Comunero rebellion. In late October, Charles had bolstered his army and reputation in Castile by appointing the constable, don Íñigo Fernández de Velasco, and the admiral, don Fadrique Enríquez de Cabrera, as cogovernors of the kingdom with Cardinal Adrian.[122] The Admiral of Castile and the Marquis of Denia numbered among the nobles loyal to Charles who entered Tordesillas 4 December 1520.[123] Although many nobles remained uncomfortable with the Burgundian succession, they eventually allied with Charles in order to defend their families' traditional privileges. Rather than opposing the Habsburgs, the grandees returned to competing and arguing with each other.

Conflicts soon emerged between Denia and Enríquez. Their disagreements revealed competition for the spoils of victory as well as genuine philosophical differences. Fiercely loyal to Charles, the marquis resented the admiral's long-term support for the queen and access to her. Much to Denia's dismay, Juana often summoned the admiral and conversed with him for hours at a time. Denia accused the admiral of attempting "to raise Lazarus from the dead again" by curing the queen, a matter that, he believed, should not even receive consideration without orders from Charles.[124] Equally disturbed by Denia's actions, Enríquez declared that the marquis treated Juana's servants too severely, and attempted to punish them without recourse to justice.[125]

In the same spirit, Enríquez cautioned Charles about the dangers of immoderate retaliation against the Comuneros and their allies. Drawing upon a corporate conception of Juana's kingdoms, the admiral used well-worn metaphors to discuss their well-being:

> If any one says that the remedy requires arms, it is not good advice for the king to set his own house on fire. Nor is the physician wise who, although able to heal with light and bland medicines, uses harsh ones, which, curing the illness, expose the body to greater ills. Your Highness is the physician, and the patient [i.e., kingdom] requires that you take the remedy of coming to these realms, granting favors to those who have served you and your parents, seducing them with words and works, and showing them that you are a true Spaniard, renewing their love for you, because states maintained by love last and those sustained by force perish.[126]

The admiral extended the discussion of "health" from Juana's person to the kingdom's condition, advocating love and clemency. Enríquez continued to believe in a territorial kingdom identified with its king, while Denia defended Habsburg dynastic interests. For his part, Charles remained suspicious of a corporate conception that the Comuneros had used to challenge his authority. Supporting the plea of Enríquez for a general pardon, Adrian of Utrecht used the same metaphor to claim that "all medicine should be taken to cure this illness," although "no cure or health will endure without Your Majesty's very prompt arrival and royal presence."[127] Initially, the emperor sided with the Marquis of Denia, who favored strong medicine against the rebels,[128] withholding a general pardon until 28 October 1522.[129]

With or without imperial favor, Enríquez attempted to better Denia. Two years before issuing a general pardon, Charles sent the governors orders in his name and Juana's to proceed against lay Comuneros of any estate, declaring them "perfidious rebels and traitors unfaithful and disloyal to us and our crown." Such individuals, who had acted against royal persons as well as the royal dignity, should lose their lives, offices, and property.[130] Since the unequivocally guilty included Juana's chief steward, the admiral selected his master of the hall (*maestresala*) and a nephew of the deceased Cardinal Cisneros, Gaspar de Villaroel, for that office.[131] Yet Denia, seeking to name his own candidate, refused to admit Villaroel, and brandished a royal decree granting him authority over household appointments.[132] While Enríquez wanted Juana's household to represent her realms, Denia considered it his family's dominion. Finding himself "in the middle of the firing range," Cardinal Adrian lamented the animosity between Denia and Enríquez, which no one could assuage.[133]

By March the disagreement had escalated. Denia charged Enríquez with releasing some of the guiltiest Comuneros from jail.[134] At the same time, Enríquez accused Denia of preventing him from selling the queen's jewels in order to raise the cash needed to pay loyal troops.[135] As the admiral prepared to move north in pursuit of the rebel army, he warned Charles that the people of Tordesillas and members of Juana's household hated the marquis so much that it seemed dangerous to leave Denia there alone.[136] Aware of local hostility, Denia wanted to transport the queen to Arévalo, where her grandmother had been confined. Certain that the move would require the use of force (*premia*), the marquis claimed that Queen Isabel herself had physically coerced her daughter and that individuals in Juana's condition actually desired such punishment.[137] Although Cardinal Adrian had long favored such a move, the constable ultimately advised against it.[138] Unwilling to sanction the use of force, Charles remained silent, and Juana remained in Tordesillas.

The quarrel between Enríquez and Denia distracted neither from pursuing family interests. Claiming to have sacrificed his estate in the rebellion, the marquis advised Charles to reward the loyal with wealth confiscated from the guilty. Denia also wanted the emperor to appoint his nephew, Hernando de Tovar, as captain of the queen's elite guard in Tordesillas, claiming that the incumbent had proved too elderly to combat the Comuneros.[139] Nor did the admiral hesitate to remind Charles that he had suffered great losses retaking Tordesillas, placing his wife, the proprietary Countess of Modica, and estate at risk. In exchange, Enríquez requested specific Comuneros' confiscated goods for two of his brothers, a bond of 12,000 mrs for himself, and offices for various clients.[140] When months passed without a response from Charles, the admiral instructed his ambassador to inquire about the emperor's health, ironically suggesting that he must be ill.[141]

Competition between Denia and Enríquez permeated the women's quarters of the royal palace. As an Enríquez married to a Denia, the marquise found herself in a particularly difficult position. Initially, the admiral petitioned Charles to send doña Francisca back to Tordesillas.[142] Nevertheless, once the marquise had returned, the admiral reported that she treated Catalina harshly and anticipated a disaster.[143] In particular, he feared that the *infanta* would be driven to become a nun or to commit some other desperate act.[144] By maintaining a correspondence with the Countess of Modica, Catalina threatened the Denias' efforts to recover their monopoly over information about the queen. According to Catalina, the marquise sought to prevent her from exchanging letters or receiving visitors.[145] In her own defense, doña Francisca claimed that she had lost authority over Catalina, since the queen would only allow Juana Cortes, Leonor Gómez, "and two or three others of the same opinion" to enter the room where the *infanta* slept.[146] The Denias suspected Leonor Gómez, her husband, Diego de Ribera, and their daughters, who also served Juana, of Comunero leanings.[147] For similar reasons, the Denias tormented Juana's Franciscan confessor, fray Juan de Ávila, despite pleas from Catalina and Cardinal Adrian, until Charles dismissed the friar with a modest pension.[148] Step by step, the Denias recovered their control over Juana's household.

In January 1525 Enríquez and Denia enjoyed a final showdown at Tordesillas. The *infanta* Catalina's departure that month to marry the new king of Portugal represented a triumph for the marquis, who had urged Charles to maintain close relations with the Portuguese royal family, especially after the death of Leonor's first husband, King Manuel.[149] Fearing Juana's reaction to the *infanta*'s departure, Charles sent the admiral and the Countess of Modica to console her. In an autograph letter written from Tordesillas on 2 January, Enríquez reported discussing "very substantial matters" with the queen while a Portuguese delegation carried away the *infanta*, who allegedly fainted from sorrow at leaving her mother. Supposedly protecting Charles, Enríquez reported informing the queen that the emperor knew nothing about his sister's marriage—a fact that Juana refused to believe.[150]

Ten days later the admiral returned to his favorite corporate metaphor in a holograph letter to Charles from Medina de Rioseco. The emperor's recovery from a fever enabled Enríquez to invoke the commonplace analogy between the king and his realms: "They have written me here that Your Majesty continues improving, and since disorders during convalescence are more dangerous than those during illness, I beg Your Majesty to guard yourself." Obliquely alluding to the Comunero rebellion, Enríquez warned Charles that the kingdom's wounds had not fully healed. Nor had the admiral ceased to oppose the marquis. According to Enríquez, the queen disliked the Denias so much that she suffered more from hearing them than she had from the *infanta*'s departure. The admiral stated that he had found the queen fully rational in her opposition to the Denias, although "as disconcerted as Your Highness has seen" in other matters.[151] Focusing his resentment on Denia, Enríquez finally accepted the Habsburg succession. Juana's resolute support for her son had left the admiral—and the Comuneros—little choice.

Habsburg Expansion, Growth of the Denia Clan

Juana's refusal to sanction the Comunero program in 1520 enabled Charles to reestablish his authority in Castile and the Denias to reassert their control of Tordesillas. By endorsing Charles's succession, Juana unwillingly facilitated the Denias' ascent. After 1525 the Denias prospered alongside the Habsburgs. Their alliance, designed to govern the queen, served the expansionist aims of both families.

Castile lost an *infanta* in 1525 but gained an empress in 1526, when Charles married his Portuguese cousin, Isabel. This alliance, enthusiastically welcomed in Castile, accompanied another measure designed to secure the emperor's hold over his Iberian possessions. Before leaving Granada in 1527, Charles ordered the Marquis of Denia to convey the corpse of his father, Philippe, to that city, where it joined the remains of Fernando and Isabel.[152] Although Juana never appears to have discovered the fact, Charles had fulfilled her mission of 1507. In this way, Charles attempted to legitimize the Habsburgs' past and to guarantee their future in Spain. The following year, the empress gave birth to a son, the future Philip II. In 1529, Charles left her as regent in Spain, sending Denia instructions to obey his wife's orders "as those of my own person."[153] Isabel bore a daughter, María, the following year. By 1532, her children were old enough to travel to Tordesillas and visit their grandmother.

Queen Juana continued to favor the interests of her offspring. In February 1532 she hosted the empress, Philip, and María during an eight-day sojourn at Tordesillas. According to the Marquis of Denia, Juana received the empress and her children with great joy, treating them in an exemplary, dignified manner, "as Queen Isabel, her mother, would have" for the entire duration of their stay.[154] Nevertheless, the marquis assured Charles that, even if Juana's "disposition" were as fine as her mother's, "no one sane would ask Her Highness to undertake anything other than what pertains to a woman."[155] While the emperor struggled to defend Italy and Germany against the Turk, Juana allegedly dedicated herself to counting prayers upon rosaries that she made with her own hands.[156] To enhance these prayers, the queen requested and received two crosses of gold.[157]

Although most historians have assumed that Juana remained "a prisoner of Tordesillas" after the Comunero rebellion,[158] she actually left Tordesillas during an episode of plague. While the marquis continued to insist that such a move would require force,[159] Juana peacefully rode a mule east along the Duero River from Tordesillas to Geria to Tudela del Duero in early 1534. When Charles sent don Juan de Zúñiga, the future Philip II's *ayo* or governor and a member of the council of Castile, to Tudela, the Marquis of Denia insisted that Zúñiga visit Juana on behalf of her son. Following this interview, in which the queen impressed Zúñiga, Denia sent Charles a remarkably strong rebuke for not visiting Juana himself: "It seems to me that we [household officials] should all serve and consider her Highness as ill, and that Your Majesty should treat and visit her as your mother and healthy."[160] Although Charles did not visit Juana in 1534, he may have followed the marquis's advice by according her a certain respect. When Juana began to suffer digestive troubles later that year, according to one source, the emperor allowed her to dictate a last will and testament entrusting the Habsburg possessions in Germany and Hungary, along with valuable jewels, to her second son, Fernando, and the rest to Charles.[161] After Juana recovered, the plague reached Tudela and the queen went to Mojados, where her household remained until the pestilence had left Tordesillas.[162]

The Empress Isabel helped Charles fulfill his obligations toward the elder queen. After Juana returned to Tordesillas, the empress gave birth to a second daughter, christened Juana in her grandmother's honor. Congratulating doña Isabel, the Marquis of Denia reported Queen Juana's delight.[163] When don Bernardo de Rojas y Sandoval died in early 1536, the empress appointed the marquise and her son, don Luis de Rojas, the new marquis, governors of Juana's household during the emperor's absence.[164] Don Luis also received an annual 300,000 mrs and command of his father's captaincy.[165] Family continuity had triumphed.

Exploiting his alliance with the emperor, don Bernardo de Rojas had provided well for his descendants. By the time of his death, the marquis had placed his brother (don Hernando), each of his six sons (don Luis, don Francisco, don Enrique, don Hernando, don Diego, and don Cristobal), three daughters (doña Ana, doña Magdalena, and doña Margarita), and a nephew (don Hernando de Tovar) in the royal service.[166] Don Luis, don Enrique, and their brother, don Hernando, traveled with the emperor as gentlemen and ambassadors,[167] while don Diego and don Cristobal became royal chaplains, eventually rising to dean of Jaén and archbishop of Seville, respectively.[168] By 1534, the marquis had placed three daughters and three daughters-in-law, doña Isabel de Quiñones, doña Catalina de Zúñiga, and doña Isabel de Orençe, in Queen Juana's chambers.[169] Not surprisingly, Denia's letters to the king continually requested gifts and positions for members of his expanding family.

While ostensibly governing the queen, the marquis oversaw a series of brilliant marriages. With financial assistance from the emperor, Denia wed his daughter, doña Magdalena, to the Count of Castro.[170] The marquis then tactfully paired his son, don Luis, with doña Catalina de Zúñiga, daughter of the Count of Miranda, who directed the Empress Isabel's household and soon gained a seat on the royal council.[171] Denia's second son, don Francisco de Rojas, the Count of Lerma, married doña Isabel de Borja, the daughter of another imperial favorite, the Marquis of Lombay, Francisco de Borja. As a bride for don Enrique, Denia chose Isabel de Quiñones, sister of the Count of Luna.[172] The marquis's marriage policy and continual requests for favors strengthened ties among the different royal households.

The Marquise of Denia defended familial interests with similar dedication. In early 1523, when Adrian of Utrecht left Spain to assume the papacy, the marquise requested special favors from him. Perhaps due to tensions with the local population or obligations in the royal palace, doña Francisca sought a papal brief that would allow her, her daughters, daughters-in-law, and granddaughters to win indulgences by praying before their altars without going to church. Doña

Francisca also requested papal permission for her son, don Hernando, commander of the military order of Calatrava, not to recite the three hundred daily *pater
nosters* that his order required. Finally, the pious marquise desired a brief that
would allow her to remove one soul from purgatory for every Mass that she dedicated to that purpose.[173] When doña Francisca died in 1538, Charles granted
don Luis alone the title of governor, with an annual salary of 925,000 mrs—
200,000 mrs less than he and his mother together had received. The remaining
200,000 mrs went to doña Francisca's daughter, doña Ana, a holy woman the
empress had befriended, to supplement the 60,000 mrs that she already received
as one of Juana's ladies.[174]

Other families wishing to retain a presence in the royal household had to
cooperate with the Denias. When the marquis suspected them of Comunero ten-
dencies, Leonor de Alarcón and Diego de Ribera secured positions for their children and retired.[175] Denia also objected to Ochoa de Landa, a cousin of the Admiral of Castile and the queen's treasurer, claiming that he paid the household
poorly.[176] When Ochoa lost his job, his wife, doña Isabel de Albornoz, allegedly
lost her mind.[177] Somewhat repentant, Denia asked the emperor to help Ochoa
pay his debts.[178] When Ochoa and doña Isabel died the following year,[179] the
marquis worked to secure the treasury for their son, Luis.[180] Although Luis was
too young to exercise the office, Denia placed the principle that children should
inherit their parents' positions above other interests.

Exercising his father's former office, in April 1536 the new Marquis of Denia
informed the empress that he withheld news of don Bernardo's death from the
queen. Ostensibly promoting Juana's "service and tranquillity," don Luis simply
told her that his father was ill.[181] Continuing his father's policy of deception, the
new marquis refused to provide the queen with information that might encourage her to rule herself, her household, or even her realms. Charged with governing the queen, the Denias struggled to control her household in order to
increase their influence and importance in her kingdoms. Their interests per-
vade most sources of information about Queen Juana and her infirmity, fictitious or real.

Queen Juana resisted the Denias' ascent as tenaciously as she defended the
advancement of her own children. During the Comunero rebellion, she freed
herself from the Denias' control and staunchly defended her son, Charles V.
Without Juana's support in 1520, Charles might have lost the royal title that he
had claimed in 1516. Yet Juana endorsed the Habsburgs, rather than the rebels,

as legitimate representatives of her kingdoms. Rather than a personal, resident monarch, she gave Castile and Leon a ruling family. In spite of Juana's opposition to her governors, the Denias believed their interests entirely compatible with those of the Habsburgs. Governing the household, like the realm, became a family enterprise.

As Charles established family members in Castile, his mother became less of a focus for dissent. The emperor's alliance with the Denias, moreover, may have qualified their descendants for governing other problematic members of the royal family.[182] Somewhat paradoxically, Queen Juana's inability to govern on her own behalf also offered many Habsburg women important political roles. Among the first of these women, the Empress Isabel served as regent of Spain and taught her children to respect their grandmother. The sense of family solidarity that Juana displayed during the Comunero rebellion became emblematic of Habsburg women in later years.[183]

CHAPTER SIX

The Politics of Possession
and Salvation

The Habsburg Empire's extension over most of Europe made the task of governing too great for any single ruler and demanded a shift toward a less personal, more familial Spanish monarchy. Both Queen Juana and her Tordesillas household facilitated this transformation. Upholding the rights of her descendants, Juana entrusted Castile, Aragon, and Granada to them. She did not, however, condone the Denias' authority over her domestic space. In the queen's view, unwelcome attendants intervened in intimate aspects of her life. Servants, on the other hand, claimed that Juana prevented them from executing their jobs. In the transition from personal to dynastic rule, Juana's major liability became a refusal to be governed.

Juana's bitter conflicts with certain attendants contrasted with the queen's reportedly pleasant encounters with her offspring. In semiretirement at Tordesillas, the queen delighted in visits from members of her expanding family—the Empress Isabel, Charles V, the future Philip II and his first wife, María Manuel, María and Maximilian of Bohemia, and Juana of Austria—interrogating them about developments in her realms. The queen welcomed these family members and their gifts into a private world that she sought to control. Prudently, Juana blamed her servants for her successors' usurpations and misdeeds.

The queen, while defending members of her family, deeply resented the pretensions of her own staff. These servants, who accepted a more patrimonial, less individual, form of rule, frustrated Juana's attempts to retain her own possessions—whether emblems of royalty or repositories of specific memories. The queen did not trust household officials to guard her belongings or to supervise her religious activities. Rather, she accused them of stealing her goods and impeding her spirituality. Juana's "madness," or inability to rule herself, her household, and her realms, emerges most clearly in these conflicts with her servants.

A Queen's Possessions

Juana's possessions, recorded in a postmortem inventory of more than six hundred folios, lay at the heart of a conflict between individual and corporate conceptions of monarchy. Juana's chamberman (*camarero*), Alonso de Ribera, compiled this inventory, really a history of the queen's belongings from 1509 through 1556, in order to free himself and his family from responsibility for goods distributed among Juana's relatives. Alonso de Ribera considered himself and his father and predecessor, Diego de Ribera, responsible for Juana's possessions as part of the royal patrimony. The *camarero* accordingly attempted to record information about all articles that had entered and left the queen's chambers. To this end, Ribera formulated "charge" and "discharge" sections for each type of article (coins, jewels, silks, brocades, retables, ornaments, goblets, coats, gloves, towels, tapestries, bags, perfumes, etc.), roughly from greatest to least monetary value.[1]

Juana's view of her own possessions clashed with the Riberas's. Treasuring her belongings, the queen demanded exclusive authority over them. Among other objects, Juana perhaps considered jewels from Queen Isabel, Philippe "the Handsome," Marguerite of Austria, the Emperor Maximilian, diplomats, and even the city of Antwerp as representing some of her most important relationships. Certain belts and ribbons that she guarded may have likewise commemorated significant occasions. The queen's 116 books, 28 altar pieces, 55 rosaries, and several reliquaries provided her with sites for personal and spiritual reflection. She also treasured portraits of her mother Isabel and sister Catalina (Catherine) of Aragon.[2]

The queen's collection, established mainly before 1507, grew little after 1512, when members of the royal family began periodic raids upon it. Upset by the disappearance of her belongings, Juana blamed household officials rather than her relatives. Thus tensions emerged between Juana and those of her servants accountable to other, ruling members of the royal family. Their conflicts, recorded as early as 1497, escalated after 1518. Servants' attitudes toward Juana's possessions often revealed their lack of personal loyalty to her.

The queen's increasingly conflictive relations with her staff emerged in testimony that Juana's *camareros* collected in order to disclaim responsibility for objects lost or destroyed. In 1524 *camarero* Diego de Ribera assembled five members of the household to answer nine questions for the "proof and perpetual record" (*provança e perpetua rymemoria*) of events in Juana's chambers during the previous twenty-eight years. Of the five witnesses, Garcia del Campo and Hernando de Helin identified themselves as Juana's quartermasters of the chamber, Hernando de Mena and Lucas de Atiença titled themselves "men of the queen's chamber," and Rodrigo de Ratya, the only witness who could not sign his testimony, was simply called a "servant of the queen." After undertaking solemn oaths to provide true information, the witnesses agreed that the *camarero* had often begged the queen to permit a written record of items that she disbursed, but Juana never agreed to document such transactions. According to Rodrigo de Ratya, on one occasion Ribera went so far as to summon Juana's scribe of the chamber. Characteristically, Juana dismissed the scribe, declaring that *she* would call him when necessary. Hernando de Mena recalled that in Brussels Juana had kept the keys to the chests and trunks in her chambers since 1497, opening and closing them as she pleased. When Ribera complained that the practice impeded him from accounting for Juana's possessions, the archduchess reportedly retorted: "Who is to demand the account of you if not I?" While Ribera conceived of his job as fulfilling the demands of an office, the archduchess insisted that he serve her. Even before she became queen or "sick," Juana resisted servants' attempts to dictate how she should conduct business. In other words, she defied their efforts to govern her and her possessions.[3]

Juana's desire to control her servants and her things produced further conflicts. Diego de Ribera's witnesses agreed that the *camarero* had entrusted some of Juana's property to her attendants, Marina Ruíz and Violante de Albión during the early 1500s. Hernando de Helin even ventured the opinion that Ribera had acted properly, since these ladies served Queen Isabel. But Juana, seeking exclusive personal loyalty among her staff, ordered the ladies with her goods, among others, to return to Castile when she departed for the Low Countries in

March 1504. Although Ruíz and Albión left Juana's trunks in her possession, the princess found certain jewels missing. By sending a messenger to inquire whether the ladies had seen or found the missing items, Juana deeply offended these former servants, "who claimed that Her Highness made them thieves." Ribera felt equally aggrieved when Juana ordered him to board her trunks but refused to sign receipts for goods that she had distributed and consumed in Castile. Originally appointed by Queen Isabel, Ribera may have also felt greater loyalty to her than to Juana. Reportedly, the *camarero* became so distraught that he remained in the port of Laredo when Juana and her remaining servants embarked for Flanders and then delayed his return to Brussels for more than one year.

Juana appears to have esteemed other servants more than she appreciated the *camarero*. Lucas de Atiença reported that Juana asked him to guard her most personal possessions when they departed from Laredo in 1504 and directed him always to keep them separate from her other belongings. Among these intimate effects, Atiença listed a coffer containing jewels of gold, which Juana never opened in Ribera's presence. Garcia del Campo, who had seen Juana wearing gold to public Mass, reported saving her letter case and dressing table from a fire in Ocaña (near Toledo) and finding jewels that she had lost in Brussels and Ghent. Although the quartermaster did not mention any rewards received for these acts, he did note that Juana gave another servant a velvet vest in return for recovering a jewel that she once lost in the park of Brussels. Although capable of a magnanimous gesture, Juana suspected employees more readily than she trusted them. When traveling overland from the English coast to Windsor Castle in 1506, Rodrigo de Ratya noted that some of Juana's chests banged together and fell open. Finding an exposed trunk containing coins and bars of gold, the servant carried it before Juana, who initially accused him of opening the chest himself. After verifying all of its contents, however, the queen gained confidence in Ratya.

Among her personal servants, Juana especially favored shoemaker Tomás de Valencia in the years after Philippe's death. The shoemaker expressed corresponding loyalty to Juana. In particular, Valencia recalled that King Fernando had ordered his daughter's trunks opened and their contents inventoried in 1512. On that occasion, the shoemaker remembered, he had not wished to relinquish fur-lined boots that the queen had granted him.[4] Valencia understood that Juana did not want the household administration to regulate or to recover her gifts to loyal servants. Aware of the trust between the queen and Valencia, the Marquis of Denia asserted his authority over the shoemaker. When the queen obtained

60 ducats (22,500 mrs) in 1519, she handed the money directly to Valencia. Intervening behind the scenes, the ever-watchful marquis ordered Valencia to forgo half of the sum that Juana had given him. In this way, Denia undermined Juana's modest effort to reward a servant loyal to her, rather than solely to himself or Charles.[5]

Unlike Tomás de Valencia, to Juana's dismay, most of the queen's servants and relatives took cues for governing her from Charles V. In late 1524 the emperor had ordered Juana's trunks secretly removed from her chambers and opened in his presence. After selecting gold, pearls, silver, and precious stones from the chests, the emperor reportedly required objects of gold that he found "old and useless" melted down and divided the remaining goods with his youngest sister, Catalina. Subsequently suspecting that a certain chest had been removed and replaced, Juana ordered Alonso de Ribera to open it before her. Unable to avoid the task, the *camarero* lifted the trunk's lid to reveal only an old cloth and some bricks. The *camarero* then feigned surprise: "Oh, I am lost, for the contents of this coffer have been robbed!" Unimpressed, Juana retorted: "Jesus, Ribera, how little spirit you have! Upon my salvation, I swear!" According to an attendant of the chamber, Juan de Arganda, the queen expressed relief when she learned that the missing goods had served her son. Above all, she seemed to fear that unworthy servants would steal her possessions. Following the emperor's example, the Empress Isabel and Prince Philip helped themselves to Juana's belongings in 1532, 1534, 1536, 1548, and 1552.[6] On these occasions, however, Juana's servants may have taken the blame for items that the queen discovered missing.

Testimony that Alonso de Ribera gathered in 1555 also suggested that some of Juana's servants interpreted their jobs as finding clever ways to trick her. Since Juana prohibited any one from recording the money and other goods that she received, a scribe stationed himself outside of her chamber, where, unbeknown to the queen, he attempted to record whatever items entered the room. Another servant, Juan de Arganda, recalled that Juana had ordered trunks with her possessions burned in 1534 and lamented that the queen's vigilance had made it impossible for him to save more than one or two chests of clothing and footwear. Arganda clearly conceived of his duty as disobeying Juana's orders. When elite guard Juanes de Solares also attempted to rescue a trunk, he reported that the queen observed him from an overhead balcony, threw a brick at Solares, and demanded that he return her belongings to the fire. Another servant, Gerónimo de Medina, recalled overhearing Denia ask Juana why she had ordered her possessions burned. According to Medina, the queen responded that she would not need to carry them with her. The reasons for such destruction eluded even Juana's governor.

Other servants reported that the queen regularly ordered her apparel burned or submerged in water so long that it was ruined. Burning clothing could have been a means of preventing the spread of plague,[7] or even appeasing an angry God. But why would Juana habitually order her possessions destroyed? Such an action makes sense only in light of the extreme animosity between Juana and her attendants. The late Queen Isabel had taught Juana and her siblings to distribute articles of their own clothing among loyal servants.[8] Yet Juana, rather than giving expensive articles to servants she found unworthy, apparently ordered her own footwear and clothing destroyed. Consuming used apparel in this way may have enabled Juana to secure frequent contact with—and regular business for—loyal servants like Tomás de Valencia.

Whether intentionally or not, from her deathbed Juana turned the tables on her less favorite attendants. According to household lore, the queen kept her finest possessions, including golden jewels, precious stones, valuable coins, two silver trays, and three silver cups, in a medium-sized trunk made in Flanders.[9] Washerwoman Catalina Redonda, a widow who spent her days and nights beside the queen, retrieved the heavy coffer whenever Juana wanted it. According to Redonda, the queen kept the key to the box and ordered the washerwoman to turn her back as she opened it. Facing away from the box, Catalina could only glimpse tied bundles of white cloth and a stone that seemed to be a diamond set in gold with a gold-enameled handle. Catalina claimed to have last seen the coffer when Juana requested it around Saint Michael's day in 1554 and used the bar of gold with "a round thing" on one end to adorn herself after washing.[10] Eight days before the queen died, the Marquis of Denia ordered Alonso de Ribera and other individuals to accompany Catalina Redonda into Juana's chamber. In one of the trunks, Catalina sought and found a key to the legendary chest. The washerwoman guided her companions toward the treasure and, reaching a certain spot, exclaimed, "Oh what grief! The coffer is not here!"

Servants never found the trunk containing Juana's most treasured possessions. Attempting to recover the coffer, Ribera and Denia obtained letters from a papal nuncio excommunicating any one who withheld information about it.[11] Although witnesses rushed forth, none restored the missing trunk. Had Juana disposed of the goods before her death or had she somehow fooled the very attendants who had worked to deceive her for years? In the last instance, Juana and her possessions evaded servants' control.

"To Kiss the Royal Hands of Her Highness"

Juana's attachment to her possessions reflected a refusal to allow her servants to handle her emblems of royalty or to intervene in the family relationships that many of them represented. Although the queen often appeared hostile toward her servants, she became remarkably amicable in the company of her family. Such different attitudes toward servants and relatives entailed more than capricious or schizophrenic impulses. While honoring status distinctions, the queen responded to very different treatment on the part of her servants and her family. Although many household officials showed a lack of respect for Juana, her descendants professed reverence for the queen. Little did Juana suspect that the servants who confined her thereby allowed the Habsburgs to honor her royal *dignitas*. In other words, given the profoundly different attitudes of her servants and her descendants, Juana either failed to grasp or, more likely, refused to recognize the extent of their complicity. Shunning troublesome attendants, the queen sought greater contact with her offspring.

All three of the emperor's legitimate children—Philip, María, and Juana—learned to exercise authority in their grandmother's name as regents of Spain. During his first regency, from 1543 to 1548, Prince Philip reported on Juana's health and resolved a dispute between the Marquis of Denia and the magistrate of Tordesillas.[12] When the emperor summoned Philip to Flanders from 1548 to 1552, his daughter María and initially her husband, Maximilian of Hungary, served as Spanish regents and frequently visited Tordesillas.[13] Finally, when Philip went to England to wed Mary Tudor in 1554, his youngest sister, Juana of Austria, the newly widowed Princess of Portugal, governed Spain. Philip, María, Maximilian, and Juana all began their regencies with visits to the proprietary queen at Tordesillas, officially "to kiss the royal hands of Her Highness." Although Charles explicitly named his children governors, none of them overlooked the need for Juana's approval. Likewise, they took formal leave of the queen before departing from Spain. Of sixteen recorded visits to Tordesillas by members of the royal family from 1535 until Juana's death in 1555, specific details survive in only two cases, both of which provide rare glimpses of an amiable queen.

Engaged to the *infanta* María Manuel (daughter of Juana's youngest child, Catalina, and João III of Portugal) in 1543, Prince Philip visited Tordesillas to request Juana's blessing before meeting his bride. Accompanied by the Cardinal Juan Tavera, the Admiral of Castile, other nobles, and a court fool, the prince found his grandmother modestly dressed in floor-length burin cloth, with sleeves "like the robe of a Benedictine friar."[14] She wore a Flemish headdress beneath a veil of the same burin knotted under her chin. According to one member of Philip's party, the prince knelt before Juana and requested her hand in order to kiss it. Reportedly refusing to extend her hand, "because she does not give it to anyone," the queen asked Philip to rise two or three times. As a mark of respect, Juana then ordered chairs for the prince, the cardinal, and the admiral. Without allowing her grandson to remove his hat when speaking (another sign of reverence for her), Juana began to extract information from him. After requesting news about Charles V, the queen asked where the prince was going, and if he planned to marry. When Philip explained that he was going to meet his bride in Salamanca, his fool added that the princess was very beautiful. Looking at Philip, Juana laughed: "You will find yourself more than fooled once you see her, if she does not seem beautiful to you."[15] After further conversation, Philip took leave of his grandmother, promising to return to Tordesillas with his bride.

According to the same chronicler, after their marriage Philip and María Manuel stopped in Tordesillas and, "once they had kissed the hand of the queen," continued on to Valladolid.[16] Had Juana really allowed her grandchildren to kiss her hand? Such a concession would conflict with the chronicler's previous assertion that the queen never permitted such a gesture. Yet the expression, used in a figurative sense, may have signified paying respect to the queen, without specifying the concrete act of homage involved. It was important for Philip and his bride to offer such a gesture, and perhaps equally important for Juana to refuse it. Although such visits kept Juana informed about events in her kingdoms and enabled her to comment on political affairs, their sporadic nature demonstrated that the monarchy no longer depended on a single physical person. The royal agency apparently confined to Juana's hands in 1520, when councillors claimed that Juana's signature could either save or destroy Castile, now extended among her descendants.

During their regency, María and Maximilian also paid official respects to Queen Juana. Learning that Juana delighted in such contact, the queen's second son, Fernando, asked Maximilian to remind Juana of his filial affection. On 17 July 1550 María and Maximilian left Valladolid to visit Tordesillas, where they arrived late that afternoon. The queen, having postponed her supper, greeted the couple "with great joy and contentment." After publicly expressing pleasure and asking her grandchildren about their trip, Juana permitted them to retire. The following day, María took portraits of her own daughter, other female relatives, and the Archduke Charles to share with her grandmother. Studying the images with great interest, Juana asked María the name and age of each family member pictured, "along with other details and pleasantries." Summoning Maximilian, who had planned to see the queen that afternoon, Juana engaged the couple in two hours of conversation, "asking infinite questions" and "complaining that they had not brought Princess Ana [their daughter born in October 1549, mother of the future Philip III] to show her." The rulers explained that they had left Ana behind to protect her from the summer heat.[17]

When treated with respect, Juana responded in kind. After the royal party had left Juana's chamber, Maximilian returned to see her, accompanied by only the Licentiate Juan Alonso de Gámiz, a royal chaplain who reported to Juana's second son, Fernando. Maximilian informed the queen that Fernando had often ordered him to visit and to serve Juana, regretting that he could not see her himself. Then, as a token of Fernando's devotion, Maximilian presented the queen with a gold cross that her son had sent, and requested that she adore it while praying for her children. Examining the object, which originally belonged to the Emperor Federico, Juana remarked that she had seen similar pieces in Flanders that had once belonged to Charles "the Bold." Emphasizing that this particular crucifix came from the House of Austria, Maximilian dated it to 1451, the year inscribed on its case. After studying these details, the queen exclaimed: "In good truth, my son gives me great pleasure by remembering me and sending me such a devout and distinguished piece." Although pleased with the cross, Juana fretted over where to keep it. When Maximilian suggested that Juana hang it from a cloth in her chamber, the queen asserted that the risk of theft required greater security, since many of her other belongings had disappeared.[18] Tactfully, Maximilian changed the subject.

The co-regent noted that he had only begun to discharge his father's orders to fulfill Juana's desires. Having understood that Juana wanted her own money, Maximilian had ordered the licentiate to bring her 400 gold ducats (150,000 mrs), which he placed in her lap.[19] Grateful for the gesture, Juana nevertheless specified that she wanted funds from her own estate and would not accept any from Fernando's. Apparently, she valued access to her inheritance more than the money itself. Maximilian thereby assured the queen that the ducats came from her own patrimony. Expressing great pleasure, Juana continued to question Maximilian about Fernando and his family. When the co-regent attempted to depart, Juana called him back, reminding him to convey her gratitude to Fernando, and requesting favors for specific servants. Gámiz further informed

Fernando that Juana had referred to him on three occasions as "my son," a term that she supposedly refrained from applying to Charles.[20]

Juana apparently attempted to gain her relatives' help in her ongoing struggle against certain attendants. To this effect Fernando's loquacious informant reported that Juana's fear of theft intensified on the eve of the regents' departure from Tordesillas. Although Juana summoned Gámiz at two o'clock in the morning, he could only attend to her after Maximilian had heard Mass and left that morning. Gámiz found the seventy-one-year-old queen clutching her new cross. Visibly distressed, Juana asked Gámiz to guard the crucifix until she could obtain a secure chest, "for I would feel great sorrow if any stone or piece of it were stolen." Gámiz suggested that Juana entrust the object to either her *camarero* Alonso de Ribera or the Marquis of Denia, but the queen claimed "that they had already taken many other jewels of great value, leaving her coffers empty." Finally, Juana promised that she would have a chest made within thirty days, and Gámiz accepted her crucifix. Fearful of keeping the image, Gámiz secretly left it with Juana's treasurer and rushed to gain Maximilian's approval of his actions.[21] Simultaneously, María and Maximilian informed the emperor of their recent trip to Tordesillas, "to see the queen, our lady, and to kiss her hands," and forwarded a list of Juana's requests to Charles.[22]

Only these two recorded visits provide glimpses of the substantial, affectionate exchanges that "kissing the hands of the queen, our lady," could entail. By giving Juana a cross from her second son, Maximilian demonstrated that material objects could express and reinforce familial ties. Juana's fear that her own attendants would steal the crucifix and consequent refusal to entrust them with it reveals that she blamed these servants for previous seizures of her possessions that her descendants had authorized. Aware of Juana's fear of losing the cross, Gámiz ultimately failed to respect her will. By leaving the crucifix with Juana's treasurer, Gámiz deceived the queen and confirmed a general pattern of bypassing her authority out of loyalty to ruling members of the Habsburg family.

A Queen Possessed?

Royal status, expressed in the objects Juana treasured, entailed a special proximity to God. Whereas Juana's parents had proved their divinely sanctioned right to rule Castile on the battlefield, a more interior religiosity distanced Juana from the act of governing. The contemplative piety that facilitated Juana's exclusion from political power may have also helped her endure the ensuing situation.

Juana's *recogimiento*, moreover, appears to have encouraged growing concerns about her spiritual health among other members of the royal family.[23] Perhaps most frustrating for Juana, servants loyal to the Habsburg cause refused to recognize signs of her spiritual (or mental) health.

The books listed in Juana's inventory suggest her awareness of an interior, contemplative piety associated with the *Devotio Moderna* and popular among early sixteenth-century elites. Juana's 116 volumes, including 29 books of hours, 12 songbooks, and 7 missals, overwhelmingly comprised devotional works. Her daughter, Catalina, took a number of Juana's spiritual treatises to Portugal in 1525. Among the tracts emphasizing personal identification with the sufferings of Christ, the queen may have deliberately shared Domenico Cavalca's *Espejo de la cruz*, the *Contemptu Mundi/Imitatio Christ* by Thomas à Kempis, attributed to Jean Gersen, and Ambrosio Montesino's *Vita Christi Cartuxano* with her daughter. The queen retained most of her prayer books and a number of devotional treatises (Pedro Jiménez de Prejano's *Lucero de la vida cristiana*, Hernando de Talavera's *Vida cristiana*, Jacobus de Voragine's *Flos sanctorum*, and Alonso de Zamora's *Loor de virtudes*) until the end of her life.[24] Whether or not Juana sought the direct, unmediated connection with God advocated in many of these texts, the spread of Protestant creeds after 1520 made such interior piety increasingly suspect.

Treasuring devout objects, from rosaries to retables to crosses, Juana undoubtedly considered herself a pious Catholic. When lightning struck her palace in 1550, the queen defended herself by making crosses and chanting "Christus vincit, Christus regnat, Christus me defenda."[25] She assured the frightened Marquis of Denia (don Luis de Rojas y Sandoval since 1536) that her *Agnus Dei*—a relic with force against storms, fire, lightening, pestilence, and demonic incursions—would protect them.[26] The queen remained calm when a bolt of lightning traversed the rafters and floor of her chamber as well as the room below, where *camarero* Ribera lay suffering from gout. In contrast to Juana's serenity, Ribera and two women with him temporarily lost their senses.[27] In the midst of such incidents, however, some of Juana's servants and relatives retained their doubts about the queen's religiosity.

A series of confessors, beginning with her childhood tutor, Andrés de Miranda, had guided Juana's religious development. The bishop of Málaga, don Diego Ramírez de Villaescusa, succeeded Miranda in 1497, left Juana in 1508, and served as bishop of Cuenca before and after refusing to support Charles in the Comunero rebellion.[28] Because Juana's official confessor after 1509, fray

Tomás de Matienzo, resided with her father, Catalina's tutor, fray Juan de Ávila had attended to the queen's spiritual needs until the Marquis of Denia dismissed him in 1523.[29] The confessor or "first chaplain," in addition to his duties with the queen, officially supervised the sacristan (in charge of annual ceremonies), twelve chaplains, two to three quartermasters of the chapel, and seven chapel boys in residence at Tordesillas.[30] At times, however, this staff appeared insufficient in order to govern the queen's religiosity.

At certain critical moments Juana's servants appealed to external spiritual personnel. Clerics had entered Juana's chambers to exorcise her in 1516 and 1520, although their efforts produced little effect.[31] To make matters worse, since the dismissal of Franciscan Juan de Ávila, Juana had lived without a confessor and, consequently, without confessing. The situation particularly disturbed the Empress Isabel.[32] But was the queen really accountable for her actions and therefore capable of sin? When the council of state discussed the matter in 1532, some members hinted that allowing Juana to confess "might presume that she is in another disposition than that which she has." In other words, they suggested that responsibility for one's sins presupposed some degree of sanity. Yet the Marquis of Denia differed, considering Juana's need to confess a sign of infirmity rather than health. Unwilling to accept another resident confessor, don Bernardo de Rojas recommended that Charles send a Dominican friar (probably Denia's preference rather than Juana's) to visit the queen, extract a specific confession from her, and return to his monastery.[33]

Accordingly, the emperor dispatched a succession of friars to confess Juana. All of them failed. The first hopeful, fray Tomás de Verlanga, met Juana in Tudela del Duero in 1534. Although he waited throughout Holy Week for the queen to summon him, a stomach ailment allegedly prevented Juana from seeing Verlanga.[34] When Juana suffered a fever the following year, Denia feared for her life, and asked Charles to send fray Bartolomé de Saavedra, a former companion of Juana's first instructor and confessor, fray Andrés. Yet the queen recovered before Saavedra reached her.[35] In November 1538 the emperor directed fray Pedro Romero de Ulloa, a Carthusian who had confessed the queen after her husband's death, to visit Juana again.[36] Instead of granting Romero an audience, the queen expressed pleasure that he resided nearby and promised to send for him if she required his services.[37] Noting that Juana often declared a willingness to confess, the marquis attributed her subsequent inability to Satanic interference.[38]

In late 1551 Prince Philip visited Juana in the company of yet another potential confessor, the Jesuit Francisco de Borja, former Duke of Gandía and Marquis of Lombay. A longtime Habsburg favorite, Borja had been a page to Juana's daughter, Catalina, at Tordesillas before he entered the Society of Jesus.[39] Borja retained important ties to the Tordesillas household. His eldest daughter, Isabel, had married the Count of Lerma, don Francisco Gómez de Sandoval y Rojas, in 1548, and began receiving wages as one of Juana's official ladies-in-waiting in 1552.[40] Thus, Borja, who later became the third general of the Jesuit order and attained posthumous canonization, could visit both his family and the queen at Tordesillas.[41] Returning to see Queen Juana after Philip left her, in 1552 the Jesuit persuaded Juana to repeat the general confession of faith and to accept absolution. Pleased with such progress, the Marquis of Denia and Prince Philip hoped that Borja would eventually achieve further success with Juana.[42]

Also in 1552, Borja began writing the spiritual treatise, "Instruction for the Good Government of a Lord in His Estates," dedicated to his eldest son, but also, judging by its contents, directed to the emperor. Drawing upon the *Regimine Principum* attributed to Saint Thomas, Borja emphasized the need for a ruler to master his passions and his household before governing his people. He also suggested that a ruler unable to govern must have offended God. Through an extended allegorical reference to the biblical King David, Borja explained that David needed to defeat Goliath (the devil), overcome Saul (the passions), enter the house of Juda (confession), and capture the fortress of Sion (contemplation) before entering the city of God. In short, the Jesuit recommended rigorous self-government for any ruler seeking salvation.[43]

When Juana of Austria, the widowed Princess of Portugal, began her regency in 1554, both she and Philip requested that Francisco de Borja meet her at Tordesillas.[44] After speaking with her grandmother and the Jesuit, the princess left Borja to continue his efforts to extract a specific confession from the queen. In four letters to Philip, Borja detailed three sessions he spent with Queen Juana in May 1554 and another before her death, 12 April 1555. This correspondence depicts the personal impact of confessional conflict on members of the royal family. It also reveals the queen's willingness to argue with Borja on his own terms in an attempt to attain greater control of her household. Unlike other suspected heretics under pressure, Juana refused to confess sins that she had not committed. Instead, she struggled and ultimately failed to condemn her servants.

God had favored Juana, above all, with reproductive and dynastic success. During her lifetime, her sons, Charles and Fernando, ruled Germany, Bohemia, Hungary, the Netherlands and Milan, while her four daughters had become queens of France, Hungary, Portugal, and Denmark. In contrast, Juana's own mother, Isabel, had witnessed the death of three of her descendants and heirs to the throne of Castile in fewer than three years. Suffering a stillbirth in 1498, Marguerite of Austria never produced surviving children. In 1509 King Fernando of Aragon's second wife, Germaine de Foix, gave birth to a son who perished within one hour. The efforts of Juana's grandson, Philip, and his second wife, Mary Tudor, to produce a Catholic heir to the English throne may have heightened concern about any divine or malignant forces connected to Juana.

During Borja's first meeting with Juana in early May 1554, the Jesuit subsequently informed Philip, he emphasized the royal family's obligation to combat the spread of Protestant heresies through exemplary Catholic piety. After describing Philip's desire to serve and to satisfy the queen, Borja reported begging Juana to consider her grandson's efforts to recover England for the church through his marriage to Juana's niece, Mary Tudor. In particular, Borja admonished Juana for devotional negligence, because the English would say "since Her Highness lived like they did, without Masses and without images and without sacraments, then they could do the same because in matters of the Catholic faith what is licit for one is licit for all." The Jesuit begged Juana—now age seventy-four—to rectify the past and unburden her royal conscience through confession. Borja informed Philip that Juana had listened to him "with much attention." Although she used to confess, take Communion, hear Mass, and keep images, Juana claimed, her servants now impeded such devout practices:

> In the beginning, when she prayed, they took the book from her hands, quarreled, and ridiculed her prayer and the images that she had, which were a Saint Dominic, a Saint Francis, Saint Peter, and Saint Paul. They spat and did many filthy things in the font of holy water. During Mass they placed themselves disrespectfully before the priest, rotating the prayer book, and ordering him to do only what they wanted. . . . They have sought many times to take the relics and crucifix that she now carries with her.

Clinging to the cross that Fernando had sent her, the queen sought to indict her servants, presumably including Borja's daughter, for traffic with the devil.[45]

Although at a disadvantage, Juana skillfully solicited Borja's help against her female attendants. When the Jesuit expressed doubt that Juana's ladies had committed such evil acts, the queen followed his lead. He might well be right, she said, because her foes claimed to be dead souls and had also bothered Princess

Juana during her visit. According to the queen, the spirits showed much contempt and made many incantations, as if they were witches.

Juana's initial conversation with Borja lasted over an hour, during which time she spoke "very much to the point, without leaving the matter." Cursing once or twice, Juana carefully avoided blasphemy by assuring the priest that her words were not directed at God. She made it clear that Borja should inform Philip of what she had told him about her attendants, since they "should confess and do as Christians." Once her servants were gone, Juana insisted that she would also confess and take Communion.[46] Borja could only respond that the Holy Office of the Inquisition would apprehend her ladies, because Her Highness had reported a case of heresy, which would need to be resolved one way or another. With some success, the queen appeared to have directed Borja's suspicions toward her attendants.

Yet the Jesuit retained doubts about Juana's spiritual health. "Did the queen believe the articles of the faith, with all that the Catholic Church commanded?" he asked. Unaware of Protestant alternatives to Catholicism, Juana declared: "Do I not have to believe? Yes, certainly, I believe!" Yet Borja persisted: "Did she believe that the Son of God had come to the world to redeem them, was born, died, resurrected, and rose to heaven? Did she want to live and to die in this Catholic faith?" "Yes," responded Juana, adding that she wanted to confess and take Communion if only her "impediment" [i.e., her servants] were removed.[47] Since it was six in the evening and the queen had not yet eaten her midday meal, Borja sought to conclude their session. Juana agreed that the priest should report to Philip and return with his response to her complaints about the ladies, but seemed eager to extend the interview. As usual, she solicited information about her offspring, asking Borja when Philip would leave England and when Princess Juana would visit her again.[48] Finally, Borja presented his companion, Doctor Torres, who brought Juana a message from Queen Catalina of Portugal, the youngest of Juana's six children and her former companion in Tordesillas. Among other matters, Juana and Torres discussed the death of the Portuguese prince João.[49] Juana's affectionate regard for members of her family contrasted with her condemnation of her female attendants.

In order to evaluate Juana's complaints, Borja and Philip adopted the established practice of deceiving her. The exchanges between Borja and Philip in 1554 resembled those between Charles and the Marquis of Denia in 1518–20, with the difference that religious orthodoxy now took precedence over dynastic expansion. Reflecting on his meeting with the queen in early May 1554, the Jesuit reported knowledge of few remedies for Juana's "weak judgment" since "this disposition is already so rooted in Her Highness."[50] Although Borja found it "very clear" that Juana's tormentors were "not her servants but her enemies," he proposed an experiment so that the situation could be "judged more clearly." After consulting the Marquis of Denia, Borja suggested that the ladies be kept out of Juana's room for several days. According to Borja, the procedure would allow him to determine whether the queen experienced "an illusion of the devil in the imagination" or if she "really, with corporeal eyes, sees these figures of persons that the enemy takes in order to afflict and to persuade Her Highness." Thus Borja, suspecting Satanic interference, proposed to ascertain its nature. Philip approved the plan: the queen should be told that the Inquisition had imprisoned her ladies, and she should not see them again "until another thing appears." With these tactics, Philip thought, "the fact of the matter could be ascertained." The Jesuit also suggested that a commissioner or inquisitor be named to examine Juana's ladies, "so that it be done in the name of the Holy Office, which is the thing that inspires most fear." Philip responded that it would be good to tell Her Highness that an inquisitor had been named, but best not to share the matter with the inquisitor or anyone else until Philip had "seen the effect" of the ladies' removal.[51]

For Borja, governing the queen required urgent measures to facilitate her salvation. Against the heresy that Juana had depicted, the priest recommended further weapons: crosses and images throughout her apartments, daily Mass and Gospel readings, holy water, and exorcisms. Philip approved all but the last two measures, which he felt should not precede the experiment with the ladies. The Jesuit thought it particularly important that Her Highness "vow to live and die in the Catholic faith, renounce Satan with all his works, purify herself, say the name of Jesus, and pray to him," every day if possible. Borja also emphasized that Juana should confess, especially "if by chance she had once complied with or obeyed any of the illusions."[52] The Jesuit suspected Juana of contact with Lucifer, which he demanded that she confess. After admitting what she had done, Borja noted, the queen could return to the Catholic faith. As Juana's days drew to a close, the Jesuit thought that she might eat and dress as she liked, but she should not be indulged in matters that touched on the health of her soul. Since healing the queen had to be "more the work of God than men," Borja also recommended prayers for her in monasteries and churches throughout the kingdom. The Jesuit further proposed special Masses and pilgrimages, which

Philip left to his discretion. With the necessary secrecy, Borja thought, individuals with power over malignant spirits might be sought to combat the illusions that gave Juana such trouble, "because free of this company, she would either confess or say why she did not." If Juana still claimed to see the ladies after they had been removed, Philip requested that the priest recommend appropriate persons to treat the queen.

Borja, like Denia, became an intermediary between Juana, her servants, and her family. In a letter of 10 May, the Jesuit informed Philip that Juana's ladies had received orders to stop serving Her Highness. If the queen should ask about the maids, other servants had been instructed to respond that the women were publicly said to be detained or imprisoned. This done, the Jesuit entered Juana's room to communicate her grandson's response. He expressed Philip's sympathy for the troubles with her servants and claimed that the women had been arrested, "placing much value on it and selling this service to Her Highness as well as I knew how." Borja then reminded Juana about her part of the deal: since her servants had been removed, she should "reveal on the outside the Catholic spirit that she had within." Juana declared that Borja had justly requested exactly what she wanted to do. The Jesuit begged Juana to declare often her intentions of living and dying in the Catholic faith, which she affirmed as she had during their previous visit. Free of her female attendants, Juana even heard Mass and accepted holy water throughout her apartments.[53]

Yet Borja continued to suspect Satanic interference. Informing Juana that she could have been excommunicated for failing to confess for so long or for having had contact with witches, Borja advised the queen to absolve herself of this censure with the greatest caution. After reminding the Jesuit that he had absolved her two years earlier, Juana accepted yet another absolution. The queen further satisfied Borja by reciting from the Gospels of Saint John and Saint Mark. Having demonstrated piety, Juana reminded Borja of her dislike for her former attendants. Asking Borja if the ladies' return was being discussed, Juana insisted that such a measure would come to no good. Borja could only respond that another father, fray Luis de la Cruz, had been named to handle the matter. After answering her questions about fray Luis, Borja left the queen.[54]

While Juana attempted to demonstrate her piety, Borja's report of 10 May suggested that servants continued to provoke her. Venturing into the corridor where she heard Mass, Borja noted that Juana observed new curtains on the altar, took offense, and demanded their removal. The Jesuit described the new altar covering as "a little cloth of gold with the mystery of the adoration of the three kings [*reyes magos*]," which he found "convenient for the decency of the altar." After attempting to retain the new cloth for two hours, the Jesuit removed it only when Juana refused to eat. Although Borja found no objection to the altar cloth, the queen clearly rejected a change made without consulting her and may have seen the three kings as eastern astrologers who defiled the altar.[55] While Juana's heretics wore Islamic garb, the Jesuit sought Protestants. In a further attempt to discredit Juana, her servants informed Borja that the queen had once rejected holy candles, "saying that they smelled." They reported, moreover, that Juana closed her eyes during Mass when the Eucharist was raised and transformed into the body of Christ, suggesting an aversion to the sacrament. Yet when Borja sent the queen candles that had been blessed, she accepted them without complaint. Furthermore, when a chaplain approached Juana at the climax of the Mass, the queen saw him and signaled him to step aside. According to Borja, subsequent tests confirmed his earlier findings. Despite the assertions of certain attendants, the queen could not be proved Satan's ally.

Unable to condemn Juana for traffic with the devil, the Jesuit found it equally impossible to admit evidence of the queen's good sense. Dismissing Juana's arguments, Borja wrote Philip on 10 May: "With regard to the disposition of the queen, she has told me that, since the ladies have been imprisoned, she has not seen any of those figures that presented themselves. It seems that now no other thing can be judged than that which has been thought at other times: these [visions] are imaginations and weakness of the head, which all proceed from the principal root of the illness that Her Highness has had for so many years." Rather than a trial, Borja, Denia, and Philip had designed a "foolproof" way of exonerating Juana's attendants. These ladies, Borja stated, could reenter the royal chambers after fray Luis arrived. In the kindest manner possible, "so that she once again receives it with patience," Juana should be informed of their innocence. Perhaps deliberately, Borja and Philip deceived themselves more than the queen.

Unlike Borja and Philip, Juana remained convinced that her female attendants were her enemies. A few days after Borja's second letter, fray Luis de la Cruz visited Juana, who immediately urged him to discipline her ladies. According to Cruz:

> I entered to visit the queen our lady and Her Highness asked if the ladies were well confined, charging me many times to punish them with great rigor. To this end Her Highness said one thousand things that they had committed in her disservice:

that they had impeded the use of the sacraments, devotions of the hours, and rosary, Mass, and holy water, and that they had her degraded [*chusmada*]—this word she said many times.[56]

Reversing Juana's version of cause and effect, Cruz defended the attendants. The servants' license and daring, he argued, came from seeing Her Highness not receive the sacraments or undertake measures their religion ordained for the type of difficulties she experienced. Once again, Juana insisted that "deformed and shameless" servants had prevented her from carrying out such practices. Self-righteously, Juana declared, "I trust that it will not be as it has been before, that they remove them [the ladies] from me and then three days later free them again, so that the [royal] person cannot do what her soul requires." In spite of the queen's best efforts, fray Luis continued siding with the servants who had offended her: "The emperor and the prince our lords have us here to serve Your Highness and relieve you of these ladies who offend you. But since Your Highness does not help by doing your part, as a Catholic and Christian queen and our lady should, how can we, your servants, serve or give contentment?" The queen responded coolly: "Certainly, father, you are not right to insist so much on this." For most of their session, Juana criticized the former servants, while the friar used "all means human and divine" to turn the argument against her.[57]

In a second meeting with Cruz two hours after the first, Juana refined her tactics. When Cruz begged her "with great insistence," she recited the sacred mysteries of Jesus Christ and the Catholic faith. According to the friar, Juana proceeded to say strange things that revealed her indisposition:

> She told me a very long history of how a civet cat had eaten the *infanta* of Navarre and the Queen doña Isabel, our lady, and had bitten the Catholic king, our lord, and many other things of this quality. And that the ladies had already brought this evil cat, which was very close to her chamber, in order to do her the same wrong and injury they used to. And Her Highness so much enjoyed telling me these histories that she ordered me to sit and to be at ease, saying that she was very [well] served by my coming.

Juana apparently took pleasure in the dramatic effect of her story. Relishing an audience, she seems to have portrayed a battle between good and evil, in which the devil took the form of a cat, attacking her predecessors.[58] Although the removal of her servants had ended the queen's afflictions, she sensed that the ladies remained a threat. Both priests confirmed Juana's impression that her attendants might return. Consequently, the queen sought the fathers' help against evildoers lurking outside her room.

Fray Luis expressed difficulty formulating a response for Philip. Considering everything "very attentively and measured[ly] by the rules of natural and moral philosophy and of sacred scripture and theology," Cruz emphasized, above all, his loyalty to Philip. The friar found Juana "so far from being reduced to the observance of the sacraments" that he pronounced her capacity to receive them "an impossible and closed case." Nor, stated Cruz, would any Christian man administer the sacraments to Juana without fearing that they would be injured and profaned. Somewhat contradictorily, Cruz then claimed that the subject of Juana's spiritual condition altered and awakened men's judgments, "which in this matter, as in the rest, are as diverse as their faces."[59] In truth, the friar stated, Her Highness was so sincere and innocent of pain and guilt that she should be envied rather than pitied. With the approval of Denia and Borja, Cruz returned to his monastery after 15 May 1554.

Although the attendants Juana despised returned to her chamber, death soon and irrevocably freed the queen from their company. In a personal note of February 1555 Juana of Austria reported "great sorrow" upon learning that her grandmother's health deteriorated.[60] The regent asked her secretary to have the Marquis of Denia request King Philip's permission for her to go to Tordesillas "to cure and to serve" the ailing queen.[61] Although Queen Juana's condition appeared to improve, in early March, the marquis traveled to Valladolid to inform Princess Juana that her grandmother's health declined again.[62] After visiting Tordesillas, the regent summoned Francisco de Borja and Domingo de Soto, a famous Dominican theologian, to help her grandmother achieve a pious death.[63]

Having administered Extreme Unction before Juana's end, Borja described "the great favor that our Lord granted Her Highness, in her illness, by having given her . . . a very different sense of the things of God than had been known in Her Highness up until then."[64] According to the Jesuit, Juana pronounced the particularly edifying last words, "Jesus Christ crucified, be with me."[65] The queen's death on Good Friday, when her suffering might recall the savior's passion, seemed especially propitious. Receiving the news in Brussels on 9 May, Charles V informed his brother, Fernando, that the queen made no specific confession before her death.[66] Juana's battles with her servants, reflecting their mutual refusal to be governed, had finally come to an end.

The Household Never Dies

The queen's final peace with God left her servants clamoring to retain their offices and salaries. In 1554 Philip had left instructions for Juana's household to continue functioning if Juana died before he or the emperor returned to Spain. In the event of Juana's death, Philip commanded the Marquis of Denia to "sustain and preserve and order the household, servants, and ladies to stand in the service and estate that they are and were" until Charles and Philip made other provisions for them.[67] Following Juana's death, Denia implored Philip to confirm these orders, reminding him that the household could not continue without pay. Although the best accountants had been working to sustain the household, they could not provide much for its members, who the marquis claimed were leaving every day. Denia suggested that poverty might force Juana's former attendants to serve outside of the royal household,[68] endangering its corporate continuity. While begging Philip to confirm his previous instructions, the marquis sent accountant Juan Pérez de Arizpe to ask the emperor to arrange for the servants to be paid. To prevent Juana's former servants from rushing to Brussels in person, Arizpe also carried letters presenting their petitions.[69]

The royal chapel, if nothing else, justified the continuity of Juana's household in Tordesillas as long as her corpse remained there.[70] As during the queen's lifetime, her chaplains sang the hours during Lent, erected a monument for Holy Week, and commissioned preachers for Advent. They even continued to receive the queen's annual offering of 375 mrs on the day of Saint Sebastian.[71] Since the queen assiduously had celebrated All Saints' Day during her lifetime, Princess Juana allotted 12,500 mrs for that purpose each year as long as her grandmother's body remained in the Royal Monastery of Saint Claire.[72]

While committed to maintaining Juana's household, which he and Philip inherited, the emperor attempted to limit its costs. Accordingly, royal secretary Francisco de Eraso compiled a list of Juana's former servants, including their salaries, rations, cost-of-living supplements, dates of entry into the household, and claims for favor (usually poverty or loyalty). The secretary then adjusted and standardized the annual wages for nearly all of the 204 servants listed, while ensuring continued payments for the relatives and heirs of 41 deceased employees.[73] Seeing their incomes reduced, many of Juana's former servants complained, and the matter remained unsettled for years. For his part, the Marquis of Denia reminded Philip II that God held him accountable for rewarding the queen's servants, and suggested that the matter might even impact Juana's salvation.[74] Interceding on behalf of the Denias, Princess Juana argued that the emperor should reward and maintain their loyalty.[75]

Notwithstanding their complaints about reduced wages, members of Juana's household obtained important fringe benefits following her death. The emperor promised them and their relatives privileged access to future offices. Moreover, the queen's former servants who claimed poverty gained priority in the distribution of 10,000 ducats to benefit her soul from a special reserve in Simancas.[76] Members of Juana's household also received some of her erstwhile belongings. Before leaving Spain in 1554, Philip had promised the Marquis of Denia two of Juana's most valuable rings, the golden cross that Fernando had sent her, and 1,500 ducats that were supposedly in Juana's possession. Because hardly any coins were found among the queen's belongings, the marquis had to accept a collection of rings, images, silk, ornaments, retables, relics, tapestries, books, rosaries, glass, games, footwear, mirrors, combs, pins, folders, and boxes worth slightly less. He also appropriated the *Agnus Dei* that had protected him and Juana from lightening in 1550. Managing this distribution of the queen's possessions, Princess Juana authorized *camarero* Ribera to dispose of old and broken objects left in Juana's chambers as he wished,[77] and granted sacristan Pedro de Ayala the queen's chalices and silver to continue using them in her chapel.[78] Allowing for corporate continuity, Juana's successors would ultimately distribute the queen's servants, laden with her remaining possessions, among themselves.

As governess, Juana of Austria appropriated more than the "remainder" of her grandmother's belongings, including liturgical ornaments and modest clothing, that King Philip had assigned her.[79] To the dismay of household personnel, the princess kept her grandmother's rosaries, books of hours and song, religious images (including one with Saint Isabel holding a book alongside the Virgin and Child), retables, and portraits of Queen Isabel of Castile and Queen Catalina (Catherine) of England.[80] While Philip II labeled such items "trinkets and things of little value,"[81] Princess Juana apparently treasured their spiritual and dynastic meaning.

Memory and Authority

Informing municipal officials of Queen Juana's death, Juana of Austria requested obsequies for her grandmother throughout Spain. In some cities, local officials went beyond Princess Juana's instructions and also declared a period of mourning, prohibiting feasts and dances, until the celebration of funeral honors.[82] Princess Juana personally attended such services in the spacious Monastery of Saint Benedict of Valladolid. For the vespers on 26 May 1555, prelates, grandees, and gentlemen in the city accompanied Prince Philip's son, don Carlos, members of the royal councils, and the monastic orders from the royal palace to Saint Benedict. Leaving the monastery in unison, the municipal justice, councillors, and religious orders conducted a separate procession with crosses, blazons, and a pennant lowered to the ground. The following day, Benedictine father Vadrillo delivered a commemorative sermon on the theme, "Fear God, Honor Kings."[83] Other cities and towns informed Princess Juana that they had enacted similar rituals to memorialize the queen.[84]

The most detailed surviving account of obsequies for Juana describes those performed in Brussels on 16 and 17 September 1555. These honors, which Philip, in England at the time, requested postponed so that he could attend them, took place in the Church of Saint Gudule, where Juana had been proclaimed Queen of Castile following her mother's obsequies in 1505. Philip, who would become King of Spain upon his father's abdication one month later, led a mourning procession from the Palace of Coudenberg to Saint Gudule behind a horse with a female saddle bearing the crown. Although Philip filled part of the ceremonial role of Juana's successor, he was not proclaimed as such. Thus Philip acted as a member of the Habsburg family rather than as his grandmother's direct or immediate successor. Rather than enacting the transfer of power from one ruler to another, Juana's exequies in Brussels represented its continuity among the queen's offspring.

The funeral sermon in Saint Gudule, which Dominican friar Anthoine Hamet pronounced on 17 September, described Juana as a link between her illustrious parents and her numerous progeny. Hamet emphasized the queen's role as a wife and mother. Her husband's death in the flower of youth, according to Hamet, miraculously convinced Juana of the ephemeral nature of earthly things. After Philip's death, Hamet stated, the queen retired from the world as a chaste widow, aspiring to the heavenly kingdom and leaving her mundane possessions to Charles V. In this way, Juana shared "the royal dignity" conferred upon her "by the providence of God to administer and govern the world, and to execute the divine providence." Among the queen's numerous descendants, Hamet particularly praised her daughters, Leonor, Queen of France, as "Queen of Peace" and Mary of Hungary, regent of the Low Countries, for "virile courage, knowledge, prudence, and magnanimity." The Dominican also described Juana's grandsons, Philip and Maximilian, as "Christianity's expectation, support, and hope for its defense and exaltation. " Making several allusions to the impact of Protestant creeds, Hamet repeatedly emphasized that Juana's obsequies demonstrated belief in the "universal resurrection of the flesh" and the efficacy of prayer for saving souls of the deceased. Such rituals made Juana's pious death a victory for the Catholic cause.[85]

The archbishop of Sassari, don Martín de Ayala, delivered a similar funeral sermon for Queen Juana in his cathedral on the island of Sardinia. Like Hamet, Ayala praised Juana's humble retreat from worldly desires after the death of her husband. Devoting particular attention to Juana's offspring, the archbishop noted that God had selected them to rule most of Europe and to sustain the Catholic Church. "After God," Ayala declared, "we owe this lady [gratitude for] all of the benefit and sustenance that Christianity has received from her fruit. Thus, with great reason, we can apply the Holy Scripture's praise of the strong and manly woman to this lady, telling her, 'Many daughters have amassed all types of riches, above all the possession of great offspring, but you have surpassed all of them.'" Juana, who had sacrificed so much for her children, would have appreciated such an elegy.[86]

To Granada at Last

Juana's death solved a number of political problems for the Habsburgs. In particular, it promised a greater correspondence between titular rights and practical authority than possible under a queen who did not govern. In May 1555 Ruy Gómez de Silva, Philip's personal attendant, wrote secretary Francisco de Eraso that the queen's death "has assured certain matters including the succession of Naples and other things, which we suspect the King of the Romans [Fernando] would like."[87] Although Charles had named Philip King of Naples prior to his son's marriage to Mary Tudor, the aging emperor subsequently recalled that the title belonged to his own mother.[88] While removing this uncertainty over Naples, Juana's death also allowed Charles to renounce his other titles and possessions in favor of his son, Philip, and Fernando, his brother. Charles could finally retire to the Jeronimite monastery of Yuste in Extremadura, following the type of precedent that Juana had established and Philip II would later adopt in the palace and monastic complex of El Escorial.

Juana's death officially completed the transition to Habsburg rule in Spain. Charles V had commissioned funeral monuments for his parents as early as 1519. The effigies, designed by Bartolomé Ordóñez, reached Granada twenty years later. Yet these sculptures could hardly appear alongside those of Isabel and Fernando in the royal chapel while Juana remained alive. The ornate Renaissance figures therefore went to Granada's royal hospital. Meanwhile, the corpses of Queen Isabel, Prince Miguel, King Fernando, King Philippe I, Empress Isabel, Princess María Manuel, and Philip II's infant brothers, Fernando and Juan, accumulated in the crypt beneath the Catholic monarchs' monument. Juana's body remained in the Royal Monastery of Saint Claire in Tordesillas until Philip II made room in the chapel of Granada by ordering the bodies of his mother, wife, and brothers transferred to the Escorial.[89] Juana's inclusion in the royal chapel at Granada would bridge the dynastic gap between Queen Isabel, King Fernando, and the grandson they never knew.

The royal monastery and palace, San Lorenzo de El Escorial, constituted one of Philip II's most famous projects as king. Attentive to every detail at San Lorenzo, Philip made typically meticulous provisions for the royal mausoleum. Excluding his grandparents, Philippe and Juana, this notable monument presented Charles V, like David in Borja's spiritual treatise, as the founder of a new dynasty. As Borja had written: "Although David did not build the Lord's temple, it was nevertheless ordered and built out of the gold and wealth that David left."[90] Thus Philip, often compared with David's son, Solomon, envisioned his father as the founder of a new dynasty in Spain. Juana remained a problematic figure—fully allied with neither her parents nor her offspring.

Philip II expected his grandmother's body to find its final resting place alongside that of her husband. The king initially ordered grandees and prelates to transfer Juana's body to the royal chapel of Granada in the spring of 1568 but then deferred the act on account of the oncoming summer heat.[91] Finally, in the fall of 1573, Philip ordered the Duke of Infantado and the bishop of Salamanca to convey his grandmother's corpse to El Escorial.[92] After instructing the president of the royal council to oversee the removal of Juana's body from Saint Claire, the king suggested that an *alcalde* from the chancellery of Valladolid accompany the corpse to the Escorial. From San Lorenzo, other officers would escort Juana's body to Granada.[93]

Deposited in the royal chapel of Granada in 1574, Juana's corpse remained separate from her funeral sculpture, which lay, apparently forgotten, in the royal hospital of that same city. In 1591, however, Philip II ordered certain officials to search the royal hospital for the effigies of Juana and her husband, Philippe. After restoring the sculptures—specifically repairing four of Philippe's fingers, two of Juana's, and the head of Juana's patron saint, John the Baptist—these officials redesigned the royal chapel to accommodate the impressive effigies along-side those of Juana's parents. The funerary images of Philippe and Juana joined their corporal remains in the royal chapel twelve years later.[94]

Juana's effigy, restored and placed alongside those of her parents in 1603, pre-serves little trace of the queen's long-term conflicts with her servants. The re-clining figure, serenely bearing crown and scepter, appears fully capable of gov-erning herself, her household, and her realms. Molded puppies at her feet suggest a domestic tranquillity that Juana herself rarely, if ever, enjoyed. Nearly fifty years after her death, Juana recovered the royal dignity long separated from her physical person. Her body, nevertheless, remained distant from those of the Habsburg descendants whose succession she had assured.

Conclusions

In 1502 Juana "the Mad" carried the first relic of Saint Leocadia from the Benedictine abbey of Saint Gislen outside of Mons to the cathedral of her birthplace, Toledo. According to Miguel Hernández (1591), Juana donated the original bone, "as a most precious gift," to the Cathedral of Toledo. Perhaps learning about the saint from Juana, the queen's grandson Philip II and the Jesuit Francisco de Borja subsequently sent Hernández to Mons and sponsored the repatriation of Leocadia's other bones. The reception of all the relics in Toledo—finally achieved, after several false starts, in 1587—featured a triumphal arch representing four kings: Alfonso VI, who captured Toledo from the Muslims; Fernando III, who founded the Cathedral of Toledo; Philip II, Borja's protector; and Philip I (Philippe), who received credit for restoring the saint's first relic. Associating Philip II with his male namesake, the public festivities in 1587 elided Juana's historical role. The history of Leocadia's remains, written by a friar aware of Queen Juana's protagonism, testifies to the early, deliberate deformation of the historical record about her.[1]

Often written out of history, Juana "the Mad" has long inhabited the realm of legend. So why attempt to recover her historical circumstances? Why exchange a romantic heroine for a queen who never governed? Or, in other words: How does the study of a "mad queen" enhance our understanding of Spanish and European history? I would like to suggest that Juana's historical experience—to the extent that texts, documents, and other remains of her time preserve it—contributes to three areas of historiographical and methodological concern. First, my research examines changing concepts of monarchical authority and relationships between royal persons at the apogee of the Spanish empire. Second, it offers a practical inquiry into the nature of Renaissance queenship. Finally, it illuminates the dangers of applying the values of one age to another.

Previous scholars have examined the theory of a king's two bodies as a legalist device and a ceremonial principle. In the Spanish transition to Habsburg rule, I argue, the idea of a dual royal persona guided assertions and contestations of royal authority. Juana's separation from the kingdoms of Castile and Aragon began with her 1496 marriage to Philippe "the Handsome," whose powerful councillors limited Juana's financial resources and control over her own servants. Although somewhat typical for a bride overseas, Juana's political isolation continued when she became proprietary Queen of Castile. After the death of Isabel "the Catholic" in 1504, Philippe used his personal authority over Juana to claim possession of Castile, Leon, and Granada. Following Philippe's death in 1506, Juana's father asserted his own right to direct the young widow and her realms. Like Philippe, Fernando adopted the idea of corporate territories bound to a royal individual to justify governing Juana's lands and subjects as his personal duty. In 1518 Juana's son Charles attempted to do the same by emphasizing his filial obligations to the queen and, therefore, her realms.

Yet the theory of the monarch's two bodies, which encompassed corporate territories attached to a "natural ruler," could also justify resistance to authority. As we have seen, in 1520 delegates from thirteen cities declared themselves a "Holy Assembly" representing the corporate kingdom of Castile and attempted to "liberate" their queen. Although initially impressed by the Comuneros' declarations, Juana ultimately rejected their program. For one thing, the queen identified her kingdoms with the royal council and the great nobles as much as the would-be Cortes. Juana, furthermore, conceived of her realms in dynastic terms. By withholding support from the Comuneros, Juana affirmed the overriding corporate interests of the Habsburgs. However reluctantly, she sanctioned the de facto disjunction between her titular rights and actual authority. Nominally, the queen governed Naples, Sicily, Spain, and the Americas. In practice, she could not even control her domestic servants. This unusual alienation of authority from a proprietary ruler, although common for a queen, dramatically illustrates the potential separation, and therefore the existence, of the monarch's individual and corporate persons in early Habsburg Spain.

The concept of a sovereign's two bodies, which originated in Christ-centered kingship, retained important sacral dimensions in sixteenth-century Burgundy, Castile, and Aragon. Official oaths in Cortes, described as coronations and sacraments,[2] public worship, funeral rites, and even formal meals, displayed the sacred nature of rulership. The sovereign's two bodies provide an intellectual framework for interpreting these events as well as the behavior of a "mad queen." According to prevailing beliefs, a monarch considered unfit to govern must have offended God. The fundamental bond between Juana and her realms further meant that the sins of one could affect the other's salvation. Thus Juana's contemporaries invoked the divine will to explain as well as to justify her separation from the government.

Juana's inability or unwillingness to rule and consistent defense of her offspring also facilitated a shift toward a more corporate and familial, less territorial or individual, idea of royal authority in early Habsburg Spain. At the beginning of the sixteenth century the demand for a "natural," native ruler remained powerful in the Low Countries, Castile, and Aragon. The subjects of Isabel "the Catholic" and Philippe "the Handsome" overwhelmingly attached legitimate authority to their ruler's personal, physical presence. Itinerant rule, featuring "joyous" entries and other public acts, reinforced the ties between sovereigns, their lands, and their subjects. The succession of Juana and Philippe, the archdukes of Austria and dukes of Burgundy before they became the monarchs of Castile and Leon, followed by the regency of Fernando, King of Aragon, and the succession of Charles, another Duke of Burgundy, challenged this constitutional configuration. Juana's refusal to remarry and retirement to Tordesillas after 1509 facilitated the implantation of a more dynastic, less personal, form of rule in Castile. The legitimate queen's attitude toward her offspring left subjects like the Comuneros little choice other than to accept a "foreign," often absentee, king. Juana's support for her descendants enabled them to control much of Europe as kings, queens, and regents through incessant travel as well as the delegation (and division) of authority among themselves. Philip II would eventually establish an administrative center in Madrid—a decision that none of his predecessors would have considered. In the construction of a family mausoleum nearby at El Escorial, Philip II asserted a dynastic right rather than a territorial identification with the far-flung domains that he had inherited.

Juana's inability to govern herself, her household, and her realms provides further insight into the challenges facing sixteenth-century queens. The claim that Juana's relatives prevented her from governing "because she was a woman" appears far too simplistic. I suggest, rather, that a female body as the "head of state" provoked fear and instability unless balanced or checked by appropriate male authority. Juana's mother, Isabel, avoided this problem by marrying Fernando, the closest male heir to the throne of Castile. Although Juana attempted similar alliances, her husband, father, and son successively increased their authority at her expense. Other Habsburg women who exercised authority— including Marguerite of Austria, the Empress Isabel, Mary of Hungary, and Juana of Austria—only ruled as regents, appointed by and accountable to male kings. Queen Juana's proprietary rights and political independence compelled ambitious relatives to govern her.

Other heiresses of Juana's day, including Elizabeth of York and Anne of Brittany, also transmitted their legitimate rights to their husbands and offspring. Early sixteenth-century kings did their best to acquire the territories that women inherited by marrying them. The consolidation and centralization of power made it increasingly difficult for women to retain their proprietary rights and potential independence in the presence of acceptable male contenders. Henry VII forced the legitimate heiress to the English crown, Elizabeth of York, to marry him in 1485, and importuned Juana to the same effect in 1508. Similarly, Anne of Brittany had no choice other than to marry Charles VIII, whose administrators quickly seized control of her duchy.[3] After the death of her first husband, Anne could negotiate her marriage to Louis XII from a stronger position.[4] Juana, upon becoming a widow herself, successfully avoided a second marriage. One scholar's conclusion that the "political judgment" of Anne of Brittany "was impaired not only by divided loyalties but by the narrowness of her focus"[5] may also apply to Juana. While Juana's parents, husband, and offspring struggled to govern her, the queen chose to blame their offenses and her plight on her servants.

Like marriage, motherhood potentially restricted the proprietary queen. Juana's procreative success not only freed her of the obligation to rule Castile and Aragon, as Charles V argued—it deprived her of that very right. The Renaissance revival of classical models often degraded female capacities and/or reduced them to motherhood. Exceptional "manly" women could emerge in the absence or in the service of acceptable male alternatives. Renaissance queens who managed to rule, like Isabel of Castile or Elizabeth I of England, competed with other female aspirants to their respective thrones rather than male candidates with direct claims to them. Whether through chastity or conjugal fidelity, queens who managed to rule neutralized their female identities.

Even if Renaissance assumptions and political centralization complicated matters, heiresses had rarely, if ever, followed a clear path to political power. In addition to her spiritual models, Isabel of Hungary and Isabel of Portugal, Juana may have found a political model in Berenguela, a thirteenth-century proprietary Queen of Castile. According to the queen's collaborator, the archbishop of Toledo, Rodrigo Jimenez de Rada, in spite of her unquestionable right to rule, Berenguela, "taking refuge behind the walls of shame and modesty, above all the women in the world, did not wish to rule the kingdom."[6] Rather than ruling in her own right, Berenguela secured the succession of her son, Fernando, to the kingdoms of Castile and Leon.[7] Might Juana have pursued a similar strategy?

In 1939 the German sociologist Norbert Elias asserted that the study of historical actors often rested upon modern-day individualistic assumptions. According to Elias, a fuller understanding of past individuals required analysis of their social roles and dependencies on others. The position of king, Elias argued, constrained even the most "absolute" monarch, who necessarily subjected himself to an elaborate etiquette used to control his court and, by extension, his realms. Elias challenged historians of earlier periods to overcome their post-Enlightenment attachment to the autonomous individual.[8]

The application of modern values to premodern societies that Elias contested has also hindered attempts to recover Queen Juana's historical experience. Starting in the nineteenth century, historians have tended to interpret events in Juana's life largely according to the interests of their own times. Led by Antonio Rodríguez Villa, romantically inclined scholars fascinated by love, death, mourning, and madness overlooked political motives for Juana's famous attachment to her husband's corpse.[9] Eager to identify roots of a "Spanish nation" in the past, scholars such as Michael Prawdin depicted the queen as national figure and ignored evidence of her overriding dynastic, familial commitments.[10] The queen's deference to her father and refusal to support the Comuneros against her son may appear equally irrational from a modern perspective.[11] Finally, efforts to persuade Juana to confess a relationship with Satan before her death reveal sixteenth-century maladies poorly suited to twenty-first-century diagnoses. I do not argue that Juana's contemporaries considered her "sane" but rather that they depicted her "madness" based on shifting political interests. Madness, like gender, proved a flexible concept in the realm of sovereignty.

This study may disappoint readers eager to discover "whether or not Juana was *really* mad." The task becomes complicated by the fact that Renaissance authors from Desiderius Erasmus to Sebastian Brant to Pietro Martire d'Angleria denied the "madness" of madness itself—depicting folly as a necessary, pious, and even reasonable escape from social conventions and political responsibilities.[12] Did Juana seek such an escape? The historical record provides little, if any, information about the queen's individual psyche. Instead, it illuminates Juana's attachments to members of her family, conflicts with her servants, and religious concerns.[13] A "lack of health" allegedly prevented Juana from governing herself, her household, and her realms. The sources have pushed me to see Juana's "madness" as a product as well as a cause of conflict with attendants who supposedly served her. Servants' lack of respect for the queen ensured that she would not exercise royal authority. On the other hand, attendants may have refused to treat Juana like a queen precisely because she failed to act like one. Yet even if Juana cursed, swung a metal bar, threw a brick, or brandished a broom, her contemporaries appeared far more concerned about the queen's aberrant ways of eating, sleeping, dressing, and worshiping.

In spite of great efforts and even physical coercion Juana's servants never overcame her *recogimiento* or ascetic spirituality. The most popular ascetic manual of the sixteenth century, the *Abecedario espiritual* of Francisco de Osuna, cited Psalm 44 to describe "withdrawl of the senses into the innermost heart, where the king's daughter, a Catholic soul, has her glory," in an apparent reference to Juana's disdain for external luxury. Osuna further compared the *recogido* to a porcupine "reduced and withdrawn into himself, without concern for the external"[14]—a comparison that servants accustomed to the "prickly" queen would have appreciated.[15] In 1523 the Emperor Charles referred to his mother as "indisposed and *recogida*."[16] Twenty years later, the emperor's son, Prince Philip, and other nobles found the queen "in the manner of a Benedictine friar," concealing and mortifying her personal, female body.[17] In yet another reference to Juana's asceticism, the archbishop of Sassari, don Martín de Ayala, noted, "in life she wore the habit of Saint Francis that her mother wore in death."[18] Juana's piety, drawing upon the devotional practices of saintly queens and previous duchesses of Burgundy, went beyond that of her mother. Whereas Queen Isabel based her sacred rulership on external display as much as internal devotion, Juana's pious seclusion made her the first in a line of inaccessible, even invisible, Spanish Habsburgs.[19]

Queen Juana's decision to reside alongside the Claires of Tordesillas set a precedent that many of her descendants followed. One year after Juana's death, her son, Charles V, abdicated and retired to the monastery of Yuste in Extremadura, while her daughters, Leonor and Mary, entered convents in Spain. Juana's grandson, Philip II, built and frequented a monastic complex at El Escorial, while the queen's granddaughter and namesake, Princess Juana, founded a convent of discalced Claires in Madrid. Juana of Austria and her elder sister, the Empress María, subsequently resided in that convent. Habsburgs including Charles V, Philip II, Juana of Austria and the Empress María emulated the queen whose *recogimiento* had enabled them to rule.

No doubt Juana's voluntary and enforced inaccessibility proved her greatest liability as queen. The queen's seclusion during much of her lifetime has made her frustratingly elusive for historians, who find Juana's public, immortal person infinitely more accessible than her enigmatic, personal self. By setting Juana within the household around her, I have attempted to avoid creating an individual where the data are absent or misleading. On the other hand, precisely Juana's tendency to conceal her physical person leads to fresh evidence and a less scandalous, less romantic vision of the queen. This vision, rather than combating Juana's voluntary and forced confinement, acknowledges it.

The queen's fasts, vigils, and solitude may have entailed devotional practices as well as strategies to secure specific personal and political demands. As a young Duchess of Burgundy, Juana established relationships with observant female Franciscans and even obtained a papal bull to convert the convent of Bethlehem into a house of Poor Claires. Nevertheless, as in the case of the translation of the relics of Saint Leocadia, Juana's role has been effaced. Franciscan accounts published since 1501 entirely exclude the archduchess and barely mention the bull that she secured.[20] Nor do they note that Juana and her female attendants visited the cloister of discalced Claires outside of Bruges in early 1501 or the Claires of Rejas outside Madrid in 1502–3. Juana's preferred confessors, Andrés de Miranda, Pedro Romero de Ulloa, and Juan de Ávila, permitted her to pursue a discreet, secluded piety.

The piety that Juana initially developed in the Low Countries intensified upon the death of her mother in 1504 and her husband in 1506. Might Queen Isabel have foreseen her daughter's contemplative inclinations upon considering that Juana might be "unable or unwilling" to govern?[21] In any case, Juana first demanded solitude upon receiving reports of her mother's moribund condition in 1504 and remained secluded for months following Isabel's death.[22] Her rejection of any but the most humble female company also dates from that period.[23]

After Philippe's death, Juana again shunned royal councillors and municipal delegates who demanded a meeting with her.[24] Nevertheless, after the birth of her sixth child, Juana received the Franciscan companion of Francisco Jiménez de Cisneros, fray Francisco Ruíz, who wrote that Juana "always shows me much love" and declared "that she is better than ever."[25] Even in moments of seclusion, Juana received men known for their holiness.

On the other hand, political turmoil, which intensified pressures for royal visibility, also augmented Juana's conflicting desire for pious retreat. Ultimately, the queen may have directed attention to her deceased husband in an attempt to reconcile competing dynastic and devotional interests. The Carthusians who accompanied Juana with her husband's coffin in 1506 and 1507 perhaps helped her harmonize the competing demands of ascetic withdrawal and royal display. By directing attention to the corpse of her deceased spouse, Juana publicized his status as king of Castile, Leon, and Granada in order to secure the inheritance of their eldest son, Charles. The queen's notorious nocturnal pilgrimages enabled her to combine public demands for royal display with her personal desire for seclusion. In compliance with the Carthusian rule, as discussed in chapter 3, Juana excluded nonroyal women from the presence of the monks. Rather than being dominated by necrophilic jealousy, the queen simply respected Carthusian norms. Once fray Pedro Romero and his followers returned to their monastery in Burgos, Juana had no compunction about depositing Philippe's remains with the female Claires of Tordesillas.

In fact, Juana exercised a measure of authority before the abbess and nuns of the Royal Monastery of Saint Claire in Tordesillas. As seen in chapter 4, the queen made donations to the convent for particular holidays and intervened in renovations planned for the principal chapel. She also maintained from three to six friars from Ávila's Monastery of Saint Francis in Saint Claire, where they prayed for her husband's soul from 1509 through 1523.[26] With the same monastery's guardian, fray Juan de Ávila,[27] and his companion, before 1514 the number of monks from Saint Francis of Ávila in Tordesillas reached eight, more than one-third of the twenty-three friars pertaining to that monastery, at least based on its composition in 1494.[28]

How did these Franciscans live? Thanks to the historian José García Oro, we know that in 1494 the friars of Saint Francis of Ávila solicited permission from their general vicar and provincial (the same Francisco Jiménez de Cisneros) to reform their monastery beneath the observant rule.[29] The early introduction of religious reform in Juan de Ávila's subsequent monastery indicates that an observant friar likely versed in *recogimiento* directed the queen's spirituality until 1523. Interestingly enough, the bishop of Ávila, fray Francisco Ruiz, who had always received "much love" from the queen, also had financed a cloister in the Monastery of Saint Francis. Juana's ties to the small and devout monastery may have begun in April 1503, when Queen Isabel, with Juana in her court, gave the guardian of Saint Francis 15,000 mrs to offset the costs of a provincial chapter held there.[30]

The Franciscans of Avila remained important for Juana's descendants. Among Juan de Avila's successors as guardians numbered illustrious royal servants including fray Antonio de Guevara, bishop of Mondoñedo; fray Juan de Zumárraga, archbishop of Mexico; fray Sebastián de Arcualo, confessor of Madrid's Descalzas Reales, bishop of Mondoñedo and Osma; and fray Antonio Cardona, archbishop of Valencia.[31] In particular, fray Antonio de Guevara, chronicler and royal councillor, dedicated his book *Marcus Arelius with the Princes' Timepiece*, which Juana also possessed, to the Emperor Charles V. Purportedly referring to the Emperor Marcus Aurelius and his maternal inheritance, Guevara highlighted a noblewoman who piously retired from the world. According to an epithet, which the Franciscan appears to have invented, "she wished to remain chaste and to be confined 46 years, rather than to be free and to marry the king of Trinacria." Uncannily, the elegy appears to allude to Juana.[32]

While constitutional thought and gender analysis allow us to approach the queen, we can only enter her household, observe its internal conflicts, and reach the royal person through her *recogimiento*. Spiritual withdrawal, however troubling in a proprietary monarch, may have helped Juana reconcile conflicting commitments to her parents, her husband, and their offspring. In fact, the tension between royal austerity and magnificence that initiated with Juana would persist through the sixteenth and seventeenth centuries.

Reluctant to be a heroine and unwilling to become a victim, Juana struggled to uphold her children's rights in Castile and Aragon. On their behalf, she relinquished her own claim to exercise royal authority in exchange for a reclusive, contemplative life. This sacrifice constituted Juana's most important and least-recognized effort to govern herself and thereby direct her realms. Long ruled by the members of her household, the "mad queen" showed little of the inclination to public life usually associated with royal authority. Endowed with unique capacities and burdened by uncommon constraints, Juana challenges assumptions governing our view of the past.

Chronology of Events

27 June 1506	Fernando agrees to leave Castile in the Treaty of Villafáfila
25 September 1506	Death of Philippe of Burgundy
18 December 1506	Juana annuls Philippe's grants
14 January 1507	Birth of Catalina (future Queen of Portugal) in Torquemada
28 August 1507	Juana and Fernando meet; Fernando assumes government
16 February 1509	Juana moves to Tordesillas
23 January 1516	Death of Fernando
4–11 November 1517	Leonor and Charles visit Tordesillas
29 August 1520	Comunero rebels reach Tordesillas
4 December 1520	Imperial troops retake Tordesillas
2 January 1525	Catalina leaves Tordesillas for Portugal
10–19 February 1532	Empress Isabel, Prince Philip, and the *infanta* María in Tordesillas
February–April 1534	Juana and her household in Tudela del Duero
December 1536	Charles V joins his family in Tordesillas
18–25 March 1537	Charles V and the Empress Isabel in Tordesillas
2–4 November 1543	Prince Philip in Tordesillas
19–20 October 1548	María and Maximilian, Kings of Bohemia, in Tordesillas
17–18 July 1550	María and Maximilian return to Tordesillas
May 1554	Francisco de Borja and Queen Juana meet three times
12 April 1555	Death of Queen Juana

Abbreviations

ACA	Archivo de la Corona de Aragón, Barcelona
ADM	Archivo Ducal de Medinaceli
ADN Lille	Archives du Département du Nord à Lille
AGRB	Archives Générales du Royaume à Bruxelles
Audience	Papiers d'Ètat et d'Audience
CC	Chambre des Comptes
Gachard	Papiers Gachard
AGS	Archivo General de Simancas
CC	Cámara de Castilla, Cédulas
CJH	Consejo y Juntas de Hacienda
CMC	Contaduría Mayor de Cuentas
CSR	Casa y Sitios Reales, Obras y Bosques
Estado	Estado, Castilla
GA	Guerra Antigua
PR	Patronato Real
AHN	Archivo Histórico Nacional, Madrid
Clero	Secular Regular
Diversos	Diversos Colecciones
Osuna	Papeles de Osuna
AHN Nobleza	Archivo Histórico Nacional, Sección Nobleza, Toledo
AMG	Archivo del Real Monasterio de Guadalupe (Cáceres)
AMS	Archivo Municipal de Sevilla
ANTT	Arquivo Nacional da Torre do Tombo, Lisbon
ASV	Archivio Segreto Vaticano, Rome
BFZ	Biblioteca Francisco de Zabálburu, Madrid
BL	British Library, London
BN Madrid	Biblioteca Nacional, Madrid
BN Marciana	Biblioteca Nazionale Marciana, Venice
BN Paris	Bibliothèque Nationale, Paris
BR Albert I	Bibliothèque Royale Albert I/Koninklijke Bibliotheek Albert I, Brussels
IVDJ	Instituto Valencia de Don Juan, Madrid
RAH	Real Academia de la História, Madrid

Notes

Preface

1. Michael O'Sullivan, "Mad Love," *Washington Post*, 20 September 2002, WE29.
2. Richard Dyer, "The Posthumous Passion of Juana la Loca," *Boston Sunday Globe* (3 August 2003), N3.
3. In their day such representations of Queen Isabel served to vindicate the rights of another female monarch, Isabel II. Carlos Reyero, *La pintura de historia en España. Esplendor de un género en el siglo XIX* (Madrid: Ediciones Cátedra, 1989), 142, 181. See also Carlos Reyero, *Imagen histórica de España (1850–1900)* (Madrid: Espasa-Calpe, 1987), 238. José Luis Díez, *La pintura de historia del siglo XIX en España* (Madrid: Museo del Prado, 1992), 85.
4. Díez, *La pintura de historia*, 310.

Introduction

1. *Letters, Despatches, and State Papers Relating to the Negotiations between England and Spain*, ed. G. A. Bergenroth, suppl. to vols. 1 and 2 (London: Longmans, Green, Reader and Dyer, 1868), xxv.
2. A collection of L. P. Gachard's articles in the popular press, with many of his notes on the subject, remain in the Archives Générales du Royaume à Bruxelles: AGRB Gachard 615. See also Louis-Prosper Gachard, "Sur la question de Jeanne la folle," extract, *Bulletins de l'Académie Royale des Sciences, des Lettres et des Beaux-Arts de Belgique*, 2d ser., 27, no. 5 (1869); "Sur Jeanne la folle et la publication de M. Bergenroth," extract, *Bulletins de l'Académie Royale de Belgique*, 2d ser., 27, nos. 9 et 10 (1869).
3. Louis-Prosper Gachard, "Jeanne la folle et S. François de Borja" and "Les derniers moments de Jeanne la folle," extracts, *Bulletins de l'Académie Royale Belgique*, 2d ser., 29 (1870): 290–323, 389–409.
4. Antonio Rodríguez Villa, *La Reina doña Juana la loca: Estudio histórico* (Madrid: Librería de M. Murillo, 1892), 407, 410. By the same author, see also *Bosquejo biográfico de la Reina doña Juana* (Madrid: Sucesores de Rivadeneyra, 1874).
5. Constantin von Höfler, *Donna Juana, Königin von Leon, Castilien und Granada* (Vienna, 1885), 1.
6. Museo del Prado, Casón del Buen Retiro, *Catálogo de las pinturas del siglo XIX* (Madrid, 1985), 207–8, 253–54.
7. Louis Gallait, "Jeanne la folle," Musée des beaux-arts à Tournai.
8. Manuel Tamayo y Baus, *Doña Juana la loca: Opera en cuatro actos*, based on the

drama, *Locura de amor* by Manuel Tamayo y Baus, with music by Emilio Serrano (Madrid: Viuda e Hija de Fuentenebra, 1890).

9. Ludwig Pfandl, *Juana la loca: Su vida, su tiempo, su culpa,* trans. Felipe Villaverde (Madrid: Espasa-Calpe, 1945; orig. 1930), 107. Nicomedes Sanz y Ruiz de la Peña, *Doña Juana I de Castilla, la reina que enloqueció de amor* (Madrid: Biblioteca Nueva, 1942), 256.

10. Amarie Dénnis, *Seek the Darkness: The Story of Juana la Loca* (Madrid: Sucesores de Rivadeneyra, 1969).

11. Miguel Ángel Zalama, *Vida cotidiana y arte en el palacio de la Reina Juana I en Tordesillas* (Valladolid: Universidad de Valladolid, 2000), esp. 540–46.

12. Michael Prawdin, *The Mad Queen of Spain,* trans. Eden Paul and Cedar Paul (London: George Allen and Unwin, 1938).

13. Manuel Fernández Álvarez, *Juana la loca, 1479–1555* (Palencia: Diputación Provincial, 1994), 62; Isabel Altayó and Paloma Nogués, *Juana I: La reina cautiva* (Madrid: Silex, 1985), 11.

14. For the most recent biography incorporating fictional episodes, see José Luis Olaizola, *Juana la loca* (Barcelona: Editorial Planeta, 1996).

15. Georges Minois, *Anne de Bretagne* (Lille: Fayard, 1999), 12, citing Jacques Le Gof on Saint Louis.

16. Janos M. Bak, "Introduction: Coronation Studies—Past, Present, and Future," in *Coronations: Medieval and Early Modern Monarchic Ritual,* ed. Janos M. Bak (Berkeley: University of California Press, 1989), 6.

17. Ernst H. Kantorowicz, *The King's Two Bodies: A Study in Mediaeval Political Theology* (Princeton: Princeton University Press, 1957); Ralph E. Giesey, *The Royal Funeral Ceremony in Renaissance France* (Geneva: Libraire E. Droz, 1960). See also Ralph E. Giesey, *Cérémonial et puissance souveraine: France, XVe–XVIIe siècles* (Paris: Armand Colin, 1987), esp. 9–19.

18. José Antonio Maravall, *Estudios de historia del pensamiento español* (Madrid: Ediciones Cultura Hispánica, 1973), 1:105–10, 133–36, 191–212.

19. Teófilo F. Ruiz, "Unsacred Monarchy: The Kings of Castile in the Late Middle Ages," in *Rites of Power: Symbolism, Ritual, and Politics since the Middle Ages,* ed. Sean Wilentz (Philadelphia: University of Pennsylvania Press, 1985), 109–44. By the same author, see also "L'image du pouvoir à travers les sceaux de la monarchie castillane," in *Génesis medieval del Estado Moderno: Castilla y Navarra (1250–1370),* ed. Adeline Rucquoi (Valladolid: Ámbito Ediciones, 1987), 217–27. Such a perspective finds support in Adeline Rucquoi, "De los reyes que no son taumaturgos: Los fundamentos de la realeza e España," *Relaciones* 51 (1992): 54–100.

20. José Manuel Nieto Soria, *Fundamentos ideológicos del poder real en Castilla (siglos XIII–XVI)* (Madrid: Ediciones de la Universidad Complutense, 1988), 227–28, 246; Nieto Soria, *Ceremonias de la realeza: Propaganda y legitimación en la Castilla Trastámara* (Madrid: Editorial Nerea, 1993), 20–21, 72, 171–72, 218n16, 229n45. Against the contention that fourteenth-century rulers of Castile were anointed, see Peter Linehan, *History and the Historians of Medieval Spain* (Oxford: Clarendon Press, 1993), 440–42.

21. José Manuel Nieto Soria, "Del rey oculto al rey exhibido: Un síntoma de las transformaciones políticas en la Castilla bajomedieval," *Medievalismo* 2, no. 2 (1992): 5–27.

22. Rucquoi, "De los reyes que no son taumaturgos."

23. J. H. Elliott, "A Europe of Composite Monarchies," *Past & Present* 137 (November 1992): 48–71.

24. Maravall, *Estudios de Historia del Pensamiento Español*, 1:83, 198.
25. Ibid., 1:199.
26. Jan Beneyto Pérez, ed., *Glosa castellana al "Regimiento de Príncipes" de Egidio Romano* (Madrid: Instituto de Estudios Políticos, 1947), 1:28.
27. Ibid., 3:275–76.
28. Marc Reydellet, *La royauté dans la littérature latine de Sidoine Apollinaire à Isidore de Séville* (Roma: École française de Rome, 1981), 591–93.
29. *Las siete partidas del rey Alfonso el Sabio* (Madrid: La Real Academia de Historia, 1807), II, xiii, 25.
30. Ibid., law 26.
31. "Ordenacions fetes per lo molt alt senyor en Pere Terç rey Daragon sobre lo regiment de tots los officiales de la sua cort," in *Colección de documentos inéditos del archivo general de la corona de Aragón*, ed. Próspero de Bofanull y Mascaró (Barcelona: Monfort, 1850), 5:8.
32. Ibid., 5:8–9.
33. Ibid., 5:13, 27,168–71, 184, 267–68.
34. Francesc Eiximenis, *Regiment de la cosa pública*, ed. Daniel de Molins de Rei (Barcelona: Editorial Barcino, 1927), 80.
35. Claude de Seyssel, *The Monarchy of France*, trans. J. H. Hexter (New Haven: Yale University Press, 1981), 48–49.
36. Judith M. Richards, "'To Promote a Woman to Beare Rule': Talking of Queens in Mid-Tudor England," *Sixteenth Century Journal* 28, no. 1 (1997): 105.
37. Ibid., 106.
38. BN Paris, Manuscrit Espagnol 143, fols. 44–48v; *Epistolario de Pedro Mártir de Anglería*, ed. and trans. José López de Toro (Madrid: Imprenta Góngora, 1953), 10: epist. 279.
39. Juan de Lucena, *Opúsculos literarios de los siglos XIV a XVI, Sociedad de Bibliófilos españoles*, cited in Félix de Llanos y Torriglia, *Una consejera de Estado: Doña Beatriz Galindo "La Latina"* (Madrid: Editorial Reus, 1920), 28–30.
40. Carole Levin, *"The Heart and Stomach of a King": Elizabeth I and the Politics of Sex and Power* (Philadelphia: University of Pennsylvania Press, 1994), 121–23.
41. Ibid., 123.
42. Louise Olga Fradenburg, "Rethinking Queenship," in *Women and Sovereignty*, ed. Louise Olga Fradenburg (Edinburgh: Edinburgh University Press, 1992), 4.
43. Ian Maclean, *The Renaissance Notion of Woman* (Cambridge: Cambridge University Press, 1980), 62.
44. Marie Axton, *The Queen's Two Bodies: Drama and the Elizabethan Succession* (London: Royal Historical Society, 1977).
45. Charles T. Wood, "The First Two Queens Elizabeth, 1464–1503," in Fradenburg, *Women and Sovereignty*, 129.
46. Tarsicio de Azcona, *Juana de Castilla, mal llamada la Beltraneja, 1462–1530* (Madrid: Fundación Universitaria Española, 1998), 73–77.
47. Antonia Fraser, *Mary Queen of Scots* (New York: Delacorte Press, 1978).
48. Rita Costa Gomes, *The Making of a Court Society: Kings and Nobles in Late Medieval Portugal* (Cambridge: Cambridge University Press, 2003); Gregory Lubkin, *A Renaissance Court: Milan under Galeazzo Maria Sforza* (Berkeley: University of California Press,

1994); Monique Sommé, *Isabelle de Portugal, duchesse de Bourgogne, une femme au pouvoir au quinzième siècle* (Villeneuve d'Ascq: Presses Universitaires du Septentrion, 1998).

49. Christopher Coleman and David Starkey, eds., *Revolution Reassessed: Revisions in the History of Tudor Government and Administration* (Oxford: Clarendon Press, 1986), 6, 58; David Starkey, ed., *The English Court from the Wars of the Roses to the Civil War* (New York: Longman, 1987), 7–9.

50. C. A. J. Armstrong, "The Golden Age of Burgundy: Dukes That Outdid Kings," in *The Courts of Europe: Politics, Patronage and Royalty, 1400–1800*, ed. A. G. Dickens (London: Thames & Hudson, 1977), 58.

51. Jaime de Salazar y Acha, *La casa del rey de Castilla y León en la Edad Media* (Madrid: Centro de Estudios Políticos y Constitucionales, 2000), 46–47. Such a distinction between the household and the court would not have applied in late medieval Burgundy.

52. Ronald G. Asch and Adolf M. Birke, eds., *Princes, Patronage and the Nobility: The Court at the Beginning of the Modern Age, c. 1450–1650* (London: Oxford University Press, 1991), 9.

53. M. J. Rodríguez-Salgado, "The Court of Philip II of Spain," in Asch and Birke, *Princes, Patronage and the Nobility*, 207.

54. "Corte" (from the Latin cors, cortis, o cohors, cohortis), *Diccionario de la Lengua Española* (Madrid: Real Academia, 1992), 1:583, 584, definitions 1 and 18. See also *Las siete partidas*, II, ix, 27–28.

55. Colin Gordon, "*Histoire de la folie*: An Unknown Book by Michel Foucault," in *Rewriting the History of Madness: Studies in Foucault's "Histoire de la folie*," ed. Arthur Still and Irving Velody (New York: Routledge, 1992), 239.

56. Annie Saunier, "'Hors de sens et de mémoire': Une approche de la folie au travers de quelques actes judiciaires de la fin du XIIe à la fin du XIVe siècle," in *Recueil de travaux d'histoire médiévale offert à M. le Professeur Henri Dubois*, ed. Philippe Contamine, Thierry Dutour, and Bertrand Schnerb (Paris: Université de Paris-Sorbonne, 1993), 490.

57. Of twenty-five individuals examined by the Inquisition in New Spain, two were women who had allegedly fallen into *locura* upon the death of their husbands. María Cristina Sacristán, *Locura e Inquisición en Nueva España, 1571–1760* (Mexico City: Fondo de Cultura Económica, 1992), 29, 68–69, 71. For a case of "religious madness" in sixteenth-century Spain, see Sara T. Nalle, *Mad for God: Bartolomé Sánchez, the Secret Messiah of Cardenete* (Charlottesville: University Press of Virginia, 2001).

58. H. C. Erik Midelfort, *Mad Princes of Renaissance Germany* (Charlottesville: University Press of Virginia, 1994), 16. Midelfort's subsequent insights into the relationship between demonic possession and witchcraft appear particularly applicable to Juana's case. See H. C. Erik Midelfort, *A History of Madness in Sixteenth-Century Germany* (Stanford: Stanford University Press, 1999), 9, 14, 67–68.

59. Geoffrey Parker, *Philip II* (Chicago: Open Court, 1995), 87.

60. Alonso de Palencia, *Crónica de Enrique IV* (Madrid: Atlas, 1973), I, iii, 2, fol. 62; I, viii, 4, fol. 185. For an excellent description of Isabel's *recogimiento*, see *La "Crónica de Enrique IV" del Dr. Galíndez de Carvajal*, ed. Juan Torres Fontes (Murcia: Sucesores de Nogues, 1946), 78. Francesc Eiximenis, *Carro de las donas* (Valladolid: Juan de Villaquiran, 1542), chaps. 52 and 67. This Castilian translation incorporated information posterior to the original text.

61. According to Roger Collins, conciliar legislation obliged the widows of Visigoth kings to enter religious life after the death of their husbands. Roger Collins, "Queens-

Dowager and Queens-Regent in Tenth-Century León and Navarre," in *Medieval Queenship*, ed. John Carmi Parsons (New York: St. Martin's Press, 1993), 84. See also José Orlandis, *Estudios visigóticos III. El poder real y la sucesión al trono en la Monarquía visigoda* (Madrid: Consejo Superior de Investigaciones Científicas, 1962), 105–23, and Álvaro Fernández Córdova Miralles, *La corte de Isabel I. Ritos y ceremonias de una reina (1474–1504)* (Madrid: Dykinson, 2002), 43–44.

62. Nancy E. van Deusen, *Between the Sacred and the Worldly: The Institutional and Cultural Practice of Recogimiento in Colonial Lima* (Stanford: Stanford University Press, 2001), 17–26.

63. Francisco de Osuna, *Tercer Abecedario Espiritual* (Burgos: Juan de Junta, 1544), fols. 51–58; Francisco de Osuna, *Norte de los Estados* (Burgos: Juan de Junta, 1550), fols. 148–49.

64. Elena Botinas Montero, Julia Cabaleiro Manzanedo, and María Ángeles Durán Vinyeta, "Las Beguinas: Sabiduría y Autoridad Feminina," in *Las sabias mujeres*, ed. María del Mar Graña Cid (Madrid: Al-Mudayna, 1994), esp. 284–87.

65. José María Pou y Marti, *Visionarios, beguinos y fraticelos catalanes (siglos xiii–xv)* (Madrid: Colegio "Cardenal Cisneros," 1991), 123–24.

66. Luis de Miranda, *Vida de la Gloriosa Virgen Sancta Clara con la declaración de su primera y segunda regla y un memorial de las cosas más insignes y memorables que en esta ilustrísima y sagrada religión han sucedido* (Salamanca: La Viuda de Artus Taberniel, 1610), 168; Angela Muñoz Fernández, *Mujer y experiencia religiosa en el marco de la santidad medieval* (Madrid: Al-Mudayna, 1988), 20–56.

o n e : From Isabel "the Catholic" to Juana "the Mad"

1. Nicolas Round, *The Greatest Man Uncrowned: A Study of the Fall of Don Alvaro de Luna* (London: Tamesis Books, 1986).

2. Angus Mackay, "Ritual and Propaganda in Fifteenth-Century Castile," *Past & Present* 107 (May 1985): 3–43, esp. 17–21.

3. Hispanic Society of America, New York, ms. B 1484, Hernando Pulgar and Antonio Nebrija, *Chronica de los muy altos y esclarecidos reyes catholicos Don Fernando y Doña Ysabel*, 2v–3. Pulgar and Nebrija characteristically attributed Isabel's decision not to assume the throne to her understanding of divine providence. Another version of the same chronicle appears printed in *Crónicas de los reyes de Castilla*, ed. Don Cayetano Rosell, Biblioteca de Autores Españoles 3 (Madrid: Rivadeneyra, 1878), 242–524.

4. The final line reads "obtiman partem de genere umana." *La historiografía en verso en la época de los Reyes Católicos: Juan Barba y su "Consolatoria de Castilla,"* ed. Pedro M. Cátedra (Salamanca, 1989), 221.

5. Reydellet, *La royauté dans la littérature latine de Sidoine Apollinaire à Isidore de Séville*, esp. 591–93.

6. Pérez, *Glosa castellana al "Regimiento de Príncipes" de Egidio Romano*, vols. 1–3.

7. Garrett Mattingly, *Catherine of Aragon* (Boston: Little, Brown, 1941), 187–88. Mattingly provided an excellent analysis of *Instrucción de la Muger Christiana*, which Juan Luis Vives wrote for Catherine of Aragon. See also note 37.

8. William Thomas Walsh, *Isabella the Crusader* (New York: Sheed & Ward, 1935), 22–23, 26. Juana's association with Moorish servants, although an aspect of her cultural and dynastic inheritance, would also prove debilitating.

9. BN Madrid, ms. R 9717, Martín de Córdoba, *Jardín de las nobles donzellas*, prologue.
10. Ibid., III, i.
11. Ibid. In contrast to French royal authors, Burgundian aristocratic writers joined Martín de Córdoba in defending female succession when sanctioned by custom. Paul Henry Saenger, "The Education of Burgundian Princes, 1435–1490" (Ph.D. dissertation, University of Chicago, 1972), 106, 231–32.
12. Martín de Córdoba, *Jardín de las nobles donzellas*, I, iii.
13. Ibid., III, iv–vii. For a contrasting interpretation, see Elizabeth A. Lehfeldt, "Ruling Sexuality: The Political Legitimacy of Isabel of Castile," *Renaissance Quarterly* 53 (2000): 36–37.
14. Luis Suárez Fernández, *Los Reyes Católicos: La conquista del trono* (Madrid: Bialp, 1989).
15. Alonso de Palencia, *Crónica de Enrique IV* (Madrid: Atlas, 1975), 3:155.
16. Hernando del Pulgar, *Crónica de los Señores Reyes Católicos Don Fernando y Doña Isabel de Castilla y de Aragon*, in *Crónicas de los reyes de Castilla*, ed. Don Cayetano Rosell Biblioteca de Autores Español, vol. 3 (Madrid: Rivadeneyra, 1878), 255–57. Isabel's partisans could cite (or invent) other precedents for female succession. The *sala de los reyes* in the Alcázar of Segovia identified Isabel as the sixth proprietary queen in Castile and Leon, although the degree to which her predecessors (or Isabel herself) ruled on their own behalf, without dominant husbands or sons, remains uncertain. BN Paris, Manuscrit Espagnol 200, fol. 1, "Copia de los reyes de Castilla y León desde don Pelayo hasta doña Juana."
17. See Bernard F. Reilly, *The Kingdom of León-Castilla under Queen Urraca, 1109–1126* (Princeton: Princeton University Press, 1982), and Miriam Shadis, *Political Women in the High Middle Ages: Berenguela of Castile and Her Family* (New York: Palgrave Macmillan, 2003).
18. Pulgar, *Crónica*, 256.
19. Jerónimo Münzer, *Viaje por España* (1494), cited in Vicente Rodríguez Valencia, *Isabel la Católica en la opinión de Españoles y extranjeros* (Valladolid: Instituto "Isabel la Católica" de Historia Eclesiástica, 1970), 158–59.
20. *Continuación de la crónica de Pulgar*, in Don Cayetano Rosell, *Crónicas de los reyes de Castilla*, 523.
21. Córdoba, *Jardín de las nobles donzellas*, II, x. As a possible source for Córdoba's discussion of princely justice and use of the corporal metaphor, see Juan de Salisbury, *Policratus*, ed. Miguel Ángel Ladero (Madrid: Editora Nacional, 1984), IV, 8 and 10; V, 2 and 6.
22. Pulgar, *Crónica*, 359–60.
23. María Isabel del Val Valdivieso, "La política exterior de la monarquia castellano-aragonesa en la época de los Reyes Católicos," *Investigaciones Históricas* (Universidad de Valladolid) (1996): 11–27.
24. E. Haverkamp Bergmann, "Juan de Flandes y los Reyes Católicos," *Archivo Español de Arte* 25 (1952): 246.
25. For the role of Pedro González de Mendoza, Tomás de Torquemada, Gonzálo Jiménez de Cisneros, Alfonso de Espina, and Alfonso de Oropesa, see J. Meseguer Fernández, "El período Fundacional (1478–1517): Los hechos," in *História de la Inquisición en España y América*, ed. Joaquín Pérez Villanueva and Bartolomé Escandell Bonet (Madrid: Biblioteca de Autores Cristianos, 1984), 1:82, 286.

26. Although undated, the text belongs to the moment between requests for a stronger inquisition in 1477 and its promulgation several years later. Miranda's treatise also reflects the impact of the last large-scale heretical movement, that of the Cathars in southern France, persecuted by the founder of his order, Saint Dominic. Real Biblioteca de El Escorial, ms. A. IV.15, Fray Andrés de Miranda, *Declaración de la herejía y otras cosas perteneçientes a esta materia*, fol. 13.

27. Ibid., fols. 3v, 6.

28. Ibid., fol. 6.

29. Pedro Marcuello, *Cancionero*, ed. José Manuel Blecua (Zaragoza: Institución Fernando el Católico, 1987), 26 [fol. 5v, line 70–73].

30. Ibid., 168 [fol. 75v, lines 21–30, 31–35].

31. Ibid., 92 [fol. 37v, lines 24–30].

32. Ibid., 313 [fol. 148, lines 251–60].

33. Francesc Eiximenis, *Carro de las donas*, anonymous translation (Valladolid: Juan de Villaquirqn, 1552), fol. 15; *Lo libre de les dones*, ed. Frank Naccarato (Barcelona: Curial Edicions Catalanes, 1981; ms. orig. 1427), 1:28. Juana probably possessed an early Castilian manuscript version of this text.

34. Eiximenis, *Carro de las donas*, fol. 16; *Lo libre de les dones*, 1:31.

35. Eiximenis recommended a shift from permissiveness to discipline at the age of twelve rather than seven as did other authors. Philippe Ariès, *Centuries of Childhood: A Social History of Family Life*, trans. Robert Baldick (New York: Vintage Books, 1962).

36. Eiximenis, *Carro de las donas*, fol. 16; *Lo libre de les dones*, 1:32.

37. Eiximenis, *Lo libre de les dones*, 1:33–38. According to the 1542 version, young women should be taught to serve their families. Drawing on Juan Luis Vives, the anonymous translator argued that a young maiden might also learn some grammar if she showed the capacity. Eiximenis, *Carro de las donas*, fols. 16v–18. Vives had praised Juana's fluency in Latin, which she mastered by age seventeen. Juan Luis Vives, *Instrucción de la mujer cristiana* (Buenos Aires: Espasa-Calpe Argentina, S.A., 1948), 22–23, 26–27.

38. *Cuentas de Gonzalo de Baeza Tesorero de Isabel la Católica*, ed. Antonio de la Torre and E. A. de la Torre (Madrid: Consejo Superior de Investigaciones Científicas, 1955), 1:72.

39. Ibid., 1:24, 27, 29, 36, 44, 72, 73.

40. Ibid., 1:70, 151, 197; 2:67, 70, 94, 236. In Juana's chambers sugar was also used in honey and quince preserve. Ibid., 1:250, 428. Single entries mention Inés Suáres as Juana's *ama* and doña Teresa de Benavides, perhaps erring in the last name, as her *aya*. Ibid., 1:322, 376.

41. Ibid., 1:70, 108.

42. Ibid., 1:108.

43. Ibid., 1:111, 114.

44. By Holy Friday of 1491, the *infanta* was offering 2 ducats (750 mrs). At age thirteen, Juana received a string of beads of jasper and, as her family traveled to Barcelona, donated a dress ornament worth 3,000 mrs to the Monastery of San Jerónimo de la Murta. For her own use, Juana received four images of the Virgin. Ibid., 1:249, 376; 2:80, 95, 119.

45. Juana's instructor received the same salary as her elder sister's tutor, Pedro de Ampudia, although half that of their brother's instructor, Diego de Deza. Earlier in 1487 Fernando and Isabel had obtained a bull from Innocent VIII allowing them to elect their

children's teachers, even without permission from the friars' superiors. Antonio de la Torre, "Maestros de los hijos de los Reyes Católicos," *Hispania* 63 (1956): 256–66.

46. *Cuentas de Baeza,* 1:364; 2:260.

47. Ibid., 1:151.

48. Ibid., 1:300; Boecio, *La consolación de la filosofía* (Madrid: Sarpe, 1985).

49. Although Münster never saw Juana, he did manage to address a few lines of Latin to Prince Juan. A problem with his lower lip and tongue supposedly impeded the prince from responding. Jerónimo Münzer, "Itinerarium sive peregrinatio per Hispaniam, Franciam et Alemaniam," in *Viajes de extranjeros por España y Portugal,* ed. J. García Mercadal (Madrid: Aguilar, 1952), 406–7. Juana's preceptor had received 10,000 mrs for his wardrobe before meeting Münster, *Cuentas de Baeza,* 2:142, 153.

50. Queen Isabel summoned Latin scholar Beatriz Galindo to the court and sponsored her marriage to the royal secretary and artillery captain, Francisco Ramírez de Madrid. Galindo retired to conventual life after the deaths of her husband (1501) and Queen Isabel (1504). Llanos y Torriglia, *Una consejera de Estado,* 26–37.

51. *Cuentas de Baeza,* 1:197. The most recent study of "La Latina" provides little information about Isabel's court beyond noting that both Juana and Catalina (Catherine of Aragon) surpassed their mother in Latin learning. Cristina de Arteaga, *Beatriz Galindo "La Latina"* (Madrid: Espasa-Calpe, 1975), 31.

52. Manuel Serrano y Sanz, *Apuntes para una biblioteca de escritoras españolas* (Madrid: Sucesores de Rivadeneyra, 1903), 1:443.

53. AGS CMC 1a época, leg. 1213, Juana's inventory, 1555.

54. Alonso Ortiz, *Diálogo sobre la educación del Príncipe Don Juan, hijo de los Reyes Católicos,* trans. Giovanni María Bertini (Madrid: Studia Humanitatis, 1983). Ortiz used the fictional device of a dialogue between Queen Isabel and Cardinal Pedro González de Mendoza.

55. Ibid., 106–7.

56. Ibid., 161–65.

57. Gonzalo Fernández de Oviedo, *Libro de la cámara real del Príncipe Don Juan e oficios de su casa e serviçio ordinario* (Madrid: Sociedad de Bibliófilos Españoles, 1870), 182; Altayó and Nogués, *Juana I: La reina cautiva,* 22–23.

58. *Cuentas de Baeza,* 1:24, 112, 154.

59. Ibid., 1:24, 197.

60. Ibid., 1:248–49. Carmen Bernis, *Trajes y modas en la España de los Reyes Católicos* (Madrid: Instituto Diego Velázquez, 1978), 1:22.

61. *Cuentas de Baeza,* 1:250, 400.

62. Ibid., 1:249, 250; 2:239, 296.

63. Pulgar, *Crónica,* 426, 427, 437, 441, 499, 507.

64. Ibid., 505–6.

65. *Cuentas de Baeza,* 1:377.

66. Pulgar, *Crónica,* 510–11.

67. Ángel Alcalá and Jacobo Sanz, *Vida y muerte del Príncipe Don Juan* (Valladolid: Junta de Castilla y León, 1999), 38–40, 106; Pulgar, *Cróncia,* 507.

68. On the subject of Juan's martial instruction, see Alcalá and Sanz, *Vida y muerte del Príncipe Don Juan,* 106–10, 121.

69. *Cuentas de Baeza,* 1:249.

70. AGS CMC 1a época leg. 267, "Las cosas que Alonso de la Torre mercader dio en

el Real sobre Granada por mandamiento de la Reyna . . .," 1491–92; *Cuentas de Baeza,* 1:308, 400, 405; 2:48, 106, 141, 149.
71. Fernández de Oviedo, *Libro de la cámara real,* 97.
72. *Cuentas de Baeza,* 1:111, 197.
73. Ibid., 1:197, 249, 299, 377, 378; 2:29.
74. Ibid., 1:201.
75. Ibid., 2:142, 297.
76. *Las siete partidas,* II, ix, 1.
77. Ibid.
78. Fernández de Oviedo, *Libro de la cámara real,* 30.
79. Ibid., 31.
80. Ibid., 60.
81. Ibid., 180.
82. Ibid., 86, 106.
83. *Las siete partidas,* II, IX, xi, 186.
84. Fernández de Oviedo, *Libro de la cámara real,* 117–18.
85. Ibid., 14, 16, 104, 180, 182.
86. Ibid., 6, 18.
87. AGS Estado 26-164, "Memorial para oficiales de la casa de la Sra. Archiduquesa" [1496].
88. *Cuentas de Baeza,* 1:66, 69, 74, 75, 116, 117, 145, 159, 206, 259, 260, 304, 317, 326, 363, 385, 396.
89. Ibid., 1:309; 2:47, 95, 341.
90. Ibid., 1:266, 298; 2:121, 197, 199, 306, 313, 317.
91. Padilla listed doña Beatriz de Tavara, Countess of Camino [Caminas], doña Ana de Viamonte [Beaumont], doña María de Villegas, doña María de Aragon, doña Blanca Manrique, doña María Manuel, doña María Manrique, doña Francisca de Ayala, doña Aldara de Portugal, doña Beatriz de Bobadilla, and doña Angela de Villanova. Lorenzo de Padilla, "Crónica de Felipe I llamado el hermoso," in *Colección de documentos inéditos para la historia de España,* ed. Miguel Salvá and Pedro Sainz de Baranda (Madrid: Imprenta de la viuda de Calero, 1846), 8:35–36. Padilla may have omitted one name, since a normal entourage usually contained twelve ladies.
92. AGS Estado 26-194, "Memorial para oficiales de la casa de la sra archiduquesa" [1496].
93. Alcalá and Sanz, *Vida y muerte del Príncipe Don Juan,* 121–26.
94. Fernández de Oviedo, *Libro de la cámara real,* 117.
95. Alfonso de la Torre, "Visión delectable de la filosofía y artes liberales, metafísica y filosofía moral," in *Curiosidades Bibliograficas,* ed. Adolfo de Castro(Madrid: Biblioteca de Autores Españoles, 1950), 395.
96. *Continuación de la crónica de Pulgar,* 520–21.
97. In 1489 the King of Scotland also sought Juana as a bride. Although Queen Isabel generously rewarded his messenger, the marriage negotiations failed to progress. AGS PR 52-91, "Sobre el casamiento de la hija del Rey de España"; *Cuentas de Baeza,* 1:282.
98. By resisting French incursions into Flanders and Burgundy, Maximilian offered to help Fernando recover Cerdeña and Roussillon. Pulgar, *Crónica,* 480. Curiously enough, the Dauphin Charles of France had considered marriage to Marguerite of Austria as well as to Juana, before he finally wed Anne of Brittany. *Documentos sobre relaciones interna-*

cionales de los Reyes Católicos, ed. Antonio de la Torre (Barcelona: CSIC, 1951), 3: doc. 25 (20 March 1491).

99. AGS Estado I-ii nos. 360–63, "Minutas de casamientos del príncipe don Juan y de la Infanta doña Juana"; AGS PR 56:2, "Capitulaciones entre el emperador Maximiliano y los Reyes Católicos"; AGS PR 56:3, "Carta de libre y quito de la dote de madama Margarita," 18 November 1495; AGS PR 56:4, "Carta de libre y quito de la dote de la infanta Juana," 18 November 1495.

100. Houghton Library, Harvard University, *Coplas fechas sobre el casamiento de la hija del rey de España* (Burgos: Frederich Biel, 1496), fols. 1–iv.

101. One of these ambassadors, Juan de Salazar, carried a letter of credence from Philippe and Marguerite. BN Paris, Manuscrit Espagnol 318, no. 59, Philippe and Marguerite to Juan and Juana, 16 December 1495.

102. *Coplas fechas sobre el casamiento de la hija del rey de España* (Burgos: Friedrich Biel, 1496), fols. 1–iv.

103. Isabel took pains to reward these ambassadors with two mules and a horse, which would ease their return over difficult roads. *Cuentas de Baeza*, 2:318.

104. Louise Roblot-Delondre, *Portraits d'infantes, XVIe siècle. Étude iconographique* (Paris: Van Oest, 1913), 10–13, esp. fig. 6.

105. In Laredo, the queen faced and overcame a rebellion of Viscayan sailors' discontent with their pay. AGS CSR 10, f. 229, Petition of the heirs of Juan Martínez de Ibarra [undated]. Professor Miguel Ángel Ladero Quesada has recently analyzed the armada's dispatch, recorded in AGS Estado I-ii, no. 356, "Relación de las cosas que se ha proveydo para el armada que enbie o ha de yr con la señora archiduquesa . . .," 1495, in *La armada de Flandes* (Madrid: Real Academia de la Historia, 2003). Seeking a stronger force, Queen Isabel wrote to her *corregidores* (local representatives of the crown) requesting additional men, "well armed and ready for war," for the armada. AHN Nobleza, Frías 18/65, Queen Isabel to Diego López de Ayala, 26 June 1496. Isabel also secured protection for Juana's fleet on the English coast in case of necessity. AGS PR 52-50, Queen Isabel to the King of England, 18 August 1496. AGS PR 52-53, Queen Isabel to Doctor de Puebla, 20 August 1496. After the armada left Laredo on 22 August, Isabel expressed anxiety for news of her daughter and the fleet. AHN Nobleza, Frías 18/75, Queen Isabel to Diego López de Ayala, 16 September 1496.

106. *Coplas fechas sobre el casamiento*, fol. 3.

107. A posterior chronicle notes two skirmishes that may have provided some basis for the embellished poetic version. According to this chronicle, the Admiral of Castile sent seven vessels along the coast of Brittany, which captured two Briton ships before rejoining the fleet. Tensions between French and Spanish caravels erupted again in the port of Middleburg, where only the locals' pleas and the admiral's orders prevented a more serious altercation. Lorenzo de Padilla, "Crónica de Felipe I," 38–39.

108. Gonzalo Fernández de Oviedo y Valdés, *Batallas y quinquagenas* (Salamanca: Ediciones de la Diputación de Salamanca, 1989), 244; *Die Cronycke van Hollande Zeelandt en Vrieslant beghinnende vandains tiden tot die geboerte ons heren jhu voertgaende tot den iare 1557*, ed. Jan van Doesborch (Antwerpen: Lombaerde veste, 1530), fol. 417. Padilla also lists 15,000 men but only 120 ships. "Crónica de Felipe I," 37. Supplies from gunpowder to barrels of fresh water, along with precautions against events from fires to shipboard disputes to enemy attacks appear in AGS Estado I-ii, fol. 356, "Relación de los aparejos y gastos para la flota que ha de conducir a Flandes a doña Juana," 1496, transcribed in

Luis Suárez Fernández, *Política internacional de Isabel la Católica: Estudio y documentos* (Valladolid: Universidad de Valladolid, 1971), 4:569–89, doc. 155.

T W O : Competing Court Cultures and the French Menace, 1496–1502

1. Padilla, "Crónica de Felipe I," 38. According to Pietro Martire a caravel collided with the Genoese carrack and also sunk. *Epistolario de Pedro Mártir de Anglería*, 9: epist. 172.

2. Jerónimo Zurita, *Historia del Rey Don Hernando el Católico: De las empresas y ligas de Italia*, ed. Ángel Canellas López (Zaragoza: Departamento de Cultura y Educación, 1989), I, ii, 32, 294–95.

3. Informed of Juana's departure in early July, from Augsburg Philippe informed the Catholic sovereigns that he had sent their ambassador, Francisco de Rojas, and nobles "of my blood" to receive her. BN Madrid, ms. 18691 (ms. res. 226), no. 99, Philippe to Fernando and Isabel, 7 July 1496.

4. Rogelio Pérez Bustamante and José Manuel Claderón Ortega, *Felipe I* (Palencia: Diputación Provincial, 1995), 37–48; Christine Weightman, *Margaret of York: Duchess of Burgundy, 1446–1503* (New York: St. Martin's Press, 1989), 194–95.

5. Isabel Morant, *Discursos de la vida buena. matrimonio, mujer y sexualidad en la literatura humanista* (Madrid: Cátedra, 2002), 20, 213, and Rosa E. Ríos Lloret, *Germana de Foix. Una mujer, una reina, una corte* (Valencia: Biblioteca Valenciana, 2003), 54.

6. Olivier de la Marche, *Mémoires* (Paris: Librairie Renouard, 1888), 3:315.

7. Marie Thérèse Caron, *La noblesse dans le duche de Bourgogne, 1315–1477* (Lille: Presses Universitaires, 1987), 130–41; Marie Claude Gerbet, *La nobleza en la corona de Castilla: Sus estructuras sociales en Extremadura (1454–1516)*, trans. María Concepción Quintanilla Raso (Salamanca: Institución Cultural "El Brocense," 1989), 168, 211.

8. Padilla, "Crónica de Felipe I," 39.

9. In September 1496 Philippe informed the Count of Nassau, the Prince of Chimay, the Ravenstines, Furnes, Meluns, Mollenbaix, and Aymeries of Juana's imminent arrival, ordering them to receive her in Bruges. ADN Lille, B 2157 no. 70941, Payment for Gerard Vanden Dalm, messenger, 4 September 1496; ADN Lille B 2157, no. 70941, Receipt of Gerard Vanden Dalm, messenger , 4 September 1496.

10. ADN Lille B 3454, no. 120569, Juana's expenses, 3 December 1496.

11. The sovereigns of the Low Countries and Spain, unlike those of France and England, remained itinerant rulers in the fifteenth century. Weightman, *Margaret of York: Duchess of Burgundy, 1446–1503*, 72.

12. *Chroniques de Jean Molinet*, ed. Georges Doutrepont et Omer Jodogne (Brussels: Palais des Académies, 1937), 3:429. Doña María Manuel, Balduin of Burgundy, and Jean de Berghes may have supplemented Juana's personnel, for Queen Isabel had only assigned Juana six trumpets. AGS Estado 26-164, "Memorial para oficiales de la casa de la señora archiduquesa" [1496].

13. Local officials eager to promote trade with Spain subsequently drafted a letter to Fernando and Isabel, informing them of Antwerp's hospitality toward Juana. *Documentos sobre relaciones internacionales de los Reyes Católicos*, ed. Antonio de la Torre (Barcelona: CSIC, 1965), 5:1497, doc. 150.

14. Zurita, *Historia del Rey Don Hernando el Católico*, I, ii, 32, 296.

15. Padilla, "Crónica de Felipe I," 41. According to another source, three thousand

to nine thousand members of Juana's overland escort and six thousand to seven thousand members of her crew died that winter. *Chroniques de Jean Molinet,* 3:31, 432. Disturbed by reports of such events, Fernando and Isabel pressured the admiral to return to Castile in great haste. RAH Salazar A-9, fols. 221–24v, "Instrucciones al obispo de Catania, para la embajada en Flandes," 1496, transcribed in Suárez Fernández, *Política internacional de Isabel la Católica,* 4:636–42, doc. 118.

16. Upon the arrival of an ambassador from Castile, Juana expressed concern about her reputation in Isabel's court. AGS PR 52-112, The Subprior of Santa Cruz to Queen Isabel, 31 July 1498.

17. *Chroniques de Jean Molinet,* 3:429–30; AGRB Gachard 611, "Extract uit het Gebodboeck der Stad Antwerpen," 20 September 1496; Jean-Marie Cauchies, "Filps de Schone en Joanna van Castilie in de Kering van de Wereldgeschiedenis" (unpublished paper, 1998).

18. Padilla, "Crónica de Felipe I," 8:40.

19. AGS PR 56-6 and AGRB Gachard 614, fols. 21–22v, "Los archiduques Felipe y Juana ratifican todos los contratos hechos con ocasión de su matrimonio," 20 October 1496, transcribed in Suárez Fernandez, *Política internacional de Isabel la Católica,* 4:646–48, doc. 190. The official act of marriage incorporated a papal dispensation for the couple's degree of kinship obtained from Alexander VI in 1493.

20. *Dits die eccellente cronike van vlanderen,* ed. Willem Vorsterman (Antwerp, 1531), fol. 283v.

21. ADN Lille, B 3454, no. 120555, Philippe's expenses, 3 November 1496; ADN Lille, B 2156, no. 70834, "Décharge donnée par l'archduc au garde de ses joyaux," 6 November 1996.

22. Jean-Marie Cauchies has placed particular emphasis on the contractual nature of "joyous entries" in the Low Countries. Jean-Marie Cauchies, "La signification politique des entrées princières dans les Pays-Bas: Maximilien d'Autriche et Philippe le Beau," in *A la Cour de Bourgogne: Le duc, son entourage, son train,* ed. Jean-Marie Cauchies (Turnhout, Belgium: Brepols, 1998), 137–52.

23. Bernard Guenée, "Les entrées royales françaises de 1328 a 1515," in *Politique et histoire au Moyen Age* (Paris: CNRS, 1968), 7–29. Also, for the subsequent period, see John Landwehr, *Splendid Ceremonies: State Entries and Royal Funerals in the Low Countries, 1515–1791: A Bibliography* (Leiden: A. W. Sijthoff, 1971).

24. ADN Lille B 3455, no. 120672, Juana's expenses, 10 June 1497; ADN Lille B 3459, no. 121115, Juana's expenses, 15 May 1501.

25. Staatliche Museen, Berlin, Kupferstichkabinett, 78 D 5, December 1496. The following works discuss this manuscript: Wim Blockmans, "Le dialogue imaginaire entre princes et sujets: Les joyeuses entrées en Brabant en 1494 et en 1496," in *Fêtes et cérémonies aux XIVe–XVIe siècles,* Publication du Centre Européen d'Études Bourguignonnes (XIVe–XVIe siècles) 34 (Neuchâtel, 1994), 37–53; Max Hermann, *Forschungen zur Deutschen Theatergeschichte: Des Mittelalters und der Renaissance* (Berlin: Weidmannsche Buchhandlung, 1914), 364–409; and Paul Wescher, *Beschreibendes Verzeichnis der Miniaturen—Handschriften und Einzelblätter—des Kupferstichkabinetts der staatlichen Museen Berlin* (Leipzig: J. J. Weber, 1931), 179–81.

26. The term *ad miraculo* perhaps invoked the use of machines for the Annunciation or Assumption of the Virgin in fifteenth-century religious plays. N. D. Shergold, *A History of the Spanish Stage* (Oxford: Clarendon Press, 1967), 14, 19, 68, 76–78.

27. Berlin Kupferstichkabinett, 78 D 5, fol. 30v. Perhaps the miracle lay in Juana's temporary ability to unite municipal groups frequently at odds: the urban patriciate and the city's forty-eight craft guilds. For discussion of a different Brussels ceremony with a similar unifying function, see Margit Thøfner, "The Court in the City, the City in the Court: Denis van Alsloot's Depictions of the 1615 Brussels 'ommegang,'" *Nederlands Kunsthistorische Jaarboek* 49 (1998): 189.

28. Berlin Kupferstichkabinett, 78 D 5, fol. 33.

29. Ibid., fol. 32v.

30. Biblical, historical, and mythological figures represented included Tecuites who murdered Achimelech, the Pharaoh's daughter who married Solomon, Michelle who wed Saul, Rebecca betrothed to Isaac, Esther, Queen of Israel, Astyages, daughter of Mandanes, Deiphilis of Thebes, Yael who stabbed Sisera, Venus, Juno, and Pallas (Athena).

31. According to Padilla, the entry into Brussels preceded a joust, with one team of three men representing Marguerite of Austria and another team dueling for Juana. At the end of the festivities, Padilla claimed, only Monsieur de Ravenstein, tilting for Juana, remained mounted. Padilla, "Crónica de Felipe I," 8:42–42v.

32. *Dits die eccellente cronike van vlanderen*, ed. William Vosterman (Antwerp, 1531), fol. 283v. After his mother's death in 1482, the people of Ghent refused to grant Maximilian custody of young Philippe and held the boy hostage. Weightman, *Margaret of York*, 144.

33. *Dits die eccellente cronike van vlanderen*, fol. 284. For a contrasting account of Juana's entry into Ghent, see "Die ontfankenisse des hertoghen in die stadt van Gentte," in *Blijde Inkomst: Vier Vlaams-Bourgondische gedichten*, ed. G. Degroote (Amsterdam: Wereldbibliotheek, 1950), 13.

34. Stadsarchief te Gent, Chartres no. 796, Juana to the Council of Flanders, 14 March 1497. As if drawing upon García de Castrojeriz, *gouvernement* in this context meant primarily self-control.

35. The Spanish community of Bruges offered two or three fountains bubbling wine for public consumption. *Dits die eccellente cronike van vlanderen*, fol. 284v. "Hoe hertoghe Philips te Bruge ontfanghen werd," in Degroote, *Blijde Inkomst*, 18.

36. ADN Lille B 3457, nos. 120863 and 120865, Juana's expenses, 26 and 30 June 1499; B 3459, no. 121091, Juana's expenses, 17 April 1501.

37. ADN Lille, B 3459, no. 121104, Expenses for Juana and her children in Bruges, 3 May 1501.

38. AGS CMC 1a época, leg. 267 [unfoliated], "Nomina q[ue] Su Alteza fizo a sus oficiales," 17 September 1496; Padilla, "Crónica de Felipe I," 35–36. Padilla mistakenly suggested that the Prince of Chimay became Juana's first "caballero de honor" in 1496 or early 1497. In fact, Chimay did not receive this post until the death of his predecessor, Berghes, in 1499. Don Rodrigo Manrique remained alongside Juana as an ambassador, receiving 18 sous per day through 1498. Padilla, "Crónica de Felipe I," 43; AGRB Gachard 615, "Wages de la maison de l'archiduchesse Jeanne d'après les originaux à Paris," 14 May 1497; ADN Lille B 3456, no. 120744, Juana's wages, 3 May 1498. The following unpublished work promises particular attention to Juana's household, although to date its author has not wished to share a copy. Lieve Reynebeau, "Het hof van een vorstin. Johanna van Castilië in de Nederlanden (1496–1506)" (Undergraduate thesis, Universitat Gent, 1998).

39. ADN Lille B 3455, no. 120659, Wages for Juana's household [first recorded],

18 March 1497. Since female courtiers rarely received daily wages in the Low Countries, this type of source provides little information about them.

40. Sommé, *Isabelle de Portugal*, 859–60.
41. Suárez Fernández, *Política internacional de Isabel la Católica*, 4:636–42, doc. 188.
42. Ibid., 137–38.
43. RAH A-8, fols. 224–25v, "Minuta de carta de Antonio de Fonseca a los Reyes Católicos" [undated], transcribed in Suárez Fernández, *Política internacional de Isabel la Católica*, 4:657–61, doc. 195.
44. AGS Estado I-ii-566, fray Andrés de Miranda to the Archduchess Juana, 1 September 1498. For another the reaction of another Spaniard, Juan Gaytán, to Burgundian festivities, see Fernández de Oviedo, *Batallas y quinquagenas*, 244–245.
45. AGS PR 52-112, Subprior of Santa Cruz to Fernando and Isabel, s.f. [1498]; PR 52-116, Subprior of Santa Cruz to Fernando and Isabel, 15 January 1499, transcribed in Suárez Fernández, *Política Internacional de Isabel la Católica*, 5:279–80, 351–56, docs. 72 and 100.
46. *Chroniques de Jean Molinet*, 431.
47. Efforts to displace, if not replace, new brides' foreign personnel would later become standard policy with Habsburg consorts. María José del Rio Barredo, "Felipe II y la Configuración del sistema ceremonial de la Monarquía Católica," in *Felipe II (1598–1998): Europa y la Monarquía Católica*, ed. José Martínez Millán (Madrid: Editorial Parteluz, 1998), 2:677–703.
48. ADN Lille, B 2173, fols. 263–64v, payment assigned to "Dame Jehanne de Comines dame de Halewin et du dit Comines dame d'honneur de madame l'archiduchesse et pardevant gouvernesse de mondisr l'archiduc et dame d'honneur de madame la princesse de castille . . .," 9 October 1499.
49. ADN Lille B 3454, no. 120576 and B 3457, no. 120837, Juana's household expenses, 31 December 1496 and 31 February 1499; B 2169, fol. 31, Payment to Jehan de la Chappelle, Philippe's councillor and Juana's master accountant, 1 July 1500.
50. ADN Lille, B 3454, no. 120565, Philippe's wages, 22 November 1496; ADN Lille, B 3454, no. 120567, Juana's expenses, 2 December 1496.
51. ADN Lille, B 3454, no. 120567, Juana's expenses, 2 December 1496. Christophe de Barronze's Portuguese origins provide only one example of Pan-European influence in the Burgundian court. Suárez Fernández, *Política internacional de Isabel la Católica*, 4:145.
52. Marche, *Mémoires*, 4:1–80.
53. ADN Lille, B 3454, nos. 120567, 120569, 120570, Juana's expenses, 2–4 December 1496; ADN Lille, B 3455, nos. 126039–49, Juana's expenses, 2 January 1497–4 February 1497.
54. ADN Lille B 3455, no. 120659, Juana's wages, 18 March 1497.
55. Werner Paravincini, "The Court of the Dukes of Burgundy: A Model for Europe?" in Asch and Birke, *Princes, Patronage and the Nobility*, 87–89.
56. AGRB Audience 22 bis, fol. 1–14, "Etat de l'hôtel de Philippe le Bel duc de Bourgogne" [posterior copy], March 1497.
57. AGRB Audience 22 bis, fol. 1–14, "Etat de l'hôtel de Philippe le Bel duc de Bourgogne" [posterior copy], March 1497.
58. ADN Lille B 3455, no. 120658, Juana's expenses, 16 March 1497.
59. ADN Lille B 3455, no. 120659, Juana's wages, 18 March 1497.

60. ADN Lille B 2165, fols. 177v–178, B 2185, fol. 141, and B 2191, fol. 264v, Payments to "Martin de Monsicque/Monchique," 5 February 1498, 14 July 1504, and 19 July 1504.

61. ADN Lille B 2164, no. 71492 and B 2191, fols. 229v–230, Payments to "Michel Francs dit Grenade," 6 August 1498 and 2 December 1504.

62. ADN Lille B 2173, f. 242v and B 2185, f. 225v–226, Payments to silversmiths, November 1501 and May 1504.

63. AGRB Audience 22, fols. 194–205v, 206–10, "L'estat de madame l'archiduchesse" [1501].

64. Flemish or Burgundian individuals are identified either by records of long-term, even multigenerational, service to the duke or by telling features in their names, such as the diminutive "quin," which indicates probable Flemish origins. Sommé, *Isabelle de Portugal*, 424.

65. AGRB Audience 22, fols. 194–205v, "L'estat de l'ostel de nre. tres chiere et tres amee compaigne l'archiduchesse" [1501].

66. Sommé, *Isabelle de Portugal*, 398.

67. AGRB Audience 22, fol. 206.

68. ADN Lille B 2165, fols. 218–81v, B 2173, fols. 189v–190 and 193v, Philippe's gifts to Juana's ladies, 13 October 1499, 1 March 1501, and 17 September 1501.

69. Sommé, *Isabelle de Portugal*, 475; Alienor de Poitiers, "Les honneurs de la cour," in *Mémoires sur l'ancienne chevalerie*, ed. La Curne de Sainte-Palaye (Paris: Girard, 1826), 143–47.

70. Gutierre Gómez de Fuensalida, *Correspondencia*, published by the Duke of Berwick and of Alba (Madrid, 1907), 143–44.

71. AGS CMC 1a época 1544, "Provança de Diego de Ribera," 27 October 1523.

72. As foreign consorts, Eleanor of Castile, Isabel of Portugal, and Margaret of York all drew upon extensive independent revenues. John Carmi Parsons, *The Court and Household of Eleanor of Castile in 1290* (Toronto: Pontifical Institute of Medieval Studies, 1977), 21; Sommé, *Isabelle de Portugal*, 857–58; Weightman, *Margaret of York*, 41.

73. AGS Estado I-ii, nos. 360–63, "Minutas de Casamientos del príncipe don Juan y de la infanta doña Juana" [1495]; AGS PR 56-2, "Capitulaciones entre el Emperador Maximiliano y los Reyes Católicos sobre casamientos ... " [1495]; AGS PR 54-5, "Aprobación y Ratificación del Emperador Maximiliano del casamiento del Archiduque Don Felipe su hijo con la ynfanta doña Juana, hija de los Reyes Católicos," 3 January 1496; ADN Lille B 432, no. 17826, Double marriage treaty, confirmed by Philippe and Marguerite, 20 January 1496.

74. ADN Lille, B 436, no. 23963, Fernando and Isabel to Marguerite of Austria, 15 April 1497.

75. Suárez Fernández, *Política internacional de Isabel la Católica*, 4:636–42, doc. 188.

76. ACA Cancilleria Reg. 3614, fols. 92v–93v, Fernando and Isabel confirming pensions negotiated by Francisco de Rojas, 5 April 1497, transcribed in Torre, *Documentos sobre relaciones internacionales de los Reyes Católicos*, 5: doc. 85. See also Suárez Fernández, *Política internacional de Isabel la Católica*, 5: doc. 47.

77. AGRB Audience 22bis, 1-14, État de l'hôtel de Philippe le Bel, duc de Bourgogne, January–February 1497.

78. Gómez de Fuensalida, *Correspondencia*, 138.

79. ADN Lille B 433, no. 17878, "Projet des lettres d'assignation de douaire pour Jeanne de Castille . . .," undated [1497].

80. BN Madrid, ms. res. 226, no. 19, "Minuta en castellano de la carta que se da a la ylustríssima señora archiduquesa," undated [1497]. A messenger Juana sent to the *receveurs* of Bois la Duc, Turnhout, and Telemont in 1504 remains the only suggestion that she may have attempted to collect her projected dowry. AGRB Audience 14, no. 348, Juana's expenses, 31 August 1504.

81. ADN Lille B 12438–42, Comptes de Olivier du Buisson, 1496–1502.

82. Sommé, *Isabelle de Portugal*, 857–58; Weightman, *Margaret of York*, 41.

83. ADN Lille B 12441, 8ème compte de Olivier du Buisson, 1500.

84. AGRB CC 1611, Compte de Jacques du Machie, 23 August 1499; ADN Lille B 12440, 7ème compte de Olivier du Buisson, 1499. Nor did Juana receive moneys collected in the crown of Aragon to celebrate her marriage. ACA Cancilleria Reg. 3537, fols. 52v–53, King Fernando to treasurer Gabriel Sánchez, 6 April 1496.

85. AGRB Audience 22, fol. 192, "Declaracion en brief a quoy montera l'estat de monseigneur, de madame et de messires leurs enffans . . .," 1 August 1504.

86. ADN Lille B 2163, no. 71323, Philippe to his Receveur General, 10 May 1498.

87. ADN Lille B 2159, fol. 274v, " . . . bailée et delivrée comptant en ses mains pour en fair son plaisir dont elle ne beut icy autre declaration estre faicte"; ADN Lille B 2161, no. 71192, "Quittance par Jeanne de Castille d'une somme de 900 livres versée entre ses mains par le Receveur general des finances," 6 May 1497; ADN Lille B 2164, no. 71425, "Quitance par Jeanne de Castille d'une somme de 200 livres . . .," 12 May 1497; ADN Lille B 2161, no. 71793, "Quittance par Jeanne de Castille d'une somme de 2100 livres . . .," 18 November 1497.

88. ADN Lille B 2167, no. 71746, "Quittance par Jeanne de Castille d'une somme de 3100 livres . . .," 31 January 1498.

89. ADN Lille B 2165, fol. 166v, Payment to Laukin Sterke, 20 November 1499.

90. ADN Lille B 2164, no. 71424, "Quittance par Jeanne de Castille d'une somme de 200 livres . . .," 12 May 1498. In the spring of 1500, a tireless messenger followed the archduchess from Ghent to Bruges to Middelburg to Zoubourg, where he finally fulfilled Philippe's command by delivering 1,000 livres. ADN Lille B 2169, fol. 81, Payment to Jaques de Thensire, 6 May 1500.

91. AGS PR 52-116, Subprior of Santa Cruz to Fernando and Isabel, 15 January 1499, transcribed in Suárez Fernández, *Política internacional de Isabel la Católica*, 5:353–56, doc. 100.

92. AGS PR 52-116, Subprior of Santa Cruz to Fernando and Isabel, 15 January 1499.

93. Ibid.

94. Ibid.

95. ADN Lille B 3457, no. 120869, Juana's wages, 12 July 1500.

96. ADN Lille, B 2156, no. 70.833, "Décharge donnée par Philippe au garde de ses joyaux . . .," 31 December 1496.

97. ADN Lille B 3495, no. 123691, "Inventoire . . . de certains joyaulx jadiz apertens a feue Madame Marie, ducesse . . .," 21 July 1482 [with posterior marginal annotations indicating pieces that Juana inherited].

98. ADN Lille B 2165, fol. 220v, Payment to Jehan van Wartenberch, sellier demourant à Bruxelles, August 1498.

99. ADN Lille B 2165, fol. 234v, Payment to Pierre de Comnixlo, October 1499.

100. ADN Lille, B 2173, fols. 170–70v, Gifts for the new year, 1 January 1501.

101. ADN Lille B 3379, no. 113579, fol. 3, "Les parties de Gilleguin de Vers, tailleur des robes et barlet de chambre . . ., " 1497–1507.

102. Ibid. , fols. 6v–13.

103. Ibid., fols. 1–2v.

104. ADN Lille B 3379, no. 113576, Marguerite of Austria and Guillaume de Croy to Vincent de Mons, 11 October 1514. This documentation, compiled after Philippe's death, does not presuppose loyalty to him as archduke. Marguerite de Vers, Gilles's sole offspring and heir, married Vincent de Mons, Juana's cook, who passed into the household of her son, Charles, where he effectively recovered part of the money due to Gilles.

105. ADN Lille B 3379, no. 113579, fol. 2, "Second terme de Gilles de Vers," 10 July 1497.

106. ADN Lille B 2165, fol. 245v, Payment to George Vander Dorpe, marchand de draps de layne demourant a Malines, February 1499; AGRB Gachard 615, "Carton 1492–1499" from the Chambre de Comptes à Lille. The Burgundian court celebrated obsequies in Saint Jacques de Coudenberg during the last two days of January. AGRB Gachard 615, "Declaration des receveurs de finance . . .," 4 February 1498.

107. Zurita, *Historia del Rey don Hernando el Católico*, II, iii, 20, 72–73. Luis Suárez Fernández, *Política Internacional de Isabel la Católica*, 5:55.

108. AGS PR 56-175, Dean of Jaén to the Doctor de Puebla, 5 June 1498.

109. AGS PR 52-112, Subprior of Santa Cruz to Fernando and Isabel, August 1498.

110. AGS Estado I-ii, no. 366, fray Andrés de Miranda to the Archduchess Juana, 1 September 1498.

111. *Chroniques de Jean Molinet*, 3:450. All due precautions for mother and child, including a visit from a Lilleoise midwife, Ysabeau Hoen, preceded Juana's delivery in Brussels. ADN Lille B 2165, fol. 205, Payment of 18 livres to "une saige femme de la ville de Lille nomée Ysabeau," September 1499. AGRB Audience 22, fol. 172, "Extrait de premier compte de Jehan van Belle," September 1502 entry "a Ysabeau Hoen saige femme de madame l'archiducesse laquelle prend chacun jour 4 s de pencion que monte pour une année entiere 73 L."

112. ADN Lille B 2165, fols. 251, 255–57, Payments to Jean le Seur and Pierre de Warenghen, August 1499. These accounts also record expenses for the newborn. In addition to four new coverlets, for example, Leonor received four refurbished ones that Mary of Burgundy had used.

113. AGS Estado 496 [unfoliated], Sancho de Avedaño to Miguel Pérez de Almazán, 13 February 1499, partially transcribed in Rafael Domínguez Casas, *Arte y etiqueta de los Reyes Católicos: Artistas, residencias, jardines y bosques* (Madrid: Editorial Alpuerto, 1993), 628–29.

114. Eric Bousmar, "La place des hommes et des femmes dans les fêtes de cour Bourguignonnes (Philippe le Bon-Charles le Hardi)," in *Fêtes et cérémonies aux XIVe–XVIe siècles*, Publication du Centre Européen d'Études Bourguignonnes (XIVe-XVIe siècles), no. 34 (Neuchâtel, 1994), 123–43.

115. ADN Lille B 3457, no. 120838, Juana's expenses, 1 March 1499.

116. AGS PR 52-116, Tomás de Matienzo to Fernando and Isabel, 15 January 1499.

117. Hélène Adhémar, *Le Musée National du Louvre, Paris: Les Primitifs Flamands* I (Brussels: Centre National de Recherches "Primitifs flamands," 1961), 90–97. See also J. Rivière, "Réévaluation du mécénat de Philippe le Beau et de Marguerite d'Autriche en

matière de peinture," in *Activités artistiques et pouvoirs dans les États des ducs de Bourgogne et des Habsbourg et les régions voisines,* ed. Jean-Marie Cauchies (Bâle: Publication du Centre Européen d'Études Bourguignonnes, XIVe–XVIe s.), 25 (1985), 103–17; M. J. Onghena, *De Iconografie van Philips de Schone* (Brussels: Paleis der Academiën, 1959), 119.

118. Stads Archief Brussel no. VIII, fols. 350v–353v, "Copie vander bullen vander clausuren vanden Graubben Zusteren," 4 September 1501 [contemporary copy]; ASV A.A.Arm. I–XVIII 4173, fols. 138v–142, Alexander VI to the convent of Bethlehem, 4 September 1501 [seventeenth-century copy].

119. ADN Lille B 3457, no. 120865, Juana's expenses, 30 June 1499.

120. ADN Lille B 2159, fol. 160v, Payment to Pierre de Nareghien, January 1500.

121. ADN Lille B 2165, fol. 171v and B 2169, fols. 104v, 177v–178, Payments to Jaspard de Beaumaux and Phelippe Cocerton, 23 December 1499 and February 1500.

122. Philippe sent his messenger to the abbey of Anchin "a extreme diligence nuyt et jour sans espargner chevaulx ne guides" to deliver letters requiring "une anneau servant a l'alegement des femmes qui traveillent d'enfant" to be sent with similar haste. ADN Lille B 2169, fol. 58v, Payment to George de Dole, 7 February 1500.

123. ADN Lille B 2169, fol. 136v, Payment for two friars of the abbey of Anchin, February 1500. The archduchess must have found the ring efficacious, for she sent for it again the following year before giving birth to a daughter, christened Isabel. ADN Lille B 2173, fol. 178v, Payment to a monk from the abbey of Anchin, July 1501; AGRB Gachard 615, Payment to a monk from the abbey of Anchin, 20 July 1501.

124. Padilla, "Crónica de Felipe I," 63. For a detailed description of the spectacular illumination, see *Chroniques de Jean Molinet,* 3:469.

125. ADN Lille B 2169, fols. 62–63, Payments to messengers, 24 and 25 February 1500. The news traveled so fast that the town crier of Ypres, sixty-five kilometers from Ghent, proclaimed it that very night. In Ypres, as throughout Philippe's realms, the occasion entailed an illuminated general procession of thanksgiving, as well as public games and other festivities. AGRB Gachard 611, "Régistre des publications à Ypres, 1494 à 1524." The destruction by fire of the Ypres archive in 1914 renders Gachard's transcription invaluable.

126. RAH A-9, fols. 142–53, "Recibimiento que se fizo a la señora prinçesa de Castilla quando vino en Gante," 5 March [1500].

127. ADN Lille B 2169, Payment to Jehan Cole, March 1500; AGRB Gachard 615, "Acquits de la recette generale des finances, 1500–1504," 25 March 1500.

128. ADN Lille B 2169, fol. 153, Payment to Maistre Josse de Leenheede, Philippe's surgeon, 3 July 1500; fol. 154, Payment to Maistre Liberal Trevisan, 4 August 1500.

129. ADN Lille B 2169, fol. 147v, Payment to "une joueur de souplesse ytalienne," November 1500.

130. Gómez de Fuensalida, *Correspondencia,* 139.

131. Juana's account of her plight confirms John Carmi Parsons's understanding of intimate relations as the basis of power for female royal (or, in Juana's case, archducal) consorts. Juan Carmi Parsons, *Medieval Queenship* (New York: St. Martin's Press, 1993), 10.

132. Gómez de Fuensalida, *Correspondencia,* 139.

133. Ibid., 143.

134. Ibid., 166.

135. Ibid., 154.

136. AHN Osuna 1982-21/3, Prince Philippe to the Duke of Infantado, 22 November 1500; Gómez de Fuensalida, *Correspondencia*, 166–67.

137. Gómez de Fuensalida, *Correspondencia*, 157–58, 162.

138. Ibid., 169.

139. Ibid., 182.

140. Ibid., 181.

141. RAH A-9, fol. 132, Bishop of Córdoba Juan Rodríguez de Fonseca to Secretary Miguel Pérez de Almazán," 12 August 1501.

142. Ibid.

143. Gómez de Fuensalida, *Correspondencia*, 174–75.

144. ADN Lille B 2173, fol. 262, Payment to Charles de Lattre, 20 July 1501.

145. ADN Lille B 2173, fol. 146, Payment for Lyon Cousin, 23 October 1501.

146. Gómez de Fuensalida, *Correspondencia*, 193–94.

147. AGRB Audience 1082, fols. 47–50v, Traicte de Parys, 23 July 1498.

148. AGS PR 52-113 and 114, Sancho de Londoño to the Catholic monarchs, 17 August 1498, transcribed in Suárez Fernández, *Política Internacional de Isabel la Católica* (1972), 5: doc. 76, 290–92.

149. AGS PR 56-19, The bishop-elect of Astorga to Fernando and Isabel, 17 August 1498.

150. SABrussel no. VIII, fol. 348, "De par l'archiduc aux burgmaistiers, eschevins, et conseil de nre ville de Bruxelles."

151. Given the sea route's strategic importance, England had represented a logical third party in the Catholic monarchs' intended alliance against France. While the dowager Duchess of Burgundy, Margaret of York, encouraged Juana not to support the Tudors, Juana admitted that she very much wished to see her younger sister upon receiving reports that Catalina might cross the channel. BN Paris, Manuscrit Espagnole 318, no. 56, Henry VII to Fernando and Isabel, 15 May 1497; AGS PR 52-189, Henry VII to the Archduchess Juana, 8 April 1497; BN Madrid, ms. 18691/121, Juana to Dr. Puebla, 19 September 1498.

152. ADN Lille B 2173, fol. 125v, Letters to Philippe de Bourgogne, 9 August 1501.

153. ADN Lille B 2173, fol. 129v, Payments for couriers, 19 August 1501.

154. In a hospitable gesture, reciprocated many times during the journey through France, the archduke paid the expenses of these guests. ADN Lille B 2173, fol. 223, Payment to Loste du Chyne, 4 May 1501.

155. ADN Lille B 2173, fol. 247, Payment to Philippe Baudberghe, November 1501. Unsuspecting, Fonseca had already sent his groom with a mule for the archduke. ADN Lille B 2173, fol. 180v, Payment to the groom of the bishop of Córdoba, 24 August 1501.

156. ADN Lille B 2173, fol. 193, Payment to Jacques [*sic*] de Riviere, 31 August 1501.

157. ADN Lille B 17791 (Castille, Jeanne . . .), Philippe to the Chambre de Comptes at Lille, 16 October 1501. Philippe used the same phrase, "tres chière et puisante compaigne," referring to Juana in his letter to the Chambre de Comptes at Lille, 4 November 1501.

160. ADN Lille B 17991 (Castille, Jeanne . . .), "Parties mises en reste pour Maîstre Aubert Thibault," undated [fall 1501].

161. AGRB Audience 22, fol. 152, "Extrait de premier compte de Jehan van Belle," entry for February 1502, "a Messire Hughes de Melun Viconte de Gand, chevalier de l'ordre et chambellan de mondisr, lequel prend chacun an durant le boiaige despaignes de

pencion 1440 L"; ADN Lille B 2186, no. 73227, Gift of 200 livres to Hughes de Melun, 28 June 1504.

160. At the head of Juana's entourage, Madame de Hallewin, went from 30 to 33 sous per day, while Juana's humblest servants, Hostelet Hamel and Jehan de Poisepo, more than doubled their pay (from 18 deniers to 4 sous per day). ADN Lille B 3459, nos. 121046, 121065, 121084, 121103, 121120, 121144, 121160, and 121183, Juana's wages, 12 February 1501, 9 March 1501, 31 March 1501, 2 May 1501, 24 May 1501, 11 July 1501, 25 July 1501, and 7 September 1501; AGRB Audience 14, no. 354, Juana's wages, 23 May 1502.

161. ADN Lille B 3459, no. 121185, Juana's wages (33 livres 14 sous 6 deniers), 8 September 1501; ADN Lille B 3459, no. 121198, Juana's wages (61 livres 13 sous), 3 November 1501.

162. *Collection des voyages de souverains des Pays-Bas*, ed. Louis-Prosper Gachard (Brussels: F. Hayez, 1876), 1:128.

163. Miguel Hernández, *Vida, martirio y traslación de la gloriosa Virgen y Mártir Santa Leocadia* (Toledo: Pedro Rodríguez, 1591), 62v–71.

164. *Collection des voyages*, 1:129.

165. Ibid., 132–34.

166. "Reise des Erzherzogs Philipp nach Spanien 1501," in *Die Handschriften der k.k. Hofbibliothek in Wien, im Interesse der Geschichte, besonders der österreichische, verzeichnet und excerpirt*, ed. Joseph Chmel (Vienna: Gedruckt und im Verlage bey Carl Gerold, 1841), 2:561.

167. Ibid., 562.

168. Ibid., 565.

169. Pfandl, *Juana la Loca*, 65.

170. From *Le cérémonial françois*, cited in *Collection des voyages*, 1:136.

171. ADN Lille B 17791, Jerome Lauwerin to the Chambre de Comptes at Lille, 19 December 1501.

172. Padilla, "Crónica de Felipe I," 83. Although less detailed with respect to Juana's activities, firsthand Burgundian accounts corroborate Padilla's assertions. *Chroniques de Jean Molinet*, 3:502–3; *Collection des voyages*, 1:137; "Reise des Erzherzogs Philipp nach Spanien 1501," 568–69.

173. Padilla, "Crónica de Felipe I," 83; "Reise des Erzherzogs Philipp nach Spanien 1501," 568.

174. Alienor de Poitiers, "Les honneurs de la cour," 170.

175. *Collection des voyages*, 137.

176. ADN Lille B 17791 (Voyage de Philipe . . .), Monsieur de Maigny to the Chambre de Comptes at Lille, 19 December 1501.

177. *Collection des voyages*, 141.

178. ADN Lille B 17791, Jerome Lauwerin to the Chambre de Comptes at Lille, 19 December 1501.

179. Padilla, "Crónica de Felipe I, " 83.

180. "Reise des Erzherzogs Philipp nach Spanien 1501," 593–94.

181. Padilla, "Crónica de Felipe I," 83.

182. RAH K-33, fols. 13v–15, Authorization of the Catholic monarchs for their ambassadors to conclude the marriage of their granddaughter, Isabel, to the Prince of Navarre, Enrique, 20 September 1503.

183. *Collection des voyages,* 148.

184. "Reise des Erzherzogs Philipp nach Spanien 1501," 601.

185. *Collection des voyages,* 152.

186. "Reise des Erzherzogs Philipp nach Spanien 1501," 608.

187. The constable's reward for his trouble and expense constituted the long-anticipated conclusion of his marriage to Fernando's illegitimate daughter, doña Juana of Aragon, and the implicit legitimization of their children in Toledo that year.

188. "Reise des Erzherzogs Philipp nach Spanien 1501," 627, 629, 633, 637.

189. *Collection des voyages,* 169.

190. Ibid., 185, 193–94.

191. "Reise des Erzherzogs Philipp nach Spanien 1501," 639. For a detailed description of the Islamic population of Burgos, see "Reise des Erzherzogs Philipp nach Spanien 1501," 609–10. Lalaing commented on the Moorish inhabitants of Granada in *Collection des voyages,* 1:208.

192. The sacrament followed a lengthy sermon and inquiry into the Moor's reasons for converting, "in order to know if he adopted Christianity out of fear or out of love that he had in God." Satisfied that the man wished to live as a good and loyal Christian, the bishop baptized him Philippe. "Reise des Erzherzogs Philipp nach Spanien 1501," 639.

193. Ibid., 642.

194. Ten years after the expulsion of 1492, this account lists "une juif resident a madril . . . avec deux ses enffans." AGRB Audience 22, fol. 178, "Extrait de premier compte de Jehan van Belle," April 1502.

195. The summons did not mention Philippe. Archivo Municipal de Toledo, Archivo Secreto, caja 8, leg. 1, núm. 65/ AS 630-12, Catholic monarchs to the city of Toledo, 8 March 1502.

196. "Reise des Erzherzogs Philipp nach Spanien 1501," 651. According to Molinet, who appropriately termed such rituals of mutual deference "mistères," Fernando positioned himself in front of both Philippe and Juana. *Chroniques de Jean Molinet,* 3:515.

197. "Reise des Erzherzogs Philipp nach Spanien 1501," 654.

198. Padilla, "Crónica de Felipe I," 87.

199. *Collection des voyages,* 1:190.

200. The Burgundians took refuge in the Monastery of Saint Bernard, where Juana's *potagier,* Francequin, later died from wounds that he had received in the quarrel.

201. *Collection des voyages,* 195–96; Desiderius Erasmus, *Obras Escojidas,* trans. and ed. Lorenzo Ribera (Madrid: Aguilar, 1956), 227n1.

202. The archbishop died shortly after Fernando and Isabel had reluctantly granted him the bishopric of Coria. Padilla, "Crónica de Felipe I," 88.

203. ADN Lille B 17795 (voyage de Philippe . . .), Philippe Haneton to the Chambre de Comptes à Lille, 28 March 1502.

204. *Collection des voyages,* 1:238.

205. This crucial exception may explain the Cortes's ready confirmation of Juana as heiress in spite of the fact that its members had refused to accept her elder sister several years before, citing Salic law, which excluded women from the succession. Gerónimo de Blancas, *Coronaciones de los serenísimos reyes de Aragón* (Zaragoza: Diego Dormer, 1641), chap. 20, fols. 252–57. Blancas considered *juramentos* coronations, since they entailed taking possession of kingdoms.

206. *Collection des voyages,* 1:239–42.

207. AHN Nobleza, Frías 17/57–58, Philippe to the Marquis of Villena, 23 October and 21 November 1502.

208. AHN Nobleza, Frías 17/59, Fernando and Isabel to the Marquis of Villena, 7 December 1502.

209. *Collection des voyages*, 1:186.

210. ADN Lille, B 3460, nos. 121326, 121327, 121333, and 121334, Juana's wages and dispense, 30 September, 1, 6, and 7 October 1502; *Collection des voyages*, 1:219.

211. ADN Lille, B 3460, nos. 121384 and 121385, B 3461, nos. 121456 and 121458, Juana's wages and dispense, 9 December 1502 and 15–16 January 1503.

212. AGS PR 27-85, "Auténtica de las reliquias de los mártires que se trajeron de Roma para la Princesa Doña Juana con facultad para poderlas colocar en iglesias," 27 October 1500.

213. Francesco Gonzaga, *De origine Seraphicae Religionis Franciscanae* (Rome: Dominici Basae, 1587), 640. On Saint Ursula and the eleven thousand virgin martyrs, see Jacobus de Voragine, *The Golden Legend*, trans. William Granger Ryan (Princeton: Princeton University Press, 1993), 2:256–60.

THREE: Renaissance Passions and Juana's Madness

1. *Epistolario de Pedro Mártir de Anglería*, 10: epist. 250. The passage cited here figures in epist. 249 of the first Latin edition. Petrus Martir de Angleria, *Opus Epistolarum* (Alcalá de Henares: Michael de Aguia, 1530), fol. 59v; Alonso de Santa Cruz, *Crónica de los Reyes Católicos*, ed. Juan de Mata Carriazo (Seville: Escuela de Estudios Hispano-Americanos, 1951), 1:255–56.

2. Fray Antonio de Guevara, *Relox de príncipes*, ed. Emilio Blanco (Madrid: CONFRES, 1994), bk 1, chap. 36, fols. 281–83, 286–87.

3. Antonio de Guevara, *Epístolas familiares* (Madrid: Joseph Pino, 1732), 7–8.

4. Niccoli Machiavelli, *The Prince*, ed. Quentin Skinner and Russell Price (Cambridge: Cambridge University Press, 1988), 59.

5. Ibid., 59–60.

6. José Luis Bermejo Cabrero, "Amor y temor al rey: Evolución histórica de un tópico político," *Revista de Estudios Políticos* 192 (November–December 1973): 107–27.

7. Hilda Grasotti, "La ira regia en León y Castilla," *Cuadernos de Historia de España* 41–42 (1965): 32, 96.

8. *Las siete partidas*, IV, xxv, 10; Grasotti, "La ira regia en León y Castilla," 37, 92.

9. The *Siete partidas* describe subjects' duty to love and fear God as well as their king. They further depict fear, "as the guardian and doorman of love," reinforcing the reciprocal obligations that love would inspire between rulers and their subjects. According to this gloss, the subject should love God and the king partly to avoid inspiring their anger and losing their love. *Las siete partidas*, II, xii and xiii, esp. título xii, 8.

10. C. Stephen Jaeger, "L'amour des rois: Structure sociale d'une forme de sensibilité aristocratique," *Annales E.S.C.* 46 (1991), 549.

11. Donald A. Beecher and Massimo Ciavolella, eds., *Eros and Anteros: The Medical Traditions of Love in the Renaissance* (Toronto: Dovehouse Editions, 1992), foreword.

12. Mary Francis Wack, "From Mental Faculties to Magical Philters: The Entry of Magic into Academic Medical Writings on Lovesickness, 13th–17th Centuries," in

Beecher and Ciavolella, *Eros and Anteros*, 9–18; Maclean, *The Renaissance Notion of Woman*, 41–46.

13. Desiderius Erasmus, *The Praise of Folly* (London: Oxford University Press, 1945), 23.

14. No complete manuscript copy of the letters survives, and the first edition, published four years after Martire d'Angleria's death, contains numerous errors in dates and titles. Certain passages appear to have been "retouched" according to events that occurred after a letter's purported date, and entire letters seem to have been invented in order to fill gaps in time. Although Martire may have began revising his earlier letters in 1512, the most substantial changes and interpolations probably occurred after his death. Antonio Marín Ocete, *Pedro Mártir de Angleria y su Opus Epistolarum* (Granada: Impr. de Francisco Román, 1943), 79–88.

15. *Epistolario de Pedro Mártir de Anglería*, 9: epist. 221.

16. Ibid., epist. 222; Petrus Martir de Angleria, *Opus Epistolarum* (1530), fol. 53v, epist. 221.

17. Although long considered a privileged source of information about the Castilian court, Martire d'Angleria's letters contain signs of revision after their purported dates of composition. Such additions and adjustments entailed common humanist practice. According to John M. Najemy, Petrarch's collected letters included "fictitious" pieces addressed to contemporaries but not necessarily sent to them as well as epistles actually sent but later revised. John M. Najemy, *Between Friends: Discourses of Power and Desire in the Machiavelli-Vettori Letters of 1513–1515* (Princeton: Princeton University Press, 1993), 26. For Jerónimo Zurita's critical assessment of Pietro Martire de Angleria's literary epistles, see Rodríguez Villa, *La Reina Doña Juana la loca*, 22n1.

18. Petrus Martir de Angleria, *Opus Epistolarum* (1530).

19. ADN Lille B 18846 (no. 29611), Pietro Martire to Claude de Cilly, undated [1505].

20. This comment, like many others, appears designed to please Charles V (ca. 1530) rather than to encourage Philippe's advisers to intercede with the archduke on Martire's behalf (ca. 1502). *Epistolario de Pedro Mártir de Anglería*, 10: Epist. 268; Petrus Martir de Angleria, *Opus Epistolarum* (1530), epist. 267, fol. 65.

21. On 17 December, after parading alongside Fernando and Philippe, the illustrious captive reached Isabel and Juana. The archduchess, like her husband but unlike her parents, humbly refused to allow the duke to perform a sign of subjection by kissing her hand. Gonzalo Fernández de Oviedo y Valdés, *Batallas y quinquagenas*, 135–36.

22. Lorenzo Galíndez de Carvajal, "Anales Breves del reinado de los Reyes Católicos," in *Crónicas de los Reyes de Castilla*, ed. Cayetano Rosell (Madrid: Rivadeneyra, 1878), 3:553.

23. *Epistolario de Pedro Mártir de Anglería*, 10: epist. 253.

24. Evelyne Berriot-Salvadore, *Un corps, un destin: La femme dans la médecine de la Renaissance* (Paris: Honoré Champion, 1993), 25.

25. *Epistolario de Pedro Mártir de Anglería*, 10: epist. 253. The standard Spanish translation reads, "no caiga en locura." For the sake of accuracy in a crucial passage, I quote from the 1530 edition. Petrus Martir de Angleria, *Opus Epistolarum* (1530), fol. 60, epist. 152 [*sic* for 252].

26. One of the few Spaniards who had remained with Juana since 1496, Diego

Ramírez de Villaescusa, received a pension from Philippe's councillors. ADN Lille B 2168, no. 71.946, "Quittance by Jaques de Ramirez," 24 June 1499.

27. For an excellent analysis of this sermon, delivered upon Isabel's "last state occasion," see Peggy Liss, *Isabel the Queen: Life and Times* (Oxford: Oxford University Press, 1991), 338.

28. Fray Prudencio de Sandoval, *Historia de la vida y hechos del Emperador Carlos V* (Madrid: Biblioteca de Autores Españoles, 1955; orig. 1604 and 1606), I, xiii, 22. In honor of Fernando's birth, Philippe sent his wife a jewel with seven large pearls—a number replete with divine significance, recalling the Virgin's seven sorrows as well as her seven joys. ADN Lille B 2182, no. 73007, Philippe's declaration discharging the jewel, 16 June 1503.

29. Banning valets and pages from dining with the *chevalier* or the *maistres*, the ordinances attempted to control costs and to enforce status distinctions.

30. Hughes de Melun received 300 livres per month for his "plate" during the Spanish sojourn. ADN Lille B 2183, no. 73099, Quittance de Hughes de Melun, 20 May 1503; ADN Lille B 2183, no. 73098, Quittance de Hughes de Melun, 30 September 1503; ADN Lille B 2188, no. 73515, Quittance de Hughes de Melun, 2 March 1504; ADN Lille B 2188, no. 23568, Quittance de Hughes de Melun, 19 April 1504.

31. AGRB Audience 22, fols. 212–12v, "Ordonnance de Phillipe l'Beau par le maison de sa femme" [December 1502].

32. AHN Nobleza, Frías 62/139, Queen Isabel to the Count of Oropesa, 10 March 1503; Archivo Ducal de Medinaceli, Toledo, Sección histórica, leg. 245, no. 96, Queen Isabel to the Count of Feria, 10 March 1503.

33. ADN Lille B 3461, no. 121463, Juana's wages, 26 January 1503 [55 livres 5 sous 6 deniers]; AGRB Audience 13, no. 336p, 7 June 1503, Juana's wages, 7 June 1503 [49 livres 8 sous 6 deniers]; ADN Lille B 3461, no. 121469, Juana's wages, 16 December 1503 [48 livres 5 sous 6 deniers].

34. ADN Lille B 3460, no. 121298, Juana's wages, 7 September 1502.

35. AGS CMC 1a época, leg. 42, fols. 379–81, Salaries of Queen Isabel, 1 November 1503.

36. These figures should be taken roughly, given the difficulty in matching French and Spanish equivalents of the same names. Individuals' charges and positions within the hierarchy have also been considered in the attempt to identify them.

37. AGS CMC 1a época, leg. 42, fols. 379–81, Pay bills of Queen Isabel, 1 November 1503.

38. "Testamentum Ochoae Perez de Loyola, S. Ignatii Fratris," in *Fontes documentales de S. Ignatio de Loyola*, Monumenta Historica Societatis Iesu (Rome: Institutum Historicum Societatis Iesu, 1977), 115:186–91 (doc. 35). This testament, written in 1508, includes references to debts that the young Loyola incurred while serving Queen Juana, as well as the sum of 200 ducats due to him for services rendered, recovered four years after his death.

39. ADN Lille B 2185, fols. 90v–91, Payments to Jaques Marchant, who traveled, at Philippe's orders, "a extreme diligence sans espargnier guides ne chevaulx aller incessanment nuyt et jour" to convey *lettres closes* to Fernando, in Catalonia, and Isabel and Juana, at Alcalá, soliciting Juana's hasty return, and then returning, after consultations in Brussels, to find Fernando in Barcelona, Isabel at Segovia, and Juana at Medina del Campo, 19 June–15 December 1503.

40. RAH Salazar A-11, fols. 380v–381, Doctors Soto, Julián, and de la Reyna to Fernando, 20 June 1503.

41. A fourteenth-century manual for governing princes described friendship (a form of love) as a remedy for fear and sadness. Biblioteca Apostolica Vaticana, Codices Urbinates Latini 1007, De Regimine Principis, cpt. 32. Another treatise of the same period advised against fear in the treatment of melancholia. Biblioteca Apostolica Vaticana, Codices Urbinates Latini 234, Haly ben Abbas, Liber totius medicinae Stephano Antiocheno interprete, fol. 123.

42. The doctors, having discussed both women's illnesses, requested that Fernando burn their letter after reading it. Apparently, they feared the political implications of royal women's maladies. RAH Salazar A-11, fols. 380v–381, Doctors Soto, Julián, and de la Reyna to Fernando, 20 June 1503.

43. Padilla, "Crónica de Felipe el Hermoso," 114.

44. False alarms about Isabel's health since November 1502 may have convinced Juana that her mother's sickness entailed more of a political strategy than a fatal threat. The Venetian ambassador, among others, suspected that Isabel suffered from a fictitious malady. *I diarii di Marino Sanuto (1496–1533). Dall'autografo Marciano Ital. Cl. VII. Codd. 419–477* (Venice: Deputazione Veneta di Sotria Patri, 1879–1902), 4:662. After all, Juana herself had survived the birth of four children and a year-long separation from her spouse in spite of warnings that she would not. She had, moreover, seen her children overcome bouts of illness that inspired great fear in the Burgundian court. Gómez de Fuensalida, *Correspondencia*, 187.

45. ADN Lille B 3379, no. 113579, List of funds owed to Gilles de Vers.

46. RAH Salazar A-9, fol. 227, Hugo de Urries to Fernando, 6 September 1503.

47. Padilla, "Crónica de Felipe I," 114–15.

48. BL Ad. ms. 28572 fols. 43–44, Queen Isabel to Princess Juana, 12 September 1503. The British Library conserves two misdated nineteenth-century copies of this supposedly holograph letter. In fact, at that very moment, the Catholic sovereigns anticipated an attack upon their fortress of Salses, where Isabel had ordered troops two days before. Aware of Philippe's French sympathies and uncertain of her daughter's, Isabel apparently concealed information from Juana. AHN Nobleza, Frías 18/127, Queen Isabel to the Count of Oropesa, 10 September 1503.

49. In this description of Juana, Pietro Martire depicted both political disloyalty and uncivilized conduct. *Epistolario de Pedro Mártir de Anglería*, 10: epist. 268.

50. Gómez de Fuensalida, *Correspondencia*, 197.

51. Padilla, "Crónica de Felipe I," 114–15.

52. Gómez de Fuensalida, *Correspondencia*, 197. The document, a contemporary copy of the original letter preserved in the Archivo de los Duques de Alba, Madrid, provides no date or information about its signatories.

53. Padilla, "Crónica de Felipe I," 115.

54. Gómez de Fuensalida, *Correspondencia*, 197.

55. Ibid., 198. At the same time, the queen informed Fernando's secretary, Lope de Conchillos, that the events in Medina del Campo should not be told or written—a late example of "Isabeline censorship." In turn, the secretary stated only that the queen was "very tired and troubled by this lady princess, God forgive her," and that the recent incident "has given me worse nights than [the siege of] Salses." Conchillos also celebrated

the news of Fernando's departure for Castile. RAH Salazar A-9, fol. 219, Lope de Conchillos to Miguel Pérez de Almazán, 2 December 1503.

56. Gómez de Fuensalida, *Correspondencia*, 210–11. For a historiographical debate regarding the events at La Mota, see Antonio Prast, "El castillo de la Mota, de Medina del Campo. Intento de 'huída' de doña Juana la Loca," *Boletín de la Real Academia de la Historia* 101 (1932): 508–22, who argued that Flemish servants persuaded Juana to disobey her mother. Although one reviewer praised this study, Felix de Llanos y Torriglia argued against its argument by referring to the letter allegedly from Queen Isabel in the Fuensalida Correspondence, which claimed that Juana's servants had urged the princess to give up her rebellion. S[áinz] de R[obles], "Reseña: Prast, Antonio.—El Castillo de la Mota . . ." *Revista de la Biblioteca Archivo y Museo del Ayuntamiento de Madrid* 10, no. 38 (April 1933): 260–61; Felix de Llanos y Torriglia, "Sobre la fuga frustrada de doña Juana la Loca," *Boletín de la Real Academia de la Historia* 102 (1933): 97–114.

57. Gómez de Fuensalida, *Correspondencia*, 211.

58. Padilla, "Crónica de Felipe I ," 115–16. Fernando and Isabel had concluded a three-year treaty with Louis XII at the end of January. ADN Lille B 368, no. 121476, "Copie de la tréve de trois ans," 30 January 1504.

59. ADN Lille B 2185, fol. 138v–139, Payment to Jehan de Courteville, "escuier, conseillier, et maistre d'ostel," 2 December 1503–9 April 1504.

60. Anxious to discuss the ensuing situation with Courteville, Philippe sent him a special messenger from Ghent, with orders that Courteville hurry north even during Holy Week and Easter. ADN Lille B 2185, fol. 78, Payment to Toussain Paielle, 3 March 1504.

61. As late as 10 April, Philippe sent messengers to Juana at Laredo. ADN Lille B 2185, fol. 96, Payment to Jaques de Mazilles, 10 April 1504. Juana's extant lists of daily expenditures were dated in Laredo from 6 March through 25 April 1504. ADN Lille B 3461, nos. 121484–90, Juana's wages and dispense, 6 March–25 April 1504.

62. AGS, CMC 1a época 1544, "Provança de Diego de Ribera camarero de la Reyna," 27 October 1523. Judging from an account of sums owed for clothing, the ladies dismissed included doña Ana de Aragon, doña María Manuel, doña Beatriz [de Bobadilla], doña María Manrique, doña Francisca [de Ayala], doña Aldara [de Aragón], Violante [de Albion], Constance, Ysabel de Bilbao, and three chamberwomen. ADN Lille B 3379, no. 113579, fol. 20v, "Les parties des damoiselles despaigne qui ont servy madame," 1 April 1504. The Princess retained at least twelve female attendants, not including slaves. ADN Lille B 2186, no. 73243, Payment to filles d'honneur, mere des filles, and femmes de chambre, 28 June 1504; ADN Lille B 2188, no. 73579, Quittance of filles d'honneur, mere des filles, and femmes de chambre, 29 June 1504.

63. AGS, CMC 1a época 1544, "Provança de Diego de Ribera camarero de la Reyna," 27 October 1523.

64. ADN Lille B 2185 fol. 152, Payment of 10 livres "pour don que mondisr lui en a fait pour une fois pour Dieu et en aulmosne pour l'aidier a entretenir a l'escole a louvain ou il estudioit" to "frere Erasme Rotterdamense religieulx de l'ordre de sr Augustin," October 1504.

65. Erasmus, *Obras Escojidas*, 206–7, 223, 264. For an abbreviated version of the panegyric omitting the main references to Juana, see Erasmus, *The Education of a Christian Prince with the Panegyric for Archduke Philip of Austria*, ed. Lisa Jardine (Cambridge: Cambridge University Press, 1997), 120–45.

66. Gómez de Fuensalida, *Correspondencia*, 200–201.

67. Erasmus, *Obras Escojidas*, 232.

68. Ibid., 237, 243.

69. Ibid., 243.

70. *Epistolario de Pedro Mártir de Anglería*, 10: epist. 272; Petrus Martir de Angleria, *Opus Epistolarum* (1530), epist. 271, fols. 66–66v.

71. BL Ad. ms. 18852, fols. 25v–26, Book of Hours, undated 1500]; Bibliothèque Royale Albert I, Brussels, ms. 9126 (précieuse), fol. 2, Cantus Missae, undated [1505].

72. Gómez de Fuensalida, *Correspondencia*, 251, 256, 265, 295. Juana had taken advantage of one of Philippe's absences from Brussels to dismiss Moxica and order him back to Spain. When the news reached Philippe, he countermanded Juana's orders and attributed the queen's anger to her condition. Philippe later wrote Moxica, "as you know, when pregnant she sometimes becomes annoyed without cause." AGSCC Cédulas 11:20v, Philippe to Moxica, 30 July 1505.

73. ADN Lille B 2185, fol. 141, Payment to Martín de Monchicque, 14 July 1504; ADN Lille B 2191, fol. 264v, Payment to "Messire Martin de Monchique chevalier [!] maistre d'ostel de la Royne," 19 July–5 December 1504. In spite of Juana's lack of satisfaction with Moxica, the Catholic monarchs' three ambassadors in Burgundy endorsed him as the most appropriate messenger for such a delicate matter. Indeed, the ambassadors appeared to align themselves with Moxica and Philippe. Discounting Juana's authority, one of these ambassadors, don Juan Manuel, joined Philippe in Holland even after the princess requested that he remain with her. Gómez de Fuensalida, *Correspondencia*, 265.

74. Gómez de Fuensalida, *Correspondencia*, 297, 304–5, 308.

75. ADN Lille B 368, no. 17932, "Instructions données a Claude de Cilly envoyé en Espagne par l'archiduc Philippe" [1504].

76. Gómez de Fuensalida, *Correspondencia*, 267.

77. Payments to don Juan Manuel appear on a list of Philippe's "secret diplomatic expenses" for 1505–6. ADN Lille B 369, no. 17945, "État des dépenses diplomatiques secrétes fait par monseigneur de Veyre, en Espagne, pour les affaires de l'archiduc," 1505–6.

78. Gómez de Fuensalida, *Correspondencia*, 297.

79. Ibid., 297–301.

80. Ibid., 304.

81. The extradition of individuals serving Juana as well as Charles hints at a possible failed conspiracy to send Juana's eldest son to Spain. ADN Lille B 2185, fols. 163–63v, Payments to Juana's four slaves and others, November 1504. Juana's first chaplain and almoner received a separate gift of 50 livres; ADN Lille B 2185, fol. 186v and B 2188, no. 73587, Payment to Jehan Yñiguez de Galarreta and his quittance, 3 and 5 November 1504; ADN Lille B 18846, no. 29598, Philippe to his "conseiller et receveur de Berbesten en Zeelande" Adrien Andres, with instructions for transporting fifteen to sixteen of Juana's servants back to Spain, 6 November 1504. Subsequently, Philippe reduced the number deported to twelve. ADN Lille B 18846, no. 29600, Philippe to Adrien Andres, with further instructions, 12 December 1504; ADN Lille B 2189, no. 73658, Quittance by Lope de Luxarra, "maistre d'une cravelle," 5 January 1505; ADN Lille B 2193, no. 74106, Declaration by Adrien Andres, 5 March 1505; ADN Lille B 2191, fols. 374–76 and B 2193, no. 74106, Payment to Adrien Andres and his declaration, March 1505. One of the children's servants, Jehanne Courtoise (Juana Cortés), was also deported. ADN

Lille B 2193, no. 74144, Philipette de la Perriere appointed to replace Jehanne Courtoise, 1 March 1505. Upon their return to Castile, Juan Íñiguez de Galarreta continued to maintain the slaves. AGS CSR 7, fol. 575, King Fernando to Ochoa de Landa, regarding payment to Juan Íñiguez de Galarreta, 4 January 1506.

82. Gómez de Fuensalida, *Correspondencia*, 305.

83. ADN Lille B 2185, fol. 179v, B 2186, no. 73342, and B 2189, no. 73659, Payment to frere Thomas Salezart, "Jacopin Espaignart," and his quittance [bearing only the secretary's signature], 3 and 6 July 1504; ADN Lille B 2186, no. 73343, Payment of 50 L more to Jehan Íñiguez de Galarreta, 3 November 1504.

84. ADN Lille B 2185, fol. 91v, Payment to Jehan Coknaes for conveying letters to the Viscountess of Furnes, 2 July 1504.

85. ADN B 2185, fols. 246v–247, Payment to George Vandidouck, December 1504.

86. ADN Lille B 2185, fol. 53, Philippe's orders to don Alfonce, *infante* of Fez, 4 July 1504; ADN Lille B 2187, no. 73441, "Commission de 'serviteur domestique,'" 4 July 1504; ADN Lille B 2185, fol. 180, Gift to don Alfonce, *infante* of Fez, 24 July 1504, also recorded in ADN Lille B 2186, no. 73282, 24 July 1504, and ADN Lille B 2189, no. 73683, Quittance of don Alfonce, infante of Fez [signed only by the secretary], 13 August 1504; ADN Lille B 2187, no. 73401, Attestation of Pierre de Lannoy, Seigneur de Fresnoy.

87. ADN Lille B 368, no. 17932, "Instructions données a Claude de Cilly envoyé en Espagne par l'archiduc Philippe" [1504]; ADN Lille B 18846, no. 29599, Philippe to the bishop of Córdoba, 13 November 1504.

88. AGRB Audience 22, fol. 188-192, "Declaracion en brief a quoy montera l'estat de monseir, de madame, et de messires leurs enffans . . .," 1 August 1504.

89. Gómez de Fuensalida, *Correspondencia*, 304.

90. Ibid., 307–10.

91. Ibid., 310.

92. AGS PR 56-18, "La carta patente de la reyna . . .," 23 November 1504.

93. Philippe ordered funeral services in more than 160 churches, including cathedrals, abbeys, and priories. BR Albert I, mss. 7386-94 (cat. 4976), fol. 17, Obsequies for Queen Isabel, 14–15 January 1505.

94. Gómez de Fuensalida, *Correspondencia*, 317–18.

95. AGS PR 70-1b, Fernando to Philippe, 8 December 1504; AGS CC Cédulas 11-9, Philippe and Juana to Fernando, 24 December 1504.

96. A manuscript preserved in the neighboring Bibliothèque Royale depicts the ceremony's careful choreography, designed to announce a transfer of power from Isabel to Philippe. According to this manuscript, the procession from the Palace of Coudenberg to the Church of Saint Gudule would begin with guildsmen carrying up to four hundred torches displaying the archduke's coat of arms. Then Brussels officials, ranked hierarchically, would precede representatives of other cities and towns. Household officers of Philippe, Juana, and Charles, collegians and churchmen, financial officers, gentlemen, and pages would follow in order of ascending importance. Behind the Spanish coat of arms, a mule draped in floor-length gold would then transport a royal crown between the Duke of Cleves and the Prince of Chimay. A *Roi d'armes* carrying a white rod would precede two ambassadors in mourning next to Philippe, in hood and cloak, sustained by knights of the Golden Fleece and his principal squire, surrounded by archers. Such an elaborate display would formally link the Kingdom of Castile to Philippe, conferring the

royal dignity upon him. BR Albert I, mss. 15381–90 (cat. 4977), fols. 45–51, Obsequies designed for Queen Isabel [December 1504].

97. Ibid.

98. ADN Lille B 2191, fols. 282–282v, "Aux dames et damoiselles tant de l'ostel de la royne comme de celles qui estoient devers messires les enffans," January 1505; ADN Lille B 2193, no. 74099, Quittance signed by Jerome Lauwerin, 6 January 1505.

99. Philippe also requested large copies of the new arms, which he proudly sent Fernando and Maximilian. ADN Lille B 2191, fols. 370v–371, Payment to maistre Jacques Van Lathem, varlet de chambre et paintre du roy, 14 January 1505. Further expenses for the obsequies appear in ADN Lille B 2191, fols. 335v, 380–81, 385v–388v, 403–4.

100. BR Albert I, ms. 9126, Cantus Missae [1505], esp. fols. 1v–2, 58v, 72–76v.

101. BR Albert I, ms. 7386–94 (cat. 4976), fol. 17, Obsequies for Queen Isabel, 14–15 January 1505.

102. ADN Lille B 18846, no. 29611, "Memoire diplomatique, anonyme," 1505. Jean-Marie Cauchies, "Voyage d'Espagne et domaine princier: Les opérations financières de Philippe le Beau dans les Pays-Bas (1505)," in *Commerce, Finances et Société (Xie–XVIe siècles): Recueil de travaux d'histoire médiévale offert à M. le Professeur Henri Dubois*, ed. Philippe Contamine, Thierry Dutour, and Bertrand Schnerb. (Paris: Université de Paris-Sorbonne, 1993), 217–24.

103. If he were to die in the Low Countries or at sea, the king wished to be buried with his mother in Bruges's Church of Our Lady, unless he recovered the Duchy of Burgundy, in which case his body should rest with those of his ancestors in Dijon's Carthusian monastery. Otherwise, if Philippe perished in Spain, he designated Granada, where his remains could join those of Queen Isabel, as his final earthly destination. ADN Lille B 458, no. 17963 (museé 122, fols. 1–6v), Philippe's testament, 26 December 1504.

104. AGS PR 69-34, "La suma de los abtos que fisieron los procuradores de las cortes de las ciudades e villas destos reynos estando juntos en las cortes generales que se fizieron en la ciudad de Toro este año de 1505." For an excellent analysis of the Cortes of 1505, see Juan M. Carretero Zamora, *Cortes, monarquía, ciudades. Las cortes de Castilla a comienzos de la época moderna (1476–1515)* (Madrid: Siglo Veintiuno, 1988), 200–204. The Cortes of Toro remain best known for formalizing private law in Castile, including the system of *mayorazgo* (primogeniture) and regulations for matrimony. According to the ordinances of 1505, a married woman could not enter into or refrain from any legal contract without the license of her husband. Nor could she appear in court without his permission. "Ordenamiento de las Cortes de Toro de 1505," in *Cortes de los antiguos reinos de León y de Castilla*, ed. La Real Academia de la Historia (Madrid: Sucesores de Rivadeneyra, 1882), 194–219. The same material appears in AGS PR 70-2, "Las leyes hechas en las cortes de la ciudad de Toro" [1505]. Fernando may have sponsored the laws on *mayorazgo* in an attempt to win over nobles who might otherwise support Philippe. For an interpretation of the 1505 Cortes as a victory for the nobility, see Bartolomé Clavero, *Mayorazgo: Propiedad feudal en Castilla 1369–1836* (Madrid: Veintiuno Editores XXI, 1974), 128.

105. Padilla, "Cónica de Felipe I," 125–29. For a slightly different version of events, see Santa Cruz, *Crónica de los Reyes Católicos*, 2:7–8; and Gómez de Fuensalida, *Correspondencia*, 349–50, 352. Philippe provided food and clothing for Conchillos and one of his servants while imprisoned in the Castel of Vilvorde. ADN Lille B 2191, fol. 400v, Payment to Capitanie du Chastel de Vilvorde, 27 February 1505.

106. Gómez de Fuensalida, *Correspondencia*, 337. Anchieta had also served as school-

master to Leonor, Charles, and Isabel. From Philippe, the chaplain received a gift of 100 livres to pay his debts and return to Spain. ADN Lille B 2195, no. 74346, Quittance of Johannes de Anchieta, 26 September 1505.

107. Gómez de Fuensalida, *Correspondencia*, 333.

108. Ibid., 389.

109. Ibid., 342–43. According to a posterior account, the confrontation in Juana's chambers hinged on the issue of her authority. In this version, the queen relied on a device that she would later employ before the Cortes of Castile: "Do you know that I am Queen of Spain, and daughter of the Catholic king?" she allegedly asked. When the gentlemen affirmed her identity, Juana supposedly continued, "then how do you dare to provide the king and archduke with such scandalous, disreputable council?" Fresnoy supposedly replied that, although Juana was queen and a great monarch, she should let herself be served and governed, ruling her kingdoms in agreement with Philippe. Juana then struck Fresnoy, ostensibly to punish his disrespectful words. BN Madrid, ms. 1253, D. Joseph Micheli Márquez, *El Consexero del desengaño. Delineado de la Breve Vida de Don Phelipe el hermoso* (1649), 165v–166.

110. Gómez de Fuensalida, *Correspondencia*, 358–59. De Veyre's father-in-law, Fresnoy, along with the Prince of Chimay, had barred Castilians from visiting Juana.

111. Bethany Aram, "Juana 'the Mad''s Signature: The Problem of Invoking Royal Authority, 1505–1507," *Sixteenth Century Journal* 39, no. 2 (1998): 331–58. Comparison of the signature on the letter to de Veyre with forty-four previously unrecognized examples of Juana's signature revealed that Juana, in fact, never signed the declaration of loyalty to Philippe. Philippe's favorite after the death of Besançon, don Juan Manuel, probably designed the forgery.

112. Gómez de Fuensalida, *Correspondencia*, 371–74.

113. Ibid., 379, 388.

114. Biblioteca Nazionale di San Marco, ms. It. cl. VII, cod. 1129 (7452), Registrum Vincentii Quirino oratoris ad Serm. Philippe Ducem Burgundie, 1505–6, fols. 61–61v, partly transcribed in Constantin von Höfler, "Die Depeschen des Venetianischen Botschafters Vincenzo Quirino," *Archiv für Österreichische Geschicte* 66 (1885): 150.

115. ADN Lille B 2191, fols. 393–94, Payment to Jacques Hyssomie, 4 September 1505.

116. AHN Nobleza, Frías 18/142, Philippe to the Count of Oropesa, 15 September 1505; ADN Lille B 2191, fol. 225v, Payment to Jehan de Paris to carry letters announcing Juana's delivery, 15 September 1505; Höfler, "Die Depeschen," 158, 161. For the first time, Juana had required the services of a physician as well as a midwife during childbirth. ADN Lille B 2195, fol. 296v–297, Payment to "Maistre Henry Vellis conseillier et phisicien du roy," November 1505; ADN Lille B 2191, fol. 326v–327; and ADN Lille B 2192, no. 74037, Payment to Jeanne Mechielle, "sage femme demourant a Lille," 9 November 1505.

117. *Chroniques de Jean Molinet*, 2:561.

118. Philippe announced the conclusion of his war on Gueldres on 4 August 1505. AGS CC Cédulas 11: 27v, Philippe to the Grandes of Castile, 4 August 1505; Höfler, "Die Depeschen," 134.

119. ADN Lille B 3462, no. 121592, Juana's dispense, 10 December 1505.

120. The "well-loved" Walerande de Brederode received 100 livres, 20 aulnes of black velour, 20 aulnes of black satin, the title of Juana's lady of honor, and a pension of

500 livres per year during the voyage. ADN Lille B 2191, fols. 323v–324, Payment to Damoiselle Walerande de Brederode, "femme d'honneur de la royne," 12 November 1505; ADN Lille B 2192, no. 74036, Pension assigned to Wallerande de Brederode, Dame de Roe, 1 January 1506. Other ladies of honor, Cornelie de Montenak and Jehanne de Hallewin, dame de Brame, secured 250 livres each. ADN Lille B 2192, no. 74045, Payment to Damoiselle Cornelie de Montenak, 15 November 1505; ADN Lille B 2191, fol. 325v, Payment to Damoiselle Jehanne de Hallewin, Dame de Brayne, 24 November 1505; ADN Lille B 2194, no. 74260, Quittance for Jehanne de Hallewin, Dame de Brayne, 4 January 1506. Philippe's secretary promised girl of honor Walburghe d'Egmonde a total of 3,750 livres over three years to advance her marriage. ADN Lille B 2192, no. 74033, Payment to Damoiselle Walburghe d'Egmonde, 30 December 1505. Somewhat disrupting the female hierarchy, both Anseline Renier, lady of the chamber, and Ysabeau de la Hameyde, Countess of Ottingen, received 62 livres 10 sous. ADN Lille B 2192, no. 73997, Gift to Anseline Renier, lady of the chamber, 3 January 1506; ADN Lille B 2195, no. 74322, Quittance for Ysabeau de la Hameyde, 5 January 1506; ADN Lille B 2195, no. 74326, Quittance for Anceline Renier, 7 January 1506.

121. Townsend Miller, *The Castles and the Crown, Spain: 1451–1555* (New York: Coward-McCann, 1963), 246.

122. With the *Julienne*'s main sail thrown into the ocean and the ship catching fire several times, Philippe and his companions resigned themselves to death while Juana showed remarkable courage—no doubt the fruit of previous sea voyages. A poem preserved in the Royal Library commemorates the dangerous occasion. BR Albert I ms. 21552–69, fol. 127, "Les regretz du Roi Philipe"; Höfler, "Die Depeschen," 193–94. According to Sandoval, *Historia de la vida e hechos de Emperador Carlos V*, I, xxii, 27: "The queen then revealed her manly spirt, for when the king told her that they would die, she dressed richly and ladened herself with monies in order to be recognized and buried." French authors, in contrast, emphasized Juana's fear and desire to die with her husband. *Chroniques de Jean Molinet*, 2:563–64; "Deuxième Voyage de Phillipe le Beau En Espagne en 1506," in *Collectión des voyages des souverains des pays-bas*, ed. Louis-Prosper Gachard (Brussels: F. Hayez, 1876), 1:417.

123. AGRB Gachard 611, "Régistre des publications" from the Archive of Ypres, 1 February 1506.

124. Philippe also relinquished custody of the Duke of Suffolk, pretender to the English throne. Public Record Office, London, E 30, 701, Agreement between Henry VII and Philippe I, 9 February 1506.

125. Public Record Office, E 30, 1082, "Promise to observe the treaty of Alliance with Henry VII of England" [signed by both Philippe and Juana], 12 February 1506. This document appears quite worn and nearly illegible.

126. AGS PR 54-33, Princess of Wales (Catalina/Catherine of Aragon) to Queen Juana, 25 October 1507.

127. Gómez de Fuensalida, *Correspondencia*, 460–61.

128. AGRB Gachard 611, Transcriptions from ms. Cocquéau, vol. 2, Philippe's letters to Valenciennes, 18 February 1506 and 13 March 1506.

129. AGS PR 56-19, Capitulations between Fernando and de Veyre, 24 November 1505; ADN Lille B 369, no. 17962, Philippe's confirmation of the treaty of Salamanca, 10 December 1505. Since Juana refused to approve the Treaty of Salamanca, Philippe argued that it should not require her signature. AGS PR 56-22, Philippe to Fernando,

9 February 1506; AGS CC Cédulas 11: 50v-51, "Sobre la capitulación del soberano entre el Rey Católico y su yerno," 10 February 1506.

130. ADN Lille B 2191, fols. 250–50v, Payment to Jehan de Warenghen, 25 November 1505, cited in *Collection des voyages*, xxiv.

131. Briefe des Grafen Wolfgang zu Fürstemberg zur Geschichte der meerfarht des Königs Philipp von Castilien (1506). Mitgetheilt von Dr. K.H. frhrn. Roth von Schreckenstein, *Vorstand des F.F. Hauptarchivs in Donaueschingen* (Freiburg, 1868), cited in *Collection des voyages*, xxiv.

132. *Chroniques de Jean Molinet*, 2:561–62; Padilla, "Crónica de Felipe I," 130.

133. Ribera received a gift of 62 livres 10 sous as well as rights over two departments. ADN Lille B 2192, no. 74060, and B 2191, fol. 327v, Payment of Diego de Ribera, 6 November 1505; AGS CC Cédulas 11: 63, Philippe to Juana's *camarero*, Diego de Ribera, granting him control over the offices of the *carneceria* (butcher) and *regatoveria* (buyer), 2 January 1506; ADN Lille B 2192, no. 74044, Pension of 6 s per day assigned to Bertrand de Fromont, 7 January 1506.

134. AGS, CC Cédulas 11: 53, Philippe to Fernando, reporting arrival, 26 April 1506.

135. Höfler, "Die Depeschen," 206–14.

136. ADN Lille B 18826, no. 24221, Philibert Naturel to Philippe, 19 June 1506.

137. At the same time, Fernando cautioned, Juana should appear well treated to prevent public scandal. BFZ Altamira 222-21, "El memorial que se dio a Mosen de Veyre," 5 April 1506.

138. ADN Lille B 18825, no. 24186, Diego de Guevara to Philippe, 1 June 1506; ADN Lille B 18825, no. 24185, Diego de Guevara to Philippe, 1–2 June 1506.

139. Padilla, "Crónica de Felipe I," 141–44.

140. BFZ Altamira 17-136, Fernando to Gonzalo Fernández de Córdoba, 1 July 1506. Philippe simultaneously courted the "Grand Captain." ADN Lille B 18826, no. 24211, Philibert Naturel to Philippe, 19 June 1506.

141. ADN Lille B 18825, no. 24198, Diego de Guevara to Philippe, 9 June 1506; ADN Lille B 18846, nos. 29628 and 29629, Diego de Guevara to Philippe [copies], 9 June 1506; ADN Lille B 18826, no. 24211 and 18846, no. 29633 and 29634, Diego de Guevara to Philippe, 14 June 1506. This increasingly frequent correspondence reflects the building tension as Fernando and Philippe's camps approached each other.

142. AGS PR 56-28 and BN Madrid, ms. 17475, fol. 59, "Capitulación hecha en Villafáfila entre el Rey don Felipe y el Rey Católico," 27 June 1506; AGRB Audience 1078, fols. 82–86v, "Traité entre Phillippe le Beau et Fernando d'Aragon," 27 June 1506.

143. AGS PR 56-27 and BN Madrid, ms. 17475, fol. 55, "Provisión que en caso que la Reyna doña Juana se quisiere entremeter en la gobernación destos Reynos no lo consintirá," 27 June 1506. A French version of the "secret" agreement remains in ADN Lille B 18826, no. 24239, "Concordat entre Fernand et Philippe," 27 June 1506.

144. BN Madrid ms. 2803, Pedro de Alcoçer, *Relación de algunas cosas que pasaron en estos reinos después de la muerte de la reina católica Doña Isabel hasta que se acabaron las comunidades en la ciudad de Toledo*; Höfler, "Die Depeschen," 237.

145. Archivo Municipal de Burgos, Sección Histórica, no. 313, King Philippe to the city of Burgos, 29 June 1506.

146. AGS PR 56-31, "Nota del Rey Cathólico en que dice lo amistosa que fué la entrevista que tuvo con su hijo político Don Felipe en Renedo," 5 July 1506. Renedo lies thirteen kilometers north of Tudela del Duero.

147. Höfler, "Die Depeschen," 243.

148. *Continuación de la crónica de Pulgar*, 524.

149. Santa Cruz, *Crónica de los Reyes Católicos*, 2:57.

150. BN Madrid, ms. 13127, "De lo que sucedió en España en cosas particulares desde la venida de Felipe I hasta su muerte," fol. 192v–195; Alcoçer, *Relación de algunas cosas*, fol. 269; Zurita, *Historia del Rey Don Fernando*, VII, vii, 1059.

151. AHN Osuna 420:1(1), Testimony of the Count of Benavente, 18 August 1506.

152. According to an anonymous French chronicle, Philippe's "government and governors" had pushed Juana's jealousy "to the point of love madness [*la rage d'amours*], an excessive and inextinguishable fury, so that in three years the good queen had no more profit or repose than a woman damned or deranged." "Deuxième voyage de Phillipe le Beau En Espagne en 1506," in *Collection des voyages*, 415, 458–59.

153. Höfler, "Die Depeschen," 240–42.

154. AGS PR 69-41 (2), "Juramento o reconoçimiento por reyes legítimos a Doña Juana y a su marido," 12 July 1506.

155. ADN Lille B 857, no. 17971, Testimony from the Cortes of Valladolid, 12 July 1506.

156. Höfler, "Die Depeschen," 244.

157. AHN Clero Secular Regular, carpeta 193, no. 3, "Indulgencia plenaria para todas las personas que se hallaron presentes a la colocación de las cabeças de las vírgenes en este convento," 20 July 1506. Royal councillor Lorenzo Galíndez de Carvajal stated that twelve heads were hung in Saint Paul on that occasion. Galíndez de Carvajal, "Anales Breves," 3:556.

158. Don Juan Manuel had recently received the fortress of Burgos along with those of Segovia, Jaén, Plasencia, and Atienza, not to mention the *contaduría mayor* of Castile. BN Madrid, ms. 13127, "De lo que sucedió en España en cosas particulares desde la venida de Felipe I hasta su muerte," fols. 190v, 197; *Epistolario de Pedro Mártir*, 10: epist. 312; Santa Cruz, *Crónica de los Reyes Católicos*, 2:56.

159. Dr. Parra to King Fernando, in *Colección de documentos inéditos*, 8:394.

160. *Continuación de la crónica de Pulgar*, 524. Another contemporary recorded the rumor that great anxiety over his financial situation precipitated the young king's death. Santa Cruz, *Crónica de los Reyes Católicos*, 2:58.

161. Whether from plague, poison, or some other cause, Philippe's sudden death remains controversial. See José M. Doussinague, *Un proceso por envenenamiento: La muerte de Felipe el Hermoso* (Madrid: Espasa-Calpe, 1947).

162. Juan de Vallejo, *Memorial de la vida de fray Francisco Jiménez de Cisneros*, ed. Antonio de la Torre y del Cerro (Madrid: Bailly-Bailliere, 1913), 113.

163. Santa Cruz, *Crónica de los Reyes Católicos*, 2:65, 89; *Epistolario de Pedro Mártir*, 10: epistles 325, 328, and 329; José García Oro, *El Cardenal Cisneros: Vida y empresas* (Madrid: Biblioteca de Autores Cristianos, 1992), 160.

164. When Juana refused to name a regent or to convoke the Cortes, the royal council summoned the Cortes in her name. Archivo Municipal de Córdoba, caja 17, doc. 22, Royal provision of doña Juana to the city of Córdoba, signed by ten members of the royal council, 6 October 1506; AMS Actas Capitulares, caja 29, carpeta 121, fols. 6 and 7, Procurators at the Cortes to the town council of Seville, 18 December 1506; Zurita, *Historia del Rey don Hernando*, VII, 22, 1067.

165. BN Madrid, ms. 18761, no. 26, "Noticia de lo que al presidente y oidores del

consejo real les pasó con la Reina doña Juana en Burgos," 26 September 1506; AMS Actas Capitulares, caja 29, carpeta 121, fols. 6 and 7, Procurators at the Cortes to the town council of Seville, 18 December 1506.

166. To some extent, her parents' 1480 revocation of King Enrique IV's "excessive favors" provided a precedent for Juana's action. *Novísima Recopilación de las leyes de España* (Madrid, 1805), III, v, x–xi. Moreover, Stephen Haliczer has argued that even the 1480 reforms proved ineffective. Stephen Haliczer, "The Castilian Aristocracy and the Mercedes Reform of 1478–1482," *Hispanic American Historical Review* 55, no. 3 (1975): 449–67.

167. AGS CC Diversos 1–12, "Revocación de las mercedes que hizo el Rey Don Phelipe I," 18 December 1506, inserted in a provision of 30 July 1507. Real Biblioteca de el Escorial, mss. castellaños Z. II.1, 62a–b, Royal mandate of doña Juana, 18 December 1506, inserted in a letter by the royal council, 26 August 1507.

168. Juana attempted to restore her mother's royal council by dismissing three councillors appointed by Philippe and don Juan Manuel. Although the queen successfully discharged one of these advisers with a witty remark, the other two remained on the court payroll as late as 1508. Zurita, *Historia del Rey Don Fernando*, VII, 38, 1080; 54, 1096. Salustiano de Dios, *El Consejo Real de Castilla (1385–1522)* (Madrid: Centro de Estudios Constitucionales, 1982), 155. Juana's revocation of Philippe's mercedes, nevertheless, appears to have remained unenforced until Fernando returned to Castile.

169. Archivo Municipal de Burgos, Sección Histórica, no. 315, Fernando to the city of Burgos, 6 November 1506.

170. Fernando eventually secured a papal bull permitting Juana to bury Philippe elsewhere. ASV Minutae BreviumArm. 39, tomo 25, fol. 420, Pope Julius II to Queen Juana, 21 September 1507.

171. AHN Osuna leg. 1523: 1, "Escritura de compromiso otorgada por el Conde de Ureña, el Arzobispo de Sevilla, y otros nobles," October 1506; BFZ Altamira 12-80, "Escritura de Alcalá la real de conformydad con el Conde de Cabra y otros grandes," 27 December 1507; ADM caja 22-97, "Confederación y pleito homenaje hecho por el conde de Tendilla, don Íñigo López de Mendoza, capitán general del reino de Granada por el cual se comprometió a guardar amistad con don Antonio Manrique, Corregidor de Baeza y Úbeda y con todos los amigos suyos que estuviesen para el servicio de la reina, " 8 April 1507.

172. "Deuxième voyage de Phillipe le Beau en Espagne en 1506," 463.

173. Indeed, Martire's account of the embalming process indicates that it would have been difficult to differentiate Philippe's feet from the rest of his remains. *Epistolario de Pedro Mártir*, 10: epist. 315.

174. Ibid., epist. 324; Petrus Martir de Angleria, *Opus Epistolarum* (1530), epist. 323, fol. 71v.

175. "Apéndice: Costumbres de la Cartuja," in *Maestro Bruno, padre de monjes* (Madrid: Biblioteca de Autores Cristianos, 1995), 350–51.

176. RAH A-12, fol. 86v, Lope de Conchillos to Miguel Pérez de Almazán, 23 December 1506.

FOUR: Forging a Legend

1. BL Add. ms. 18852, The Archduchess Juana's Book of Hours, ca. 1496.
2. AGS PR 56-17, Clause of Queen Isabel's testament charging Juana to obey and to respect her father, 12 October 1504.
3. Ibid.
4. AGS CSR 14-1/15, Queen Juana to Fernando de Arzeo, 4 March 1507; AGS CSR 14-1/16, List of Queen Juana's officials, 11 March 1507; AGS CSR 14-2/71, Queen Juana to Ochoa de Landa, 24 March 1507.
5. AGS CSR 12-10/438, Queen Juana to Pedro Núñez de Guzmán, governor of the *infante* Fernando, 3 June 1507.
6. The Marquis of Villena, who accompanied Juana declared, "I have not decided to desire or permit that the said lord and king [Fernando] come to have the government and administration [of Castile], as I have not seen or heard that the queen, our lady, has written or spoken to summon him." AHN Nobleza, Frías 18/149, Declaration of don Diego López Pacheco, Duke of Escalona and Marquis of Villena, 19 June 1507.
7. Santa Cruz, *Crónica de los Reyes Católicos*, 2:79.
8. RAH Salazar A-12, fol. 166, Queen Juana's verbal orders to members of the Royal Council, 18 August 1507. RAH Salazar A-12, fol. 167, Lope de Conchillos to Miguel Pérez de Almazán, 20 August 1507.
9. Fernando's opponents argued that the Aragonese king's second marriage invalidated the codicil of Queen Isabel's testament entrusting Fernando with her realms in the case that Juana could not or would not govern Castile. Zurita, *Historia del Rey Don Hernando el Católico*, VII, xlvi, 195; VIII, vii, 256; *I diarii di Marino Sanuto*, 7:225–26.
10. RAH Salazar A-12, fol. 167, Lope de Conchillos to Miguel Pérez de Almazán, 20 August 1507.
11. Zurita, *Historia del Rey Don Hernando el Católico*, VIII, vii, 258.
12. *I diarii di Marino Sanuto*, 7:137.
13. Juan de Vallejo, *Memorial de la Vida de Jiménez de Cisneros*, ed. Antonio de la Torre y del Cerro (Madrid: Bailly-Bailliere, 1913), 113.
14. RAH Salazar A-12, fol. 79, Lope de Conchillos to King Fernando, 10 October 1506.
15. RAH Salazar A-12, fols. 77–78, Alcalde de los Donceles to Fernando, 10 October 1506.
16. RAH Salazar A-12, fols. 86–87, Lope de Conchillos to Miguel Pérez de Almazán, 23 December 1506.
17. *Continuación de la crónica de Pulgar*, in *Crónicas de los reyes de Castilla*, ed. Don Cayetano Rosell Biblioteca de Autores Español, vol. 3 (Madrid: Rivadeneyra, 1878), 525.
18. "Deuxième voyage de Philippe le Beau en Espagne," 1:64.
19. Zurita, *Historia del Rey Don Hernando el Católico*, VIII, vii, 259.
20. Ibid., VIII, vii, 259.
21. Pedro Abarca, *Los anales históricos de los Reyes de Aragon* (Salamanca: Lucas Pérez, 1684), 2:375v–376.
22. Archivio di Stato di Mantova, Archivio Gonzaga 585, no. 65, Miguel Pérez de Almaçan to Mosen Jayme de Albion, 5 September 1507.
23. Almazán also exaggerated the landed magnates' loyalty to Fernando by claiming

that the Duke of Nájera had requested permission to kiss the king's hands. In fact, the duke continued to oppose Fernando's return. Zurita, *Historia del Rey Don Hernando el Católico,* VIII, viii, 260; *I diarii di Marino Sanuto,* 7:371.

24. *Epostolario de Pedro Mártir de Anglería,* 10: epist. 363; Petrus Martir de Angleria, *Opus Epistolarum* (1530), fols. 82v–83, epist. 362.

25. ASV Arm. 39, tomo 25, fol. 420, Pope Julius II to Queen Juana, 21 September 1507.

26. *I diarii di Marino Sanuto,* 7:180, 225–26, 235.

27. AHN Osuna 420, 1 (1), Count of Benavente and Duke of Alba to the city of la Coruña, 16 June 1507. In Juana's name, the royal council had charged Benavente and Alba with recovering Ponserrada from the Count of Lemos.

28. AGS PR 54-81, Fernando to Catherine of Aragon, November 1507.

29. Zurita notes that the army prepared for Africa bolstered Fernando's authority in Castile, where he could also employ its six thousand to seven thousand men in case of necessity. The Armada eventually left Spain in 1509, led by Francisco Ximénez de Cisneros. Zurita, *Historia del Rey Don Hernando el Católico,* VIII, x, 271–72; xxx, 357.

30. ADN Lille B 857, no. 18036, City of Sevilla to King Fernando, undated [1508].

31. Three of four basic hermetic texts that Alain Saint-Saëns cites can be identified in Queen Juana's library. In addition to Saint Jerome, Juana possessed Jacobo de Voragine's *Golden Legend,* and the multivolume *Vita Christi Cartuxano.* Fray Luis de Granada translated the fourth text, Saint John Climac's *Spiritual Ladder,* into Castilian after Juana's death. Alain Saint-Saëns, *La nostalgie du désert. L'idéal érémitique en Castille au Siècle de'Or* (San Francisco: Mellen Research University Press, 1993), 138–41.

32. *Select Letters of Saint Jerome,* trans. F. A. Wright (London: William Heinemann, 1963), 237, 241.

33. Ibid., 257.

34. An old Galician woman allegedly articulated this prophecy in 1506. Alonso Fernández de Madrid, *Silva Palentina* (Palencia: Diputación Provincial, 1973; orig. ca. 1530), 376; Sandoval, *Historia de la vida y hechos del Emperador Carlos V,* I, xxiii, 29.

35. Santa Cruz, *Crónica de los Reyes Católicos,* 2:91. Along the same lines, see also Alvar Gómez de Castro, *De las hazañas de Francisco Jimenez de Cisneros,* trans. José Oroz Reta (Madrid: Fundación Universitaria Española, 1984), 202.

36. Elena Botinas Montero, Julia Cabaleiro Manzanedo, and María Angeles Duran Vinyeta, "Las Beguinas: Sabiduría y Autoridad Feminina," in *Las sabias mujeres,* ed. María del Mar Graña Cid (Madrid: Al-Mudayna, 1994), 286–87.

37. AGS CSR 53-449, Queen Juana to Ochoa de Landa, 9 and 18 April 1507.

38. AGS CSR 14-1/8, Queen Juana to Ochoa de Landa, 19 December 1506; AGS CSR 14-1/10, 14-1/13, 14-2/81, 14-2/83, and Colección de Autógrafos no. 101 [previously Estado Castilla I-ii-475], Queen Juana to Ochoa de Landa, 30 December 1506, 4 March 1507, 5 April 1507, 22 May 1507, and 15 July 1507. Fray Pedro Romero received an additional 35,175 mrs for costs incurred in the service of the deceased monarch. AGS Estado I-ii-476, Queen Juana to Ochoa de Landa, 18 July 1507.

39. RAH A-12, fol. 208, Mosen Ferrer to Fernando, 28 October 1507. According to the 1344 ordinances of Pedro of Aragon, the number of torches used for obsequies should correspond to the rank of the deceased. "Ordenacions fetes per lo Molt alt senyor en Pere Terç rey Daragon sobre lo regiment de tots los officials de la sua cort," in *Colección de documentos inéditos del archivo general de la corona de Aragón,* 5:184.

40. Santa Cruz, *Crónica de los Reyes Católicos*, 2:280; Bartholomé Leonardo de Argensola, *Primera parte de los anales de Aragon que prosigue los del Secretario Geronimo Çurita desde el año 1516 . . .* (Zaragoza: Ivan de Lanaia, 1630).

41. Fernando even considered naming Juana's second son, Fernando, governor of her kingdoms after his own death. For an analysis of the threat that young Fernando represented for the future Charles V, see Friedrich Edelmayer, "El hermano expulsado: don Fernando," *Torre de los Luganes* 39 (June 1999): 147–61.

42. AGS PR 54-83 (i–ii), King Fernando to Doctor de Puebla [December?], 1507; Fernández de Madrid, *Silva Palentina*, 376. Fernando imprisoned the Duke of Calabria, another candidate for Juana's hand. *I diarii di Marino Sanuto*, 15: 413.

43. Gómez de Fuensalida, *Correspondencia*, 437.

44. BN Marciana, ms. It. VII, 1108, fols. 346–46v, Francesco Corner to the Doge of Venice, 6 July 1508; fols. 346v–347, Francesco Corner to the Doge of Venice, 16 July 1508.

45. AGS CSR 13-52/1374, 1375, Nomina firmada por el rey, 22 January 1508.

46. He ordered lodging prepared in Tordesillas for the entire court, including himself, Germaine, Juana, two papal nuncios, three ambassadors, and the entourage accompanying each of them, and made another attempt to move the queen's possessions and officials from Arcos to Tordesillas. AGS CC Cédulas 7, fols. 243–46v, Fernando to his quartermasters and to the town of Tordesillas, 1 July 1508; AGS CSR 14-4/197 and 198, "Nomina de los maravedíes que se cargan . . . por mandado del rey," 24 July 1508.

47. Zurita, *Historia del Rey Don Hernando el Católico*, VII, xlii, 181.

48. AHN Diversos Colecciones leg. 288, King Fernando to Queen Juana, 30 July 1508, cited in Ramón González Navarro, *Fernando I (1503–1564). Un Emperador español en el Sacro Imperio* (Madrid: Editorial Alpuerto, 2003), 104–6, and Karl Friedrich Rudolf, "Yo, El Infante—Fernando, Príncipe en España," in *Fernando I. Un infante Español Emperador*, ed. Teófanes Egido López (Valladolid: Universidad de Valladolid, 2004), 51.

49. AGS CSR 14-4/182, "Nomina del rey para la casa de su hija," 1 September 1508.

50. Zurita, *Historia del Rey Don Hernando el Católico*, VIII, xxi, 315.

51. AGS CSR 14-4/226, Nomina de los oficiales de la casa en Arcos, 30 May 1508; AGS CC Cédulas 17, fol. 3002v, Fernando to Mosen Luys Ferrer, "cerrero mayor de la casa de la serenissima reyna y princesa," 30 May 1508.

52. Accordingly, Ferrer sent nine carts to retrieve essential items taken to Tordesillas and paid one servant 9,170 mrs for having waited in Arcos in order to guide the chariot that would convey Philippe's body to Miraflores. AGS CSR 53-1, "Gastos extraordinarios pagados por cartas de Mosen Ferrer," 15 August 1508.

53. AGS CSR 53-1, "Gastos extraordinarios pagados por cartas de Mosen Ferrer," 15 August 1508.

54. By no means thwarting all of Juana desires, Ferrer provided Franciscan friars and their guardian, who took up residence in Arcos in order to serve the queen, with tunics and shawls. AGS CSR 53-2, Cuenta de Mosen Ferrer, 11 October 1508.

55. RAH A-12, fol. 262, The bishop of Málaga to Fernando, 9 October 1508.

56. AGS CSR 55-74, Fernando to the principal accountants, 3 November 1508.

57. BN Marciana, ms. It. VII, 1108 (7448), fols. 357–58v, Francesco Corner to the Doge of Venezia, 17 February 1509.

58. Zurita, *Historia del Rey Don Hernando*, VIII, xxix, 355.

59. Gómez de Fuensalida, *Correspondencia*, 495; Zurita, *Historia del Rey Don Hernando*,

VIII, xlii, 180; xlvi, 198–99; Carlos E. Corona, *Fernando el Católico, Maximiliano y la regencia de Castilla (1508–1515)* (Seville: Facultad de Filosofía y Letras, 1961), 20–32.

60. AGS PR 54-83 (i–ii), Fernando to Doctor de la Puebla, undated [December 1507?].

61. AGS PR 54-85 (iii), Fernando to his ambassador Gómez de Fuensalida, undated [1508]; *I diarii di Marino Sanuto*, 7:299.

62. Gómez de Fuensalida, *Correspondencia*, 419.

63. Ibid., 437.

64. Pressuring Fernando to cede him his daughter, Henry threatened to marry the equally unwilling Marguerite of Austria instead. AGS PR 54-47 and 48, Catherine to Fernando and "Relación de las cartas que vinieron de Inglaterra," 7 September and 4–5 October 1507.

65. Gómez de Fuensalida, *Correspondencia*, 495.

66. AGS PR 54-105, Fernando to Catherine of Aragon, 3 December 1509; ACA Cancilleria, Cartas Reales, Fern. II, caja 4, olim, 3, fols. 8–11v, Fernando to don Luys Carroz, 6 January 1510.

67. AHN Nobleza, Frías 18/149, Declaration of the Marquis of Villena, 19 June 1507; AHN Osuna 1860-27, Declaration of the Duke of Infantado, 27 October 1507.

68. Zurita, *Historia del Rey Don Hernando*, VIII, ii, 239.

69. AHN Nobleza, Frías 22/92, City of Toledo to Prince Charles, 19 May 1507; ADN Lille B 18827, nos. 24495, 24497, 24496, Andrea de Burgo to Marguerite of Austria, 17 April, 19 June, 21 June 1507.

70. ADN Lille B 370, no. 18016, Treaty between Fernando and Charles, undated [August 1508?].

71. ADN Lille B 371, no. 18.020, and AGS PR 56-48, Treaty of Blois, 12 December 1509; ACA Cancilleria, Cartas Reales: Fern. II, caja 4, olim 3, fols. 1–7, Treaty of Blois, 24 December 1509.

72. AGS PR 56-48, Treaty of Blois, 12 December 1509.

73. AHN Nobleza, Frías 17/63,"Copia simple del juramento de los grandes, perlados y cavalleros . . .," 6 October 1510; AGS PR 70-5, "Actas de las cortes," 6 October 1510. As Juan M. Carretero Zamora has noted, the Cortes confirmed Fernando as governor in the case of Juana's death only until Charles reached the age of twenty. Juan M. Carretero Zamora, "Algunas consideraciones sobre las Actas de las Cortes de Madrid de 1510," *Cuadernos de Historia Moderna* 12 (1991): 35–37.

74. Sandoval, *Historia de la vida y hechos del Emperador Carlos V,* I, xxxv, 38; Rodríguez Villa, *La Reina doña Juana la Loca,* 245–46.

75. Miranda, *Vida de la Gloriosa Virgen Saint Claire,* 69, 163.

76. AHN Diversos Colecciones 253-62, Homage of Duke of Najera, 11 April 1511.

77. M. J. Rodríguez-Salgado, "Charles V and the Dynasty," in *Charles V (1500–1558) and His Time,* ed. Hugo Soly (Antwerp: Mercatorfonds, 1999), 55.

78. Laurent Vital, *Relación del primer viaje de Carlos V a España,* trans. Bernabe Herrero (Madrid: Estades, 1958), 221–22. Juana's former palace was demolished in the eighteenth century.

79. Enrique Martínez Ruiz, "El Monasterio de Santa Clara de Tordesillas. Una aproximación sociológica," in *El tratado de Tordesillas y su época: Congreso Internacional de Historia,* ed. Luis Ribot (Valladolid: Sociedad V Centenario, 1994), 3:1868.

80. Archivo Histórico Provincial de Valladolid, sección histórica 265: 58, King Fernando to the abbess and nuns of Saint María la Real of Tordesillas, 30 May 1514.

81. Archivo del Real Monasterio de Santa Clara de Tordesillas, caja 30, no. 20, Fernando and Juana to the alcaldes, alguaziles de su casa e corte, corregidor, alcaldes e otros justicias de la villa de Tordesillas, 2 November 1517.

82. Archivo del Real Monasterio de Santa Clara de Tordesillas, microfilm 1746, caja 4915, no. 38, Catholic monarchs to Juan de Glosas, corregidor of Tordesillas, 30 June 1502.

83. Miranda, *Vida de la Gloriosa Virgen Saint Claire*, 168.

84. Muñoz Fernández, *Mujer y experiencia religiosa*, 42–56.

85. Francisco Tarín y Juaneda, *La Real Cartuja de Miraflores (Burgos): Su Historia y Descripción* (Burgos: Hijos de Santiago Rodriguez, 1896), 178.

86. Ibid., 178–79. Royal silversmith Antón López de Carrión claimed to have spent 18,392 mrs on another silver and gold lamp that Juana donated to the Monastery of Miraflores. AGS CSR 55-59, "Pliego de Carrión, Platero," 5 March 1508. Juana's postmortem inventory listed two books for drawing; AGS CMC 1a época 1213, Queen Juana's Inventory, 1555.

87. AGS CSR 53-13, Nómina de Mosen Ferrer, 25 de junio de 1512; AMG Códice 87, "Tabla de los bienhechores desta sancta casa y monasterio," fol. 5; AMG leg. 5, no. 9, King Fernando in the name of Queen Juana to their quartermasters, 30 June 1514.

88. AGS CSR 15-1/34, Mosen Ferrer to Ochoa de Landa, 5 June 1511; AGS CSR 15-1/35, Receipt of ducats for Holy Friday, 6 June 1511; AGS CSR 53-12, Nominas of Mosen Ferrer, 3 May 1512; AGS CSR 15-7/675, Receipt by Mosen Ferrer, 3 May 1512; AGS CSR 53-16, Cédulas of Mosen Ferrer, 22 April 1513; AGS CSR 15-5/533, Receipt by Mosen Ferrer, 22 April 1513.

89. AGS CSR 53-8 and 17, Payments of Mosen Ferrer, 6 June 1511 and 17 July 1513; AGS CSR 15-1/20, Mosen Ferrer to Ochoa de Landa, 12 June 1511; AGS CSR 96-553, Annual extraordinary expenses, 1512; AGS CSR 15-7/677, "Memorial de lo que se comprase para el monumento," 15 April 1512; AGS CSR 15-6/540, "Memorial de la semana santa," 29 March 1513; AGS CSR 15-5/423, Mosen Ferrer for Diego de Ribera, 17 July 1513; AGS CSR 15-7/652, Mosen Ferrer for don Alonso de Alva, 29 June 1514; and AGS CSR 15-7/693, Mosen Ferrer for the sacristan and Lorenzo, carpintero, 29 June 1514. Juana's mother, Queen Isabel, sponsored the same annual monuments. Angela Muñoz Fernández, "Notas para la definición de un model socioreligioso femenino: Isabel I de Castilla," in *Las mujeres en el cristianismo medieval*, ed. Angela Muñoz Fernández (Madrid: Al-Mudayna, 1990), 428.

90. AGS CSR 15-7/738, Mosen Ferrer to Alonso de Alva, 29 January 1515.

91. AGS CSR 15-8/864, Fernando to Ochoa de Landa, 11 July 1515; AGS CSR 96-36, Nomina de Fernando, 20 November 1515.

92. AGS CSR 15-7/655 and CSR 53-12, Mosen Ferrer to Ochoa de Landa, 5 August 1512.

93. AGS CSR 15—7/63, Mosen Ferrrer to Ochoa de Landa, 9 March 1514.

94. AGS CSR 24-46/611, Gracia de Carreño to the principal accountants, 14 July 1523.

95. Muñoz Fernández, *Mujer y experiencia religiosa*, 56.

96. AGS CSR 14-6/431–36 and 446, "Oficios y oficiales e criados de la casa de la reyna," 3 April 1509; AGS CSR 15-8/790, The king for Pedro de Quintana, 15 June

1514. In August 1514, however, King Fernando decided to reduce costs at Saint Claire by having three of Juana's regular chaplains replace three of the Franciscans praying for Philippe. AGS CSR 24-1/42, "La orden que se dió . . . en los gastos de la yglesia," 4 August 1514. New Masses and vespers for Philippe were also composed that year. AGS CSR 15-7/742 and 53-28, Mosen Ferrer for Gregorio, scribe of the books, 27 November 1514.

97. AGS CSR 96-565, "Relacion de los maravediés que montan las raciones de los oficiales de la reyna . . .," 1513.

98. AGS CSR 53-7, 8 and 11, Nominas de Mosen Ferrer, 15 December 1510, 6 June 1511 and 6 December 1511; AGS CSR 15-1/31 and 70, Mosen Ferrer to Ochoa de Landa, 24 January 1511 and 10 November 1511; AGS CSR 56-15, Cuenta de Francisco de Quartona, 24 February 1511; AGS CSR 15-1/24, Mosen Ferrer to Fray Juan de Ávila, 12 June 1511; AGS CSR 15-1/94, King Fernando to Mosen Ferrer, 28 April 1511; AGS CSR 15-1/86, Mosen Ferrer for fray Buenaventura, 6 December 1511.

99. AGS CSR 53-11, Nomina de Mosen Ferrer, 6 December 1511.

100. AGS CSR 24-1/42, "La orden que se dio . . . en los gastos de la yglesia," 4 August 1514; AGS CSR 16-1/16, Mosen Ferrer for Gonçalo Gómez, 1 October 1515.

101. *Epistolario de Pedro Mártir de Anglería*, 10: epist. 411, 431, 461; Petrus Martir de Angleria, *Opus Epistolarum* (1530), epistles 410, 430, 460.

102. Rudolf Wittkower and Margot Wittkower, *Born under Saturn: The Character and Conduct of Artists: A Documented History from Antiquity to the French Revolution* (New York: W. W. Norton, 1963), 102–4.

103. *Epistolario de Pedro Mártir de Anglería*, 11: epist. 516.

104. Ibid.; Petrus Martir de Angleria, *Opus Epistolarum* (1530), fols. 115v-116, epist. 514.

105. Miranda, *Vida de la Gloriosa Virgen Sancta Clara*, 67–69, 79, 163.

106. AGS CSR 51-45, King Fernando to his *mayordomo* and principal accountants, 10 March 1512.

107. AGS CSR 15-1/13, Mosen Ferrer to Antonio de Arévalo, 9 July 1511; AGS CSR 15-1/81, Mosen Ferrer for Bartolomé de Castellón, boticario, 23 November 1511.

108. AGS CSR 15-1/3, Mosen Ferrer to Ochoa de Landa, 10 July 1511.

109. AGS CSR 12-1/23, Mosen Ferrer to Tomas de Valençia, 16 June 1511.

110. AGS CSR 15-1/30, Mosen Ferrer for Fernando de Arzeo, 13 November 1511.

111. AGS CC Pueblos 20, "El teniente de la villa de Tordesillas," 28 March and 13 May 1509.

112. AGS CC Pueblos 20, Sancho Vázques de Çepeda, town councillor of Tordesillas to Queen Juana, 11 July 1513; Sancho Vázques de Çepeda, town councillor of Tordesillas, to Queen Juana, 29 August 1513.

113. AGS CC Pueblos 20, Royal council to the town of Tordesillas, 12 June 1515.

114. AGS CSR 15-7/648, Fernando to his principal accountants, 25 June 1514.

115. AGS CSR 15-8/805-6, Fernando to Ochoa de Landa, 26 July 1514; AGS CSR 16-2/128–29 and 130, Fernando to Ochoa de Landa, 20 November 1515.

116. AGS Estado 3-113, Creencia de Doña María de Ulloa, undated [1516].

117. AGS Estado I-II, no. 298, Mosen Ferrer to Cardinal Cisneros, 6 March 1516. In the end, the *cerrero mayor*'s claim that he had served the king faithfully appeared persuasive. Although Ferrer retired to Valencia, he continued to receive wages as a member of Juana's household.

118. In 1515 the Florentine ambassador reported that the Queen of Castile's refusal to eat had endangered her life and had sent Fernando rushing to Tordesillas. Archivio di Stato di Firenze, Otto di Practica: Legazioni e Commissarie, reg. 11, fols. 100v–101v, Dispatch by Francisco Pandulphino, 4 May 1515.

119. The next chapter discusses Juana's similar demands in 1518–19.

120. A secretary of Cardinal Cisneros sensationalistically reported: "We know that he [Ferrer] sought all possible means of making the queen worse, and that he clearly and publicly declared—for there are a thousand witnesses—the greatest ignomities ever said of a woman; and when they asked him for food for the queen he said, 'You should give this beast straw and oats and nothing else.'" From the Archivo de la Colegial de Jerez, Códice de Cartas del Cardenal Cisneros, fol. 268, Jorge de Varacaldo a Diego López de Ayala, 10 June 1516, transcribed in Manuel Giménez Fernández, *Bartolomé de las Casas* (Madrid: Consejo Superior de Investigaciones Cientificas, 1984), 1:757.

121. AGS CSR 394-7, Diego de Ribera to the Adelantado of Cazorla, 10 February 1516.

122. Ibid.

123. AGS Estado 3-113, Creencia de Doña María de Ulloa, undated [1516].

124. AGS Estado 3-354, Deciphered letter from Charles to Cisneros, 30 April 1516.

125. AGS Estado 9-93, Pedro de Ayala to Cardinal Cisneros, 12 July 1517.

126. AGS PR 29-52 (no. 2968), fols. 17–17v, Testament of King Fernando, 22 January 1516, transcribed in Ricardo del Arco, *Fernando el Católico: Artífice de la España Imperial* (Zaragoza: Editorial Heraldo de Aragón, 1939), 444.

127. Edelmayer, "El hermano expulsado: don Fernando," 152.

128. Galíndez de Carvajal, *Anales breves*, 561–65. A number of Juana's servants recalled great hostility between Juana and the archbishop of Toledo, Francisco Jiménez de Cisneros. Catalina's governess, doña Beatriz de Mendoza, even claimed that Cisneros "loved [the queen] so little that he would tie her up and would not permit her to be cleaned." Yet Juana reportedly expressed pleasure that her father had named the archbishop regent of Castile. AGS Estado 3:113, Declaration of doña María de Ulloa, undated [1516].

129. AGS PR 29-52 (no. 2968), esp. fols. 15–17v, Testament of King Fernando, 22 January 1516, transcribed in Ricardo del Arco, *Fernando el Católico*, 413–58.

130. Jerónimo de Blancas, *Comentarios de las cosas de Aragón*, trans. Manuel Hernández (Zaragoza: Imprenta del Hospicio, 1878), 254.

131. AGS PR 13-77 (Planchados 177), "Escritura otorgada por el lugarteniente del justicia de Aragón . . .," 12 March 1516.

132. Nevertheless, once secure of his succession, Charles named Alfonso *lugarteniente general* in Aragon. Arxiu Historiç Municipal, Barcelona, Consell de Cent, sèrie VII, reg. 1, fols. 6–7v, Juana and Charles to don Alfonso of Aragon, 31 May 1516. As Cardinal Cisneros grew increasingly feeble, Alfonso of Aragon also begged Charles to bestow the archbishopric of Toledo or Seville upon him. ADN Lille B 18873, nos. 32080 and 32081, Don Alonso of Aragon to Marguerite of Austria, 6 and 7 September 1516.

FIVE: Promoting Family Interests

1. On causes underlying the Comunero rebellion, see Stephen Haliczer, *The Comuneros of Castile: The Forging of a Revolution, 1475–1521* (Madison: University of Wiscon-

sin Press, 1981), 135–37, and Joseph Pérez, *La revolución de las comunidades de Castilla (1520–1521)*, trans. Juan José Faci Lacasta (Madrid: Siglo XXI, 1977), esp. 121–28.

2. *Letters, Despatches, and State Papers*, suppl., liii–lxi.

3. Pérez, *La Revolución de las Comunidades de Castilla*, 193–95, 535–36; Michael Prawdin, *The Mad Queen*, 7–8.

4. Sandoval, *Historia de la vida y hechos del Emperador Carlos V*, II, iv, 79.

5. Charles followed the precedent of his father, Philippe, who declared himself King of Castile at the conclusion of obsequies for Isabel of Castile, also celebrated in Brussels's Church of Saint Gudule. The great expenses for Fernando's funeral likewise enhanced Charles's proclamation. Laurent Vital, "Premier voyage de Charles-Quint en Espagne, de 1517 à 1518," in *Collection des voyages des souverains des Pays-Bas*, ed. Louis-Prosper Gachard and Charles Piot (Brussels: F. Hayez, 1881), 6.

6. ADM caja 40, no. 78, Don Francisco Pacheco to the Marquis of Priego, 18 February 1516.

7. ADM caja 4 (leg. 246), no. 111[a], King Charles to the Marquis of Priego, 20 March 1516; AHN Nobleza Frías 22/99, King Charles to the Count of Oropesa, 20 March 1516.

8. ADM caja 41 (leg. 283), no. 13, Minutes of the admiral, 31 March 1516.

9. Sandoval, *Historia de la vida y hechos del Emperador Carlos V*, II, vi, 80–81.

10. Argensola, *Primera parte de los anales de Aragon*, fol. 188.

11. Archivo Ducal de Medina Sidonia, Villafranca 4336; ADM caja 4 (leg. 246), no. 111b, AHN Nobleza, Frías 22/100, Archivo Municipal de Toledo, Archivo Secreto, caja 1, leg. 2, no. 62f, Francisco Jiménez de Cisneros and Adrian of Utrecht to the Marquis of Villafranca, the Marquis of Priego, the Count of Oropesa, and the city of Toledo, 3 April 1516.

12. Ruiz, "Unsacred Monarchy," 125. Ruiz sees the practice of raising the royal pennant to proclaim a new ruler as supporting the case for a single royal persona.

13. Pérez, *La revolución de las comunidades de Castilla*, 78–79.

14. Archivo Ducal de Medina Sidonia, Velez 549, "Testimonio de como el Ilustrísimo señor marqués, adelantado, y los señores conçejo de la ciudad de Murcia alçaron pendones por la Reyna y Rey, nuestros señores," 10 April 1516.

15. Archivo Histórico Provincial de Zaragoza, Casa Ducal de Hijar, I-197-2, "Testimonio a instancia del Conde de Salinas . . .," 2 May 1516.

16. AGS Estado I-ii, no. 288, "Plasencia sobre la proclamación de la Reyna Doña Juana y del Príncipe Don Carlos," 24–25 July 1516. For a transcription of this document, see *Orígenes de la monarquía hispánica: Propaganda y legitimación (ca. 1400–1520)*, ed. José Manuel Nieto Soria (Madrid: Dykinson, 1999), 444–45; Conde de Cedillo, *El Cardenal Cisneros: Gobernador del Reino* (Madrid: Real Academia de la Historia, 1921), 149.

17. RAH Salazar A-16, fols. 17–20, Instructions of don Alfonso de Aragón to Juan de Aragón, 7 March 1516, published in *Corpus documental de Carlos V*, ed. Manuel Fernández Álvarez (Salamanca: Ediciones Universidad de Salamanca, 1973–81), 1:53–56. Fearing chaos if the *infante* Enríque Trastámara or Fernando's illegitimate son, don Alfonso, asserted his own claim to the throne, *justicia mayor* Juan Lanuça III ultimately endorsed Charles. AGS PR 13-77 (Planchados 177), "Escritura otorgada por el lugarteniente del justicia de Aragón . . .," 12 March 1516.

18. ADN Lille 17876 (Castille, Jeanne la folle), King Charles to the Chambre de Comptes, 14 July 1517.

19. ADN Lille 17876 (Castille, Jeanne la folle), Juana's wages, 1 October 1501; ADN Lille 17876 (Castille, Jeanne la folle), Juana's wages, 1 April 1505.

20. Vital, "Premier voyage de Charles-Quint en Espagne," 200–201.

21. Before his death, King Fernando told procurators to the Cortes, "yo he deseado y me huelgo de fablaros a todas juntos como a todo el reyno pues lo representays." AGS PR 69-50, King Fernando to the Procurators of the Cortes, undated [June 1515].

22. AGS PR 70-52, Chapters of the Cortes, 5 January 1518. A similar version of the Cortes appears in *Cortes de los antiguos reinos de León y Castilla*, 4:260–84.

23. AGS PR 70-52, Chapters of the Cortes, 5 January 1518. Charles officially ordered young Fernando to the Low Countries on 19 April 1518, in spite of the Cortes's demands that he remain in Castile. Denia reminded Charles that he should write Fernando. AGS Estado 5-290, Denia to Charles, 27 April 1518.

24. Even before the king reached Castile, representatives of the cities and towns characterized the alienation of offices and the export of moneys as insufferable injuries, which Charles should remedy at once. Archivo Municipal de León, leg. 15, no. 392, "Ciertos capítulos e acuerdos que se asentaba entre Burgos y León y Salamanca y Valladolid sobre cosas tocantes al servicio de Dios y de Su. Magt. e bien del reino," 28 April 1517.

25. AGS PR 70-53, Capítulos de Cortes con las respuestas, 1518.

26. AGS Estado 33-112, Charles to Denia, 15 March 1518; BN Madrid, ms. 1890, fol. 297, "Poder al marqués de Denia, don Bernardo de Rojas y Sandoval, para regir y administrar la casa de la Reina doña Juana en Tordesillas," 15 March 1518.

27. As *contino* don Luis received salary and rations amounting to 70,000 mrs per year— remuneration that reflected Fernando's desire to please the marquis. ADM caja 3 (leg. 245), no. 153, King Fernando to the principal accountants, 16 March 1514.

28. Sandoval, *Historia de la vida y hechos del Emperador Carlos V*, II, i, fol. 71; II, xii, 133. Fittingly, Charles would ask the marquis to accompany the corpse of his father, Philippe, to Granada in 1525. AGS CSR 24-6/98, Charles to Ochoa de Landa, 22 August 1525; AGS Estado 13-342, Denia to Charles, 14 September 1525.

29. ADM caja 4 (leg. 246), nos. 3, 9, and 11, Charles to Denia, 7 October 1516, 17 July 1517, and 8 September 1517. Charles, in turn, asked the marquis and his wife, doña Francisca Enríquez, to support a marriage between the pro-Burgundian Count of Cabra, don Luis de Córdoba, and the Marquise of Priego, a cousin to doña Francisca. RAH A-50, fol. 21, Charles to the Marquise of Denia, 18 March 1517.

30. ADM caja 3 (leg. 245), no. 101, Royal decree, 15 July 1514.

31. ADM caja 3 (leg. 245), no. 154, King Fernando to the principal accountants, 29 March 1515. Fernando may have renewed this salary in order to encourage a prospective marriage between doña Francisca's daughter, doña Magdalena de Rojas, and don Alvaro de Mendoza, the eldest son of don Rodrigo de Mendoza, Count of Castro, with a dowry of 7,500,000 mrs. AHN Osuna 1954:1 (5), License to mortgage the town of Lerma, 12 September 1514.

32. ADM caja 4 (leg. 246), no. 14, and AGS Estado 33-113, Decree of Charles remunerating the Marquis and Marquise of Denia, 29 March 1518.

33. The *infanta* Catalina had argued on behalf of Mendoza and Castilla. ADN Lille B 18873, no. 32071, Catalina to Marguerite of Austria, 4 August 1516. The couple received an annual pension of 300,000 mrs, along with two mules in order to return to their house. AGS CSR 16-5/351–54, Ayudas de costa de los oficiales de la casa de la reyna, 27 July 1518.

34. *Epistolario de Pedro Mártir de Anglería*, 10: epist. 614; Sandoval, *Historia de la vida y hechos del Emperador Carlos V,* II, xiv, 134; Vital, "Premier voyage de Charles-Quint en Espagne," 214, 243–46.

35. Vital, "Premier Voyage de Charles-Quint en Espagne," 237–42. Upon the death of Mosen Luis Ferrer, Denia requested that Fromont receive the position of *mayordomo*, which he had exercised in practice since 1518. AGS Estado 10-60, Denia to Charles, 13 October 1522.

36. Charles also warned the Aragonese that he would request a *servicio* (tax) to offset the great costs of his voyage. Archivo Municipal de Zaragoza, Serie Facticia 20 (caja 7768), no. 1, Charles to the *jurados* of Zaragoza, 3 May 1518; Serie Facticia 121 (caja 7877), no. 1, "Juramento fecho por el Rey nuestro senyor," 1518.

37. Ricardo García Cárcel, "Las Cortes de 1519 en Barcelona, una opción revolucionaria frustrada," in *Homenaje al Dr. D. Juan Reglà Campistol,* ed. Juan Reglàversidad de Valencia, 1975), 240.

38. Arxiu Historiç Municipal de Barcelona, Concell de Cent, II-44, fols. 16v–17, "Jura del rey," 19 March 1519.

39. For an excellent discussion of the Barcelona Corts, see Àngel Casals i Martínez, "Emperor i principat: Catalunya i les seves relacions amb l'imperi de Carles V (1516–1543)" (Ph.D. dissertation, Universitat de Barcelona, 1995), esp. 86–134.

40. Ibid., 99–101.

41. Seven Castilian nobles (don Fadrique Enríquez, Admiral of Castile; don Fadrique de Toledo, Duke of Alba; don Diego López Pacheco, Marquis of Villena; don Diego Hurtado de Mendoza, Duke of Infantado; don Iñigo Velasco, Duke of Frías and Constable of Castile; don Alvaro de Zúñiga, Duke of Bejar; don Antonio Manrique, Duke of Nájera), two Aragonese (don Ferndando Ramon Folch, Duke of Cardona; don Alvaro Perez-Osorio, Marques de Astorga) and a Neapolitan (don Pedro Antonio de San-Severino, principe de Bisigniano y San-Marco) received the prestigious collar in 1519. Baron de Reiffenberg, *Histoire de l'ordre de la Toison d'Or* (Brussels: Fonderie et Imprimerie Normales, 1830), 346–47.

42. In order to win the imperial election, Charles had offered Germaine de Foix to the Marquis of Brandenburg and his sister, Catalina, to the son of the Duke of Saxony. Sandoval, *Historia de la vida y los hechos del Emperador Carlos V,* II, xxxiii, 146; AGS Estado 6, fol. 32, Charles to Denia, 12 February 1512; ADM caja 4 (leg. 246), no. 26, Charles to Denia, 27 May 1519;BL Ad. ms. 28572, fol. 212, "Reclamación y revocación de la infanta Catalina contra el matrimonio que fue contractado por ella y el Emperador con Johan Frederic, hijo del Duque de Saxonia," 2 July 1520.

43. Archivo Municipal de Córdoba, caja 3, doc. 6, Charles to the city of Córdoba, 5 September 1519; RAH N-44, fol. 545, "Carta del emperador Carlos V en la que justifica el haberse antepuesto a su madre en todos los documentos oficiales," 5 September 1519.

44. AGS Estado 5-343 and 344, Denia to Charles, undated [late 1519].

45. AGS Estado 5-303, Denia to Chièvres, 27 May 1518. Cardinal Cisneros, before his death on 8 November 1517, had urged Adrian of Utrecht to reform the royal household, eliminating posts created since the death of Queen Isabel. BN Paris, Manuscrit Espagnol 143, fols. 44–48v, Instruction from Cardinal Cisneros to Adrian of Utrecht, undated [September or October 1517]. Adrian apparently began but never finished this task, partly due to Denia's interference. AGS Estado 5-320, 317 y 312 Denia to Charles,

23 September 1518, 18 October 1518 and 29 October 1518; AGS Estado 6, fol. 132, Denia to Chièvres, 8 January 1519; AGS Estado 5-302, Charles to Denia, 27 May [1519?].

46. AGS Estado 5-331, Denia to Charles, 6 April 1518.

47. AGS Estado 5-339, Denia to Charles, 30 July 1518.

48. Ibid.

49. Ibid.

50. ADM caja 4 (leg. 246), no. 31, Charles to Juana's female attendants, 14 January 1520. At the same time, the king asked the Denias to favor Leonor Gómez on account of her services and those of her husband. RAH A-50, fol. 21v, Charles to Denia, 30 December [?] 1518; RAH A-50, fol. 22, Charles to Denia, 14 January 1520.

51. AGS Estado 5-331, Denia to Charles, 27 December 1519; ADM caja 4 (leg. 246), no. 35, Charles to doña Elvira de Rojas, 11 April 1520.

52. Seeking to reward a female servant loyal to him, the marquis sought royal favors for María de Cartama, her husband, Lope de Ordas, and their son. AGS Estado 5-146, Denia to Chièvres, undated [July 1518]; AGS Estado 5-329, Denia to Charles, 30 November 1518; AGS Estado 5-333, Charles to Denia, 8 December 1518; AGS Estado 5-291, Denia to Charles, 14 March [1520].

53. The *monteros de Espinosa* took their name from the town of origin of their founding member, credited with saving the life of don Sancho, third Count of Castile (ca. 580). Fernández de Oviedo, *Libro de la cámara real del Prínçipe Don Juan*, 126–29; Pedro de la Escalera Guevara, *Origen de los Monteros de Espinosa. Su Calidad, Exercicio, Preeminencias, Esenciones* (Madrid: Francisco Martínez, 1632), 13–14.

54. Beltrán de Fromont, *teniente de mayordomo*, and Guillem Punçon, *repostero de camas*, were among the only servants permitted to interact with the queen. Charles sent Fromont and Punçon instructions to obey orders they received from Denia, "como sy yo mysmo en persona vos lo mandase." ADM leg. 246/caja 4, núm. 25, Charles to Beltrán de Fromont and Guillem Punçon, 28 April 1519.

55. AGS CSR 56-1, Fernando and Isabel's regulations for the Monteros de Espinosa, 19 September 1495; AGS CSR 17-5/380, Denia to Ochoa de Landa for the Monteros, 15 February 1525.

56. AGS Estado 5-305, Denia to Chièvres, 12 June 1519.

57. AGS Estado 5-311, Denia to Charles, 6 April 1518. When Juana returned to the theme, Denia claimed that all grandees had fled the province due to the plague. AGS Estado 6-5, Denia to Charles, 6 July 1519.

58. AGS Estado 5-311, 302, 346, and 337, Denia to Charles, undated [6 April 1518], 27 May 1519, 26 April 1519, and 26 September 1519.

59. AGS Estado 5-294, Charles to Denia, 19 April [1518]; ADM caja 4 (leg. 246), núm. 16, Charles to Denia, 12 June 1518.

60. AGS Estado 5-299, Denia to Charles, 22 June [1518].

61. AGS Estado 5-315, Denia to Charles, 13 September 1518.

62. AHN Osuna 2116, no. 4, Charles to Denia, 24 August 1518. Denia, nevertheless, argued that an imitation coffin would be risky, especially since Juana might wish to see it opened. AGS Estado 5-346, Denia to Charles, 26 April 1519.

63. ADM caja 4 (leg. 246), no. 20, Charles to Denia, 30 October 1518.

64. AGS Estado 5-308, Denia to Charles, 10 August [1518]; AGS Estado 5-346, Denia to Charles, 26 April 1519.

65. AHN Osuna 2116, no. 4, Charles to Denia, 24 August 1518, copied in BN Madrid, ms. 2058, fol. 164; ADM caja 4 (legajo 246), no. 19, Charles to Denia, 2 October 1518; AGS Estado 5-300, Denia to Charles, 12 May 1519.

66. AGS Estado 5-315, Denia to Charles, 13 September 1518; AGS Estado 5-324, Marquis to Charles, 4 November 1518.

67. AGS Estado 5-300, Denia to Charles, 12 May 1519.

68. AGS Estado 5-301, Denia to Charles, undated [May 1519].

69. AGS Estado 6-5, Denia to Charles, 6 July 1519.

70. AGS Estado 5-308, Denia to Charles, 10 August 1518; AGS CSR 16-5/460, Denia to Ochoa de Landa, 4 September 1518; AGS CSR 18-2/81, Denia to Ochoa de Landa, 1 February 1519.

71. AGS Estado 5-312, Denia to Charles, 29 October 1518.

72. AGS Estado 5-322, Denia to Charles, 19 September 1519; AGS Estado 5-336 and 337, Denia to Charles, 26 September 1519. In accord with Denia's wishes, Charles thanked the town for its cooperation. AGS Estado 5-286, Denia to Charles, 20 April 1519; Archivo Histórico Provincial de Valladolid, Sección Histórica 265, no. 63, Charles to the town of Tordesillas, 5 May 1519.

73. AGS Estado 5-311, Denia to Charles, 6 April 1518.

74. ADM caja 4 (leg. 246), no. 29, Charles to Denia, 15 September 1519.

75. AGS Estado 5, fols. 340 and 341, Denia to Charles, undated [October 1519].

76. AGS Estado 5-287, Denia to Charles, undated [May 1520].

77. AGS Estado 5, fols. 343 and 344, Denia to Charles, undated [late 1519].

78. AGS Estado 5-301, Denia to Charles, undated [May 1519]; AGS Estado 5, fols. 343 and 344, Denia to Charles, undated [late 1519].

79. ADM caja 4 (leg. 246), no. 27, Charles to Denia, 5 July 1519; RAH A-50, fol. 22, Charles to Denia, 14 January 1520.

80. AGS Estado 6, fol. 5, Denia to Charles, 6 July [1519].

81. AGS CSR 56-546, "Información de servicios de otros oficiales de la Reyna . . .," undated [1521].

82. AGS Estado 6, fol. 5, Denia to Charles, 6 July [1519].

83. AGS Estado 5-323, Denia to Charles, undated [October 1519].

84. AGS Estado 5-340 and 341, Denia to Charles, undated [October 1519]; RAH A-50, fol. 22, Charles to Denia, 14 January 1520.

85. Among other positions, the marquis sought the bishopric of Burgos for his son, don Diego, and the office of Catalina's *maestresala* for his nephew, Hernando de Tovar. AGS Estado 5-330, Denia to Charles, undated [November 1518]; AGS Estado 6-10, Cardinal Adrian to Charles, 7 June 1519. Frequent references in Denia's correspondence to his relative Alonso de Cabeças and secretary Pedro de Aranz, who both served as personal messengers, suggest that Denia handled some requests for patronage verbally. AGS Estado 5-298, Denia to Chièvres, 7 April 1518; AGS Estado 5-303, Denia to Chièvres, 27 May 1518. While cultivating loyal clients, the marquis also sought greater authority over the royal troops led by his brother, don Hernando de Sandoval—requesting permission to move, dismiss, and appoint them at will, which Charles denied. AGS Estado 5-326 and 327, Memorial of Denia, undated [November 1518]; ADM caja 4 (leg. 246), no. 24, Charles to Denia, 3 April 1519.

86. AGS Estado 5-334, Charles to Denia, 20 November 1518.

87. ADM caja 4 (leg. 246), no. 29, Charles to Denia, 15 September 1519. Since the

taxes voted at la Coruña were never paid, the marquis requested the same funds out of ordinary revenues in order to dower his daughter, doña Magdalena. AGS PR 5-293, Denia to Charles, 25 January 1522.

88. AGS Estado 5-315, Denia to Charles, 13 September 1518. The marquis also asked Chièvres to support his right to continue receiving a salary for serving on the royal council. AGS Estado 6-132, Denia to de Chièvres, 8 January 1519. Although Charles initially claimed that Denia's salary as governor included the requested 100,000 mrs, Charles issued orders to pay the marquis an additional 100,000 mrs per year and his son, don Luis de Rojas, 70,000 mrs following the emperor's third visit to Tordesillas. AGS Estado 5-334, Charles to Denia, 20 November 1518; ADM caja 4 (leg. 246), nos. 32, 33, and 42, Charles to his principal accountants, 4 April 1520 and 24 August 1520.

89. BN Madrid, ms. 1778, fol. 42v–43v, Denia to Charles, 6 July 1520.

90. AGS Estado 5-300, Denia to Charles, 12 May 1519.

91. The Count of Benavente, on the other hand, urged the Comuneros to make their foremost demand Charles's marriage to doña Isabel, *infanta* of Portugal. ANTT Corpo Cronológico Parte I, Maço 26, no. 69, Ambassador João Rodriguez to King Manuel, 19 September 1520.

92. BN Madrid, ms. 1778, fols. 42v–43v, Denia to Charles, 6 July 1520.

93. BN Madrid, ms. 1778, fols. 44–45v, Denia to Charles, 27 July 1520.

94. José Antonio Maravall, *Las Comunidades de Castilla: Una primera revolución moderna* (Madrid: Alianza Editorial, 1984; orig. 1963), 101–3, 107–27. Echoing the Cortes of 1518, these rebels demanded offices and benefices for native Castilians and opposed the export of coin.

95. Sandoval, *Historia de la vida y hechos del Emperador Carlos V*, VI, xxv–xxvi, 271–78.

96. Vastly outnumbered, the *monteros* also lacked artillery, which the Comunero forces had seized in Medina del Campo. Denia later attributed the guards' immobility to the advanced age of their captain, Gil de Baracaldo. AGS Estado 8, fol. 165, "Creencia del Marqués de Denia con don Hernando de Tovar," December 1521.

97. AGS PR 4-72, "Escritura de cierta platica que pasaron los capitanes del ejército e gente de las ciudades de Toledo e Segovia e la villa de Madrid con la Reyna doña Juana n[uest]ra señora e Su Alteza con ellos en la villa de Tordesillas," 29 August 1520.

98. Ibid.

99. Sandoval, *Historia de la vida y hechos del Emperador Carlos V*, VI, xxvi, 279.

100. AGS PR 4-73, "La autoridad que Su Alteza dio a la junta sobre lo que Juan de Padilla le dixo," 1 September 1520.

101. AGRB Gachard 614, fol. 140, Comunero Captains to the Junta of Ávila, 30 August 1520.

102. AGS PR 2-1-14/26, Cardinal Adrian to Lope Hurtado de Mendoza, 4 September 1520; AGS PR 2-1-20/43, Cardinal Adrian to Charles, 14 September 1520.

103. AGS PR 2-1-18/38, Cardinal Adrian to Charles, 4 September 1520.

104. ANTT Corpo Cronológico Parte I, Maço 26, no. 69, Ambassador João Rodriguez to King Manuel, 19 September 1520.

105. AGS PR 2-1-21, Cardinal Adrian to Charles, 23 September 1520; AGRB Gachard 614, fols. 149–50, Junta of Tordesillas, 6 October 1520.

106. AGS PR 4-75, "Lo que pasaron con la Reyna, nuestra señora, los de la Junta quando le fueron a besar la mano," 24 September 1520, printed in Sandoval, *Historia de*

la vida y hechos de Carlos V, VI, xxx, 283–86. A similar version of the meeting exists in the BL Eg. ms. 2059, fols. 60–54v.

107. AGS PR 4-75, "Lo que pasaron con la Reyna Nra. S. los de la Junta quando le fueron a besar la mano," 24 September 1520.

108. AGRB Gachard 614, fol. 146, Comunidades de Castilla, 26 September 1520.

109. AGS PR 2-1/253, Memorial for the emperor by an eyewitness [fray Luis de León], undated [September 1520]; AGS PR 2-1-30, Cardinal Adrian to Charles, 13 November 1520; ANTT Corpo Cronológico Parte I, Maço 26, no. 85, Ambassador João Rodriguez to King Manuel, 28 October 1520.

110. AGS PR 2-1/253, Anonymous letter [fray Francisco de León] to Cardinal Adrian, undated [November 1520], transcribed in Bergenroth, *Supplement to State Papers,* doc. 67.

111. AGS PR 2-1-20/43, Cardinal Adrian to Charles, 14 September 1520; ANTT Corpo Cronológico Parte I, Maço 26, no. 85, João Rodriguez to King Manuel, 28 October 1520.

112. AGS PR 2-1-18/38, Cardinal Adrian to Charles, 4 September 1520.

113. AGS PR 2-1/253, Anonymous [fray Francisco de León] to Cardinal Adrian, undated [November 1520], transcribed in *Letters, Despatches, and State Papers,* suppl., doc. 67.

114. AGS PR 2-1-25, Cardinal Adrian to Charles, 21 October 1520; AGS PR 2-1-32, Cardinal Adrian to Charles, 17 November 1520; AGS PR 2-1-38, Cardinal Adrian to Charles, 6 December 1520.

115. AGS PR 2-1/253, Anonymous letter [fray Francisco de León] to Cardinal Adrian, undated [November 1520].

116. AGS Estado 7, fol. 222, Lope Hurtado to Charles, 16 December 1520; AGS PR 2-1-45, Cardinal Adrian to Charles, 20 December 1520.

117. AGS PR 2-36/55, Lope Hurtado de Mendoza to Charles, 10 December 1520.

118. AMG leg. 5, no. 1503, Prior of the monastery of la Mejorada to the prior of Our Lady of Guadalupe, 13 December 1520.

119. AGS PR 2-36/55, Lope Hurtado de Mendoza to Charles, 10 December 1520.

120. AGS PR 2-1-45, Adrian of Utrecht to Charles, 20 December 1520.

121. Juan Ignacio Gutiérrez Nieto, *Las comunidades como movimiento antiseñorial* (Barcelona: Editorial Planeta, 1973), 314–22.

122. When the Comuneros criticized the Constable of Castile, Juana declared that his house had always been very loyal to the crown and that don Íñigo Fernández de Velasco would act as his predecessors had. In this way, she restated her belief in governmental tradition and family continuity. AGS PR 2-1/253, Anonymous [fray Francisco de León] to Cardinal Adrian, undated [November 1520].

123. AGS PR 1-96/60, Admiral of Castile and Count of Benavente to Charles, 4 December 1520; AGS PR 1-106/242, Count of Haro to Charles, 5 December 1520; AGS PR 2-36/53, Lope Hurtado to Charles, 6 December 1520; AGS PR 2-36/55, Lope Hurtado to Charles, 10 December 1520.

124. AGRB Gachard 614, fol. 186, Denia to Charles, 21 February 1521.

125. AGS PR 1-96/42, Instructions of the Admiral of Castile for Angelo de Bursa, 26 January 1521.

126. BL Ad. ms. 8219, fols. 11–14v, Instructions of the Admiral of Castile for Angelo de Bursa, undated.

127. AGS PR 2-1-79, Cardinal Adrian to Charles, 9 April 1521.

128. AGS PR 2-1-51, Cardinal Adrian to Charles, 16 January 1521.

129. RAH N-43, fols. 270–81, General pardon and exceptions, 28 October 1522.

130. AGRB Gachard 614, Charles to the governors of Castile, 17 December 1520.

131. AGS PR 1-96/97, Admiral of Castile to Charles, 23 December 1520.

132. AGS PR 2-1-68, Cardinal Adrian to Charles, 21 February 1521.

133. AGS PR 2-1-69, Cardinal Adrian to Charles, 23 February 1521.

134. AGRB Gachard 614, fol. 189, Denia to Charles, 16 March 1521; AGRB Gachard 614, fol. 194, Denia to Charles, 14 April 1521.

135. AGS PR 1-96/77, Instructions of the admiral for Angelo de Bursa, 28 March 1521.

136. AGS PR 1-96/24, Instructions of the admiral for Angelo de Bursa, 16 March 1521; AGS PR 1-96/46, Instructions of the admiral for Angelo de Bursa, 16 March 1521.

137. AGS PR 4-48, Denia to Charles [deciphered], undated [January 1521].

138. AGS PR 2-1-85 and 2-1-87, Cardinal Adrian to Charles, 8 August 1521; AGS Estado 27-235, Constable to Charles, 8 December 1521.

139. AGS Estado 8-165, Instructions of Denia for Don Hernando de Tovar, December 1521.

140. AGS Estado 5-276, Instructions of the admiral for Angelo de Bursa, 23 May 1521.

141. AGS PR 1-96/140, Instructions of the admiral for Angelo de Bursa, 27 August 1521.

142. AGS PR 1-96/24, Instructions of the admiral for Angelo de Bursa, 16 March 1521.

143. AGS PR 1-96/52, Instructions of the admiral for Angelo de Bursa, 21 June 1521.

144. AGS PR 1-96/105, Instructions of the admiral for Sancho Núñez de Legoa, 5 July 1521.

145. AGS Estado 8-122, Catalina to Charles, 19 August 1521.

146. AGS Estado 8-164, Minutes of letters from Denia to Charles, 28 July and 5 August 1521; AGS Estado 8-114, Marquise of Denia to Charles, 30 July 1521.

147. AGS Estado 8-165, Instructions of Denia for don Hernando de Tovar, December 1521.

148. AGS Estado 8-125 and 192, The *infanta* Catalina and fray Juan de Ávila to Charles, 26 January and 19 August 1521; AGS PR 2-1-93, Cardinal Adrian to Charles, 18 September 1521, and AGS Estado 5-101, Juan de Ávila to Charles, 27 September 1521; ADM caja 4 (leg. 246), no. 53, Charles to Denia, 16 September 1523. The Franciscan Juan de Ávila, at Tordesillas since 13 January 1513, should not be confused with the more famous mystic, Juan de Ávila (1502–69), who began studies in Salamanca in 1516. *Archivo biográfico de España, Portugal y Iberoamérica*, ed. Victor Herrero Mediavilla (Munich: Saur, 1995), 90.

149. ADM caja 4 (leg. 246), no. 43, Charles to Denia, 22 September 1520; AGS PR 5-293, Denia to Charles, 25 January 1522. The Habsburgs needed another Portuguese marriage, and the emperor's confessor, Francisco García de Loaisa, accordingly found Catalina free of obligations to the Marquis of Brandenburg and the Duke of Saxony. AGS Estado 12-241, Denia to Charles, 15 June 1524; AGS Estado 8-143, Fray García de Loaisa to Charles, 15 July [1524].

150. AGS Estado 13-270, Admiral to Charles, 2 January 1525.

151. AGS Estado 13-14, Admiral to Charles, 15 January 1525.
152. AGS Estado II-i-157, Denia to Charles, 8 November 1526.
153. ADM caja 4 (leg. 246), no. 82, Charles to Denia, 28 July 1529.
154. AGS Estado 24-291, Denia to Charles, 20 February 1532.
155. AGS Estado 24-290, Denia to Charles, 20 March 1532.
156. AGS Estado 22-122, Denia to Charles, 10 May 1531. The records for Juana's household include summaries of the benefits of "blessed accounts," in Sion and England. AGS CSR 12-19/609, 610, 611, "Memorial de lo que se gana en rezar las cuentas de ynglaterra," 1530.
157. AGS CSR 18-5/351, Denia to Ochoa de Landa, 1 June 1531; AGS Estado 22-254, Denia to Charles, 27 June 1531.
158. Sandoval, *Historia de la vida y hechos del Emperador Carlos V,* I, xxvii, 79; Jan Brans, *De Gevangene van Tordesillas* (Leuven: Davidsfonds, 1962); and, most recently, Manuel Fernández Álvarez, *Juana la loca: La cautiva de Tordesillas* (Madrid: Espasa Calpe, 2000). For a particularly bleak view of Juana's alleged captivity, see Miller, *The Castles and the Crown, Spain,* 347–48.
159. AGS Estado 27-161, Denia to the emperor, 12 May 1533.
160. AGS Estado 36-243, Denia to Charles, 20 February 1534.
161. The act of dictating a testament required a sound mind, which potentially explains why the document in question, if it ever existed, no longer remains in the Archivo General de Simancas. AGS Estado 29-196, Denia to Charles, 12 April 1534; *El Emperador Carlos V y su corte según las cartas de Don Martín de Salinas, embajador del infante Don Fernando (1522–1539)* (Madrid: Real Academia de la Historia, 1903–5), 565.
162. AGS CMC 1a época 1544, "Provança de Alonso de Ribera," 20 August 1555.
163. Asking Isabel to send him news of her health and that of Charles as he embarked upon the conquest of Tunis, Denia asserted that the well-being of all Christianity depended on them. AGS Estado 32-69, Denia to Isabel, 8 July 1535, transcribed in *Corpus documental de Carlos V,* 2:433–34.
164. AGS CSR 24-26/310, Draft of orders from the empress to the Marquise of Denia and the Marquis don Luis, undated [early 1536].
165. AGS Estado 35-29, Charles to the Empress Isabel, 5 March 1536; AGS GA 8-103, "Memorial de las cosas que tocan a la casa de la reyna, n.s." [1536].
166. AGS CSR 17-2/7–9, Payroll signed by the Marquis of Denia, [1522]; AGS Estado 13, fol. 275, Denia to Charles, 25 October 1525; AGS CSR 18-1/3, Payroll signed by the Empress Isabel, 20 July 1528.
167. AGS Estado 21-335, Minutes of a letter from Charles to Denia, 31 July 1530. Carrying recommendations from both the marquis and the admiral, don Hernando de Rojas joined Charles in Brussels in January of 1531. AGS Estado 20-134, Admiral to Charles, 12 November 1530; AGS Estado 20-135, Denia to Charles, 14 November 1530; AGS Estado 22-292, Minutes of letters from the king, 27 January 1531.
168. Denia had sought the bishopric of Burgos and archbishopric of Tarragona for his clerical sons. Although don Diego lost royal favor for poor conduct, don Cristobal became one of Juana's chaplain. AGS GA 8-102, "Memorial de la casa de la reyna n.s." [1536]; AGS Estado 24-291, Denia to Charles, 20 February 1532; AGS Estado 26-84, Denia to Charles, 15 January 1533; Alonso López de Haro, *Nobiliario genealógico de los reyes y títulos de España* (Madrid: Luis Sánchez, 1622), 1:164–65.

169. AGS CSR 18-3/221, "Sumario de todos los oficiales de la casa de la reyna . . ." [1534].

170. AGS CSR 12-5/62, Denia to Andrés Martínez de Ondarça, 21 June [1533?].

171. AGS Estado 38-199, Denia (don Luis) to the Empress Isabel, 4 July 1536.

172. AGS Estado 22-254, Denia to Charles, 27 June 1531. In 1532, when both doña Catalina de Zúñiga and Isabel de Quiñones were pregnant, the marquis requested permission for don Enrique and don Luis to visit them at Tordesillas. AGS Estado 24-242, Denia to Charles, 8 October [1532].

173. AGS CSR 24-30/387 and 388, Marquise of Denia to Pope Adrian, undated [1523].

174. AGS Estado 24-20, Marquise of Denia to the Empress Isabel, 14 November 1532; ADM caja 4 (leg. 246), no. 85, Charles to Denia (don Luis), 18 September 1538.

175. An account of household personnel from the late 1520s lists María and Francisca de Ribera, as well as doña Catalina de Alarcon, her daughter doña Beatriz, and her sister, doña Fermina, among Juana's female attendants. AGS CSR 24-72/901 a 912, "Relación del tiempo que cada un criado de la Reyna, Nra. Sa., sirve a Su. Al. . . .," undated. In addition to his father's office, Alonso de Ribera gained a position for his wife, doña Marina de Vargas, among the queen's female attendants. AGS CSR 18-3/221, "Sumario de todos los oficiales de la casa de la reyna . . ." [1534].

176. AGS Estado 14-28, Denia to Charles, 22 April 1526; AGS CSR 12-2/16, Admiral to Ochoa de Landa, 12 March 1522.

177. Documentation regarding this interesting case can be found in AGS CSR 12-19/566-567, "Recebta del Clerigo de Contrasta para el mal de mi muger"; AGS, CSR 12-19/567, "Para la tentación diabolica"; and AGS, CSR 24-38/510, "Lo que la comadre syente del mal desta señora . . ."

178. AGS Estado 20-103, Denia to Charles, 2 October 1530.

179. AGS CSR 12-19/568-570, "Reçebta e regimiento del Doctor de Valladolid," April 1531; AGS CSR 24-40/510, Denia to the Empress Isabel, 21 May 1531; AGS CSR 25-13/457 to 460, "Gastos hechos en las exequias de Ochoa de Landa," June 1531.

180. AGS CSR 12-5/78, Denia to Andrés Martínez de Ordança, 11 June 1531.

181. AGS Estado 36-211, Denia (don Luis) to the Empress Isabel, 9 April 1536.

182. In 1568, the Count of Lerma, and four other trusted nobles, led by Ruy Gómez de Silva, pledged to guard don Carlos, son of Philip II, according to the king's orders, confining the prince to his room and preventing him from communicating with outsiders. IVDJ 38, Oath of don Francisco de Rojas y Sandoval, Conde de Lerma, 25 January 1568.

183. At the court of Philip III the Empress María, Marguerite of Austria, and Margaret of the Cross would find themselves at odds with Denia's descendant, the Duke of Lerma. Magdalena S. Sánchez, *The Empress, the Queen, and the Nun: Women and Power at the Court of Philip III of Spain* (Baltimore: Johns Hopkins University Press, 1998).

s i x : The Politics of Possession and Salvation

1. Biblioteca del Palacio Real, microfilm 79 [Cámara de Seguridad II/3283], "Inventario de Doña Juana," undated [1565]. Earlier copies of the same inventory can be found in AGS CMC 1a época 1213 and 1544.

2. On the intimate memories contained in personal objects, see Orest Ranum, "The

Refuges of Intimacy," in *A History of Private Life*, ed. Roger Chartier (Cambridge, Mass.: Belknap/Harvard University Press, 1989), 3:206–63.

3. AGS CMC 1a época 1544, "Provança de Diego de Ribera," 27 April 1524.

4. AGS CMC 1a época 1544, "Provança de Alonso de Ribera," 20 August 1555.

5. AGS Estado 5, fol. 323, Denia to Charles, undated [October 1519]; AGS CMC 1a época 1544, "Provança de Alonso de Ribera," 20 August 1555.

6. Certain items apparently caught the Empress Isabel's attention during her first visit to Tordesillas. Denia sent Camarero Alonso de Ribera to carry these goods to the empress along with an order, requesting her to sign for them. Aware that the bureaucratic measure could cause offense, the marquis asked Isabel to forgive such trivial details (*nonadas*). AGS Estado 12-38, Denia to the empress, 23 February 1531. Juan de Arganda reported that Philip had ordered additional silver and gold removed from the queen's trunks when he returned to Spain in 1552. AGS CMC 1a época 1544, "Provança de Alonso de Ribera," 20 August 1555.

7. Denia also correctly believed that cloth could transmit plague. AGS Estado 36-245, Denia to Charles, 29 May 1534.

8. See Chapter 1.

9. AGS CMC 1a época, 1544, "La fe del Marqués de Denia sobre el cofre para el Sr. Camarero," 11 August 1555.

10. Rather than a slovenly recluse, the washerwoman portrayed a queen who cared about her appearance. A noblewoman who had witnessed the scene from a distance, doña Francisca de Alba, thought that she had seen a luminous piece of gold about the shape of a real and the length of a palm. Strangely enough, no witness identified the object as a mirror.

11. AGS CMC 1a época, 1544, Don Leonardo Marino to the clerics of Tordesillas, 4 July 1555.

12. Deciding in favor of the marquis, Philip granted Tordesillas independent jurisdiction and empowered the marquis to select its *corregidor*. AGS Estado 76-28 and 29, Charles to Philip, 19 October 1548; AGS Estado 76-173–76, Juan Vázquez to Philip, 4 December 1548; AGS Estado 76-159, Denia to Philip, 18 December 1548. Philip also reported Juana's bouts of illness to Charles. AGS Estado 69-37, Minutes of letters from Philip to Charles, 5 May 1545; AGS Estado 75-270 (2), Philip to Denia, 1 January 1548.

13. In late 1550, Maximilian returned to Germany, and María remained in Spain as the sole regent. AHN Nobleza, Frías 22/105, Maximilian and María in the name of Charles to the Count of Oropesa, 28 October 1550.

14. Alonso Enríquez de Guzmán, *Libro de la vida y costumbres*, ed. Hayward Keniston (Madrid: Atlas, 1960), 242.

15. Ibid.

16. Enríquez de Guzmán, *Libro de la vida y costumbres*, 241–44.

17. AGRB Gachard 615 [unfoliated], Licentiate [Gámiz] to Fernando, 4 August 1550, cited from the Haus-, Hof- und Staatsarchiv, Viena, Spanien, Diplomatishche Korrespondenz, Karton 2 (alt. Fasz. 2), by José Luis Cano de Gardoqui García, *Tordesillas 1494* (Valladolid: Electa, 1994), 226.

18. AGRB Gachard 615 [unfoliated], Licentiate [Gámiz] to Fernando, 4 August 1550.

19. The queen frequently requested, and occasionally received, funds delivered directly to her, bypassing the regular household structure. Treasurer Ochoa de Landa delivered 32,000 mrs "in the royal hands of her Highness" in January 1529 and deposited an addi-

tional 200 ducats or 75,000 mrs "in her royal hands" nine months later. AGS CSR 18-2/82, Denia to Ochoa de Landa, 9 January 1529; AGS CSR 18-2/85, Denia to Ochoa de Landa, 3 September 1529. In 1536 the queen received "in her hands" 300 gold ducats out of the entire household's allotment of 400 ducats for "extraordinary" costs. AGS Estado 40-79, marquise and Denia to Charles, 27 March 1537; AGS CSR 25-51/149, Consultations with the emperor, March 1537.

20. AGRB Gachard 615 [unfoliated], Licentiate [Gámiz] to Fernando, 4 August 1550. In fact, Juana's attitude toward her eldest son remains difficult to ascertain. Although Charles's memoirs recorded several visits "to kiss the hands of the queen, his mother," the terse formula disclosed little about their relationship. *Corpus documental de Carlos V,* ed. Manuel Fernández Álvarez, vol. 4 (Universidad de Salamanca, 1979), 487, 491, 503

21. AGRB Gachard 615 [unfoliated], Licentiate [Gámiz] to Fernando, 4 August 1550.

22. AGS Estado 81-43, María and Maximilian to Charles, 4 August 1550.

23. On the "infectious and demonic potential of royalty," see David Nirenberg, *Communities of Violence: Persecution of Minorities in the Middle Ages* (Princeton: Princeton University Press, 1996), 61–62.

24. AGS CMC 1a época, leg. 1213, Juana's inventory, 1555.

25. For a discussion of the motto *Christus vincit, Christus regnat, Christus imperat,* see Ernst H. Kantorowicz, *Laudes Regiae: A Study in Liturgical Acclamations and Mediaeval Ruler Worship* (Berkeley: University of California Press, 1946), 1–3, 180–83. Juana's adjustment to the third phrase appears particularly significant.

26. Sebastián de Covarrubias Orozco, "Agnusdéi," in *Tesoro de la Lengua Castellana o Española,* ed. Felipe C. R. Maldonado (Madrid: Editorial Castalia, 1995), 25.

27. Lightning bolts reportedly claimed ten lives in Tordesillas. When the storm began on 23 June 1550, Denia went to Juana's chamber and lit holy candles. AGRB Gachard 615 [unfoliated], Licenciate [Gámiz] to Fernando, 9 July 1550.

28. Sara T. Nalle, *God in La Mancha: Religious Reform and the People of Cuenca, 1500–1650* (Baltimore: Johns Hopkins University Press, 1992), 22–30.

29. ADM caja 4 (leg. 246), no. 53, Charles to Denia, 16 September 1523.

30. AGS CSR 14-6/435–36, Salaries paid by King Fernando, 3 April 1509; AGS CSR 17-2/7–9, Salaries paid by Denia, undated [1522]; CSR 56-931–36, Charles to Denia, 11 September 1523; AGS Estado 26-134, "Relación de todas maneras de oficios e oficiales e otros gastos de la casa real de la reyna Doña Ysabel . . . y de la casa de la Reyna Doña Juana," undated [1533]. Denia increasingly filled these offices with members of his own family as well as the offspring of Juana's other attendants. AGS CSR 24-26/278, Asiento de capellán para Fernando, hijo del Doctor Santa Cara, médico, undated [after 1524]; AGS Estado 18-165, Consulta tocante a particulares, 1534; AGS GA 8-102, "Memorial de la Casa de la Reyna," 1536.

31. AGS Estado 3-113, Creencia de Doña María de Ulloa, undated [1516]; AGS PR 2-1/253, Anonymous [fray Francisco de León] to Cardinal Adrian, undated [November 1520].

32. AGS Estado 12-38, Denia to the Empress Isabel, 23 February [1532?]; AGS Estado 12-39, Denia to the Empress Isabel, 23 February [1531?].

33. AGS Estado 24-290, Denia to Charles, 20 March 1532.

34. AGS Estado 29-196, Denia to Charles, 12 April 1534; AGS Estado 29-180, Denia to Charles, 22 April 1534.

35. AGS Estado 36-214, Denia to Nicolás de Sosa, 7 May 1535.

36. AGS Estado 42-145/1, Charles to Denia, 6 November 1538.

37. BN Madrid, ms. 1778, fols. 70v–71v, and RAH G-23, fols. 74v–75r, Denia to Charles, 25 November 1538.

38. AGS Estado 24-292, Denia to Charles, 24 April 1532.

39. In 1528, Borja entered the service of the Empress Isabel and soon married one of her favorite attendants. Naming their first child after the emperor, Borja and his wife selected three-year-old Prince Philip for the godfather. When the Empress Isabel died in 1539, Borja and Philip accompanied her corpse from Toledo to Granada—an experience that allegedly inspired the former to take religious vows. He nevertheless continued to serve the royal family as Viceroy of Catalonia and subsequently *mayordomo* to the emperor's daughter, María, charged with governing her household and property. Archivo de la Casa Ducal del Alburquerque, caja 49, IV, leg. 5B, núms. 23 and 24, Cédulas del Emperador, 22 April 1543.

40. ADM caja 4 (leg. 246), no. 107, Charles to Doña Isabel de Borja, 27 December 1551.

41. During one visit to his daughter Isabel, Borja allegedly commented upon worldly vanities as the family dined. When a bone in her food dislodged one of Isabel's teeth, the Jesuit remarked that the countess appeared quite ugly without the tooth. Raising his eyes to heaven, Borja then replaced the tooth, advising his daughter that it would not fall out again. After Isabel's death the tooth that Borja had touched allegedly remained intact while the others rotted. *Sanctus Franciscus Borgia Quartus Gandiae Dux et Societatis Jesu Praepositus Generalis Tertius* (Roma: Monumenta Historica Societatis Jesu, 1894), 1:625–26.

42. AGS Estado 89-344, Denia to Prince Philip, 9 May 1552.

43. Saint Francis de Borja, "Instrucción para el buen gobierno de un señor en sus estados," in *Tratados Espirituales*, ed. Candido de Dalmases (Barcelona: Juan Flors, 1964), 165–219.

44. Marcel Bataillon, "Jeanne d'Autriche, Princesse de Portugal," in *Études sur le Portugal au temps de l'humanisme* (Coimbra: University of Coimbra, 1952), 267. Borja's reluctance to accept the worldly commission did not prevent him from admiring Juana of Austria's dedication to the government, which he found unusual for her age and gender. Princess Juana expressed a desire to take vows in the Jesuit order, perhaps to avoid a second marriage. Referring to the princess as "Mateo Sánchez," Francisco de Borja and Ignatius Loyola discussed reservations about admitting a woman to the order. While unable to refuse such an illustrious personage, the Jesuits insisted on "scholarly vows" that would allow the princess to contract a second marriage if necessary.

45. AGS Estado 109-331, Francisco de Borja to Philip, undated [early May 1554].

46. Unbeknown to the Jesuit, more than thirty years earlier Juana had made a comparable agreement to convince Comuneros occupying the royal palace to remove her ladies. See Chapter 5.

47. The impediment would have been caused by the servants' malicious acts. Did Juana believe her servants were witches, or was she trying to manipulate the friar? Probably both, since religious faith and politics were entirely compatible. Almost everyone believed in Satan, and his interference was also a logical way to explain the servants' abuse of their queen.

48. Queen Juana wondered when Philip II would be returning to Spain. Princess

Juana of Portugal may have informed the queen that she would reside in Valladolid. Borja did not mention how he handled either inquiry.

49. Archivum Societatis Iesu, Rome, Epp. NN. 57, no. 70, Francisco de Borja to Ignatius de Loyola, undated.

50. AGS Estado 109-331, Francisco de Borja to Philip, undated [early May 1554].

51. Ibid.

52. The distinction here is between the queen being a witch and being bewitched. Satan could have possessed Juana even if her contact with him had been involuntary.

53. AGS Estado 109-330, Francisco de Borja to Philip, 10 May 1554.

54. Ibid.

55. Support for this interpretation can be found in Pedro Ciruelo, *Reprovacion de las supersticiones y hechizerias*, ed. Alva V. Ebersole (Valencia: Artes Gráficas Soler, 1978; orig. 1530), 9, 48.

56. AGS Estado 109-253, Luis de la Cruz to Philip, 15 May 1554.

57. Ibid.

58. Ciruelo had warned his readers about Satan in feline form, which the devil could adopt. Pedro Ciruelo, *Reprouacion de las supersticiones y hechizerias*, 49. Historian Carlo Ginzburg notes a number of instances in which women were believed to have transformed themselves or others into cats. See Carlo Ginzburg, *The Night Battles: Witchcraft and Agrarian Cults in the Sixteenth and Seventeenth Centuries*, trans. John Tedeschi and Anne Tedeschi. (London: Routledge & Kegan Paul, 1983), 86, 89, 99, 106, 142. Animal forms were also appropriate for queens' apocalyptic visions. Historian Peggy Liss quotes Juana's mother, Isabel, at the end of her life, asking the archangel Michael to receive and defend her soul "from that cruel beast and old serpent who will then want to devour me." According to Liss, the beast and the serpent represented the Antichrist and the Devil from the Revelation of Saint John the Evangelist. Liss, *Isabel the Queen*, 346.

59. AGS Estado 109-253, Luis de la Cruz to Philip, 15 May 1554.

60. AGS CC 363, Juana of Austria to Juan Vázquez, her secretary [holograph], undated [mid-February 1555].

61. AGS CC 363, Juana of Austria to Juan Vázquez, her secretary [holograph], undated [mid-February 1555].

62. AGS Estado 109-324, Denia to Charles, 17 March 1555.

63. On views of death in early modern Spain, see Fernando Martínez Gil, *Muerte y sociedad en la España de los Austrias* (Madrid: Siglo Veintiuno, 1993), and Carlos M. N. Eire, *From Madrid to Purgatory: The Art and Craft of Dying in Sixteenth-Century Spain* (New York: Cambridge University Press, 1995).

64. AGS Estado 109-263, Francisco de Borja to Charles, 19 May 1555.

65. Ibid.

66. AGRB Gachard 615, Charles V to Fernando, 10 May 1555.

67. AGS CJH 27-221, Prince Philip to Denia, 10 April 1554; AGS CSR 24-33/243, Prince Philip to Denia, undated copy [April 1554].

68. AGS Estado 109-260, Marquis to Philip, undated [1555].

69. AGS Estado 109-259, Denia to Charles, 26 May 1555. Folios 259 through 269 of Estado 109 in Simancas list various demands for funds after Juana's death.

70. AGS CSR 34-8/278–76, Philip to Luis de Landa, 16 February 1560.

71. AGS CSR 19-17/1704, Denia to Luis de Landa, 15 April 1555.

72. AGS CSR 66-212, Princess Juana in the name of King Philip to their governor and principal accountants, 8 November 1556.

73. BN Madrid, ms. 670, fols. 160–77, "Los offiçiales y mugeres, capellanes y criados de la casa de la reina, nuestra señora, questa en gloria . . ."

74. AGRB Gachard 614, fol. 367, Denia to King Philip, 10 February 1556.

75. AGS Estado 109-262, Princess Juana to Charles, 31 May 1557.

76. AGS PR 29-17, "Cuaderno de la distribución de 10 V ds que el Emperador mandó dar para bien del anima de su madre . . .," 10 September 1555.

77. AGS CC 366-45, "Fé de las cosas viejas e quebradas que quedan en la cámara de Su. Al.," 1557.

78. AGS PR 29-17, "Cuaderno de la distribución de 10 V ds que el Emperador mandó dar para bien del anima de su madre . . .," 10 September 1555.

79. AGS CMC 1a época, Charge and discharge of Diego and Alonso de Ribera, 1555.

80. AGS CC 132, fols. 291–92v, Philip II to his principal accountants, 11 March 1561.

81. AGS CC 132, fols. 291–92v, Philip II to his principal accountants, 11 March 1561.

82. In Seville, moreover, master carpenters constructed a giant tomb to commemorate the queen. Biblioteca Colombina, Sevilla, ms. 59-1-3, fols. 148–88, "Exequias de la Reyna N[uest]ra Señora doña Juana, madre del emperador don Carlos V, celebradas en esta muy noble y muy leal ciudad de Sevilla," 1555.

83. Archivo de la Real Chancilleria de Valladolid, Libro de Acuerdo 2, fols. 132–35, "Discurso de lo que se hizo en esta real audiençia quando fallesció la majestad de la reyna doña Juana . . . " April–May 1555.

84. AGS GA 56-86, City of Gibraltar to Princess Juana, 20 May 1555; AGS Estado 108-138 and 109-157, Princess Juana to Charles, undated [June 1555].

85. IVDJ libro 26–II-10, fols. 128v–134v, Exequies for Queen Juana in Brussels, 16–17 September 1555.

86. *Sermón hecho por el ilustrísimo y reverendísimo señor Arçobispo de Saçer en su yglesia metropolitana, en las honras de la Serenísima y Católica Reyna Doña Juana madre del Emperador y Rey, nro. señor* (Valencia: Casa de Antón Sanahuja, 1556).

87. AGRB Gachard 614, fol. 357, Ruy Gómez de Silva to Francisco de Eraso, 15 May 1555.

88. AGS PR 42-19, "Registro original del protesto que el rey d. Felipe II hizo sobre la reservación del derecho de la Reina Da Juana su abuela al reino de Nápoles," 6 May 1555.

89. Antonio Gallego Burin, *La capilla real de Granada* (Granada: Paulino Ventura Traveset, 1931), 70, 76, 85, 199. See also Duque de T'Serclaes, "Traslación de cuerpos reales de Granada a San Lorenzo de El Escorial y de Valladolid a Granada: Siete cartas inéditas del rey D. Felipe II," *Boletín de la Real Academia de la Historia* 60, no. 1 (January 1912): 5–24.

90. Francisco de Borja, "Instrucción para el buen gobierno," 209.

91. AHN Nobleza, Frías 24/61, Philip to the Count of Oropesa, 21 April 1568; AHN Nobleza Frías 24/62, Philip to the Count of Oropesa, 5 May 1568.

92. AHN Osuna 1976-27 (1), Philip to the Duke of Infantado, 5 October 1573.

93. IVDJ Envio 7 (II), Instructions for the removal and transport of royal bodies, 12 April 1573.

94. BNM ms. 18654, no. 42, "Provisión de los sepulcros de D. Felipe . . . y Da. Juana a la capilla de los Reyes Católicos," 15 December 1591.

Conclusions

1. Hernández, *Vida, martirio y traslación de la gloriosa Virgen y Mártir Santa Leocadia,* fols. 73v, 224–24v.

2. Blancas, *Coronaciones de los serenísimos reyes de Aragón. I diarii di Marino Sanuto,* 25:426.

3. Minois, *Anne de Bretagne,* 244, 335, 348.

4. Ibid., 377–78.

5. Pauline Matarasso, *Queen's Mate: Three Women of Power in France on the Eve of the Renaissance* (Aldershot: Ashgate, 2001), 291.

6. Rodrigo Jiménez de Rada, *Historia de los hechos de España o historia gótica* (Madrid, 1989), 336–37.

7. Miriam Shadis, *Political Women in the High Middle Ages: Berenguela of Castile and Her Family* (New York: Palgrave Macmillan, 2003).

8. Norbert Elias, *The Court Society,* trans. Edmund Jephcott (Oxford: Basil Blackwell, 1983; orig. 1939), 3–4, 16.

9. Rodríguez Villa, *La Reina Doña Juana la loca,* esp. 410–11. See also Emilia Pardo Bazán, *Hombres y Mujeres de Antaño (Semblanzas)* (Barcelona: López, editor, ca. 1889), 119–41.

10. Prawdin, *The Mad Queen.*

11. Pérez, *La revolucion de las comunidades de Castilla,* 193–94.

12. Erasmus, *The Praise of Folly,* 94, 114, 118, 120–24; Sebastian Brant, *The Ship of Fools,* trans. Edwin H. Zeydel (New York: Columbia University Press, 1944); *Epistolario de Pedro Mártir,* 10: epist. 516.

13. In part my approach to these sources draws on the recent use of inquisitorial documents for revealing larger social conflicts rather than heresy (or insanity) itself. Jaime Contreras, *Soto contra Riquelmes: Regidores, inquisidores y criptojudios* (Madrid: Anaya and M. Muchnik, 1992).

14. *Vulgata aedito veteris ac Novi Testamenti* (Venice, 1542), Psalm 44, f. 35; Francisco de Osuna, *Abecedario espiritual* (Burgos: Juan de Junta, 1544), 3:56v. Osuna's third volume, first published in 1527, appears to have been written during the lifetime of King Fernando, since Charles V's first daughter was born in 1530. The 1527 version's dedication to the Marquis of Villena, who knew Juana well, also indicated that the marquis had "loved" and "appropriated" the book before its publication.

15. Osuna, *Abecedario espiritual,* 3:56v.

16. AGS CSR 56-931–936, King Charles regarding his mother's household, 11 September 1523.

17. Enríquez de Guzmán, *Libro de la vida y costumbres,* 242.

18. *Sermón hecho por el ilustrísimo y reverendísimo señor Arçobispo de Saçer en su yglesia metropolitana, en las honras de la Serenísima y Católica Reyna Doña Juana.*

19. J. H. Elliott has noted a tendency to isolate the Spanish king through court ceremonial giving him access to only a few aristocrats and otherwise ensuring his seclusion. J. H. Elliott, "The Court of the Spanish Habsburgs: A Peculiar Institution?" in *Spain and Its World, 1500–1700* (New Haven: Yale University Press, 1989), esp. 148–49, 154, 160–61.

20. The only history that mentions this bull makes no reference to Juana. Alexandre

Henne and Alphonse Wauters, *Histoire de la Ville de Bruxelles*, ed. Mina Martins (Brussels 1968–72; orig. 1845), 4:161. Most Franciscan histories credit Father Theodore of Munster with reforming the Brussels Claires. Henrici Sedulii, "Chronicon Werthense," in *Collectanea Franciscana* XVI–XVII, ed. David de Kok (1946–47; orig. 1620), 66; J. Goyens, "Passage de soeurs grises de Bruxelles à l'Ordre de Sainte Claire," *Archivum Franciscanum Historicum* 36 (1943), 227–34; Heribert R. Roggen, *De Clarissenorde in de Nederlanden (Instrumenta Franciscana)* (Sint-Truiden: Instituut voor Franciscaanse Geschiedenis, 1995), 195–99. Although Franco-Habsburg domination of Spain appeared a greater threat during Juana's lifetime, subsequent opposition to Spanish rule may have dissuaded the Brussels Claires from acknowledging their patroness.

21. AGS PR 56-18, "Carta patente de la reyna de gloriosa memoria," 23 November 1504.

22. Gómez de Fuensalida, *Correspondencia*, 312–13, 327.

23. Ibid., 297–301.

24. BN Madrid, ms. 18761, no. 26, "Noticia de lo que al presidente y oidores del consejo real les pasó con la Reina doña Juana en Burgos," 26 September 1506; AMS Actas Capitulares, caja 29, carpeta 121, fols. 6 and 7, Procurators at the Cortes to the town council of Seville, 18 December 1506.

25. RAH Salazar A-12, fol. 130, Fray Francisco Ruiz al secretario Miguel Pérez de Almazán, 9 de marzo de 1507, transcribed in Rodríguez Villa, *La Reina Doña Juana la Loca*, 464–65.

26. AGS CSR 53-5, 15-1/24 y 70, Mosen Ferrer to Ochoa de Landa, 16 May 1509, 12 June and 10 November 1511; AGS CSR 53-15, Mosen Ferrer to the Bachiler Torisco, resident of Tordesillas, 29 January 1513; AGS CSR 24-1/42 and 24-6/95, King Ferdinand on the costs of the church and memorial regarding the service of the chapel, 4 August 1514 and undated [1524].

27. On fray Juan de Ávila, see Manuel de Castro, "Confesores franciscanos en la corte de los Reyes Católicos," *Archivo Ibero Americano* 34 (1974): 55–126, esp. 102–7.

28. AHN Universidades 1224F, f. 105r, "Carta de los religiosos del convento de Avila al Vicario General para pasar a la observancia," 29 July 1494, transcribed in José García Oro, *Cisneros y la reforma del clero español en tiempo de los Reyes Católicos* (Madrid: CSIC, 1977), 175.

29. AHN Universidades 1224F, f. 105r, "Carta de los religiosos del convento de Avila al Vicario General para pasar a la observancia," 29 July 1494.

30. *Cuentas de Gonzalo de Baeza*, 2:82, cited in J. Meseguer Fernández, "Franciscanismo de Isabel la Católica," *Archivo Ibero Americano* 19 (January–June 1959): 1–43.

31. Leonardo Herrero, "El sepulcro de los padres de Santa Teresa en la iglesia del exconvento de Saint Francis de Avila," *Boletín de la Real Academia de Historia* 71 (1917): 534–35.

32. Guevara, *Relox de Príncipes*, 87.

Archival and Manuscript Sources

BARCELONA
Archivo de la Corona de Aragón
  Cancilleria Reg. 3537, 3546, 3569, 3573, 3577, 3614, 3584, 3896, 3897, 3908, 3909,
    3912, 3973, 4011, 4012
  Cancilleria, Cartas Reales, Fer. II, caja 1, 2, 3, 4
  Cancilleria Pergamins 355, Carlos I
Arxiu Historiç Municipal
  Consell de Cent, Sèrie II, reg. 44; Sèrie VI, reg. 42–44; Sèrie VII, reg. 1; Sèrie IX,
    Subsèrie A, c. 6–7

BERLIN
Staatliche Museen. Kupferstichkabinett
  ms. 78 D 5

BRUSSELS
Archives Générales du Royaume à Bruxelles
  Papiers d'État et d'Audience 13, 14, 22, 34, 73, 1078, 1082
  Chambre des Comptes 7218, 7220, 15733f, 15751b, 15760b, 15765b, 15773b,
    16606–7, 16611–12, 16617, 30705
  Papiers Gachard 611–15
  Manuscrits Divers 1678, 1726
Bibliothèque Royale Albert 1/Koninklijke Bibliotheek Albert 1
  mss. 3749, 7376–77, 9126, 10329–65, 10898–952, 14517–21, 21552–69; II 240, 569;
    III 1087
Stads Archief Brussel
  No. VIII, X

BURGOS
Archivo Municipal de Burgos
  Sección Histórica 312–17, 3027

CAMBRIDGE, MASS.
Harvard University, Houghton Library
  Inc 9593.7, Ms Lat 204, Ms Typ 443.1

CÓRDOBA
Archivo Municipal de Córdoba
  caja 3, 7, 15, 17

CUELLAR, SPAIN
Archivo de la Casa Ducal de Alburquerque
  varios 29, 32; leg. 1; cajas 2, 7, 46, 49

EL ESCORIAL
Real Biblioteca de El Escorial
  mss. A. IV. 15, Z. II. 1

FLORENCE
Archivio di Stato di Firenze. Otto di Practica
  Legazioni e Commissarie, Reg. 11

GENOA
Archivio di Stato di Genova
  Archivio Segreto 2793, 2707B, 2707C, 2718

GHENT
Rijksarchief
  No. 892, 900
Stadsarchief
  Chartres no. 796

GUADALUPE, SPAIN
Archivo del Real Monasterio de Guadalupe (Cáceres)
  Códice 87; leg. 4, 5, 42

JEREZ DE LA FONTERA
Colegiata de Jerez
  Ms. 043

LEÓN
Archivo Municipal de León
  leg. 15

LILLE
Archives du Département du Nord à Lille
  B 368, 369, 370, 371, 432, 433, 435, 458 (Museé 122), 857, 1287, 2364, 2156–2196,
    2204, 2228, 2364, 3379, 3380, 3382, 3454–63, 3495, 3507, 12438–42, 17782,
    17791, 17795, 17799, 17802, 17822, 17823, 17825, 17876, 18825, 18826, 18827,
    18846, 18873, 19262, 20156, 20160

LISBON
Arquivo Nacional da Torre do Tombo
  Corpo Cronológico Parte I, Maço 3, 5, 26
  Gaveta Antiga 17, Maço 2

LONDON
British Library
  Ad. ms. 8219, 9926, 9929, 17280, 18851, 18852, 28572
  Eg. ms. 307, 442, 489, 544, 1875, 2059
  Harley ms. 3569
Public Record Office
  E 30

MADRID
Archivo de la Villa de Madrid
  Sección 2, leg. 311, 393, 397, 447
  Sección 3, leg. 64
Archivo Histórico Nacional
  Clero Secular Regular, leg. 982–86, 988, 994, 998, 1001, 1002; carpeta 192, 193
  Diversos Colecciones, leg. 246, 253, 288, 291
  Universidades, legs. 712–14, 741, 757
  Biblioteca Francisco de Zabálburu
  Altamira 12, 17, 18, 114, 119, 222, 241, 245–46
  Miró 23–24
Bilbioteca del Palacio Real
  ms. II/3283 [microfilm 79]
Biblioteca Fundación Lázaro Galdiano
  ms. 386
Biblioteca Nacional
  ms. res. 226; ms. 670, 1253, 1759, 1778, 2058, 2803, 2993, 6020, 6170, 131237,
    17475, 18654, 18691, 18697, 18761, 19699
Instituto Valencia de Don Juan
  38, "Don Carlos pliego"; ms. 26–II-10; Envio 7
Real Academia de la História
  Colección de Salazar y Castro A-8, 9, 11, 12, 16, 50; G-23; K-33; N-34, 43, 44

MANTOVA
Archivio di Stato di Mantova
  Archivio Gonzaga Busta 583, 585

MODENA
Archivio di Stato di Modena
  Cancelleria Ducale. Ambasiatore. Spagna. Busta 1

NEW YORK
Hispanic Society of America
  B 1484; B 2861

PALENCIA
Archivo Municipal de Palencia
  Emb. 27

PARIS
Bibliothèque Nationale
  Manuscrits Espagnols 143, 144, 200, 318
  Moreau 409, 417

ROME
Archivio Segreto Vaticano
  A.A.Arm I–XVIII, nos. 4167, 4172, 4173, 4179, 4197, 4205, 6129, 6154, 6185
  Minutae Brevium Arm. 39, tomo 25
  Reg. Vat. 833, 837
Archivum Societatis Iesu
  Epist. Ext. 25, Epist. NN. 57, NN. 65 (I)
Biblioteca Apostolica Vaticana
  Codices Urbinates Latini 1007, 1198, 1258, 1569
  Codici Capponiani 73.VII, 73.VIII

SANLUCAR DE BARRAAMEDA, SPAIN
Archivo Ducal de Medina Sindonia
  Martorell 529
  Medina Sidonia 931, 933
  Villafranca 4336, 4355
  Velez 537, 549

SEVILLE
Archivo General de las Indias
  Casa de Contratación 4674, 5009, 5103, 5873
  Indiferente General 418
Archivo Municipal de Sevilla
  Actas Capitulares, caja 29, carpetas 119, 121
Biblioteca Colombina
  ms. 59-1-3, fol. 148–88

SIMANCAS, SPAIN
Archivo General de Simancas
  Cámara de Castilla, Cédulas, libros 3, 7–8, 11–12, 16–18, 132, 363, 366; Diversos
    353; Personas leg. 2, 6–10, 15, 24, 26; Pueblos leg. 9, 20
  Consejo y Juntas de Hacienda 2, 11, 27–29
  Contaduría Mayor de Cuentas, 1a época, 42, 267, 1213, 1544
  Casa y Sitios Reales, Obras y Bosques 7–20, 24–25, 34, 46, 48–49, 51, 53–61, 65–66,
    95–98, 394, 396
  Estado, Castilla 1–18, 20–33, 35–36, 38, 40, 44–46, 50, 53–54, 60–61, 64–65, 69 70,
    72–73, 75–77, 81, 89, 108–13, 496

Guerra Antigua 2, 7, 8, 56, 57
Patronato Real 1–5, 13, 27, 29, 41–43, 50, 52, 54, 56, 69, 70
Quitaciones de Corte leg. 27, 35
Registro General de Sello XII.1506; I.1507; IV.1520

TOLEDO
Archivo de la Catedral de Toledo
 Actas Capitulares 3
Archivo Ducal de Medinaceli
 Sección histórica, leg. 246, 256–58, 263, 266, 270, 282–84, 341, 342, 347–48; cajas
  22–24, 40–41
Archivo Histórico de la Provincia de Toledo de la Compañia de Jesús (Alcalá de
  Henares)
 I-2; IV-1
Archivo Histórico Nacional, Sección Nobleza
 Frías 17, 18, 21, 22, 24, 62, 91, 180, 181, 2
 Papeles de Osuna, leg. 326, 420, 1523, 1860, 1954, 1976, 1982, 2116
Archivo Municipal de Toledo
 Alacena 2, leg. 2
 Archivo Secreto, caja 1, leg. 1,2; caja 5, leg. 6; caja 7, leg. 1; caja 8, leg. 1

TORDESILLAS
Archivo del Real Monasterio de Santa Clara de Tordesillas
 caja 30; caja 4915 (microfilm 1746)

VALLADOLID
Archivo de la Real Chancilleria de Valladolid
 Libros de Acuerdo 1, 2
Archivo Histórico Provincial de Valladolid
 Protócolos 4396–4401
 Sección Histórica 242, 265
Archivo Municipal de Valladolid
 Actas 2
Biblioteca de Santa Cruz
Incunable 343

VENICE
Archivio di Stato di Venezia
 Misc. Ducali e atti diplomatici, Busta 21, 20bis, 47
 Senato Secreto, Reg. 39–40
Biblioteca Nazionale Marciana
 ms. It. VII, 1108; ms. It. VII, 1129

WASHINGTON, D.C.
Library of Congress
 John Boyd Thacher Collection 1435, 1437

ZARAGOZA
Archivo Municipal de Zaragoza
    Serie Facticia 20, 27, 121
Archivo Provincial de Zaragoza
    Casa Ducal de Híjar, Sala I, leg. 17, 19, 33, 34, 93, 116, 186, 197; Sala IV, leg. 37

Select Bibliography

PRINTED PRIMARY SOURCES

Abarca, Pedro. *Los anales históricos de los reyes de Aragon.* Vols. 1 and 2. Salamanca: Lucas Pérez, 1684.

Agustin, San. *Obras completas.* Ed. Victorino Capanaga. Vols. 1, 3, 40, and 41. Madrid: Biblioteca de Autores Cristianos, 1969, 1971, 1995.

Argensola, Bartholomé Leonardo de. *Primera parte de los anales de Aragon que prosigue los del Secretario Geronimo Çurita desde el año 1516* . . . Zaragoza: Ivan de Lanaia, 1630.

Ayala, Martín de. *Sermón hecho por el illustrissimo y reverendissimo señor Arçobispo de Saçer en su yglesia metropolitana, en las honrras de la Serenissima y Catholica Reyna Doña Juana madre del Emperador y Rey, Nro. Señor.* Valencia: Casa de Antón Sanahuja, 1556.

Azpilcueta Navarro, Martín de. *Manual de confessores y penitentes.* Valladolid: Francisco Fernández de Córdova, 1570.

Bernáldez, Andrés. *Memorias del reinado de los Reyes Católicos.* Ed. Manuel Gómez-Moreno and Juan de Mata Carriazo. Madrid, 1962.

Blancas, Gerónimo de. *Comentarios de las cosas de Aragón.* Trans. Manuel Hernández. Zaragoza: Imprenta del Hospicio, 1878.

———. *Coronaciones de los serenísimos reyes de Aragón.* Zaragoza: Diego Dormer, 1641.

———. *Modo de proceder en las cortes de Aragón.* Zaragoza: Diego Dormer, 1641.

Blijde Inkomst vier Vlaams-Bourgondische Gedichten. Ed. G. DeGroote. Amsterdam: Wereldbibliotheek, 1950.

Boethius. *La consolación de la filosofía.* Madrid: Sarpe, 1985.

———. *The Consolation of Philosophy.* Trans. Richard Green. New York: Macmillan, 1962.

Calendar of Letters, Despatches, and State Papers Relating to the Negotiations between England and Spain. Ed. G. A. Bergenroth. Nendeln, Liechtenstein: Kraus-Thomson, 1969. Originally published 1862.

Cartas del Cardenal Fray Francisco Jiménez de Cisneros dirigidas a Don Diego López de Ayala. Ed. Pascual de Gayangos and Vicente de la Fuente. Madrid: Imprenta del colegio de sordo-mudos y de ciegos, 1867.

Cartas de los secretarios del Cardenal D. Fr. Francisco Jiménez de Cisneros. Ed. Vicente de la Fuente. Vols. 1 and 2. Madrid: Viuda e hijo de D. Eusebio Aguado, 1875–76.

Cartas de San Jerónimo. Edicion bilingüe. Ed. Daniel Ruiz Bueno. Madrid: Biblioteca de Autores Cristianos, 1962.

La casa de Isabel la Católica. Ed. Antonio de la Torre. Madrid: Selecciones Gráficas, 1954.

Cavalca, Domenico. *Espejo de la Cruz.* Trans. Alfonso de Palencia. Seville: Antón Martínez, 1486.

Cicero, Marcus Tulius. *Letters to Atticus.* Ed. Shackleton Bailey. Cambridge: Cambridge University Press, 1970.

Ciruelo, Pedro. *Reprouacion de las supersticiones y hechizerias.* Ed. Alva V. Ebersole. Valencia: Artes Gráficas Soler, 1978.

Colleción de documentos inéditos para la historia de España. Vol. 8. Ed. Miguel Salvá and Pedro Sainz de Baranda. Madrid: Imprenta de la viuda de Calero, 1846.

Collection des voyages des souverains des Pays-Bas. Ed. Louis-Prosper Gachard. Brussels: F. Hayez, 1876.

A Collection of Ordinances and Regulations for the Government of the Royal Household, Made in Divers Reigns from King Edward III to King William and Queen Mary. London: Society of Antiquaries, 1790.

Coplas fechas sobre el casamiento de la hija del rey de España. Burgos: Friedrich Biel, 1496.

Córdoba, Fray Martín de. *Jardín de las nobles donzellas.* ca. 1542.

———. *Jardin de nobles doncellas.* Madrid: Joyas Bibliográficas, 1953.

Corpus Documental de Carlos V. Ed. Manuel Fernández Alvarez. Vols. 1–5. Salamanca: Ediciones Universidad de Salamanca, 1973–81.

Cortes de los antiguos reinos de León y Castilla. Ed. La Real Academia de la Historia. Vol. 4. Madrid: Sucesores de Rivadeneyra, 1882.

Cota, Sancho. *Memorias.* Ed. Hayward Keniston. Cambridge, Mass.: Harvard University Press, 1964.

Crónicas de los reyes de Castilla. Ed. Don Cayetano Rosell. Biblioteca de Autores Españoles, vol. 3. Madrid: Rivadeneyra, 1878.

Cuentas de Gonzalo de Baeza Tesorero de Isabel la Catolica. Ed. Antonio de la Torre and E. A. de la Torre. Vols. 1 and 2. Madrid: Consejo Superior de Investigaciones Científicas, 1955.

Datos documentales para la historia del arte español: Inventarios reales. Ed. José Ferrándis. Vol. 3. Madrid: Consejo Superior de Investigaciones Científicas, 1943.

Daza, fray Antonio. Quarta parte de la chronica general de San Francisco. Valladolid, 1611.

"Die Depeschen des Venetianischen Botschafters Vincenzo Quirino." Ed. Constantin von Höfler. *Archiv für Osterreichische Gestchicte* 66 (1885): 53–248.

I diarii di Marino Sanuto (1496–1533). Dall'autografo Marciano Ital. Cl. VII. Codd. 419–477. Vols. 1–58. Venezia: Deputazione Veneta di Sotria Patri, 1879–1902.

Dits die excellente cronike van Vlanderen. Ed. William Vorsterman. Antwerpen, 1531.

Documentos sobre relaciones internacionales de los Reyes Católicos. Ed. Antonio de la Torre. Vols. 3 and 6. Barcelona: Consejo Superior de Investigaciones Científicas, 1951 and 1966.

Eiximenis, Francesc. *Carro de las donas.* Anonymous translation. Valladolid: Juan de Villaquiran, 1542.

———. *Com usar bé de beure e menjar: Normes morals contingudes en el "Terç del Crestia."* Jorge J. E. Gracia, ed. Barcelona: Curial, 1983.

———. *Regiment de la cosa pública.* Ed. Daniel de Molins de Rei. Barcelona: Editorial Barcino, 1927.

Enríquez de Guzmán, Alonso. *Libro de la vida y costumbres.* Ed. Hayward Keniston. Madrid: Atlas, 1960.

Erasmus, Desiderius. *The Education of a Christian Prince with the Panegyric for Archduke Philip of Austria.* Ed. Lisa Jardine. Cambridge: Cambridge University Press, 1997.

————. *The Praise of Folly.* London: Oxford University Press, 1945.

————. *Obras Escojidas.* Trans. and ed. Lorenzo Ribera. Madrid: Aguilar, 1956.

Fernández de Oviedo, Gonzalo. *Batallas y quinquagenas.* Salamanca: Ediciones de la Diputación de Salamanca, 1989.

————. *Libro de la cámara real del Príncipe Don Juan e ofiçios de su casa e serviçio ordinario.* Madrid: Sociedad de Bibliófilos Españoles, 1870.

Flos Sanctorum: La vida de nuestro señor Jesu Christo y de su santissima madre, y de los otros santos segun la orden de sus fiestas. Alcalá de Henares: Casa de Andres de Angulo, 1572.

Fontes documentales de S. Ignatio de Loyola. Monumenta Historica Societatis Iesu, vol. 115. Rome: Institutum Historicum Societatis Iesu, 1977.

Furió Ceriol, Fadrique. *El consejo y consejeros del príncipe y otras obras.* Ed. Diego Sevilla Andrés. Diputación Provincial de Valencia, 1952.

García de Castrojeriz, fray Juan. *Glosa castellana al "regimiento de príncipes" de Egidio Romano.* Ed. Jan Beneyto Pérez. Vols. 1–3. Madrid: Instituto de Estudios Políticos, 1947.

Garibay y Zamalloa, Esteban. *Los quarenta libros del compendio historial de las chronicas y universal historia de todos los reynos de España.* Barcelona: Sebastían de Cormellas, 1628.

Gerson, Jean. *Tratado de contemptu mundi . . . del menosprecio de todas las vanidades del mundo.* Seville: Compañeros Alemanes, 1496.

Girón, Pedro. *Crónica del Emperador Carlos V.* Madrid: Consejo Superior de Investigaciones Científicas, 1964.

Gómez de Fuensalida, Gutierre. *Correspondencia.* Published by the Duke of Berwick and of Alba. Madrid, 1907.

Guevara, Antonio de. *Menosprecio de Corte y Alabanza de Aldea.* Madrid: Ediciones "La Lectura," 1928.

————. *Velox de príncipes.* Ed. Emilio Blanco. Madrid: CONFRES, 1994.

Historia crítica y documentada de las comunidades de Castilla. Ed. Manuel Danvila y Collado. Vols. 35–40. Madrid: Tipografía de la viuda e hijos de M. Tello, 1897–1900.

Huarte de San Juan, Juan. *Examen de ingenios para las ciencias.* Ed. Esteban Torre. Madrid: Editora Nacional, 1976. Originally published 1575.

Jerome, Saint. *Select Letters.* Trans. F. A. Wright. London: William Heinemann, 1963.

Jiménez de Prejano, Pedro. *Luzero de la vida Chrisiana.* Burgos: Fadrique Biel, 1495.

Kempis, Thomas à. *The Imitation of Christ.* Trans. Leo Sherley-Price. Middlesex, England: Penguin Books, 1973.

Lalaing, Antoine de. "Voyage de Philippe le Beau en Espagne." *Collection des voyages des souverains des pays-bas.* Ed. Louis-Prosper Gachard. Vol. 1. Brussels: F. Hayez, 1876.

Leonardo de Argensola, Bartholomé. *Primera parte de los anales de Aragon que prosigue los del Secretario Geronimo Çurita desde el año 1516 . . .* Zaragoza: Ivan de Lanaia, 1630.

Letters, Despatches, and State Papers Relating to the Negotiations between England and Spain Preserved in the Archives of Simancas and Elsewhere. Ed. G. A. Bergenroth. Suppl. to vols. 1 and 2. London: Longmans, Green, Reader and Dyer, 1868.

Liber Regie Capelle. A manuscript in the Biblioteca Publica, Evora. Ed. Walter Ullmann. Cambridge: Harvard University Press, 1961.

"El Libro de los Doze Sabios o Tractado de la Nobleza y Lealtad [c.a. 1237]." In *Anejos del boletín de la Real Academia Española.* ed. John K. Walsh. Suppl. XXIX. Madrid, 1975.

Lisboa, fray Marcos de. *Tercera parte de las chronicas de la orden de los frayles menores del*

Seraphico Padre Sant Francisco. Trans. Fray Diego Navarro. Salamanca: Casa de Alexandro de Canova, 1570.

López de Villalobos, Francisco. *Algunas obras.* Madrid: Sociedad de Bibliofilos Españoles, 1886.

Machiavelli, Niccoli. *The Prince.* Ed. Quentin Skinner and Russell Price. Cambridge: Cambridge University Press, 1988.

Manrique, Gómez. *Regimiento de príncipes y otras obras.* Ed. Augusto Cortina. Buenos Aires: Esapsa-Calpe, 1947. Originally published ca. 1478.

Marcuello, Pedro. *Cancionero.* Ed. José Manuel Blecua. Zaragoza: Institución Fernando el Católico, 1987. Originally published 1502.

————. *Rimado de la conquista de Granada.* Complete facsimile edition of manuscript 604 (1339) XIV-D-14 of the library of the Musée Condé, Chantilly castle. Madrid: Edilan, 1995.

Mariana, Juan de. *Del rey y de la institución real.* Vol. 31. Madrid: Biblioteca de Autores Españoles, 1950.

Marineo Siculo, Lucio. *Cosas memorables de España.* Alcalá de Henares: Casa de Miguel de Eguia, 1530.

————. *Sumario de la clarísima vida y heroycos hechos de los Catholicos Reyes don Fernando y doña Ysabel.* Toledo: Casa de Juan de Ayala, 1546.

Mártir de Angleria, Pedro. *Epistolario.* Trans. José López de Toro. In *Documentos inéditos para la historia de España,* vols. 9–12. Madrid: Imprenta Góngora, S.L., 1953.

————. *Opus Epistolarum.* Alcalá de Henares: Michael de Aguia, 1530.

Mexía, Pedro. *Historia del Emperador Carlos V.* Madrid: Espasa Calpe, 1945.

————. *Relación de las comunidades de Castilla.* Barcelona: Muñoz Moya y Montraveta, 1985.

————. *Silva de varia lección.* Ed.. Antonio Castro. Madrid: Ediciones Cátedra, 1989.

Miranda, Luis de. *Vida de la Gloriosa Virgen Sancta Clara con la declaración de su primera y segunda regla y un memorial de las cosas más insignes y memorables que en esta ilustrísima y sagrada religión han sucedido.* Salamanca: La Viuda de Artus Taberniel, 1610.

Montesino, Ambrosio. *Vita Christi Cartuxano Romançado.* Vols. 1–3. Alcalá de Henares, 1502–3.

Muñoz, Andrés. *Viaje de Felipe Segundo a Inglaterra.* Madrid: Sucesores de Rivadeneyra, 1877.

Opera inedite di Francesco Guicciardini, ambasciatore a Ferdinando il Cattolico, 1512–1513. Ed. Giuseppe Canestrini. Vol. 6. Florence: Presso M. Cellini, 1864.

Ortiz, Alonso. *Diálogo sobre la educación del Principe Don Juan, hijo de los Reyes Católicos.* Trans. Giovanni María Bertini. Madrid: Studia Humanitatis, 1983.

Padilla, Lorenzo de. "Crónica de Felipe I llamado el hermoso." In *Colección de documentos inéditos para la historia de España,* ed. Miguel Salvá y Pedro Sainz de Baranda, vol. 8. Madrid: Imprenta de la viuda de Calero, 1846.

Pere III (Pedro IV). "Ordenacions . . . sobre lo regiment de tots los officials de la sua cort." In *Colección de documentos inéditos del Archivo General de la Corona de Aragón,* ed. Próspero de Bofaroll y Mascaró, vol. 5. Barcelona: Monfort, 1850.

Poitiers, Alienor de. "Les Honneurs de la Cour." In *Mémoires sur l'ancienne chevalerie,* ed. La Curne de Sainte-Palaye, 2:143–219. Paris: Girard, 1826.

Pulgar, Fernando. *Crónica de los Reyes Católicos.* Ed. Juan de Mata Carriazo. Vols. 1 and 2. Madrid: Espasa- Calpe, 1943.

Rayssius, Arnoldus. *Hierogazophylacium Belgicum sive Thesaurus Sacrum Reliquiarum Belgii.* Colonia: Gerardum Pinchon, 1628.

"Reise des Erzherzogs Philipp nach Spanien 1501." In *Die Handschriften der k.k. Hofbibliothek in Wien, im Interesse der Geschichte, besonders der österreichische, verzeichnet und excerpirt,* ed. Joseph Chmel, 2:554–655.Vienna: Gedruckt und im Verlage bey Carl Gerold, 1841.

Relazioni degli Ambasciatori Veneti al Senato. Ed. Eugenio Albèri. Vol. 1. Florence: Tipografia All'Insegna di Clio, 1839.

Ribadeneyra, Pedro de. *Vida del P. Francisco de Borja.* Madrid: P. Madrigal, 1592.

Salazar, Pedro de. *Crónica de la Provincia de Castilla.* Madrid: Editorial Cisneros, 1977. Originally published c. 1610.

Salinas, Martín de. *El Emperador Carlos V y su corte.* Madrid: Real Academia de la Historia, 1903–5.

Salisbury, John of. *Policratus.* Ed. Miguel Ángel Ladero. Madrid: Editora Nacional, 1984.

Sandoval, Prudencio de. *Historia de la vida y hechos del Emperador Carlos V.* Pamplona: Casa de Bartholome Paris Mercader Librero, 1618.

———. *Historia de la vida y hechos del Emperador Carlos V.* Vols. 1, 2, and 3. Madrid: Biblioteca de Autores Españoles, 1955. Originally published 1604 and 1606.

Santa Cruz, Alonso de. *Crónica de los Reyes Católicos.* Ed. Juan de Mata Carriazo. Vols. 1 and 2. Seville: Escuela de Estudios Hispano-Americanos, 1951.

Sepúlveda, Juan Ginés de. *Obras completas: Historia de Carlos V.* Trans. and ed. E. Rodríguez Peregrina. Vols. 1 and 2. Pozoblanco, Córdoba: Ayuntamiento, 1995.

Siete partidas del rey Alfonso el Sabio. Madrid: Imprenta Real, 1807.

Talavera, Hernando de. *Breve y muy provechosa doctrina cristiana.* Granada: Juan Pegnitzer y Meinardo Ungut, ca. 1496.

Torre, Alfonso de la. "Vision delectable de la filosofía y artes liberales, metafísica y filosofía moral." In *Curiosidades bibliográficas,* ed. Adolfo de Castro, 339–402. Madrid: Biblioteca de Autores Españoles, 1950.

Vallejo, Juan de. *Memorial de la vida de fray Francisco Jiménez de Cisneros.* Ed. Antonio de la Torre y del Cerro. Madrid: Bailly-Bailliere, 1913.

Viajes de extranjeros por España y Portugal. Ed. J. García Mercadal. Madrid: Aguilar, 1952.

Villena, Enrique de. *Obras completas.* Madrid: Turner Libros, 1994.

Vital, Laurent. *Relación del primer viaje de Carlos V a España.* Trans. Bernabe Herrero. Madrid: Estades, 1958.

———. *Relation du premier voyage de Charles-Quint en Espagne.* Ed. Louis-Prosper Gachard and CharlesPiot. Brussels: F. Hayez, 1881.

Voragine, Jacobus de. *The Golden Legend.* Trans. William Granger Ryan. Princeton: Princeton University Press, 1993.

Zamora, Alonso de. *Flor de virtudes. Tratado de varias sentencias y doctrinas de la Sagrada Escriptura, y de otros sabios antiguos.* Lisboa: Antonio Alvarez, 1601.

———. *Loor de virtudes nuevamente impresso.* Alcalá de Henares: Miguel de Eguia, 1525.

Zúñiga, Francisco de. *Crónica burlesca del Emperador Carlos V.* Ed. José Antonio Sánchez Paso. Salamanca: Universidad de Salamanca, 1989.

Zurita, Jerónimo. *Historia del Rey Don Hernando el Católico: De las empresas y ligas de Italia.* Ed. Angel Canellas López. Vols. 1–5. Zaragoza: Departamento de Cultura y Educación, 1989–96.

SECONDARY SOURCES

Alcalá, Ángel, and Jacobo Sanz. *Vida y muerte del Príncipe don Juan*. Valladolid: Junta de Castilla y León, 1999.

Alenda y Mira, Don Jenaro. *Relaciones de solemnidades y fiestas públicas de España*. Madrid: Sucesores de Rivadeneyra, 1903.

Altayó, Isabel, and Paloma Nogués. *Juana I: La reina cautiva*. Madrid: Silex, 1985.

Alvar Ezquerra, Alfredo. *Isabel la Católica. Una reina vencedora. Una mujer derrotada*. Madrid, 2002.

Andrés Martín, Melquíades, ed. *Los recogidos: Nueva visión de la Mística Española (1500–1700)*. Madrid: Fundación Universitaria Española, 1976.

Aram, Bethany. "Juana 'the Mad's' Signature: The Problem of Invoking Royal Authority, 1505–1507." *Sixteenth Century Journal* 29, no. 2 (1998): 333–61.

———. "Juana 'the Mad,' the Clares, and the Carthusians: Revising a Necrophilic Legend in Early Habsburg Spain." *Archiv für Reformationsgeschichte* 93 (2002): 172–91.

———. "Representing Madness: Text, Gender and Authority in Early Habsburg Spain." In *Women, Texts and Authority in the Early Modern Spanish World*, ed. Marta V. Vicente and Luis R. Corteguera, 73–90. Aldershot: Ashgate Publishing, 2003.

Arco, Ricardo del. "Cortes aragonesas de los Reyes Catolicos." *Revista de Archivos, Bibliotecas y Museos* 60, no. 1 (1954): 77–103.

———. *Fernando el Católico: Artífice de la España Imperial*. Zaragoza: Editorial Heraldo de Aragón, 1939.

Armstrong, C. A. J. *England, France and Burgundy in the Fifteenth Century*. London: Hambledon Press, 1983.

Arnade, Peter. *Realms of Ritual: Burgundian Ceremony and Civic Life in Late Medieval Ghent*. Ithaca: Cornell University Press, 1996.

Axton, Marie. *The Queen's Two Bodies: Drama and the Elizabethan Succession*. London: Royal Historical Society, 1977.

Azcona, Tarsicio de. *Isabel la Católica: Estudio crítico de su vida y su reinado*. Madrid: Biblioteca de Autores Cristianos, 1964.

———. *Juana de Castilla, mal llamada la Beltraneja, 1462–1530*. Madrid: Fundación Universitaria Española, 1998.

Barrio Gonzalo, Maximiliano. "El archivo de la casa ducal de Alburquerque: Panorama general de sus fondos documentales." *Universidad de Valladolid. Separata de Investigaciones Historicas* 8 (1988): 309–13.

Bataillon, Marcel. *Érasme et l'Espagne*. Geneva: Librairie Droz, 1991.

Bates, Catherine. *The Rhetoric of Courtship in Elizabethan Language and Literature*. Cambridge: Cambridge University Press, 1992.

Beecher, Donald A., and Massimo Ciavolella, eds. *Eros and Anteros: The Medical Traditions of Love in the Renaissance*. Toronto: Dovehouse Editions, 1992.

Belenguer, Ernst. *Fernando el Católico*. Barcelona: Ediciones Peninsula, 1999.

Beneyto Pérez, Juan. "Magisterio político de Fernando el Católico." *Instituto de Estudios Políticos* (1944): 451–73.

Benitez de Lugo, Antonio. "Doña Juana la loca, más tiranizada que demente." *Revista de España* 100 (10 and 29 October 1885): 378–403, 536–71.

Bergenroth, G. A. "Jeanne la Folle." *Revue de Belgique* (Brussels) 1 (1869): 81–112.

Bermejo Cabrero, José Luis. "Amor y temor al Rey: Evolución Histórica de un Tópico Político." *Revista de Estudios Políticos* 192 (November–December 1973): 107–27.

———. *Máximas, principios y símbolos políticos (una aproximación histórica)*. Madrid: Centro de Estudios Constitucionales, 1986.

———. *Los oficiales del concejo en León y Castilla. De los orígenes al Ordenamiento de Alcalá*. Madrid: Gráficas Cóndor, 1973.

Bernis, Carmen. *Trajes y modas en la España de los Reyes Católicos*. Madrid: Instituto Diego Velázquez, 1978.

Berriot-Salvadore, Evelyne. *Un corps, un destin: La femme dans la médecine de la Renaissance*. Paris: Honoré Champion, 1993.

Berry, Philippa. *Of Chastity and Power: Elizabethan Literature and the Unmarried Queen*. New York: Routledge, 1989.

Bertelli, Sergio. *Il corpo del re. Sacralità del potere nell'Europa medievale e moderna*. Florence: Ponte Alle Grazie, 1990.

Bilinkoff, Jodi. "A Spanish Prophetess and Her Patrons: The Case of María de Santo Domingo." *Sixteenth Century Journal* 23, no. 1 (1992): 21–34.

Blockmans, Wim. "The Devotion of a Lonely Duchess." In *Margaret of York, Simon Marmion, and the Visons of Tondal*, ed. Thomas Kren, 29–46. Malibu, Calif.: J. Paul Getty Museum, 1992.

———. "Le dialogue imaginaire entre princes et sujets: Les joyeuses entrées en Brabant en 1494 et en 1496." In *Fêtes et cérémonies aux XIVe–XVIe siècles*, 37–53. Publication du Centre Européen d'Études Bourguignonnes (XIVe–XVIe siècles) 34. Neuchâtel, 1994.

———. "La joyeuse entrée de Jeanne de Castille à Bruxelles en 1496." *Diálogos Hispánicos* 16 (1995): 27–42.

Blockmans, Wim, and Walter Prevenier. *The Promised Lands: The Low Countries under Burgundian Rule, 1369–1530*. Ed. Edward Peters. Philadelphia: University of Pennsylvania Press, 1999.

Boruchoff, David A., ed. *Isabel la Católica, Queen of Castile: Critical Essays*. New York: Palgrave Macmillan, 2003.

Boureau, Alain. *Le simple corps du roi: l'impossible sacralité des souverains français, XVe–XVIIIe siècle*. Paris: Les Éditions de Paris, 1988.

Bouza Álvarez, Fernando. *Locos, enanos y hombres de placer en la corte de las Austrias*. Madrid: Ediciones Temas de Hoy, 1991.

Bouwer, J. *Johanna de Waanzinnige: Een Tragische Leven in Een Bewogen Tijd*. Amsterdam: J. M. Meulenhoff, 1958. Originally published 1940.

Brandi, Karl. *The Emperor Charles V*. Trans. C. V. Wedgwood. London: Jonathan Cape, 1963.

Brans, Jan. *De Gevangene van Tordesillas*. Leuven: Davidsfonds, 1962.

Bullón y Fernández, Eloy. *El concepto de la soberanía en la Escuela jurídica española del siglo XVI*. Madrid: Librería General de Victoriano Suárez, Rivadeneyra, 1936.

Cardaillac, Louis. *L'Espagne des rois catholiques. Le prince don Juan, symbole de l'apogée d'un règne, 1474–1500*. Paris: Éditions Autrement, 2000.

Caro Baroja, Julio. *Las formas complejas de la vida religiosa: Religión, sociedad y carácter en la España de los siglos XVI y XVII*. Madrid: Akal Editor, 1978.

Caron, Marie Thérèse. *La noblesse dans le duche de Bourgogne, 1315–1477*. Lille: Presses Universitaires, 1987.

Carreras Panchon, Antonio. *La peste y los médicos en la España del Renacimiento.* Salamanca: Universidad de Salamanca, 1976.

Carretero Zamora, Juan M. "Algunas consideraciones sobre las Actas de las Cortes de Madrid de 1510." *Cuadernos de Historia Moderna* 12 (1991): 13–45.

————. *Cortes, monarquía, ciudades. Las cortes de Castilla a comienzos de la época moderna (1476–1515).* Madrid: Siglo Veintiuno, 1988.

Cartellieri, Otto. *The Court of Burgundy: Studies in the History of Civilization.* New York: Haskell House Publishers, 1970.

Casado Alonso, Hilario. "Oligaquía urbana, comerico internacional y poder real: Burgos a fines de la Edad Media." In *Realidad e imágenes del poder: España a fines de la Edad Media,* ed. Adeline Rucquoi. Valladolid: Ámbito, 1988.

Casals i Martínez, Àngel. "Emperor i principat: Catalunya i les seves relacions amb l'imperi de Carles V (1516–1543)." Ph.D. dissertation, Universitat de Barcelona, 1995.

Cátedra, Pedro M. *Dos estudios sobre el sermón en la España medieval.* Barcelona: Universidad Autónoma de Barcelona, 1981.

Cauchies, Jean-Marie, ed. *A la cour de Bourgogne: Le duc, son entourage, son train.* Turnhout, Belgium: Brepols, 1998.

————. "L'Archiduc Philippe d'Autriche dit le Beau (1478–1506)." In *Handelingen van de Koninklijke Kring voor Oudheikunde, Lettern en Kunst van Mechelen,* ed. R. de Smedt, 46–55. Mechelen, 1992.

————. "Die burgundischen Niederlande unter Erzherzog Philipp dem Shönem (1494–1506), ein doppelter Integrationsprozess." In *Europa 1500, Integration prozesse im Widerstreit,* ed. F. Seibt and W. Iberhard, 27–52. Stuttgart: Integrationsprozesse, 1987.

————. "Filps de Schone en Johanna van Castilië in de kering van de wereldgeschiedenis." Ed. Lira Elegans. *Liers Genootschap voor geschiedenis. Jaarboek* VI (1996): 69–89.

————. *Philippe le Beau. Le dernier duc de Bourgogne.* Turnhout, Belgium: Brepols, 2003.

————. "La signification politique des entrées princières dans les Pays-Bas: Maximilien d'Autriche et Philippe le Beau." In *A la Cour de Bourgogne: Le duc, son entourage, son train,* ed. Jean-Marie Cauchies, 137–52. Turnhout, Belgium: Brepols, 1998.

————. "Voyage d'Espagne et domaine princier; les opérations financières de Philippe le Beau dans les Pays-Bas (1505–1506)." In *Commerce, Finances et Societé, Xie–XVIe siècles: Recueil de travaux d'histoire medievale offerts à M. le Profeseur Henri Dubois,* Philippe Contamine, Thierry Dutour, and Bertrand Schnerb, 217–44. Paris, 1993.

Cazaux, Yves. *María de Borgoña: Testigo de una gran empresa en los orígenes de las nacionalidades europeas.* Trans. María Luisa Pérez Torres. Madrid: Espasa-Calpe, 1972.

Cepeda Adan, José. *En torno al concepto del estado en los Reyes Católicos.* Madrid: Consejo Superior de Investigaciones Científicas, 1956.

Cirac Estopañán, Sebastián. *Los procesos de hechicerías en la Inquisición de Castilla la Nueva (Tribunales de Toledo y Cuenca).* Madrid: Consejo Superior de Investigaciones Científicas, 1942.

Clanchy, M. T. *From Memory to Written Record: England, 1066–1307.* Cambridge: Harvard University Press, 1979.

Clavero, Bartolomé. *Mayorazgo: Propiedad Feudal en Castilla (1369–1836).* Madrid: Siglo Veintiuno Editores, 1974.

Cedillo, el Conde de. *El Cardenal Cisneros: Gobernador del Reino.* Madrid: Real Academia de la Historia, 1921.

Cerro Bex, Victoriano del. "Itinerario seguido por Felipe el Hermoso en sus dos viajes a España." *Chronica Nova* (Granada) 6 (1973).

Clemencín, Diego. *Elógio de la Reina Católica Doña Isabel.* Madrid: Imprenta de Sancha, 1820.

Coleman, Christopher, and David Starkey, eds. *Revolution Reassessed: Revisions in the History of Tudor Government and Administration.* Oxford: Clarendon Press, 1986.

Comas Ros, María. *Juan López de Lazarraga y El Monasterio de Bidaurreta.* Barcelona: Ediciones Descartes, 1936.

Congreso de historia de la corona de Aragon V. Fernando el Católico: Pensamiento político, política internacional y religiosa. Zaragoza: Institución "Fernando el Católico," 1956.

Córdova Miralles, Álvaro Fernández. *La corte de Isabel I. Ritos y ceremonias de una reina (1474–1504).* Madrid: Dykinson, 2002.

Corona, Carlos E. *Fernando el Católico, Maximiliano y la regencia de Castilla (1508–1515).* Seville: Facultad de Filosofía y Letras, 1961.

Cosandey, Fanny. *La reine de France: Symbole et pouvoir.* Paris: Editions Gallimard, 2002.

Costa Gomes, Rita. *The Making of a Court Society: Kings and Nobles in Late Medieval Portugal.* Cambridge: Cambridge University Press, 2003.

Dalmases, Candido de. *El Padre Francisco de Borja.* Madrid: Biblioteca de Autores Cristianos, 1983.

Dénnis, Amarie. *Seek the Darkness: The Story of Juana la loca.* Madrid: Sucesores de Rivadeneyra, 1969.

Dézert, G. Desdevises du. *La Reine Jeanne la folle d'après l'étude historique de D. Antonio Rodriguez Villa.* Toulouse: Imprimerie et Librairie Édouard Privat, 1892.

Díaz Martín, Luis Vicente. "Los inicios de la política internacional de Castilla (1360–1410)." In *Realidad e imágenes del poder: España a fines de la Edad Media,* ed. Adeline Rucquoi. Valladolid: Ámbito, 1988.

Dios, Salustiano de. *Gracia, Merced y Patronazgo Real: La Cámara de Castilla entre 1474–1530.* Madrid: Centro de Estudios Constitucionales, 1993.

Domínguez Casas, Rafael. *Arte y etiqueta de los Reyes Católicos: Artistas, residencias, jardines y bosques.* Madrid: Editorial Alpuerto, 1993.

———. "Ceremonia y simbología Hispano-Inglesa, desde la justa real celebrada en el palacio de Westminster en el año 1501 en honor de Catalina de Aragón, hasta la boda de Felipe II con María Tudor." *Boletín de la Real Academia de Bellas Artes de San Fernando* 79 (1994): 197–228.

Doorslaer, G. van. "La chapelle musicale de Philippe le Beau." *Revue Belge d'archéologie et d'histoire de l'art* 4 (1934): 21–57.

Doussinague, José M. *Un proceso por envenenamiento: La muerte de Felipe el Hermoso.* Madrid: Espasa-Calpe, 1947.

Duquenne, Xavier. *Le parc de Bruxelles.* Brussels: CFC Editions, 1993.

Edwards, John. *The Spain of the Catholic Monarchs, 1474–1520.* Oxford: Blackwell, 2000.

Eire, Carlos M. N. *From Madrid to Purgatory: The Art and Craft of Dying in Sixteenth-Century Spain.* New York: Cambridge University Press, 1995.

Elias, Norbert. *The Court Society.* Trans. Edmund Jephcott. Oxford: Blackwell, 1983. Originally published 1939.

Elías de Tejada, Francisco. *Las doctrinas políticas en la Cataluña Medieval.* B`rcelona: Ayma, 1950.

Fagel, Raymond. *De Hispano-Vlaamse Wereld: De contacten tussen Spanjaarden en Nederlanders, 1496–1555.* Brussels: Archives et Bibliothèques de Belgique, 1996.
————. "Juana y Cornelia. Flamencos en la corte de Juana la Loca en Tordesillas." *El Tratado de Tordesillas y su época: Congreso internacional de historia,* ed. Luis Ribot, 3:1855–66. Valladolid: Sociedad V Centenario, 1994.
Ferdinandy, Miguel de. *El Emperador Carlos V: Semblanza de un hombre.* Trans. Salbavor Giner. Rio Piedras, Puerto Rico: Editorial Universitaria, 1964.
Fernández, Felix Sagredo. *La Cartuja de Miraflores.* Leon: Editorial Everest, 1973.
Fernández Albaladejo, Pablo. *Fragmentos de Monarquía.* Madrid: Alianza, 1992.
Fernández Álvarez, Manuel. *Juana la loca, 1479–1555.* Palencia: Diputación Provincial 1994.
Feros, Antonio. *Kingship and Favoritism in the Spain of Philip III, 1598–1621.* Cambridge: Cambridge University Press, 2000.
Florez, Henrique. *Memorias de las reynas cathólicas.* Vols. 1–2. Madrid, 1770.
Foucault, Michel. *Histoire de la folie à l'âge classique.* Paris: Gallimard, 1972. Originally published 1965.
Fradenburg, Louise Olga, ed. *Women and Sovereignty.* Edinburgh: Edinburgh University Press, 1992.
Fuentes, Carlos. *Terra Nostra.* Mexico City: Editorial Joaquín Mortiz, 1975.
Gachard, Louis-Prosper. "Les derniers moments de Jeanne la folle." Extract. *Bulletins de l'Académie Royale des Sciences, des Lettres et des Beaux-Arts de Belgique,* 2d ser., 29. Brussels: M. Hayez, 1870.
————. "Jeanne la folle défendue contre l'imputation d'hérésie." Extract. *Bulletins de l'Académie Royale des Sciences, des Lettres et des Beaux-Arts de Belgique,* 2d ser., 27, no. 6. Brussels: M. Hayez, 1869.
————. "Jeanne la folle et Charles Quint," pt. 1. Extract. *Bulletins de l'Académie Royale des Sciences, des Lettres et des Beaux-Arts de Belgique* 24, no. 6. Brussels: M. Hayez, 1870.
————. "Jeanne la folle et Charles-Quint," pt. 2. Extract. *Bulletins de l'Académie Royale des Sciences, des Lettres et des Beaux-Arts de Belgique* 33, no. 1. Brussels: M. Hayez, 1872.
————. "Jeanne al folle et S. François de Borja." Extract. *Bulletins de l'Académie Royale des Sciences, des Lettres et des Beaux-Arts de Belgique,* 2d ser., 29. Brussels: M. Hayez, 1870.
————. "Sur Jeanne la folle et les documents concernant cette princesse." Extract. *Bulletins de l'Académie Royale des Sciences, des Lettres et des Beaux-Arts de Belgique,* 2d ser., 27, no. 3. Brussels: M. Hayez, 1869.
————. "Sur Jeanne la folle et la publication de M. Bergenroth." Extract. *Bulletins de l'Académie Royale des Sciences, des Lettres et des Beaux-Arts de Belgique,* 2d ser., 28, nos. 9 and 10. Brussels: M. Hayez, 1869.
Gallego Burin, Antonio. *La capilla real de Granada.* Granada: Paulino Ventura Traveset, 1931.
Gan Gimenez, Pedro. *El consejo real de Carlos V.* Granada: Universidad de Granada, 1988.
García Cárcel, Ricardo. "Las cortes de 1519 en Barcelona, una opción revolucionaria frustrada." In *Homenaje al Dr. D. Juan Reglà Campistol,* ed. Juan Reglà. Valencia: Universidad de Valencia, 1975.
————. *Herejía y sociedad en el siglo XVI: La inquisición en Valencia 1530–1609.* Barcelona: Ediciones 62, 1980.
García Carraffa, Alberto, and Arturo García Carraffa. *Heraldico y genealogico de apellidos españoles y americanos.* Vol. 80. Madrid: Hauser y Menet, 1959.

García de Valdeavellano, Luis. *Curso de historia de las instituciones españolas de los orígenes al final de la Edad Media.* Madrid: Alianza, 1982. Originally published *1968.*

García Gallo, Alfonso. *Historia del derecho español.* Vol. 1. Madrid, 1943.

García Oro, José. *El Cardenal Cisneros: Vida y empresas.* Madrid: Biblioteca de Autores Cristianos, 1992.

Gerbet, Marie Claude. *La nobleza en la corona de Castilla: Sus estructuras sociales en Extremadura (1454–1516).* Trans. María Concepción Quintanilla Raso. Salamanca: Institución Cultural 'El Brocense,' 1989.

Gibert, Rafael. "La sucesión al trono en la monarquia española." *Recueils de la Société Jean Bodin* 21 (1969): 447–546.

Giesey, Ralph E. *Cérémonial et puissance souveraine: France, XVe–XVIIe siècles.* Paris: Armand Colin, 1987.

———. "Inaugural Aspects of French Royal Ceremonials." In *Coronations: Medieval and Early Modern Monarchic Ritual,* ed. János M. Bak. Berkeley: University of California Press, 1989.

———. "The Juristic Basis of Dynastic Right to the French Throne." *Transactions of the American Philosophical Society* 51, no. 5 (1961): 3–48.

———. *The Royal Funeral Ceremony in Renaissance France.* Geneva: Libraire E. Droz, 1960.

———. "Rules of Inheritance and Strategies of Mobility." *American Historical Review* 82, no. 2 (April 1977): 271–89.

Giménez Fernández, Manuel. *Bartolomé de las Casas* . Vol. 1: *Delegado de Cisneros para la Reformación de las Indias (1516–1517);* Vol. 2: *Capellán de S. M. Carlos I Poblador de Cumana (1517–1523).* Madrid: Consejo Superior de Investigaciones Científicas, 1984.

Ginzburg, Carlo. *Ecstasies: Deciphering the Witches' Sabbath.* Trans. Raymond Rosenthal. London: Hutchinson Radius, 1990.

———. *The Night Battles: Witchcraft and Agrarian Cults in the Sixteenth and Seventeenth Centuries.* Trans. John Tedeschi and Anne Tedeschi. London: Routledge & Kegan Paul, 1983.

González Duro, Enrique. *Historia de la locura en España.* Madrid: Ediciones Temas de Hoy, 1994.

González Herrera, Eusebio. *Tragedia de la Reina Juana.* Tordesillas: Gráficas Andrés Martín, 1992.

González Navarro, Ramón. *Fernando I (1503–1564). Un Emperador español en el Sacro Imperio.* Madrid: Editorial Alpuerto, 2003.

Gordon, Colin. "*Histoire de la folie*: An Unknow book by Michel Foucault." In *Rewriting the History of Madness: Studies in Foucault's "Histoire de la folie,"* ed. Arthur Still and Irving Velody. New York: Routledge, 1992.

Goyens, J. "Passage de soeurs grises de Bruxelles à l'Ordre de Sainte Claire." *Archivum Franciscanum Historicum* 36 (1943).

Graham, Thomas F. *Medieval Minds: Mental Health in the Middle Ages.* London: George Allen & Unwin, 1967.

Graña Cid, María del Mar, ed. *Las sabias mujeres: Educación, saber y autoria (siglos iii–xvii).* Vols. 1 and 2. Madrid: Asociación Cultural Al-MUDAYNA, 1994–95.

Grasotti, Hilda. "La ira regia en León y Castilla." *Cuadernos de Historia de España* 41–42 (1965): 5–135.

Griffin, Clive. *The Crombergers of Sevilla: The History of a Printing and Merchant Dynasty*. Oxford: Clarendon Press, 1988.

Guenée, Bernard. "Les entrées royales françaises de 1328 à 1515." In *Politique et histoire au Moyen Age*. Paris: CNRS, 1968.

Häbler, Konrad. "Die Streit Ferdinands des Katholischen und Philipp I um die Regierung von Castilien 1504–1506." Ph.D. dissertation, Dresden, 1882.

Hale, John. *The Civilization of Europe in the Renaissance*. New York: Simon & Schuster, 1993.

Haliczer, Stephen. *The Comuneros of Castile: The Forging of a Revolution, 1475–1521*. Madison: University of Wisconsin Press, 1981.

Harsgor, Mikhaël. "L'essor des bâtards nobles au XVe siècle." *Revue Historique* 253 (1975): 319–54.

Hermann, M. *Forschungen zur deutschen Theatergeschichte des Mittelalters und der Renaissance*. Berlin: Weidmannsche Buchhandlung, 1914.

Heusch, Luc de. *Escrits sur la royaute sacrée*. Brussels: Editions de l'Université de Bruxelles, 1987.

Hocart, A. M. *Kingship*. Oxford: Oxford University Press, 1927.

Höfler, Constantin von. "Antoine de Lalaing, Seigneur de Montigny, Vicenzo Quirino und don Diego de Guevara als Berichterstatter unter König Philipp I in den jahren 1505, 1506." *Sbb Akad Wein* 104 (1883): 433–510.

———. *Donna Juana, Königin von Leon, Castilien und Granada*. Vienna, 1885.

Hofmann, Christina. *Das Spanische Hofzeremoniell von 1500–1700*. Frankfurt: Peter Lang, 1985.

Hugenholtz, F. W. N. "Filips de Schöne en Maximilianns twede regenischap 1493–1515." *Algemene geschiedenus der Nederlanden*. Utrech-Amberes: W. de Haan, 1952.

Hulst, Henri d'. *Le Mariage de Philippe le Beau avec Jeanne de Castille à Lierre le 20 Octobre 1496*. Anvers: Imprimeries Generales Lloyd Anversois, 1958.

Jackson, Stanley W. *Melancholia and Depression: From Hippocratic to Modern Times*. New Haven: Yale University Press, 1986.

Jaeger, C. Stephen. "L'amour des rois: Structure sociale d'une forme de sensibilité aristocratique." *Annales E.S.C.* (1991): 547–71.

Jean, Mireille. *La Chambre des Comptes de Lille: L'institution et Les Hommes (1477–1667)*. Paris: École des Chartes, 1992.

Jordan, Annemarie. "The Development of Catherine of Austria's Collection in the Queen's Household: Its Character and Cost." Ph.D. dissertation, Brown University, 1994.

Juvyns, Marie-Jeanne. *Le couvent des Riches-Claires à Bruxelles*. Mechelen: Sint-Franciskusdrukkerij, 1967.

Kagan, Richard L. *Lucrecia's Dreams: Politics and Prophecy in Sixteenth-Century Spain*. Berkeley: University of California Press, 1990.

Kantorowicz, Ernst H. *The King's Two Bodies*. Princeton: Princeton University Press, 1957.

Keniston, Hayward. *Francisco de los Cobos: Secretary of the Emperor Charles V*. Pittsburgh: University of Pittsburgh Press, 1960.

Klibansky, Raymond, Erwin Panofsky, and Fritz Saxl. *Saturn and Melancholy: Studies in the History of Natural Philosophy, Religion, and Art*. London: Nelson, 1964.

Kohler, Alfred. "La doble boda de 1496/97: Planeamiento, ejecución y consecuencias dinásticas." In *Reyes y mecenas: Los reyes católicos, Maximiliano I, y los inicios de la casa de Austria en España*, 253–72. Toledo: Ministerio de Cultura, 1992.

Ladero Quesada, Miguel Ángel. *La armada de Flandes. Un episodio en la política naval de los Reyes Católicos (1496–1497)*. Madrid: Real Academia dela Historia, 2003.

———. "La hacienda real de Castilla en 1504. Rentas y gastos de la corona al morir Isabel I." *Hispania* 16 (1976): 311–29.

———. "El proyecto político de los Reyes Católicos." In *Reyes y mecenas: Los Reyes Católicos, Maximiliano I, y los inicios de la casa de Austria en España*, coord. Mercedes Aznar Lópêz and Luz Gaztelu y Quijano, 79–100. Toledo: Electra, 1992.

Lafuente, Modesto. *Historia general de España*. Vol. 2. Barcelona: Montaner y Simón, 1879.

Lagomarsino, Paul David. "Court Factions and the Formulation of Spanish Policy towards the Netherlands (1559–67)." Ph.D. dissertation, Cambridge University, 1973.

Larregla, Santiago. "'El médico de guardia de Da Juana la Loca." *Yatros* (1957–58): 1–16.

Lehfeldt, Elizabeth A. "Ruling Sexuality: The Political Legitimacy of Isabel of Castile." *Renaissance Quarterly* 53 (2000): 31–56.

Levin, Carole. *"The Heart and Stomach of a King": Elizabeth I and the Politics of Sex and Power*. Philadelphia: University of Pennsylvania Press, 1994.

Linehan, Peter. "Frontier Kingship: Castile, 1250–1350." In *La Royauté sacrée dans le monde chrétien*, ed. Alain Boureau and Claudio Sergio Ingerflom. Paris: École des Hautes Études en Sciences Sociales, 1992.

———. *History and the Historians of Medieval Spain*. Oxford: Clarendon Press, 1993.

Lisón Tolosana, Carmelo. *La imagen del rey: Monarquía, realeza y poder ritual en la casa de los Austrias*. Madrid: Espasa-Calpe, 1991.

Liss, Peggy K. *Isabel the Queen: Life and Times*. Oxford: Oxford University Press, 1992.

Llanos y Torriglia, Félix de. *Una consejera de Estado: Doña Beatriz Galindo "La Latina."* Madrid: Editorial Reus, 1920.

———. *En el hogar de los Reyes Católicos y cosas de sus tiempos*. Madrid: Ediciones Fax, 1953.

———. "No tan aína: Suposición histórica." *Ateneo* 2, no. 17 (May 1907): 395–406.

———. "Sobre la fuga frustrada de doña Juana la Loca." *Boletín de la Real Academia de la Historia* 102 (1933): 97–114.

López de Haro, Alonso. *Nobiliario genealógico de los reyes y títulos de España*. Madrid: Luis Sánchez, 1622.

MacDonald, Michael. *Mystical Bedlam: Madness, Anxiety, and Healing in Seventeenth-Century England*. Cambridge: Cambridge University Press, 1981.

Mackay, Angus. "Ritual and Propaganda in Fifteenth-Century Castile." *Past & Present* 107 (May 1985): 3–43.

Maclean, Ian. *The Renaissance Notion of Woman*. Cambridge: Cambridge University Press, 1980.

Maravall, José Antonio. *Estudios de historia del pensamiento español*. Vols. 1 and 2. Madrid: Ediciones Cultura Hispánica, 1973–84.

Marcos Martín, Alberto. "Los estudios de demografía histórica en Castilla la Vieja y León (siglos XIV–XIX). Problemas y resultados." In *Demografía histórica en España*, ed. Vicente Pérez Moreda and David-Sven Reher. Madrid: Fundación José Ortega y Gasset, 1988.

Marin, Louis. *Portrait of the King*. Trans. Martha H. Houle. Minneapolis: University of Minnesota Press, 1988.

Martín García, Juan Manuel. *Arte y diplomacia en el reinado de los Reyes Católicos*. Madrid: Fundación Universitaria Española, 2002.

Martínez Gil, Fernando. *Muerte y sociedad en la España de los Austrias*. Madrid: Siglo Veintiuno Editores, 1993.

Martínez Millán, José et al. *La corte de Carlos V*. Vols. 1–5. Madrid: Sociedad Estatal para la Conmemoración de los Centenarios de Felipe II y Carlos V, 2000.

Matarasso, Pauline. *Queen's Mate: Three Women of Power in France on the Eve of the Renaissance*. Aldershot: Ashgate, 2001.

Mayer, Ernesto. *El antiguo derecho de obligaciones español según sus rasgos fundamentales*. Barcelona: Libreria Bosch, 1926.

———. *Historia de las instituciones sociales y políticas de España y Portugal durante los siglos V a XIV*. Vol. 1. Madrid: Anuario de Historia del Derecho Español, 1925.

Mayer, Rita Maria. "Die politischen Beziehungen König Maximilians I zu Philipp dem Schönen und den Niederlanden 1493–1506." Undergraduate theses, Graz, 1969.

McKendrick, Melveena. *Woman and Society in the Spanish Drama of the Golden Age: A Study of the Mujer Varonil*. Cambridge: Cambridge University Press, 1974.

Menéndez Pidal, Ramón. "The Significance of the Reign of Isabella the Catholic, According to Her Contemporaries." In *Spain in the 15th Century*, ed. Roger Highfield, 380–404. London: Macmillan, 1972.

Merriman, Roger B. *The Rise of the Spanish Empire in the Old World and in the New*. Vols. 2 and 3. New York: Macmillan, 1936.

Midelfort, H. C. Erik. *A History of Madness in Sixteenth-Century Germany*. Stanford, Calif.: Stanford University Press, 1999.

———. *Mad Princes of Renaissance Germany*. Charlottesville: University Press of Virginia, 1994.

Miller, Townsend. *The Castles and the Crown, Spain: 1451–1555*. New York: Coward-McCann, 1963.

Minois, Georges. *Anne de Bretagne*. Lille: Fayard, 1999.

Moorman, John. *A History of the Franciscan Order from its Origins to the Year 1517*. Oxford: Clardendon Press, 1968.

Morant, Isabel. *Discursos de la vida buena. Matrimonio, mujer y sexualidad en la literatura humanista*. Madrid: Cátedra, 2002.

Muñoz Fernández, Angela. *Mujer y experiencia religiosa en el marco de la santidad medieval*. Madrid: Al-Mudayna, 1988.

———. "Notas para la definición de un modelo socioreligioso femenino: Isabel I de Castilla." In *Las mujeres en el cristianismo medieval*, ed. Angela Muñoz Fernández, 45–434. Madrid: Al- Mudayna, 1989.

Muñoz Fernández, Angela, and Maria del Mar Graña, eds. *Religiosidad femenina: Expectativas y realidades (ss. 8–18)*. Madrid: Asociación Cultural Al-Mudayna, 1991.

Nader, Helen. "Habsburg Ceremony in Spain: The Reality of the Myth." *Historical Reflections/Reflexions Historiques* 15, no. 1 (1988): 293–309.

———. *The Mendoza Family in the Spanish Renaissance, 1350–1550*. New Brunswick, N.J.: Rutgers University Press, 1979.

Nalle, Sara T. *God in La Mancha: Religious Reform and the People of Cuenca, 1500–1650*. Baltimore: Johns Hopkins University Press, 1992.

———. *Mad for God: Bartolomé Sánchez, the Secret Messiah of Cardenete*. Charlottesville: University Press of Virginia, 2001.

Nieto Soria, José Manuel. *Ceremonias de la realeza: Propaganda y legitimación en la Castilla Trastámara.* Madrid: Editorial Nerea, 1993.

————. *Fundamentos ideológicos del poder real en Castilla, siglos XIII al XVI.* Madrid: Ediciones de la Universidad Complutense, 1988.

————, dir. *Orígenes de la monarquía hispánica: Propaganda y legitimación (ca. 1400–1520).* Madrid: Dykinson, 1999.

Nirenberg, David. *Communities of Violence: Persecution of Minorities in the Middle Ages.* Princeton: Princeton University Press, 1996.

Noreña, Carlos G. *Juan Luis Vives and the Emotions.* Carbondale: Southern Illinois University Press, 1989.

Norton, Frederick J. *La imprenta en España, 1501–1520.* Ed. Julián Martín Abad. Madrid: Ollero & Ramos, 1997.

Onghena, M. J. *De iconografie van Phlips de Schone.* Brussels: Paleis der Academiën, 1959.

Orlandis, José. *Estudios visigóticos III. El poder real y la sucesión al trono en la monarquía visigoda.* Madrid: Consejo Superior de Investigaciones Científicas, 1962.

Le palais de Bruxelles: Huit siécles d'art et d'histoire. Ed. Arlette Smolar-Meynart et al. Brussels: Crédit Communal, 1991.

Paravicini, Werner. "The Court of the Dukes of Burgundy: A Model for Europe?" In *Princes, Patronage & the Nobility: The Court at the Beginning of the Modern Age, c. 1450–1650,* ed. Ronald G. Asch and Adolf M. Birke, 69–102. London: Oxford University Press, 1991.

————. "'Ordonnances de l'Hôtel' und 'Escroes des gaiges.' Wege zu einer prosopographischen Erforschung des burgundische Staats im fünfzehnten Jahrhundert." In *Medieval Lives and the Historian: Studies in Medieval Prosopography,* ed. Neithard Bulst and Jean-Philippe Genet. Kalamazoo, MI: Medieval Institute Publications, 1986.

Parker, Geoffrey. *Philip II.* Chicago: Open Court, 1995.

————. *The Grand Strategy of Philip II.* New Haven: Yale University Press, 1998.

Parsons, John Carmi. *The Court and Household of Eleanor of Castile in 1290.* Toronto: Pontifical Institute of Medieval Studies, 1977.

————, ed. *Medieval Queenship.* New York: St. Martin's Press, 1993.

Paz y Espeso, Julian. "Casa de Doña Juana la loca en Tordesillas." *Revista de Archivos, Bibliotecas y Museos* 61, no. 2 (1955).

Penella, Manuel A. *Juana la loca.* Madrid: Amigos de la Historia, Editions Ferni Genéve, 1975.

————. "La Reina Juana no estaba loca." In *Grandes enigmas históricos españoles.* Madrid: Amigos de la Historia. Editions Ferni Genéve, 1979.

Pérez, Joseph. "El desconocido reinado de Felipe I El Hermoso y de Juana I la loca." *Torre de los Lujanes* 39 (June 1999): 135–46.

————. *La révolution des "comunidades" de Castille (1520–1521).* Bordeaux: Féret & Fils, 1970.

————. *La revolución de las comunidades de Castilla (1520–1521).* Trans. Juan José Faci Lacasta. Madrid: Siglo XXI, 1977.

Pérez-Bustamante, Rogelio, and José Manuel Calderon Ortega. *Felipe I 1506.* Palencia: Editorial Olmeda, 1995.

Pérez Villanueva, Joaquín, and Bartolomé Escandell Bonet. *Historia de la Inquisición en España y América. El conocimiento científico y el proceso histórico de la Institución (1478–1834).* Vol. 1. Madrid: Biblioteca de Autores Cristianos, 1984.

Petitjean, Bernadette. *Les conseillers de Philippe le Beau (1495–1506) d'après les comptes de la recette générale des finances. Essai de prosopographie.* Louvaine: Undergraduate thesis, 1991.

Pfandl, Ludwig. *Juana la loca: Su vida, su tiempo, su culpa.* Trans. Felipe Villaverde. Madrid: Espasa Calipe, 1943. Originally published 1930.

Pou y Marti, José María. *Visionarios, beguinos y fraticelos catalanes (Siglos xiii–xv).* Madrid: Colegio "Cardenal Cisneros," 1991.

Prast, Antonio, "El castillo de la Mota, de Medina del Campo. Intento de 'huída' de doña Juana la Loca." *Boletín de la Real Academia de la Historia* 101 (1932): 508–22.

———. *Sobre la fuga frustrada de Doña Juana la Loca: A propósito de unos comentarios con fotografías* . . . Madrid: Imp. S.P.N., 1933.

Prawdin, Michael. *The Mad Queen of Spain.* Translated by Eden Paul and Cedar Paul from *Johanna die wahrsinnige, Habsburgs Weg zum Weltreich.* London: George Allen and Unwin, 1938.

Prescott, William H. *History of the Reign of Ferdinand and Isabella the Catholic.* Boston: Charles Little & James Brown, 1837.

———. *The History of the Reign of the Emperor Charles the Fifth.* Ed. William Robertson. Philadelphia: J. B. Lippincott, 1845.

Prodi, Paolo. *Il sacramento del potere. It giuramento politico nella storia costituzionale dell'Occidente.* Bologna: Società editrice il Mulino, 1992.

Phillips, Carla Rahn. "Spanish Merchants and the Wool Trade in the Sixteenth Century." *Sixteenth Century Journal* 14, no. 3 (1983): 259–82.

Phillips, William D. "Local Integration and Long-Distance Ties: The Castilian Community in Sixteenth-Century Bruges." *Sixteenth Century Journal* 17, no. 1 (1986): 33–49.

Pirenne, Henri. "Une crise industriele au XVIe siècle: La draperie urbaine et la 'nouvelle draperie' en Flandre." In *Histoire économique de l'Occident médiéval,* 621–43. Bruges: Desclée de Brouwer, 1951.

Ranum, Orest. "The Refuges of Intimacy." In *A History of Private Life,* ed. Roger Chartier, 3:206–63. Cambridge: Belknap/Harvard University Press, 1989.

Redondo, Agustin. *Antonio de Guevara (1480?–1545) et l'Espagne de son temps.* Geneva: Librairie Droz, 1976.

Reiffenberg, Baron de. *Histoire de l'ordre de la Toison d'Or.* Brussels: Fonderie et Imprimerie Normales, 1830.

Reilly, Bernard F. *The Kingdom of León-Castilla under Queen Urraca, 1109–1126.* Princeton: Princeton University Press, 1982.

Reydellet, Marc. *La royauté dans la littérature latine de Sidoine Apollinaire à Isidore de Séville.* Rome: École française de Rome, 1981.

Riera, Juan. *Cirujanos, urólogos, y algebristas del Renacimiento y Barroco.* Valladolid: Universidad de Valladolid, 1990.

Ríos Lloret, Rosa E. *Germana de Foix. Una mujer, una reina, una corte.* Valencia: Biblioteca Valenciana, 2003.

Rodríguez-Salgado, M. J. *The Changing Face of Empire: Charles V, Philip II and Habsburg Authority, 1551–1559.* Cambridge: Cambridge University Press, 1988.

Rodríguez Valencia, Vicente. *Isabel la Católica en la opinión de Españoles y extranjeros.* Vols. 1 and 3. Valladolid: Instituto "lsabel la Católica" de Historia Eclesiastica, 1970.

Rodríguez Villa, Antonio. *Bosquejo biográfico de la Reina Doña Juana.* Madrid: Sucesores de Rivadeneyra, 1874.

————. "Observaciones y documentos relativos a la Reina Doña Juana." *Revista de Archivos, Bibliotecas y Museos* (15 November 1873): 321–25.

————. "Observaciones y documentos relativos a la Reina Doña Juana, conclusión." *Revista de Archivos, Bibliotecas y Museos* (30 November 1873): 337–40.

————. *La Reina doña Juana la loca: Estudio histórico.* Madrid: Librería de M. Murillo, 1892.

Roelker, Nancy Llyman. *Queen of Navarre: Jeanne d'Albret, 1528–1572.* Cambridge: Harvard University Press, 1968.

Rogren, Heribert R. *De Clarissenorde in de Nederlande (Instrumenta Franciscana).* Sint-Truiden: Instituut voor Franciscaanse Geschiedenis, 1995.

Rosen, George. *Madness in Society: Chapters in the Historical Sociology of Mental Illness.* London: Routledge & Kegan Paul, 1968.

Round, Nicolas. *The Greatest Man Uncrowned: A Study of the Fall of Don Alvaro de Luna.* London: Tamesis Books Limited, 1986.

Rubin, Miri. *Corpus Christi: The Eucharist in Late Medieval Culture.* Cambridge: Cambridge University Press, 1991.

Rucquoi, Adeline. "De los reyes que no son taumaturgos: Los fundamentos de la realeza en España." *Relaciones* 51 (1992): 54–100.

Rudolf, Karl Friedrich. "Yo, El Infante—Fernando, Príncipe en España." In *Fernando I. Un infante Español Emperador,* ed. Teófanes Egido López, 41–67. Valladolid: Universidad de Valladolid, 2004.

Ruíz, Teófilo F. "Unsacred Monarchy: The Kings of Castile in the Late Middle Ages." *Rites of Power: Symbolism, Ritual, and Politics Since the Middle Ages,* ed. Sean Wilentz, 109–44. Philadelphia: University of Pennsylvania Press, 1985.

Rumeu de Armas, Antonio. *Itinerario de los Reyes Católicos: 1474–1516.* Madrid: CSIC, 1974.

Rummel, Erika. *Jiménez de Cisneros: On the Threshold of Spain's Golden Age.* Temple: Arizona Center for Medieval and Renaissance Studies, 1999.

Sacristán, María Cristina. *Locura e Inquisición en Nueva España, 1571–1760.* Mexico City: Fondo de Cultura Económica, 1992.

Saenger, Paul Henry. "The Education of Burgundian Princes, 1435–1490." Ph.D. dissertation, University of Chicago, 1972.

Sahlins, Peter. *Boundaries: The Making of France and Spain in the Pyrenees.* Berkeley: University of California Press, 1989.

Saint-Saëns, Alain. *La nostalgie du désert. L'idéal érémitique en Castille au Siècle de'Or.* San Francisco: Mellen Research University Press, 1993.

Salazar y Acha, Jaime de. *La casa del rey de Castilla y León en la Edad Media.* Madrid: Centro de Estudios Políticos y Constitucionales, 2000.

Sánchez, Magdalena S. *The Empress, the Queen, and the Nun: Women and Power at the Court of Philip III of Spain.* Baltimore: Johns Hopkins University Press, 1998.

————. "Melancholy and Female Illness: Habsburg Women and Politics at the Court of Philip III." *Journal of Women's History* 8, no. 2 (summer 1996): 81–102.

————. "Pious and Political Images of a Habsburg Woman at the Court of Philip III (1598–1621)." In *Spanish Women in the Golden Age: Images and Realities,* ed. Magdalena S. Sánchez and Alain Saint-Saëns. Westport, CT: Greenwood Press, 1996.

Sánchez Cantón, Francisco Javier. *Libros, tapices y cuadros que coleccionó Isabel la Católica.* Madrid: Consejo Superior de Investigaciones Científicas, 1950.

————. *Los retratos de los reyes de España*. Barcelona: Ediciones Omega, 1948.

Sanctus Franciscus Borgia Quartus Gandiae Dux et Societatis Jesu Praepositus Generalis Tertius. 5 vols. Rome: Monumenta Historica Societatis Jesu, 1894–1911.

Sanz y Ruiz de la Peña, Nicomedes. *Doña Juana I de Castilla en su palacio de Tordesillas*. Madrid: Ediciones de Conferencias y Ensayos, n.d.

————. *Doña Juana I de Castilla, la reina que enloqueció de amor*. Madrid: Biblioteca Nueva, 1942.

Scholz Williams, Gerhild. *Defining Dominion: The Discourses of Magic and Witchcraft in Early Modern France and Germany*. Ann Arbor: University of Michigan Press, 1995.

Schramm, Percy E. *Las insignias de la realeza en la Edad Media española*. Trans. Luis Vázquez de Parga. Madrid: Instituto de Estudios Políticos, 1960.

Seaver, Henry Latimer. *The Great Revolt in Castile: A Study of the Comunero Movement of 1520–1521*. London: Constable, 1928.

Segura Graiño, Cristina. "Las mujeres y el poder real en Castilla. Finales del siglo XV y principios del XVI." In *Las mujeres y el poder. Representaciones y prácticas de vida*, ed. Ana I. Cerrada Jiménez and Cristina Segura Graiño, 135–46. Madrid: Al-Mudayna, 2000.

Serrano y Sanz, Manuel. *Apuntes para una biblioteca de escritoras españolas*. Madrid: Sucesores de Rivadeneyra, 1903–5.

Siraisi, Nancy G. *Medieval and Early Renaissance Medicine: An Introduction to Knowledge and Practice*. Chicago: University of Chicago Press, 1990.

Sobré, Judith Berg. *Behind the Altar Table: The Development of the Painted Retable in Spain, 1350–1500*. Columbia: University of Missouri Press, 1989.

Sommé, Monique. "Les délegations de pouvoir a la duchesse de Bourgogne." In *Les princes et le pouvoir au Moyen Age*, 285–301. Paris: Sorbonne, 1993.

————. "Les déplacementes d'Isabelle de Portugal et la circulation dans les Pays Bas bourguignons au milieu du XVe siècle." *Revue du Nord* 52 (1970): 183–97.

————. *Isabelle de Portugal, duchesse de Bourgogne, une femme au pouvoir au quinzième siècle*. Villeneuve d'Ascq: Presses Universitaires du Septentrion, 1998.

————. "La jeunesse de Charles le Téméraire d'après les comptes de la cour de Bourgogne." *Revue du Nord* 64, nos. 254–55 (Julyt–December 1982): 731–50.

Suárez Fernández, Luis. *Política internacional de Isabel la Católica: Estudio y documentos*. Vols. 4 (1494–96) and 5 (1497–99). Valladolid: Universidad de Valladolid, 1971–72.

Szasz, Thomas S. *The Manufacture of Madness: A Comparative Study of the Inquisition and the Mental Health Movement*. New York: Harper and Row, 1970.

Tentler, Thomas N. *Sin and Confession on the Eve of the Reformation*. Princeton: Princeton University Press, 1977.

Thompson, I. A. A. "The Nobility in Spain, 1600–1800." In *The European Nobilities in the Seventeenth and Eighteenth Centuries*, ed. H. M. Scott. London: Longman, 1995.

Torre, Antonio de la. "Maestros de los hijos de los Reyes Católicos." *Hispania* 63 (1956): 256–66.

Toussaert, Jacques. *Le sentiment religieux en Flandre à la fin du Moyen-Age*. Paris: Librairie Plon, 1963.

Urquijo Urquijo, María Jesús. "Archivo General de Simancas, Casa y Sitios Reales: Casa de la Reina Juana en Tordesillas." *Boletín de Archivos* 2 (1978): 201–8.

Vallejo-Nájera, Juan Antonio. *Locos egregios*. Madrid: Editorial Dossat, 1981.

Val Valdivieso, María Isabel del. "Ascenso social y lucha por el poder en las ciudades castellanas del siglo XV." *En la España Medieval* (Editorial Complutense) 17 (1994), 157–84.

———. "La herencia del trono." In *Isabel la Católica y la política*, ed. Julio Valdeón Baruque, 15–49. Valladolid: Instituto de Historia Simancas, 2001.

———. "La política exterior de la monarquia castellano-aragonesa en la época de los Reyes Católicos." *Investigaciones Históricas* (Universidad de Valladolid) 17 (1996): 11–27.

van Deusen, Nancy Elena. *Between the Sacred and the Worldly: The Institutional and Cultural Practice of Recogimiento in Colonial Lima*. Stanford, Calif.: Stanford University Press, 2001.

Varela, Javier. *La muerte del rey: El ceremonial funerario de la monarquía española, 1500–1885*. Madrid: Turner, 1990.

Vega, Jesusa. "Impresores y libros en el orígen del renacimiento en España." In *Reyes y mecenas: Los Reyes Católicos, Maximiliano I, y los inicios de la casa de Austria en España*, 199–232. Toledo: Electa, 1992.

Vicens Vives, Jaime. "The Economy of Ferdinand and Isabella's Reign." In *Spain in the 15th Century*, ed. Roger Highfield, 248–75. London: Macmillan, 1972.

———. *Fernando el Católico, príncipe de Aragón, rey de Sicilia, 1458–1478*. Madrid: Consejo Superior de Investigacioens Científicas, 1952.

———. *Historia crítica de la vida y reinado de Fernando II de Aragon*. Vol. 1 (through 1481). Zaragoza: Institución "Fernando el Católico," Diputacion Provincial, 1962.

Wack, Mary Frances. *Lovesickness in the Middle Ages: The Viaticum and Its Commentaries*. Philadelphia: University of Pennsylvania Press, 1990.

Walker Bynum, Caroline. *Holy Feast and Holy Fast: The Religious Significance of Food to Medieval Women*. Berkeley: University of California Press, 1987.

Weightman, Christine. *Margaret of York: Duchess of Burgundy, 1446–1503*. New York: St. Martin's Press, 1989.

Weir, Alison. *Eleanor of Aquitaine: By the Wrath of God, Queen of England*. London: Jonathan Cape, 1999.

Willard, Charity Cannon. "The Concept of True Nobility at the Burgundian Court." *Studies in the Renaissance* 14 (1967): 33–48.

Wittkower, Rudolf, and Margot Wittkower. *Born under Saturn: The Character and Conduct of Artists: A Documented History from Antiquity to the French Revolution*. New York: W. W. Norton, 1963.

Yarza, Joaquín. "El arte de los Países Bajos en la España de los Reyes Católicos." In *Reyes y mecenas: Los Reyes Católicos, Maximiliano I, y los inicios de la casa de Austria en España*, coord. Mercedes Aznar Lópêz and Luz Gaztelu y Quijano, 133–50. Toledo: Electa, 1992.

Yndauráin, Domingo. *Humanismo y Renacimiento en España*. Madrid: Ediciones Cátedra, 1994.

Zalama, Miguel Ángel. "Doña Juana 'la loca' con el cortejo fúnebre de su esposo por tierras de Palencia." In *Actas del III Congreso de Historia de Palencia*, IV:551–53. Palencia, 1996.

———. "Juana I de Castilla y el Monasterio de Santa Clara de Tordesillas." *Reales Sitios* 39, no. 151 (2002): 14–27.

———. *Vida cotidiana y arte en el palacio de la Reina Juana I en Tordesillas*. Valladolid: Universidad de Valladolid, 2000.

Zalama, Miguel Ángel, and Rafael Domínguez Casas. "Jacob Van Laethem, Pintor de Felipe 'el hermoso' y Carlos V: Precisiones sobre su obra." *Boletín del Seminario de Estudios de Arte y Arqueologia* 61 (1995): 347–58.

Zilboorg, Gregory. *The Medical Man and the Witch During the Renaissance.* New York: Cooper Square Publishers, 1969. Originally published 1935.

Index